NOT QUITE US

MCGILL-QUEEN'S STUDIES IN THE HISTORY OF RELIGION
Volumes in this series have been supported by the Jackman Foundation of Toronto.

SERIES ONE: G.A. RAWLYK, EDITOR

1 Small Differences
  Irish Catholics and Irish Protestants, 1815–1922
  An International Perspective
  Donald Harman Akenson

2 Two Worlds
  The Protestant Culture of Nineteenth-Century Ontario
  William Westfall

3 An Evangelical Mind
  Nathanael Burwash and the Methodist Tradition in Canada, 1839–1918
  Marguerite Van Die

4 The Dévotes
  Women and Church in Seventeenth-Century France
  Elizabeth Rapley

5 The Evangelical Century
  College and Creed in English Canada from the Great Revival to the Great Depression
  Michael Gauvreau

6 The German Peasants' War and Anabaptist Community of Goods
  James M. Stayer

7 A World Mission
  Canadian Protestantism and the Quest for a New International Order, 1918–1939
  Robert Wright

8 Serving the Present Age
  Revivalism, Progressivism, and the Methodist Tradition in Canada
  Phyllis D. Airhart

9 A Sensitive Independence
  Canadian Methodist Women Missionaries in Canada and the Orient, 1881–1925
  Rosemary R. Gagan

10 God's Peoples
   Covenant and Land in South Africa, Israel, and Ulster
   Donald Harman Akenson

11 Creed and Culture
   The Place of English-Speaking Catholics in Canadian Society, 1750–1930
   Edited by Terrence Murphy and Gerald Stortz

12 Piety and Nationalism
   Lay Voluntary Associations and the Creation of an Irish-Catholic Community in Toronto, 1850–1895
   Brian P. Clarke

13 Amazing Grace
   Studies in Evangelicalism in Australia, Britain, Canada, and the United States
   Edited by George Rawlyk and Mark A. Noll

14 Children of Peace
   W. John McIntyre

15 A Solitary Pillar
   Montreal's Anglican Church and the Quiet Revolution
   Joan Marshall

16 Padres in No Man's Land
   Canadian Chaplains and the Great War
   Duff Crerar

17 Christian Ethics and Political Economy in North America
   A Critical Analysis
   P. Travis Kroeker

18 Pilgrims in Lotus Land
   Conservative Protestantism in British Columbia, 1917–1981
   Robert K. Burkinshaw

19 Through Sunshine and Shadow
   The Woman's Christian Temperance Union, Evangelicalism, and Reform in Ontario, 1874–1930
   Sharon Cook

20 Church, College, and Clergy
A History of Theological
Education at Knox College,
Toronto, 1844–1994
Brian J. Fraser

21 The Lord's Dominion
The History of Canadian Methodism
Neil Semple

22 A Full-Orbed Christianity
The Protestant Churches and Social
Welfare in Canada, 1900–1940
Nancy Christie and Michael Gauvreau

23 Evangelism and Apostasy
The Evolution and Impact
of Evangelicals in Modern Mexico
Kurt Bowen

24 The Chignecto Covenanters
A Regional History of Reformed
Presbyterianism in New Brunswick
and Nova Scotia, 1827–1905
Eldon Hay

25 Methodists and Women's
Education in Ontario, 1836–1925
Johanne Selles

26 Puritanism and Historical
Controversy
William Lamont

SERIES TWO: IN MEMORY OF GEORGE RAWLYK
DONALD HARMAN AKENSON, EDITOR

1 Marguerite Bourgeoys and Montreal,
1640–1665
Patricia Simpson

2 Aspects of the Canadian
Evangelical Experience
Edited by G.A. Rawlyk

3 Infinity, Faith, and Time
Christian Humanism and
Renaissance Literature
John Spencer Hill

4 The Contribution of Presbyterianism
to the Maritime Provinces of Canada
*Edited by Charles H.H. Scobie
and G.A. Rawlyk*

5 Labour, Love, and Prayer
Female Piety in Ulster Religious
Literature, 1850–1914
Andrea Ebel Brozyna

6 The Waning of the Green
Catholics, the Irish, and Identity
in Toronto, 1887–1922
Mark G. McGowan

7 Religion and Nationality
in Western Ukraine
The Greek Catholic Church
and the Ruthenian National
Movement in Galicia, 1867–1900
John-Paul Himka

8 Good Citizens
British Missionaries and Imperial States,
1870–1918
*James G. Greenlee and
Charles M. Johnston*

9 The Theology of the Oral Torah
Revealing the Justice of God
Jacob Neusner

10 Gentle Eminence
A Life of Cardinal Flahiff
P. Wallace Platt

11 Culture, Religion, and Demographic
Behaviour Catholics and Lutherans
in Alsace, 1750–1870
Kevin McQuillan

12 Between Damnation and Starvation
Priests and Merchants
in Newfoundland Politics,
1745–1855
John P. Greene

13 Martin Luther, German Saviour
German Evangelical Theological
Factions and the Interpretation
of Luther, 1917–1933
James M. Stayer

14 Modernity and the Dilemma
of North American Anglican
Identities, 1880–1950
William H. Katerberg

15 The Methodist Church on
the Prairies, 1896–1914
George Emery

16 Christian Attitudes towards
the State of Israel
Paul Charles Merkley

17 A Social History of the Cloister
Daily Life in the Teaching
Monasteries of the Old Regime
Elizabeth Rapley

18 Households of Faith
Family, Gender, and Community
in Canada, 1760–1969
Edited by Nancy Christie

19 Blood Ground
Colonialism, Missions, and the Contest
for Christianity in the Cape Colony
and Britain, 1799–1853
Elizabeth Elbourne

20 A History of Canadian Catholics
Gallicanism, Romanism, and
Canadianism
Terence J. Fay

21 The View from Rome
Archbishop Stagni's 1915
Reports on the Ontario Bilingual
Schools Question
*Edited and translated by
John Zucchi*

22 The Founding Moment
Church, Society, and the
Construction of Trinity College
William Westfall

23 The Holocaust, Israel, and
Canadian Protestant Churches
Haim Genizi

24 Governing Charities
Church and State in Toronto's
Catholic Archdiocese, 1850–1950
Paula Maurutto

25 Anglicans and the Atlantic World
High Churchmen, Evangelicals,
and the Quebec Connection
Richard W. Vaudry

26 Evangelicals and the
Continental Divide
The Conservative Protestant Subculture
in Canada and the United States
Sam Reimer

27 Christians in a Secular World
The Canadian Experience
Kurt Bowen

28 Anatomy of a Seance
A History of Spirit Communication
in Central Canada
Stan McMullin

29 With Skilful Hand
The Story of King David
David T. Barnard

30 Faithful Intellect
Samuel S. Nelles and
Victoria University
Neil Semple

31 W. Stanford Reid
An Evangelical Calvinist
in the Academy
Donald MacLeod

32 A Long Eclipse
The Liberal Protestant
Establishment and the Canadian
University, 1920–1970
Catherine Gidney

33 Forkhill Protestants and Forkhill
Catholics, 1787–1858
Kyla Madden

34 For Canada's Sake
Public Religion, Centennial
Celebrations, and the Re-making
of Canada in the 1960s
Gary R. Miedema

35 Revival in the City
The Impact of American
Evangelists in Canada, 1884–1914
Eric R. Crouse

36 The Lord for the Body
Religion, Medicine, and
Protestant Faith Healing in
Canada, 1880–1930
James Opp

37 Six Hundred Years of Reform
   Bishops and the French Church,
   1190–1789
   J. Michael Hayden and
   Malcolm R. Greenshields

38 The Missionary Oblate Sisters
   Vision and Mission
   Rosa Bruno-Jofré

39 Religion, Family, and Community
   in Victorian Canada
   The Colbys of Carrollcroft
   Marguerite Van Die

40 Michael Power
   The Struggle to Build the Catholic
   Church on the Canadian Frontier
   Mark G. McGowan

41 The Catholic Origins of Quebec's
   Quiet Revolution, 1931–1970
   Michael Gauvreau

42 Marguerite Bourgeoys and the
   Congregation of Notre Dame,
   1665–1700
   Patricia Simpson

43 To Heal a Fractured World
   The Ethics of Responsibility
   Jonathan Sacks

44 Revivalists
   Marketing the Gospel in
   English Canada, 1884–1957
   Kevin Kee

45 The Churches and Social Order
   in Nineteenth- and Twentieth-
   Century Canada
   Edited by Michael Gauvreau
   and Ollivier Hubert

46 Political Ecumenism
   Catholics, Jews, and Protestants in
   De Gaulle's Free France, 1940–1945
   Geoffrey Adams

47 From Quaker to Upper Canadian
   Faith and Community among Yonge
   Street Friends, 1801–1850
   Robynne Rogers Healey

48 The Congrégation de Notre-Dame,
   Superiors, and the Paradox of Power,
   1693–1796
   Colleen Gray

49 Canadian Pentecostalism
   Transition and Transformation
   Edited by Michael Wilkinson

50 A War with a Silver Lining
   Canadian Protestant Churches
   and the South African War,
   1899–1902
   Gordon L. Heath

51 In the Aftermath of Catastrophe
   Founding Judaism, 70 to 640
   Jacob Neusner

52 Imagining Holiness
   Classic Hasidic Tales in Modern Times
   Justin Jaron Lewis

53 Shouting, Embracing, and
   Dancing with Ecstasy
   The Growth of Methodism in
   Newfoundland, 1774–1874
   Calvin Hollett

54 Into Deep Waters
   Evangelical Spirituality and
   Maritime Calvinist Baptist
   Ministers, 1790–1855
   Daniel C. Goodwin

55 Vanguard of the New Age
   The Toronto Theosophical
   Society, 1891–1945
   Gillian McCann

56 A Commerce of Taste
   Church Architecture in
   Canada, 1867–1914
   Barry Magrill

57 The Big Picture
   The Antigonish Movement
   of Eastern Nova Scotia
   Santo Dodaro and Leonard Pluta

58 My Heart's Best Wishes for You
   A Biography of Archbishop
   John Walsh
   John P. Comiskey

59 The Covenanters in Canada
   Reformed Presbyterianism
   from 1820 to 2012
   Eldon Hay

60 The Guardianship of Best Interests
   Institutional Care for the Children
   of the Poor in Halifax, 1850–1960
   Renée N. Lafferty

61 In Defence of the Faith
Joaquim Marques de Araújo,
a Brazilian Comissário in the
Age of Inquisitional Decline
James E. Wadsworth

62 Contesting the Moral High Ground
Popular Moralists in Mid-
Twentieth-Century Britain
Paul T. Phillips

63 The Catholicisms of Coutances
Varieties of Religion in Early
Modern France, 1350–1789
J. Michael Hayden

64 After Evangelicalism
The Sixties and the United
Church of Canada
Kevin N. Flatt

65 The Return of Ancestral Gods
Modern Ukrainian Paganism
as an Alternative Vision
for a Nation
Mariya Lesiv

66 Transatlantic Methodists
British Wesleyanism and
the Formation of an Evangelical
Culture in Nineteenth-Century
Ontario and Quebec
Todd Webb

67 A Church with the Soul of a Nation
Making and Remaking the United
Church of Canada
Phyllis D. Airhart

68 Fighting over God
A Legal and Political History
of Religious Freedom in Canada
Janet Epp Buckingham

69 From India to Israel
Identity, Immigration, and the Struggle
for Religious Equality
Joseph Hodes

70 Becoming Holy in Early Canada
Timothy G. Pearson

71 The Cistercian Arts
From the 12th to the 21st Century
*Edited by Terryl N. Kinder
and Roberto Cassanelli*

72 The Canny Scot
Archbishop James Morrison
of Antigonish
Peter Ludlow

73 Religion and Greater Ireland
Christianity and Irish Global
Networks, 1750–1950
*Edited by Colin Barr and
Hilary M. Carey*

74 The Invisible Irish
Finding Protestants in the Nineteenth-
Century Migrations to America
Rankin Sherling

75 Beating against the Wind
Popular Opposition to Bishop Feild
and Tractarianism in Newfoundland
and Labrador, 1844–1876
Calvin Hollett

76 The Body or the Soul?
Religion and Culture in a Quebec
Parish, 1736–1901
Frank A. Abbott

77 Saving Germany
North American Protestants and
Christian Mission to West Germany,
1945–1974
James C. Enns

78 The Imperial Irish
Canada's Irish Catholics Fight the Great
War, 1914–1918
Mark G. McGowan

79 Into Silence and Servitude
How American Girls Became Nuns,
1945–1965
Brian Titley

80 Boundless Dominion
Providence, Politics, and the Early
Canadian Presbyterian Worldview
Denis McKim

81 Faithful Encounters
Authorities and American Missionaries
in the Ottoman Empire
Emrah Şahin

82 Beyond the Noise of Solemn Assemblies
The Protestant Ethic and the Quest
for Social Justice in Canada
Richard Allen

83 Not Quite Us
Anti-Catholic Thought in English
Canada since 1900
Kevin P. Anderson

NOT QUITE US

Anti-Catholic Thought in English Canada since 1900

KEVIN P. ANDERSON

McGill-Queen's University Press
Montreal & Kingston • London • Chicago

© McGill-Queen's University Press 2019

ISBN 978-0-7735-5654-6 (cloth)
ISBN 978-0-7735-5655-3 (paper)
ISBN 978-0-7735-5755-0 (ePDF)
ISBN 978-0-7735-5756-7 (ePUB)

Legal deposit first quarter 2019
Bibliothèque nationale du Québec

Printed in Canada on acid-free paper that is 100% ancient forest free (100% post-consumer recycled), processed chlorine free

This book has been published with the help of a grant from the Canadian Federation for the Humanities and Social Sciences, through the Awards to Scholarly Publications Program, using funds provided by the Social Sciences and Humanities Research Council of Canada.

We acknowledge the support of the Canada Council for the Arts, which last year invested $153 million to bring the arts to Canadians throughout the country.

Nous remercions le Conseil des arts du Canada de son soutien. L'an dernier, le Conseil a investi 153 millions de dollars pour mettre de l'art dans la vie des Canadiennes et des Canadiens de tout le pays.

Library and Archives Canada Cataloguing in Publication

Anderson, Kevin P., 1985–, author
  Not quite us: anti-Catholic thought in English Canada
since 1900 / Kevin P. Anderson.

(McGill-Queen's studies in the history of religion. Series two; 83)
Includes bibliographical references and index.
Issued in print and electronic formats.
ISBN 978-0-7735-5654-6 (cloth). – ISBN 978-0-7735-5655-3 (paper). –
ISBN 978-0-7735-5755-0 (ePDF). – ISBN 978-0-7735-5756-7 (ePUB)

  1. Anti-Catholicism – Canada – History. 2. Catholics – Canada – History. 3. Canada – Religion. I. Title. II. Series: McGill-Queen's studies in the history of religion. Series two; 83

BX1766.A53   282'.71   C2018-906471-4
                           C2018-906472-2

This book was typeset by Marquis Interscript in 10.5/13 Sabon.

Dedicated to Willa Jean, the best person I barely know

Contents

Tables and Figures xiii

Abbreviations xv

Acknowledgments xvii

Introduction: Anti-Catholicism and Identity 3

1 Corrupting Democracy: French Canada, Immigration, and Anti-Catholicism in the "Progressive Era," 1900–1929 27

2 Fascism and the "Revenge of the Cradle": Anti-Catholicism and the Great Depression 69

3 Conscription and the "Omnicompetent State": The Second World War and Anti-Catholicism 111

4 What It Means to Be (Truly) Canadian: Cold War Anti-Catholicism and the Transformation of Britishness in Canada, 1945–1965 155

5 Anti-Catholicism, 1970s–1990s: The Strange Survival of an Old Prejudice 199

Conclusion: Not Quite Us? 240

Notes 243

Bibliography 297

Index 321

Tables and Figures

TABLES

0.1 Canadian Catholic population, as percentage of the overall Canadian population   11
1.1 French population of Canada   47
1.2 Overall population of the western provinces   55
2.1 Population of Canada with French as mother tongue (1931–1941)   82
3.1 Population of Canada with French as mother tongue (1941–1951)   118
4.1 Immigration from predominantly Catholic and/or Communist continental Europe   158
4.2 Religious composition of immigration to Canada, by percentage   158
4.3 Population of Canada with French as mother tongue (1951–1971)   160
5.1 Foreign-born population, descending from non-European areas   201
5.2 Religious composition of immigration as percentage of immigration   201

FIGURES

0.1 Kaufman portrays himself as a frightened bystander to the "whole Church of Rome." Reproduced with permission of University of Waterloo Library. Special Collections and Archives. A.R. Kaufman fonds   4

0.2 Kaufman saw the "Church of Rome" and the medical profession as joint forces preventing birth control due to their "Self Interest." Reproduced with permission of University of Waterloo Library. Special Collections and Archives. A.R. Kaufman fonds, box 1, file 23   5

0.3 Kaufman fears that Protestants are not paying enough attention to the political activities of the Catholic Church. Reproduced with permission of University of Waterloo Library. Special Collections and Archives. A.R. Kaufman fonds, box 1, file 23   6

0.4 The Liberals parade jubilantly into the legislature. Reproduced with permission of University of Waterloo Library. Special Collections and Archives. A.R. Kaufman fonds, box 1, file 23   7

2.1 "The Quints at Queen's Park." Library and Archives Canada/George Drew fonds/e011183965   93

5.1 Bill Davis sits in place of William III on his white horse. *Maclean's*, 16 February 1981. Reproduced with permission from Geoff Peterson   216

Abbreviations

APEC	Alliance for the Preservation of English in Canada
BCSH	Birth Control Society of Hamilton
CCC	Canadian Council of Churches
CCCC	Committee on Cooperation in Canadian Citizenship
CCF	Co-operative Commonwealth Federation
CCNWO	Commission on the Church, Nation and World Order
CCRL	Catholic Civil Rights League
CPA	Canadian Protestant Association
CPL	Canadian Protestant League
DCR	Defence of Canada Regulations
DPS	displaced persons
EFC	Evangelical Fellowship of Canada
ESC	Eugenics Society of Canada
FCSO	Fellowship for a Christian Social Order
GMA	Guelph Ministerial Association
ICC	Inter-Church Committee on Protestant–Roman Catholic Relations
LSR	League for Social Reconstruction
MCSC	Montreal Catholic School Commission
MSA	Military Service Act
NAC	National Association of Canada
NCSB	New Canadian Service Bureau
NDP	New Democratic Party
NRMA	National Resources Mobilization Act
OCAC	Ontario Coalition for Abortion Clinics
PC	Progressive Conservative Party
PIB	Parents' Information Bureau

PQ	Parti Québécois
SSCC	Social Service Council of Canada
WCC	World Council of Churches
WEA	Wartime Elections Act
WIB	Wartime Information Board

Acknowledgments

There are so many people to thank for helping me through the long process of publication. I would like to thank the L.R. Wilson Institute for Canadian History and McMaster University for support during the doctoral research stages of this project. I also received significant support from SSHRC and the Ontario Graduate Scholarship program. I would like to thank Library and Archives Canada, Queen's University Archives, the Esther Clark Wright Archives at Acadia University, the University of Waterloo Archives, the United Church of Canada Archives, the Glenbow Museum Archives in Calgary, the Archive of the Jesuits in Canada, the Anglican Diocese of Toronto Archives, and Local History and Archives Hamilton. This project would also not have been as successful without the hard work and resourcefulness of the Interlibrary Loan staff at McMaster University and the University of Calgary.

I would like to thank the two anonymous reviewers who looked over this manuscript and provided invaluable feedback. Both have made this work infinitely better. Kyla Madden, Finn Purcell, and Kathleen Fraser from McGill-Queen's University Press also greatly aided in improving this manuscript, helping to transform it from a dissertation and making this complex process much easier to understand. Patricia Kennedy's eye for detail in the copy-editing stages cannot be overstated. In this spirit, I thank the reviewers and editors from the *Journal of Religious History*, *Historical Studies*, *History Compass*, and *History of Intellectual Culture* for helping me think through and streamline my work to a digestible length and narrative form.

Sections of Chapter 1 appeared in article form as "The Cockroaches of Canada: French Canada, Immigration, and Nationalism, Anti-Catholicism in English Canada, 1905–1929," *Journal of Religious History* 39 (March, 2015): 104–22. Sections of Chapters 3 and 4 appeared in article form as "I am ... the very essence of a Protestant: Arthur Lower, Anti-Catholicism, and Liberal Nationalism, 1939–1959," *Historical Studies* 81 (2015): 7–30. Sections of Chapter 4 appeared in article form as "The Farthing Brothers and the Narrativization of a Conservative Canada," *History of Intellectual Culture* 11 (2014–2016).

Without the guidance of Michael Gauvreau, this project never would have existed. I thank him for all of his support over the last several years, as a doctoral supervisor, a prolific and thought-provoking scholar, and as a friend. Nancy Christie provided a keen editorial eye as well, encouraging me when I was frustrated and helping me clarify my sometimes-murky thinking. I am grateful to both of you.

I would like to offer thanks to my doctoral committee, namely Stephen Heathorn and Martin Horn. I appreciated all of your feedback. I also appreciate how you stayed on my committee, even if Canadian history was not your focus, as it encouraged me to pursue a more transnational perspective. My external advisor, Paul Litt, also challenged me to rethink my ideas of nationalism and to make my assertions bolder. I thank him for his continued support. Paul Stevens and William Westfall at York University also oversaw this material in its very early stages, when I was first experimenting with writing about anti-Catholicism over a decade ago. I thank both of them.

I could continue listing people to whom I am indebted for pages, so I will only mention a few here from McMaster. Ryan Vieira helped me think about complex questions of causality, discourse, and ideology, while still remaining someone I want to hang out with. The same can be said for Jennifer Tunnicliffe, with whom I have had the privilege of both working on scholarly panels and chatting about family life. Devon Stillwell-Bowley also helped me think about history, while remaining a close friend.

My family, of course, remains my most steadfast and valuable support. My parents, while not always consistent in understanding the purpose of my project (particularly Dad), have always been enthusiastic. Mom continues to read everything I write, even if she is troubled by these attitudes toward Catholics. It was your mixed religious marriage that first got me interested in this topic, as did my brother's fascination with Northern Ireland and sectarian politics there. You never wavered in your encouragement, and I thank you. My in-laws, David Oakleaf and Anne McWhir, have provided not only their keen editorial eyes and advice, but a loving support system out here on the Prairies. I thank them for welcoming me so warmly. Last but certainly not least, I thank my wife, Catherine. Without you I never would have had the confidence to actually finish this work or find the right words. I am forever in the active voice now. I cannot believe that you tolerated me discussing anti-Catholicism for this long, but I think this is a testament to your patience and your character. Love is not a strong enough word. The arrival of Willa Jean has only made us stronger. This is dedicated to the two of you.

NOT QUITE US

INTRODUCTION

Anti-Catholicism and Identity

A.R. Kaufman, an eccentric and wealthy rubber manufacturer, birth-control activist, and promoter of sterilization during the Great Depression, was not shy about his opinions of the Catholic Church and its role in blocking the progress of these and other causes. In 1936–37 he attended the bitter legislative debates over a revision of the separate-school tax in Ontario, producing bizarre-yet-illuminating collages of his experience in a scrapbook he kept of the sessions, mostly containing cutouts from Attilio Mussino's classic 1901 illustrations for *Pinocchio*. Kaufman linked the lobbying of the Church on funding for separate schools to its opposition to birth control and sterilization, as both campaigns revealed the political power of the Church. His cartoons portray the Church in many threatening forms. In one, it was a sinister snake with its eyes on the legislature, blocking advances from good citizens like Kaufman and plotting to use its unlimited money, massive organization, and "gently persuasive powers on the leaders of the Liberal Party now in power" (see Figure 0.1). In another, the Church was an amorphous spectre labelled "Pope," holding Kaufman back from entering the building with members of the (self-interested) medical industry (see Figure 0.2). In perhaps the most disturbing cartoon, the Church is a crow with what appears to be blood on its beak, taking advantage of a slumbering Canadian Protestantism, represented as a plump, contented sheep (see Figure 0.3). In this latter collage, "Conservatism" occupies the lowly "Do Not Disturb" mat, while the menacing crow is labelled "Liberal R.C. Group." In another illustration, Kaufman portrays the Liberal Party as a dancing line of animals, enthusiastically, even recklessly, following the dictates of its Catholic masters – the caption reads "The Roman Church leads the rejoicing procession" – with little to no opposition

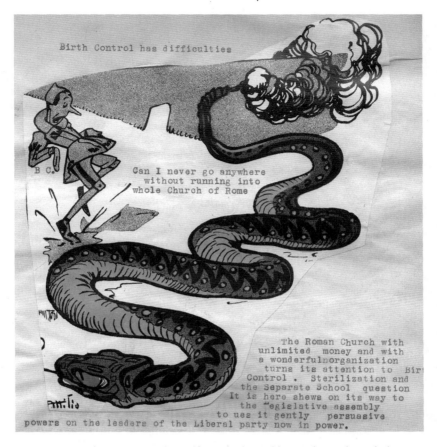

Figure 0.1 Kaufman portrays himself as a frightened bystander to the "whole Church of Rome," which is a sinister snake travelling to the Ontario legislature to "use its gently persuasive powers" on the Liberal Party. He adds, "The Church of Rome with unlimited money and with a wonderful organization turns its attention to Birth Control, Sterilization, and the Separate School Question."

(see Figure 0.4). For Kaufman, the political control the Catholic Church exercised, either through open manipulation or the apathy of Tories and Protestants, was more than obvious and explained to him why his crusade to better the country was stymied.[1]

Anti-Catholicism has proven to be an underdeveloped topic of study within Canadian history, especially its twentieth-century manifestations, despite its important role as a cultural and intellectual force

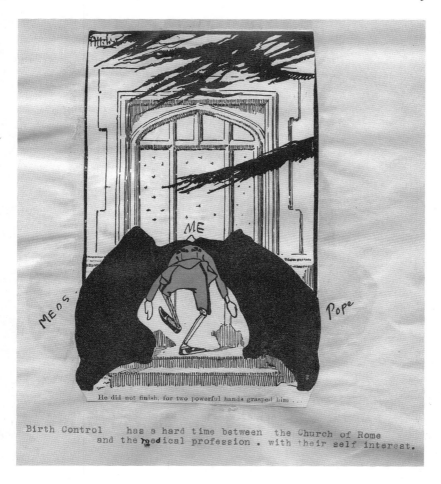

Figure 0.2 Kaufman saw the "Church of Rome" and the medical profession as joint forces preventing birth control due to their "Self Interest." Here he is being prohibited from entering the legislature by shadowy figures labelled "Meds" and "Pope."

helping to shape English-Canadian discourses of national identity.[2] Anti-Catholicism was not confined simply to the "lunatic fringe," such as the Ku Klux Klan or the Orange Order. It was also not just a remnant of a more sectarian nineteenth century, polarized by the execution of Riel or the Manitoba Schools Crisis. Instead, anti-Catholicism was central to the world views of mainstream intellectuals, such as Arthur Lower and C.E. Silcox; politicians, such as Robert

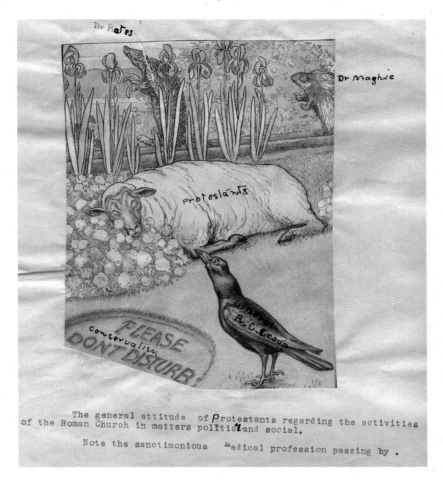

Figure 0.3 Kaufman fears that Protestants are not paying enough attention to the political activities of the Catholic Church (and its Liberal allies), portrayed as a crow with what appears to be blood on its beak. Slumbering contentedly, the sheep-Protestants are matched by a Conservatism that does not want to fight this force.

Borden and George Drew; civic/church organizations, like the "ecumenical" Inter-Church Committee on Protestant–Roman Catholic Relations (ICC); and private citizens expressing themselves through letters to the editor or letters to politicians. Anti-Catholicism was also evident among prominent leftist intellectuals and activists at different times, such as Eugene Forsey, F.R. Scott, and J.S. Woodsworth, who promoted caricatured perceptions of the Catholic Church as harmful

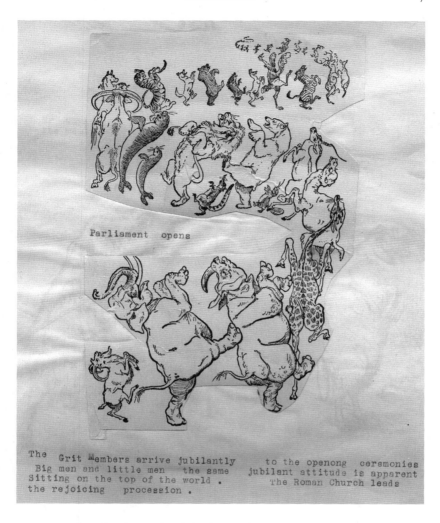

Figure 0.4 The Liberals parade jubilantly into the legislature, according to Kaufman, being easily led by the Roman Catholic Church.

to the Canadian body politic. What linked these figures from across the political, ideological, and social spectrum, beyond their status as English-speaking Protestants of various levels of devoutness and denomination, was a commitment to a vision of Canada couched in a teleological understanding of world history in which the Catholic Church was an irredeemably regressive, authoritarian, and medieval force, which bred a dual allegiance in its followers by demanding unquestioning loyalty to a foreign power, namely the pope in Rome. It had been – and needed to continuously be – countered by the enlightenment, individualism, and inherent democracy of the Reformation. Those in the Canadian context linked Canada's British heritage to this grand narrative, (re)iterating a synonymy of Britishness, Protestantism, and democracy. As these diverse intellectuals, public figures, and private Canadians negotiated and constructed Canada's national identity during the first several decades of the twentieth century, the prevalence and consistency of anti-Catholicism demonstrates that the allegedly secular/civic Canadian nationalism that emerged during this period was in fact deeply religious, specifically Protestant, and fundamentally British.

This book is an intellectual history of anti-Catholicism in Canada. It takes a "culturalist approach" to intellectual history, focusing not only on the thinking and writing of public intellectuals and the elites, but on the history of the idea of anti-Catholicism and how its various manifestations circulated through English Canada, constantly reinscribing an Anglo-Protestant conception of Canadian national identity.[3] I take seriously the ideas present in and/or underlying letters from the editor, editorials, doggerel poetry, cartoons, correspondence, legal defences, public lectures, "fringe" religious literature, and lengthy dissertations on liberalism. Patterns of anti-Catholicism changed with the socio-cultural context, as ideas are inextricably tied to socio-cultural reality, and I examine how a broad range of anti-Catholic tropes were part of the intellectual and cultural landscape of twentieth-century Canada.

I have found innumerable examples of anti-Catholic sentiment in studies of specific figures and organizations, yet they have rarely been studied as part of an explicit pattern of anti-Catholicism. I became convinced that this warranted study as a phenomenon itself, and one that has contained a variety of different strains over the course of the twentieth century. The figures I have chosen to focus on – many of whom were "respectable" people who contributed to public discourse and often shared social networks, though they spanned the political, ideological, and denominational spectrum – are representative of these strains. For example, Eugene Forsey was from the left, George Drew and Charlotte Whitton from the right, and Arthur Lower from the liberal centre; T.T. Shields came from fundamentalist circles, C.E. Silcox from the United Church, and Watson Kirkconnell from Baptist ranks; then there were well-known figures like F.R. Scott and Emily

Murphy, and more obscure actors, such as the Farthing brothers. I am influenced in my choice of examples by Dror Wahrman, who has posited a means by which historians, who are often accused of creating a "weak collage" from disparate "cultural *loci*," can evaluate and present their evidence as more than just a collection of eclectic representations. By focusing on the repetition and resonance of language and practices, in other words its relative consistency and presence as "commonsense," the historian can discern important – albeit uneven – patterns from an intentionally eclectic evidentiary base.[4] It is my contention that these figures, supplemented by more popular manifestations of anti-Catholicism, are representative of a wide spectrum of English-Canadian political and ideological opinions, and demonstrate the resonance anti-Catholicism had in twentieth-century Anglo-Protestant Canada.

This study builds on the work of Canadian historians J.R. Miller and Nancy Christie and that of American historians Mark Massa and Philip Jenkins. Not much has been written about Canadian anti-Catholicism since Miller's pioneering work in the 1970s and 1980s, when he focused largely on the late-nineteenth century and specific manifestations of anti-Catholicism (that is, D'Alton McCarthy and the Equal Rights Association). Christie is an influential exception, bringing the study of anti-Catholicism into the twentieth century and linking it to the immediate postwar intellectual milieu. Her study is quite brief, however, and not dedicated to a sustained analysis of anti-Catholicism.[5] Massa and Jenkins have contributed to the recognition of anti-Catholicism as a tradition with a long history and contemporary currency in the United States. Jenkins's contention that anti-Catholicism remains salient because of its almost infinite flexibility has proven influential to this study, as has his discussion of the role of the institutional Catholic Church in fuelling anti-Catholicism. According to Jenkins, critics of Roman Catholicism feel relatively comfortable denouncing a hierarchical institution, especially in the fiercely democratic United States, without fear of significant public reprisal. This perspective largely ignores the central place of the papacy and the Vatican in the Catholic faith, taking for granted that most "reasonable people" reject the Church's hierarchical structure.[6]

Relatedly, Massa links anti-Catholicism to the deep currents of American civic culture, namely Americans' commitment to individualism and how Catholicism was believed to violate (and sometimes *did/does* self-consciously reject) this commitment. Massa also notes how the Church's claims to comprehensiveness in civil life and morality often challenge modern assumptions of the separation of church and state, causing problems for Catholics and the Church in "secular" democratic nations. The Church and faith are thus agents in Massa's work, although he is certainly not blaming anti-Catholicism on Catholics (a theme that does appear in my work).[7] My study borrows from these scholars, applying their insights to an intellectual history that examines a specifically twentieth-century English-Canadian identity and nationalism through the lens of anti-Catholicism. Anti-Catholicism in Canada often pulled many of the figures into international/Anglosphere debates occurring at various historical moments (for example, Progressivism, the two world wars, the Spanish Civil War, the battle against communism). Canadian anti-Catholicism thus had domestic characteristics, derivative characteristics (from a general Anglo-Protestant reading of history and influenced by Canada's place in the North Atlantic triangle), and characteristics forged through reacting to international affairs. These strains combined to create a distinctly twentieth-century, Anglo-Protestant, and Canadian anti-Catholicism.

While not a detailed social history of how anti-Catholicism affected the everyday lives of Catholics and Protestants in Canada (see Table 0.1), I have not completely ignored the relationship of ideas to lived reality. The relationship between text and context is fundamental to the function of ideas in society. As John Porter noted in his landmark sociological study *The Vertical Mosaic*, Catholics (including but not limited to French-speaking Catholics) tended to be underrepresented in the upper echelons of Canadian society and in positions of socio-political influence in the first several decades of the twentieth century.[8] A casual discrimination existed against Catholics as being "not quite" Canadian, a prejudice documented in the chapters that follow. The objective of this study is to examine how anti-Catholicism – specifically how perceptions of Catholics – shaped discourses of national identity. It is my contention that these discourses facilitated a social reality (and vice versa) that was often exclusionary and prejudicial toward Catholics. In other words, it influenced how Catholics and Protestants *lived* anti-Catholicism.

Although I have sought sources across a broad spectrum, some voices are more dominant than others – especially the voices of men. The gendered nature of the public sphere continued deep into the twentieth century, and was historically contingent, not a reflection of

Table 0.1
Canadian Catholic population, as percentage of the overall Canadian population

Year	Percentage of population, Catholic
1901	41.5
1911	39.3
1921	38.5
1931	39.5
1941	41.7
1951	43.4
1961	45.7
1971	46.2
1981	47.3
1991	45.2
2001	43.2

K.G. Basavarajappa and Bali Ram, "Section A: Population and Migration," Series A1 and A164-184, *Historical Statistics in Canada*, 2nd Edition (Social Science Federation of Canada, Statistics Canada, 1983); *2001 Census: Analysis Series, Religions in Canada* (Statistics Canada, 2003), 18. *1981 Census of Canada: 20 Per Cent Data Base* (Statistics Canada, 1983), 16. Calculations done by author.

any lack of opinion, expertise, or "unsullied purity" on the part of women concerned with the socio-political and cultural influence of the Catholic Church. However, I have sought to include the voices and perspectives of women wherever possible (such as Emily Murphy, Kate Foster, and Charlotte Whitton). Whether expressing anger toward the Church's position on contraception, sterilization, and/or abortion (a thread that can be traced throughout this story), attacking the Church's patriarchal structure or its (at best) ambivalence toward – if not outright rejection of – feminist conceptions of women's rights, or simply being anti-Catholics who happened to be women, women were part of these debates.

The story is centred largely in Central Canada (Ontario and Quebec). The relative influence of Central Canada on the national narrative during much of this period, due to the concentration of population and the associated cultural, intellectual, and political sway of the region, remains the primary focus. Many intellectual, cultural, and political institutions were "headquartered" in Central Canada for much of the period studied here (from the CBC, to *Maclean's* and *Saturday Night*, to the *United Church Observer*). I do not simply equate Canada with Ontario; I do explore how Anglo-Protestant Ontarians, particularly Ontario-based intellectuals and politicians, embraced a self-appointed status as the defender of the British tradition in Canada against the incursions of a foreign Catholicism, largely stemming from Quebec and Southern and Eastern Europe. The ardency of this feeling manifested itself most obviously in the extended importance of the Orange Order to the Ontario socio-political milieu, into at least the 1970s, much longer than almost anywhere else in Canada.[9]

There are significant exceptions, however, that I believe allow this to be more than a regional study. For example, Chapter 1 deals extensively with the Prairies (Manitoba, Saskatchewan, and Alberta), focusing on the reactions to the massive influx of non-Protestant immigrants during the first decades of the twentieth century and how this would shape hopes for Western Canada as the future of the nation. Chapter 2 deals extensively with Quebeckers, albeit Anglo-Protestant Quebeckers, emphasizing their discomfort with Catholicism. British Columbia, with its small Catholic population relative to the rest of Canada (17.4 per cent of the population as of 2001, the smallest percentage in the country), is little discussed, although its use by anti-Catholics as an idealized province, escaping from the sectarian divides of Central Canada (only 8 per cent French-speaking population as of 2006) is examined, if briefly.[10] Anti-Catholicism did have an important place in the socio-cultural and political environment of twentieth-century Atlantic Canada, embodied in the continuing salience of the Orange Order in Newfoundland, the Protestant-Catholic tensions related to a growing Acadian population in New Brunswick, and the political divisions that often operated along denominational lines in many of the provinces.[11] Watson Kirkconnell, Ontario-born but later president of Acadia University in Wolfville, Nova Scotia, and some Maritime Baptist sources are used. The narratives of national identity in this story, however, tended to "look West" from the centre, seeing in the settlement of the Prairies the future of Canada's peculiar British democracy threatened by the presence of the Catholic Church. Many other figures detailed here (especially Arthur Lower) saw Canada's destiny in the "solving" of the historic divide between Catholic Quebec and Protestant English Canada, although some constructed New Brunswick as a component of a feared French-Catholic "Papal state" in Canada. Anti-Catholicism reflected the predominance of "the

French question" (what role French Canadians should play in Canadian affairs and identity) in public life, along with the concomitant regional and historic tensions between English Canada and French Canada, with the fortresses of each in this battle residing in Ontario and Quebec. Anti-Catholicism did not exist only in the minds of Ontarians, but it was often Ontarians who believed it was their role to publicly defend the nation against Catholic malfeasance.

A detailed analysis of anti-Catholicism challenges long-standing assumptions about the history of Canadian nationalism, which typically posit a teleological narrative that tells of a Canada moving from an exclusive form of nationalism based in explicitly British ideals to an open civic nationalism based on universal values and allegiance to a neutral state.[12] Historian José Igartua argues for this perspective most recently in his study *The Other Quiet Revolution: National Identity in English Canada, 1945–71*. Igartua positions ethnic nationalism as conservative and particularistic, privileging the British connection, and civic nationalism as "universalist," embracing liberty and allegiance to the state, with the latter suddenly supplanting the former in the 1960s. While Igartua is careful not to conceive of a total divide between ethnic and civic nationalism, he still presents the former as "bad" and the latter as "good" and assumes the rapid disappearance of ethnic nationalism in the face of an enlightened civic challenge.[13] Conservative intellectual C.P. Champion has offered a sustained critique of Igartua, accusing him of continuing a long Canadian tradition of condemning Britishness as archaic, racist, and representing a "pre-Canadian" heritage. Champion sees Canadian intellectuals, politicians, and popular culture as adhering to traditions of Britishness throughout the postwar era, yet he ultimately overcorrects. Champion theorizes that the perpetuation of civic nationalism was the fulfillment, rather than the rejection of, the liberal conception of Britishness, causing him to assume proclamations of tolerance to be evidence of them.[14] This perspective echoes that of intellectuals during the 1940s and 1950s who believed Britishness itself represented universalized values.

Yet intellectuals, public figures, and civic organizations that identified themselves as perpetuating liberal and progressive ideals, or conservative and fundamentalist ones for that matter, were in fact often unable to accept Catholicism as a valid component of the modern nation, due to its perceived authoritarianism and its alien place in the

"Canadian tradition." These actors used an implicitly and explicitly Protestant understanding of history, freedom, tolerance, and liberty to argue against the full inclusion of Catholicism and Catholics within Canadian society. As scholars Paul Bramadat and David Seljak have noted, even while English-Canadian nationalism was transforming in the later twentieth century, and embracing religious tolerance as a central value, these same Protestant values remained as a core tenet of some vague sense of ethnic Canadianism for many Anglo-Protestants because of Protestantism's long associations with English-Canadian culture and nationhood. This caused Catholics, other non-Protestant Christians, and non-Christians to find it difficult to fit into English-Canadian society.[15] Anti-Catholicism as an analytical framework through which to examine nationalism demonstrates that the historiographical dichotomization of civic and ethnic nationalism, the positioning of civic nationalism as inherently liberal, and the concomitant understanding of Canadian nationalism as becoming increasingly tolerant of difference does not allow for the flexibility and nuance of such ideologies in Canada's intellectual, cultural, and political history.

This study positions itself between these schools of thought, calling for a better understanding of Britishness, and its constant companion Protestantism, as an important component of Canadian identity, without either valorizing the British connection or rejecting it as evidence of a "colonial mentality." Anti-Catholicism in Canada demonstrates the elision between civic and ethnic nationalism, as well as the potentially exclusionary nature of "universal" concepts of nationalism, by tracing the changing relationship between Britishness, Protestantism, and national identity throughout twentieth-century Canada. By paying close attention to the discourses of Anglo-Protestant intellectuals, politicians, religious leaders, and private citizens in this period, I demonstrate that, far from abandoning the ethno-religious prejudices of the past, these figures reconstituted these narrowly British values and institutions as "universal." In his study of nationalism, Bernard Yack has claimed that conceptions of civic nationalism simply "redescrib[e] contingent communities of memory and experience as if they were nothing more than voluntary associations of individuals, united by their shared attachment to a body of moral and political principles."[16] This imposition of order upon conflicting – and often excluded – identities or memories replicates that of ethnic nationalism; it is simply not as explicitly based upon blood and claims a neutral, voluntary character. For Yack, civic nationalism is itself rife with ethnocentrism, embodying the historical and cultural baggage of the American and French revolutions. In other words, the "civic nation" is not neutral, as some Canadian scholars have posited, but laden with assumptions about "rational" and "voluntary" citizen participation. The central myth of the civic nation that Yack refutes as false is the assumption of the total freedom of choice for citizens belonging or participating in a civic nation as it refuses to recognize the continuation of, and even intrinsic reality of, marginalization. This Western conceit, for Yack, represents "a mixture of self-congratulation and wishful thinking."[17]

Indeed, the Anglo-Protestants discussed in this study centred much of their criticism of Catholics and the Church on the apparent inability of Catholics to exercise rational choice, that central reality of a modern civic-minded democracy, simultaneously claiming for Protestants (or at least non-Catholics) the realm of unadulterated rational choice. Through the prism of anti-Catholicism, it becomes apparent that civic and ethnic nationalism, far from being oppositional, frequently co-exist within nationalistic discourses. The universality proclaimed and cherished by civic nationalists is, in other words, a contingent universality when those calling for inclusion do not "fit" into the prescribed mould, in this case a British-Protestant mould, and certainly not when they are believed to embody a "foreign" institution, in both the ethnic/cultural sense of that term and the civic/political.[18]

Britishness, along with nationalism and anti-Catholicism, is a complex concept, which shifts in meaning when used by different individuals, political parties, or interest groups. Yet an appeal to British traditions and British institutions, explicit or not, underlay much of the anti-Catholic sentiment of this period in Canada. I understand Britishness as serving as a "collective inheritance," containing a constellation of ideas, symbols, and myths that posit the normative character, if not superiority, of British values and institutions.[19] English Canadians were intimately interwoven into this "inheritance," constantly borrowing from and contributing their own ideas, symbols, and myths to the fabric of the whole. Even if the mother country was perceived as aloof or inward-looking, many English Canadians emphasized their continued devotion to British ideals. As Jonathan Vance has noted in his study of Canadians serving and living in Britain during and between the world wars, many Canadians held that it was Canada's responsibility to represent traditional British values in the face of the complacency of the mother country. These values, such as democracy and social order, were necessary for the proper functioning of not only society but in fact of the international community.[20] Anti-Catholicism fit into this process of self-definition, as it was also central to what many perceived as the traditional British identity. Britishness in Canada thus reflected trends in Britain and the Empire/Commonwealth (the Anglosphere), but socio-political developments on the home front determined its shape. It was not just derivative of Britain, but was a component of a reciprocal relationship in which English Canadians saw themselves – in the words of James Belich – as potentially "Better Britons," separated from the crass politics of the mother country, yet dependent on it for their heritage.[21] Protestantism remained central to this identity in Canada through the first several decades of the twentieth century, and influenced attitudes towards Catholics and the place of Catholicism within the Canadian body politic. If only Canada could rise above harmful sectional conflicts, in this case believed to be caused by the presence of the Church and its power among New and French Canadians, it could act as a model nation, embodying the eternal values of the United Kingdom.

Although often based on an explicit dedication to preserving the British connection and British institutions or the superiority of Protestantism as a faith tradition, anti-Catholicism was just as often expressed through a subtler language, arguing that the heritage of the modern nation, indeed the modern world itself, was grounded in a reading of history in which the Reformation served as the foundational moment. This foundational moment, even in ostensibly secular discourse that rejected traditionalist interpretations of Protestant theology, signalled the emergence of liberty, individualism, and eventually democracy, ideals exclusive of Catholicism. The linking of Protestantism with liberty, democracy, and individualism in both secular and explicitly religious sources helps explain the concern many Anglo-Protestant Canadians felt in the face of a changing nation, particularly the perceived eclipsing of Protestantism by rival faiths and the declining Anglo-Protestant birth rate. It was through this conception of the world and the importance of Protestantism to it that mainstream intellectuals could vilify the Catholic Church internationally and in Canada (particularly in Quebec) by using civic, universalist values emptied of overt ethnic references. English-Canadian claims that Canada outgrew a narrowly ethnic nationalism and embraced an inclusive civic nationalism at roughly mid-century neglect the extent to which Anglo-Protestantism, with its attendant anti-Catholicism, shaped discourses of English-Canadian identity throughout the twentieth century and provided roots for a changing language into later, more "secular," decades.

But what is anti-Catholicism? At its simplest, it is hostility to Catholicism as a belief system, the Catholic Church as an institution, and/or to Catholics as adherents to this belief system. Yet anti-Catholicism consists of much more than offering criticisms of the Church or individual Catholics over their theological traditions or position on social, cultural, and moral issues. Jenkins characterizes the difference between legitimate criticism and anti-Catholicism as occurring when an essential feature of the belief system and/or institution is held to perpetuate some form of behavioural evil, inevitably and forever.[22] Anti-Catholicism also engages with a coterie of stereotypes, tropes, and themes with a particular historical significance that can present Catholicism as a false faith (as not truly Christian), but more often challenges its ability to function in modern society, positioning the Church and Catholicism as one of – if not *the* – enemy of progress, individualism, and democracy. The Church and doctrine, in this understanding, is hopelessly authoritarian and purposely creates followers that are incapable of self-realization and independent thought, the cornerstones of democracy, and reduces the Catholic Church to a power-hungry caricature, attempting to dominate world affairs and nations for its own benefit.[23] Similar to the understanding of Islam in Islamophobia, anti-Catholic discourses distort whether Catholicism is actually a faith tradition or a political ideology dedicated to establishing an alien "way of life" in certain nations.[24] Mark Massa has identified three major forms of anti-Catholicism. Cultural anti-Catholicism proclaims certain cultures to be specifically Protestant (synonymous with democratic) in "ordering" and composition, emphasizing allegedly Protestant values like freedom of thought and access to the "true" Gospel. Catholicism, on the other hand, is "European" (Continental) and authoritarian in nature. Intellectual anti-Catholicism portrays Catholic traditions and theology as inherently opposed to various formative historical moments, such as the Reformation and the Enlightenment, and therefore hostile to the secular state. Social-scientific anti-Catholicism is hostile to Catholicism because it is an impediment to the development of a truly pluralist, religiously privatized society. Proponents of this perspective, according to Massa, engage in a process of "boundary-making," whereby the Church is castigated for its continuing assertion of authority in the public sphere over sexual and moral issues and its undemocratically rigid hierarchy.[25]

It is impossible, however, to sever Massa's three main types of anti-Catholicism from each other. It is a multi-faceted phenomenon, with numerous competing thematic elements that often overlap. In addition, there is a stricter theological strain of anti-Catholicism that understands the pope to be the biblical Antichrist and the faith itself as anti-Christian and pagan, although this tradition, dating back to the Reformation and Luther himself, was often limited in Canada to fundamentalist circles. More common was an ideological form of anti-Catholicism, embraced by, but certainly not confined to, the Orange Order or the Canadian Protestant League (CPL), which saw Rome as lurking behind all social relations, political decisions, and limitations of liberty. Adherents of this view were unable either to recognize social forces as independent of the Church or to allow for Catholics to act outside the dictates of the faith. Ideological anti-Catholics tied the blind loyalty of Catholics to their hierarchy and its "foolish" doctrines to the nationally detrimental actions of individual Catholics. The faith of these Catholics thus prevented them from being able to participate in civil society, a society defined by its devotion to "non-Catholic" values such as freedom, liberty, and democracy.

Like Islamophobia and its distortion of Islam, anti-Catholicism is a "way of thinking" about Catholicism that essentializes the faith and the faithful as a backward Other, "incompatible with modernity" and its corollary, democracy.[26] According to Medhi Semati, Islamophobia is a "cultural-ideological outlook" seeking to explain the ills of the world through an easy, but horrifying, narrative.[27] Chris Allen has provided a useful and workable definition of Islamophobia that translates well to this discussion of anti-Catholicism: "Islamophobia is an ideology, similar in theory, function and purpose to racism and other similar phenomena, that sustains and perpetuates negatively evaluated meaning about Muslims and Islam ... shaping and determining understanding, perceptions and attitudes in the social consensus – the shared languages and conceptual maps – that inform and construct thinking about Muslims and Islam as Other."[28] Anti-Catholicism shares with Islamophobia its status as a means of knowing, in this case knowing, understanding, and producing Catholicism that becomes commonsensical, in the way that Orientalism produces the Orient/Islam through allegedly objective analysis of "the facts" surrounding Catholicism. Catholicism is not a "free subject of thought or action," in the mind of the anti-Catholic or within the anti-Catholic tradition, but is used to elaborate "the self" in a specific context; Catholicism is ascribed meanings that become anchored in the matrices of ideas and symbols that compose everyday life. Anti-Catholicism is an umbrella term for – again borrowing from recent analysis of Islamophobia – "that which perpetuates and sustains those meanings which are relevant and acknowledged in the shared languages and conceptual maps of today's setting" about Catholicism.[29]

Unlike the discourses of Islamophobia that obfuscate the realities of Islamic history, however, Catholicism is undeniably central to European history and culture, and this is acknowledged even by the most ardent anti-Catholics. How then does one construct the "Catholic-as-Other" when Catholicism is so integral to the existence of the Western European project? Even if Catholic cultural contributions are demeaned and dismissed, as often occurs in anti-Catholicism, Catholicism is still present; it still exists. Where Islamophobia and anti-Catholicism again resemble each other is in the solution to this conundrum: Catholicism becomes for modern Western Europe and North America the "distorted mirror of its own past," as it threatens the universalist foundations of modernity, such as the sovereign individual, capitalist social relations, and the separation of church and state. It signals a return to a dark age of development, impossible in the teleological understanding of civilizational progress, that modernity has left behind. In Islamophobia, the West and universality are equated; in anti-Catholicism, Protestantism – or at least the values associated with Protestantism, as the discourse does not require an explicitly theological basis – and universality/secularity are equated. Catholicism, in other words, violates what is accepted as normal and good in modern Western society.[30]

The latter point is important, because anti-Catholicism being/becoming a commonsense cultural reference point makes it difficult for commentators on Catholicism to operate outside of the meanings it produces. The narratives and tropes inflect otherwise legitimate criticisms of the Church, forcing many discussions of Catholicism and the Church to be carried out within the framework(s) of anti-Catholicism and periodically undermining these criticisms. This is not to say that it is impossible to criticize the Church and faith without being anti-Catholic. It is to say that anti-Catholicism often provides the pre-existing "rules of the game" with which subsequent discourse(s) engage.

A sustained analysis of anti-Catholic sentiment in Canada also reveals a lot of similarity between so-called "vulgar" and "genteel" forms of anti-Catholicism. In revising this rigid divide, I borrow from Alan Mendelson's study of anti-Semitism among the Anglo-Canadian elite. Mendelson argues that "genteel" anti-Semites strove to differentiate themselves from the "vulgar" anti-Semitism of Nazis and street gangs by presenting their understanding of Jews as having been gained through reason, and they did not promote or engage in physical violence. For Mendelson, "genteel" anti-Semitism is perhaps even more insidious, as it masks itself in a veneer of objectivity, thereby making anti-Semitism respectable. Both types of anti-Semitism rely upon prejudicial, caricatured assumptions about Jews.[31] I am not equating the horrors resulting from anti-Semitism with anti-Catholic attitudes, just as I am not equating contemporary Islamophobia with anti-Catholicism. The "way of thinking" that produces these strains have a "family resemblance," however; there is no essentialist core defining them, yet the pattern is recognizable and familiar.[32]

Mendelson's model lends itself well to the anti-Catholicism that existed in Canada in the twentieth century. Many intellectuals, prominent Protestant figures, and private citizens engaged in an "objective" condemnation of Catholicism, while simultaneously expressing outrage at the unpatriotic excesses of the Orange Order or the fiery fundamentalist Rev. T.T. Shields. Yet this reveals a glaring irony, because their conclusions were often the same: Catholicism was a "fossilized faith,"[33] hindering the development of Canada in the modern world. In addition, some Protestant Canadians perceived Catholicism as a rival form of (counter-)modernity, providing a systematic alternative to liberal democracy, which Protestantism was potentially unable to match. This elicited anxiety among some that, while Catholicism was gaining in social respectability and sheer numbers, the Protestant tradition was losing its vitality due to the increased materialism and affluence of Protestants (concomitantly lowering the Protestant birth rate) and the inherent divisions within Protestantism. Allison O'Mahen Malcom has noted that studies of the Orange Order in Canada have tended to separate the anti-Catholicism of groups labelled as extremist from mainstream Protestant opinion, perpetuating the historical assumption that mainstream Protestants did not share the vehement hostility to Catholicism. For Malcom, this divide is artificial, as elements, if not the language, of these "extremists" were present throughout society, even into the twentieth century.[34] Malcom's ideas have proven influential to my study, as I focus on the sentiments of mainstream figures, comparing them periodically to the sentiment of "extremists" to reveal previously unexamined continuities. Protestants of all denominations, ideology, and societal positions felt the Catholic threat to their values, as these very values were believed to be the sole jurisdiction of Protestantism.

As Michael Gross's study *The War against Catholicism: Liberalism and the Anti-Catholic Imagination in Nineteenth-Century Germany* has shown, this seemingly paradoxical situation, where one must oppose Catholicism as "unfit" for the modern democratic society in the name of civil and religious liberty, represents the historical problem of using anti-Catholicism as a means of formulating liberal identity and a particular concept of modernity. According to Gross, anti-Catholicism "was not derivative but constitutive of liberalism."[35] It provided the means through which to express one's democratic bona fides – one's commitment to preserving a modern social order based on individual choice and representative government – in a rapidly changing world. Catholicism needed to be challenged, reformed (with all the Protestant connotations of this word), or, in perhaps the major difference between "vulgar" and "genteel" anti-Catholicism, even expunged from the nation in general. It simply did not "fit."

Anti-Catholicism, in the words of historians Yvonne Maria Werner and Jonas Harvard, has served as a "unifying other" in many predominantly Protestant nations, including Canada. This "unifying other" embodies the traits deemed undesirable and/or unacceptable in a modern citizenry, in turn constructing an idealized self/citizen by expelling these taints. Anti-Catholicism provides a "shared symbolic language," steeped in European history and culture, that both transcends national boundaries and allows people of varying perspectives to communicate their understanding of not only the citizen but of "the nation." It allows commentators to apply and adapt this flexible language and historical framework to changing domestic issues and national contexts while remaining consistent in its overarching narrative. Its exact manifestation is thus contingent on specific concerns and events of specific times, but the interior logic of anti-Catholicism remains dedicated to constructing a faith, an institution, and a congregation as not quite "Us."[36]

In the Canadian context, the "Us" being defined in contrast to Catholicism are what I will often call Anglo-Protestants. This is not to position this group as a monolithic whole, as one of the major themes of this study is to critique and deconstruct how Catholicism was "monolithized." As mentioned, I will be discussing English-speaking Protestants from various denominational backgrounds, levels of devoutness, political ideologies, public recognition, social standing, and careers. I will also demonstrate that different figures had different criticisms of Catholicism and the Church, with some, such as F.R. Scott, advocating moderate levels of rapprochement with the Church, and others rejecting any chance of compromise. What unites these figures in my study is their concern with the influence of the Church and Catholicism on the proper functioning of the nation, on the future of Canada in the modern world and the democratic values believed to serve as the foundations of the Canadian nation. All of them, in one way or another, engaged with anti-Catholicism as a lens through which to understand the Church and the faith.

Inextricable with the Catholic "Other" in Canada were concerns about the ethnic and racial composition of the nation and the consequences this held for the health of Canadian democracy. Hostility toward immigrants, often from Central, Southern, and Eastern Europe, as well as racism, intersected with the web of tropes, symbols, meanings, and historical assumptions anti-Catholicism represents. These people – with all the problematic connotations of that phrase – represented alien traditions, an uneducated peasantry steeped in the authoritarianism of their Mother Church, and a barrier to national unity/homogeneity. In other words, it was not *just* the skin colour or the "climatic conditions" of those arriving in Canada that elicited xenophobia; it was not only an issue of race. Assumptions about the religious traditions of immigrants, whether affiliated with Catholicism, Orthodoxy, or other non-Protestant branches of Christianity, intersected with this racial essentialism to construct for many a hopelessly alien population incapable of fulfilling the obligations of democracy.

Perhaps an even greater threat to national unity, however, lay in the fortress of Catholicism: Quebec. Anti-Catholicism and anti-French Canadianism were so entangled in much of this period that it is difficult, if not impossible, to separate them. At the core of attitudes toward Quebec in English Canada was the deterministic power of the Catholic Church. Being French Canadian meant being not only Catholic, but a particularly insular form of Catholic. French Canadians, in this framework, could not escape the authority of the Church, which was assumed to control all aspects of Quebec society. Even after the Quiet Revolution and the widespread acceptance in English

Canada of the narrative of sudden secularization in Quebec, the historical influence of the Church was viewed as harmful, producing an immature and angry *nationalisme*. Yet Quebec also had an enormous amount of influence over the socio-political realities of Canada, especially in the Liberal Party, and thus had to be dealt with seriously if Canada was to achieve its destiny as a united modern nation. If this Catholic "Other" had a face, it was the face not only of an institution foreign to the traditions of the modern world and a British nation, but of "foreigners," including French Canadians, who could not "fit."

Anti-Catholicism was not static. It was, rather, a dynamic component of English-Canadian nationalism in the period covered in this study. The first chapter examines the period from 1900 to 1929, specifically how anti-Catholic rhetoric focused on the preponderant influence this "backward" religion had upon the nation, undermining the hopes of Progressive Era reformers who advocated for increased democracy and efficiency. This progressive anti-Catholic mode singled out Quebec during the First World War as disloyal and anti-progressive, while attacking largely Catholic (or Orthodox) immigrants in Western Canada as hindering national development, particularly in the 1920s. Many leftist intellectuals clung to progressive anti-Catholicism into the 1930s, something detailed in Chapter 2, as they saw Catholicism as a barrier to democratic progress – or indeed as a threat to its very existence. Catholicism, in their minds, was a reactionary force facilitating demagoguery and corruption, particularly in Quebec. Those who ascribed to this brand of anti-Catholicism also believed it to be the foremost enemy of another progressive *cause célèbre*, contraception, along with the more extreme practice of eugenics. Progressive anti-Catholicism also contained an explicit/implicit devotion to British institutions and traditions. Indeed, British civic values, held to be universal, were tinged with an ethnicity that became evident when "other" groups, such as French Canadians and non-British European immigrants, were assumed to be irreconcilable to these fundamentally British values, since Catholics stubbornly maintained their religious traditions. Chapter 2 thus explicitly connects the anti-Catholicism of progressives to that of more traditionally conservative actors.

With the outbreak of the Second World War, anti-Catholicism was politicized, as I outline in Chapter 3, becoming notably embraced by the Progressive Conservative (PC) party and particularly George Drew. Catholic Quebec was the target of the majority of anti-Catholic sentiment, perceived as disloyal due to the authoritarian and alien nature of the French-Canadian Church and French-Canadian hostility to conscription. It was actively preventing Canadian unity for the prosecution of the war effort. The war revived a fierce nationalism in English Canada, which allowed anti-Catholicism to become an important discursive strategy in the fight for Canada and Britain. Drew and his coterie continued to utilize anti-Catholicism for political capital after the war ended, but the Cold War witnessed the "universalizing" of anti-Catholicism away from the Tories' narrow ethnic focus on French Canadians.

This early Cold War "universalization" is the focus of Chapter 4 (roughly covering 1945 to 1970). Anti-Catholic sentiment began to encompass broader concerns about Catholic illiberality as the national narrative moved increasingly toward a self-conscious (albeit often superficial) religiously neutral identity. The polarization of the world between atheistic totalitarianism and liberal democracy catalyzed this universalization, the latter perceived as fundamentally Christian and Reformationist, but in a Canada rethinking its attitudes toward institutional religion and the linkages of sectarian identity, national identity, and the public sphere. The first thirty postwar years saw a long, inconsistent process of decoupling religious identity from national identity for many Canadians, a result of postwar affluence, a generational embrace of the individual, and the primacy of personal choice. As Gauvreau and Christie discuss, this does not mean that secularization was inevitable, sudden, or total; it *does* mean that personal belief in God and other Christian tenets slowly became paramount over communal rituals in many Christian communities.[37] Yet these were the very values understood for years to be the historical inheritance of Protestants, especially British Protestants, so an important tension emerged within nationalist discourse. In this period, the last manifestations of mainstream ethnic nationalism in English Canada began to bleed into civic nationalism, particularly by the 1960s, as the overt Britishness and Anglo-Protestantism of the past came to be subsumed in a broader discourse of "liberties" and "freedoms."

While Christianity and explicit proclamations of Britishness may have become a less-potent force in public culture by the 1970s, anti-Catholicism persisted into the 1990s and beyond, as is demonstrated in Chapter 5. This is not to suggest that Britishness disappeared. Many Canadians still held the traditionalist Anglo-Protestant suspicion of the Church and its role in a fundamentally British nation. The de-ethnicization, or "universalization," of historically Anglo-Protestant values did continue, on the other hand, as what Bramadat and Seljak call the "personality" of official Canada became relatively secularized.[38] Immigration dramatically changed in this period, and older fears of Catholic demographic dominance through migration largely faded. It was often replaced by hostility toward the newer non-Christian, non-white population arriving on Canada's shores as the "points-system" of immigration was implemented. Similarly, Protestantism, Christianity, and religion in general did not disappear from public life in post-1960s Canada in the face of an increasingly state-centred approach to multiculturalism. The linkage between Christianity and Canadianism instead shifted, messily, with polite "official" identity embracing a multifaith "unity through diversity" narrative.[39]

Those frustrated with these changes to the traditional structure of Canadian religious identity, as with the "decline" of the British connection, blamed the increasingly polyglot religious landscape of non-European, non-Christian immigrants, not necessarily Catholics.[40] As an organizing mental framework and ideological and cultural reference point, anti-Catholicism became inextricably linked to the promotion of progressive, liberal values, with or without explicit reference to religion or ethnicity, as Canada was, allegedly, secularized and multicultural. Catholicism was an alien and regressive force, invading and challenging the modern, secular space of civil society for influence and allegiance. Outside of some conservative fundamentalist Protestant manifestations that were increasingly on the fringe, anti-Catholicism became even more coded in this period, severed as it was from strictly theological and overt ethnic references. As stated earlier, the meanings and narrative produced by anti-Catholic discourses often set the "rules of the game" when discussing the Church and faith, hindering otherwise important criticisms of the Church's position on LGBTQ rights, abortion, and women's rights, issues that served to unite some conservative evangelicals and Catholics and overcome traditional theological divides.[41] What remained in this period was a vision of a faith and Church fundamentally at odds with a modern democratic nation; yet this vision was steeped in the language of an old prejudicial tradition that most contemporary progressives would reject as coming from the "bad old times" of Canada's past. Post-1960s progressive anti-Catholicism thus represented a form of ironic liberal Anglo-Protestantism.

Literature scholar Raymond Tumbleson positions hostility to Catholicism as fundamental to expressing faith in the teleological progress from medieval times to the superior character of modern society. Tumbleson answers his rhetorical question "What is anti-Catholicism?" with the following: "It is the ghost in the machine, the endless neurotic repetition by self-consciously rational modernity of the primal scene in which it slew the premodern as embodied in the archetypal institution [the Catholic Church], arational and universal, of medieval Europe."[42] Modern national, religious, or cultural identities are complex and multi-faceted. Studying anti-Catholicism as a historical subject containing its own logic and within specific contexts reflects how Anglo-Protestant Canadians viewed and organized their world. This sentiment was common and consistent, revealing, through the tropes and rhetoric of a dynamic anti-Catholicism, the shifting nature of an English-Canadian national identity coming to terms with the rapid changes of the times throughout the twentieth century.

I

Corrupting Democracy: French Canada, Immigration, and Anti-Catholicism in the "Progressive Era," 1900–1929

Again, we claim that Rome is a national peril. The Church of Rome is the sworn enemy of our liberties and our principles.[1]

J.S. Woodsworth (1909)

While serving at an internment camp for enemy aliens in Kapuskasing, Ontario, during the First World War, future public intellectual and president of Acadia University Watson Kirkconnell sent a particularly vitriolic letter to his father expressing his unconditional support for Robert Borden's victorious Union government in the 1917 election. Kirkconnell was adamant that no "French Catholic curs" be allowed into Borden's cabinet, adding, "I used to think that Aunt Jane might be exaggerating in her denunciation of the French, but we know Quebec now. Colonel Date calls them 'the cockroaches of Canada' and he is not far out." In Kirkconnell's opinion, the arrival of the Union government not only pitted Catholic against Protestant in Canada: it was going to result in the elimination of petty partyism and the selfish influence of the French Catholic. The exclusion of French Catholics from influence in government was central for Kirkconnell, as they had proven their disloyalty to the cause of English Canada in the war, and he claimed that thousands of "French scum" were hiding in Northern Ontario "at the direction of the clergy," armed with guns and provisions to avoid being enlisted. These cowards, according to Kirkconnell, "would not even come out to vote for Laurier and the Pope."[2]

In the early twentieth century, Anglo-Protestant Canadians like Kirkconnell believed Catholics to be antipathetic to a nation dedicated to British – implicitly Protestant – ideals of freedom, liberty, and self-sufficiency. Anti-Catholicism in the years from 1900 to 1929 served to solidify an emerging Canadian identity, yet it was a complex and multi-faceted identity, contingent upon the understanding of the nature of the threat Catholicism presented. Fundamentalist Protestants in Canada maintained a strict theological anti-Catholicism, although this strain became increasingly marginalized in the early-twentieth century as the major concern became the Catholic desire to control the destiny of the nation by overwhelming good British stock by increasing Catholic immigration or refusing conscription. There was, however, constant slippage between these two categories in this period, as Catholics were portrayed as easily controlled by a selfish, power-hungry hierarchy, dedicated to keeping its followers in spiritual *and* social ignorance in an increasingly progressive era.

The intellectual currents of progressivism and "New Liberalism," which stressed equal political and individual rights guaranteed by a moderate activist state, was one of the defining characteristics of Canada in the first three decades of the twentieth century.[3] The specific flavour of "New Liberalism" echoed the belief expressed by social scientists that a scientific approach to government was indispensable to the ensuring of a modern, liberal-democratic society by serving to craft rational public policy.[4] Efficiency was the watchword of the day, and many understood partisan politics to be destructive. The Borden Tories, for their part, embraced this rhetoric and were determined to stamp out the corrupt and inefficient tradition of patronage and brokerage politics, desiring instead to create a national politics that transcended party loyalty and sectional interests.[5] Protestantism was not simply a traditionalist remnant within this progressivism and the English-Canadian nationalism that accompanied it, but in fact nourished these sentiments, positioning Catholicism as a disruptive element within the body politic, due to its conservative, reactionary, and authoritarian nature.[6]

Another aspect of Canadian anti-Catholicism in this period is the shift from focusing on all Catholics to concentrating on French Canada and recent immigrants largely from continental Europe. Hostility toward English-speaking Catholics (or Catholics of Anglo-Celtic origin), which in Canada in this period was comprised mostly of the Irish and Scottish, was rarer within the intellectual community or organizations dedicated to the reforming of Canadian society, outside of the Orange Order. This reflects what historian Mark McGowan has described as the slow integration of Irish Catholics into the mainstream Anglo-Protestant socio-economic milieu of English Canada in this period.[7] While McGowan is perhaps overly optimistic in his account of Irish-Canadian integration, as demonstrated recently by historian Robert McLaughlin,[8] French Catholics and the "foreign hordes" of Western Canada were certainly beyond the pale of true belonging, especially during the First World War, when they were perceived as potentially disloyal.

This focus on Catholic immigrants and French-speaking Canadians demonstrates the fluid nature of anti-Catholicism; it was not a monolithic framework. It constructed vague categories in which to place certain values, traditions, and practices, and through which one could express fears and concerns regarding the modern world. Some values were good, understood as emanating from the Reformation and Britain, while some were bad, encompassed in what Steven Pincus terms "popery," connoting arbitrary power, decadence, mass docility, and dual allegiance.[9] The latter belonged to a Catholicized realm inimical to freedom and liberty. This malleable concept of Catholicism allowed those wielding it to attack other Protestants, such as ritualistic High Church Anglicans, to conflate Orthodox Christianity with Catholicism due to its Otherness, or even to accept, cautiously, some Catholics, if they behaved "appropriately." Continental Europeans and French Canadians, however, were perceived as refusing to participate in Anglo-Protestant society, and even stressed their Otherness through language, culture, traditions, and, of course, religion. These Catholics were objects to act upon and fix, while good Anglo-Protestant Canadians were subjects to protect, cultivate, and include.

The discourse surrounding continental immigrants thus demonstrates the mutually reinforcing nature of the racial/ethnic theories of the period and anti-Catholicism, particularly the overriding concern that immigrants could not be trusted with the obligations of democracy. These various groups (Italians, Slavs, Ruthenians, Galicians, Ukrainians, etc.) were separated into races that had certain intrinsic characteristics differentiating them from the existing Anglo-Protestant population, and these were largely determined by biology, geography, and climate. Yet there was also a cultural/historical component, what historian Mariana Valverde has labelled a "synthesis of hereditarian and environmental arguments," that explained the nature of these peoples.[10]

Religion was at the forefront of the environmental side of "the foreigner," reflecting and shaping the historical and racial reality: a race or an individual embraced (or simply tolerated) Catholicism because they were prone to authoritarianism, ignorance, and oppression, but they were prone to authoritarianism, ignorance, and oppression because of their very nature. This circular thinking informed much of the Anglo-Protestant reaction to non-Protestant immigrants, whether from exclusionists and nativists dedicated to a strict quota system or from those who recognized the reality of mass immigration, but who wanted to shape the population in their own image. It also demonstrates the important place of religion in discourses of ethnicity, race, and immigration in Canada. When commentators denounced the ignorance and primitiveness of an immigrant, these statements were loaded with religious presumptions and narratives about the possible coexistence of democracy and Catholicism. This continued long into the twentieth century.

What was occurring was the continued normalization of the synonymy of Protestantism and a democratic civic character as the base of English-Canadian nationalism in the face of a potential Catholic threat. Explicit pronouncements of Protestant opposition to Catholicism on theological grounds became rarer throughout the twentieth century, but the linkages between Protestantism and "being Canadian" remained, growing subtler as the decades wore on. This analysis reveals little distinction between a conservative ethnic nationalism and a progressive civic nationalism based on universal rights. Unless they liberated themselves from the troublesome aspects of their religion, namely the authority of priests, the power of the hierarchy, and the upholding of ritual and seemingly archaic traditions, Catholics were unsuitable for these rights. It was feared that Catholicism was gaining in influence, threatening the continuance of the Anglo-Protestant traditions of individual liberty and democracy. English-Canadian nationalism was thus inherently exclusionary, despite exhortations of inclusion and tolerance, as nationalists became concerned with the religious and racial composition of the nation in an industrialized modern world.

Anti-Catholicism, or at least the exoticization of Catholicism, was part of the atmosphere and culture of early-twentieth-century Anglo-Protestant Canada. One early example is contained in Emily Murphy's first book released under her pen name, Janey Canuck, *The Impressions* of *Janey Canuck Abroad*. Murphy, who would later become the first female magistrate in the British Empire, an eloquent crusader for women's rights, and a staunch supporter of sterilization and Anglo-Saxonism, wrote this travelogue while accompanying her husband, Anglican minister Arthur Murphy, to England in 1898–99 (it was released in 1901 and established her as a popular author).[11] While in the mother country, Murphy wrote of the conflict between High Church ritualists and Low Church evangelicals in the Church of England, a conflict in which she sided vociferously with the latter. The High Church was corrupted in its effeminacy, sensuousness (characterized by the pre-eminence of scarlet as a ubiquitous colour of ritual), and foreignness: at a "Ritualistic church" she attended in Liverpool, Murphy referred to the minister as a figure of "ambiguous sex," who was wearing what appeared to be an "inverted tea-cosy." Upon entering another High Anglican church, Murphy complained that she had entered "Oriental quarters," unrecognizable to a good Protestant such as herself, lit by dozens of waxen tapers and filled with lush scarlet curtains acting as ominous screens throughout the room. Roman Catholicism for Murphy was not Christianity. She made it clear that the theatricality of the rituals and "Roman materialism" of candles, scarlet, and incense, was "spiritual pabulum," it was "playing at religion" and was "trivial and vulgar." The Ritualists were "wandering in formulae" that had long ago "lost its meaning." Instead, it revelled in a dead formalistic exercise bereft of spiritual value and belonging in the dark reaches of the past. When characterizing the "church crisis" while in London, Murphy starkly stated that "Ritualism is simply the recurrence of the lifeless Pharisacial [sic] of Judaism in the heart of the Church of England."[12]

Murphy presented this conflict as more than just a battle between a living faith and the hollowness and formalism of an archaic Catholicism. It was between the true spirit of the Reformation (evangelicals), which was always moving forward toward the fulfillment of Christian liberty and truth, and those attempting to reverse history by turning toward Rome and tyranny. Upon visiting Smithfield, Murphy recalled laying laurels on the stones in commemoration of "the memory of these saints, and that of my own good ancestors, who suffered and died for the sake of the Protestant religion, and the liberties of England" during the reign of Queen Mary I. She performed her own ritual, reciting the lines "Lest we forget," clearly referring to the current crisis she was witnessing between the forces of Rome and those of the English Reformation. She continued this line of thinking during the one-hundredth anniversary meeting of the Church Missionary Society in London; attendees were, as during the Reformation, burning with enthusiasm for Protestantism, unlike the effete, mumbling Masses she had attended in Ritualistic churches. Quoting the Whig opponents of James II, who was long one of the symbols of Romish excesses in British history, Murphy stated that "Protestantism has not forgotten her baptism of fire and blood," and that "when the suffering and memory of her Martyrs shall no longer be objects of deepest veneration, surely 'it requires no spirit of prophecy to fortell that English liberty will be fast approaching to its final consummation.'" This was a simple calculus for Murphy: Catholicism meant a return to the dark ages of not only superficial faith, but of social and political tyranny that had been thankfully destroyed by the liberation of the Reformation. Protestantism was synonymous with progress, with democracy, and thus with the true meaning of Britishness. How could these Ritualists, ostensibly fellow Anglicans, cater to this foolishness and invite back Romish materialism and dictatorship into the fold? When attending a Mass on Ash Wednesday, Murphy could no longer hide her disgust and stomped out before communion. She saw in the smearing of ashes on congregants' foreheads a metaphor for the "spiritual dyspepsia" of Anglo-Catholics. The ashes "graphically symbolized the spiritually oxidized religion he [the minister] taught. It is a religion barren, and without life – a mere refuse, fit for nothing but to be trodden under foot of man."[13]

Murphy would repeat these sentiments when visiting a small French-Canadian community in the Northwest in *Seeds of Pine*, one of her trilogy of pro-Western-settlement books published between 1910 and 1914. She admitted her ignorance of the meaning of the Catholic service she attended, as she was versed in the "Thirty-nine Articles of the English church instead of the Rosary of the Blessed Virgin." She did gain, however, "languorous impressions of golden robes, silver censers ... the odour of lilies and lilacs ... a suspended cross with an agonized Christ ... of purple and scarlet cloths ... and smoke of incense, but, most of all, there was a music that mothered you and stayed with you. In some way or other these old plaintive songs of Egypt seem fitted to the boreal regions, but why I cannot explain." For Murphy, Catholicism was sensory/sensual and certainly Other. It was not *of* the Western world but *of* the fragrant East (Oriental), fitting into the New World but beyond the understanding of a

Protestant versed in the simple faith of Jesus. It was not the admittedly "flat-wash view of pleasure and religion" that she preferred, but something else, seemingly decadent in nature.[14]

Eugene Forsey echoed some of these sentiments in a visit to Rome as a young man in the 1920s. Later to become one of Canada's most eminent constitutional experts and leftist thinkers, involved as he was with the early years of the League for Social Reconstruction (LSR) and the Co-operative Commonwealth Federation (CCF), Forsey experienced the Vatican first-hand, and his reactions are revealing. In a letter to his mother, Forsey referred to a visit to the cathedral at Ragusa, portraying the Catholic congregation in patronizing tones, reducing them to a quaint, exceedingly reverent, group handling relics while absurdly believing them to cure illnesses.[15] In another letter to his mother, Forsey is more explicit about his disdain for Catholicism, ridiculing the policies of the churches in Verona that prevented women from wearing immodest dress out of respect for a house of God. For Forsey, this was sheer hypocrisy: "Magnificent example of the Roman Church's amiable habit of straining at gnats and swallowing camels. Another prevalent notice runs: 'Out of respect for the house of God, do not spit on the floor.' Delightful customs! ... All this sort of thing nearly made go [sic] berserk."[16] The Catholic Church in his opinion was addressing petty issues instead of the pressing "camels" they were forced to swallow.

One can speculate that Forsey was referring to certain traditions within Catholicism, such as the relics he had witnessed earlier. Scholar Frank Milligan has described Forsey's theology as heavily influenced by the social gospel, which conceived of personal liberty and Christian liberty as synonymous. If one lived right, which was by Christ's example, then the individual's freedom would be preserved and the society would benefit.[17] The perceived blind adherence of the Catholic to the whims of the hierarchy and lack of focus on the living Christ was therefore problematic and interpreted as not fitting into this social-gospel world view. While attending Oxford on a Rhodes scholarship in the early 1920s, Forsey engaged in a spirited debate with his colleagues, claiming he acted as the sole defender of the Christian tradition, as he found himself "the solitary defender of Methodism, Anglicanism, High Churchism [sic], and Catholicism." He was quick to note "(These last two of course only in certain particulars – chiefly as to sincerity and sanity of at least some of their members)."[18] In Forsey's view, the ritualistic traditions of Catholicism and High Church

Anglicanism were only defensible in that they were aspects of the Christian tradition, although they were extremely flawed. Forsey admitted later in the letter that, while he agreed with the Catholic position on divorce and birth control, citing his conviction as to the sanctity of marriage and of life, there was "Uproarious laughter from my friends at the idea that I should have a good word to say for those people." He ended this section of the letter defending his action by theorizing that the values he defended were not exclusively Catholic but broadly Christian, reassuring his mother that he had not come under the sway of the local priest. Indeed, Forsey mentioned that he had met only a small number of Catholics at Oxford, and that "those people"[19] did not discuss religion openly. While Catholicism may have been part of the Christian tradition in Forsey's opinion, it was a backward interpretation.

Journalist Robert Sellar represents a less-philosophical, more-conspiratorial strand of anti-Catholicism in this period, promulgated through his Anglo-Quebec newspaper the *Huntington Gleaner* and his 1907 book *The Tragedy of Quebec: The Expulsion of Its Protestant Farmers*.[20] Historian Justin Nordstrom believes that journalists were central to the Progressive Era battle against corruption and decadence in an industrializing society and in adapting earlier, familiar anti-Catholic tropes to an industrialized nation in America.[21] Sellar was prolific in his role of disseminator of anti-Catholic and progressive rhetoric, editing the *Gleaner* from the 1860s until after the First World War. He was fixated on the idea that the Church in Quebec, and in Canada in general, was plotting to prevent Protestants from farming properly, allowing Catholics to take over their land, beginning in the Eastern Townships and slowly moving across the nation. He communicated this in his magnum opus, *The Tragedy of Quebec*.

The Orange-leaning *Toronto Telegram* was convinced that Sellar's exposé would be "as deadly to ecclesiastical privilege in Can[ada] as 'Uncle Tom's Cabin' was to slavery in the U.S.," positing the common anti-Catholic trope that Catholicism was akin to slavery.[22] Sellar, dubbed "Fanatic Bob" by his francophone opponents in his home region,[23] believed this Catholic plot was doubly harmful, as Protestants were inherently superior farmers, since they were not "kept in fetters" by the Church, like the habitants of Quebec. The Protestant farmer was hard-working, productive, and useful, while the Catholic habitant, poor, stupid, and ignorant, contributed little to the nation. The

Catholic Church and its followers thus hurt Canada's potential future greatness. For Sellar, this was not just a contemporary problem. He conceptualized an entire historical framework within which the demands of the Catholic Church in Quebec would forever be harmful. According to Sellar, Canada's greatest mistake was conceding the right of Catholics to worship and providing the Church a legitimate place in society in the Quebec Act, an Act passed by an ignorant Anglican British parliament, which could not conceive of religion outside of an Establishment. This Act was against liberty, since Catholicism perpetuated slavery.[24] In addition, concessions to the Catholic Church in the Quebec Act were directly responsible for the American Revolution, as these concessions angered the Patriots and ruined the opportunity for a great global English-speaking alliance.[25] Catholicism was a medieval aberration in modern times, as "Wolfe's victory preserved in the New World what the Old World soon afterwards destroyed – the clerical and temporal institutions of feudal France." The reactionary religion that the French Revolution destroyed was very much alive in Canada because of these short-sighted politicians. In fact, Catholicism was not about spirituality at all, unlike Protestantism, but was instead an organized political system dedicated solely to gaining and achieving power through any means necessary.[26]

Another intolerable concession were the separate schools, used, according to Sellar, for the teaching of priestly propaganda, allowing them to maintain a stranglehold over the politics of Quebec and the nation. Sellar presented these schools as the site where the hierarchy taught about creating a papal state, secluding pupils from their families, and crushing their individuality. This destructive sentiment was present in the alleged huge increase in separate schools and religious orders across Canada, particularly in the newly settled Prairie region, which undermined the spread and maintenance of Anglo-Protestant conceptions of liberty. The schools were inculcating prejudice against Protestants and manipulating the legal system in Quebec to expand canon law to formerly Protestant farming areas. Many Protestants that witnessed this takeover of Quebec were, in Sellar's mind, moving to the United States for fear that Canada would soon be an entirely papal country. In the conclusion of his book, Sellar became increasingly shrill in his denunciations of Catholicism and bolder in his claims about the grandiosity of the Catholic plot in North America. Sellar believed that the suppression of Protestant farmers in Quebec and the inevitable establishment of a papal state was the initial salvo in a wider plot to take over all New England, where French-speaking Catholics had already integrated into the manufacturing sector. The priests, by manipulating habitants through separate schools, and by convincing them that their language and religion were the only means of their cultural survival, aspired to create an enormous papal state consisting of Eastern Ontario, the Northwest, and New England. This fantastic scenario complicates the claims of his biographer, Robert Hill, that Sellar was simply a staunch proponent of the nineteenth-century liberal ideal of separation of church and state and, like D'Alton McCarthy, an authentic representative of English-Canadian nationalism who engaged in excesses of rhetoric. While Sellar admitted "[t]hat in this twentieth century, on a continent the very air of which is democratic, a body of men ... labouring to bring about the creation of a Papal nation sounds incredible," he was convinced that he was witness to this plot.[27]

Sellar warned Anglo-Protestant Canadians that they needed to vote specifically for any candidate who opposed clericalism, as this was the greatest crisis facing the nation. Canada in general was becoming increasingly pluralistic in its composition, a development Sellar vociferously opposed, as "these people" were bringing to Canada hatreds and prejudices that did not "fit" into a British society. To vote against clericalism was to vote for a British, as opposed to a papal, Canada. True British Canadians represented a "motive [that] is no narrow one; it is, by destroying privilege, to bestow equality on all. Shall Canada be a land of equal rights, or shall it not? What say you?"[28] This was a familiar call for Anglo-Protestant Canadians in the early-twentieth century. It resembled that of the Equal Rights Association of the 1880s, founded in opposition to the passing of the Jesuits' Estates Act and the privileges it allegedly bestowed upon a subversive Catholic hierarchy, as well as McCarthy's rogue Francophobic Toryism. Sellar, in the same vein, wanted one Canada, in which all were treated "equally." Yet equality here meant destroying the privileges of special-interest groups like the Church and preserving the equality inherent in a British democracy.[29]

Present in Sellar's work is the intersection of theological anti-Catholicism and a socio-political hostility. Catholicism's alleged superstitious, static dogma created a population easily controlled by a hierarchical clergy motivated by self-interest and power. Prominent revivalist Oswald Smith, who was active from around 1910 to the late 1950s, was one of the most public proponents of a strictly theological anti-Catholicism in Canada, one that was common within emerging fundamentalist circles, but which bled into Anglo-Protestant nationalist discourses.[30] Smith was devoted to an intense personal experience of God and the fundamentalist concept of premillennial dispensationalism.[31] Within this latter concept was a fixation on prophetic biblical texts, mined for contemporary symbols and events that signalled the coming apocalypse. In an early edition of *Is the Antichrist at Hand?* Smith speculated about whether Mussolini was the foretold Emperor of the revived Roman Empire, a figure who was, according to this theological strain, the Antichrist.[32] In Smith's writing, the Antichrist/Emperor would gain political dominance in Europe and quickly align himself with the Catholic Church, as these two institutions represented the civil and ecclesiastical Babylons discussed in the biblical Book of Revelation. The concept of Rome representing "two Babylons" was not novel in anti-Catholic literature, as clergyman Alexander Hislop's infamous and widely popular nineteenth-century tract *The Two Babylons* promoted the idea that the Vatican was Babylon itself, the lineal descendent of the pagan mystery religions of the Bible.[33] Smith simply updated the references, believing that the "Rome-ward" turn of many nations, for example that of the United Kingdom, which had recently appointed an envoy to the Vatican, was an initial step in the Vatican's consolidation of its ecclesiastical control over Europe. Smith denied that the pope himself was likely Antichrist, a common trope among earlier anti-Catholics and other fundamentalists.[34] Instead, the Emperor would betray the pope and the Catholic Church, a result of the Church's gross apostasy in refusing to preach the word of God. Smith warned against the pretensions of the Catholic Church and its growing influence in North America. In language directly referencing the bloody religious conflicts surrounding the Reformation, yet resembling that of Janey Canuck, Smith concluded that if the Church "had the power, today, she would rise and massacre the Protestants just as eagerly as in the days gone by ... The spirit of tolerance is at present seen, but given the opportunity and it will be no more."[35]

Smith was not an isolated crank. He was, in fact, a member of a conservative fundamentalist network. Smith worked for Roland V. Bingham, founder of the successful Sudan Interior Mission and editor of the often anti-Catholic fundamentalist periodical *The Evangelical Christian*, and they remained good friends for the rest of Bingham's life.[36] Bingham's periodical often professed similar opinions to Smith's, certainly influencing him in his formative years. Bingham was unequivocal about the threat of Catholicism and the inherent disloyalty of Roman Catholics. For example, he believed that the Catholic Church aided the Central Powers during the First World War, that it was behind the Easter Rebellion in Ireland in 1916, and, like Sellar, that it was dispossessing Protestants of property.[37] With this network and his growing following, Smith was able to build Toronto Gospel Tabernacle, which quickly changed its name to the People's Church, with the major financial contribution of the intensely spiritual owner and publisher of the *Globe*, William G. Jaffray. This church eventually became the largest independent church in Toronto.[38] While Smith may not have been part of the theological and cultural mainstream, he was a popular figure, whose eschatological vision of the Catholic Church as an internationally influential force carried currency. Smith, however, evidently did not seem to be overly concerned with Canadian politics in his writings, unlike journalists such as Sellar, reflecting the ambivalence with which fundamentalists in this period treated domestic political engagement.[39] Sellar, and other secular public figures within the Progressive Era, envisioned a Catholic Church that was not only an international concern to Protestantism at a theological level but a political and social system operating principally out of Quebec and dedicated to dominating Canada.

In his famous study of immigration in Western Canada, *Strangers within our Gates; or, Coming Canadians*, J.S. Woodsworth repeated from a progressive perspective concerns about the influence of Catholicism at a socio-political level. Woodsworth is justly remembered as one of the pre-eminent figures in the Canadian left, writing *Strangers* during what sociologist Jane Pulkingham has referred to as the first phase of his massive influence on Canadian affairs: as a pioneering social worker in Winnipeg.[40] In *Strangers* he bemoaned the infiltration of the Catholic Church into civic life, violating cherished values of the separation of church and state and the "neutrality" of civic institutions. Specifically, as with Sellar, he saw the separate school as allowing the priest to exert total control over Catholics, preventing them from achieving independent thought and self-realization. For Woodsworth, these institutions were the most dangerous obstacle to the unified nationality he desired, and they hindered the underlying assumption of that nationality, namely assimilation of differences.[41] As literature scholar Daniel Coleman has stated, Woodsworth was a "progressive liberal" who had a vision for an improved Canada that included foreigners, even Catholics; but this liberal inclusivity relied on the assumption that the foreign Catholic hordes would need to be "improved" through education and contact with the pinnacle of civilization, Britain.[42] A fusing of racial assumptions, Protestant triumphalism, and English-Canadian nationalism allowed for individuals of all political, intellectual, and denominational stripes to believe that assimilation of Catholics was necessary for the health of Canada.[43] For Woodsworth, as for others in this period, race, ethnicity, and religion were intimately connected components of the Otherness of these groups and individuals. In fact, they were hurdles that needed to be simultaneously overcome to create a more democratic and unified Canada.

Woodsworth believed deeply in the importance of Protestantism for improving the nation. Ensuring the national development of Canada required converting "these people" to "pure Christianity," as opposed to the "baptized Paganism" of Catholicism. Woodsworth questioned the ability of Catholic immigrants to practise responsible citizenship, as they were accustomed to the inherent "serfdom" of Catholicism. He even wanted to restrict the franchise for Catholic immigrants at the time of authoring *Strangers* to prevent the manipulation of Canadian politics by the Vatican and "priest-craft." Woodsworth explicitly outlined that Protestantism was *the* necessary component for the creation of an informed and progressive people, capable of self-realization and able to enjoy the civic gifts of the nation. He consistently straddled the line between those who believed in the potential redemption of Catholics exposed to the liberties and freedom of an Anglo-Protestant country and those who saw the Church and Catholicism as the ultimate enemy. This is embodied in the following statement: "Independence means that people are taught to think for themselves ... it means that the people ally themselves with the Protestants rather than the Catholics. *Independence affords the opportunity for reformation.*"[44] The significance of the term "reformation" and its synonymity with independence and freedom is clear. It is also simple: Protestantism meant progress, liberty, and the future, while Catholicism meant regression, oppression, and the past. His understanding of national destiny was thoroughly Protestant and anti-Catholic, along with being undergirded by racial essentialism. Woodsworth states his anti-Catholicism most succinctly when declaring "Again, we claim that Rome is a national peril. The Church of Rome is the sworn enemy of our liberties and our principles."[45]

The apparent danger that Catholicism represented is also present in a short story by Presbyterian clergyman Rev. Charles Gordon, better known by his pen name, Ralph Connor.[46] Coleman identifies Connor as in the same "progressive liberal" camp as Woodsworth regarding immigrants and Catholics; they did not necessarily want to exclude but improve them to achieve a unified nation. Released in cooperation with the Canadian Presbyterian Church's Board of French Evangelization in the early-twentieth century, "The Colporteur" follows the investigation of the small Quebec town of Ste Marie by a professor, a businessman, and an "aesthetic young lady." Throughout the story, the professor analyzes the symbols of Catholicism as relief for a simple people, while the gaudy manifestations of the faith enthrall the woman. Tellingly, the businessman is concerned with the lack of progress in the village and with the effeminacy suggested by the woman's admiration of the symbols and relics, to the point where he finds it difficult to remember that he is in Canada. After stopping in a quaint café, they meet a young, pox-ridden man, who identifies himself as a Presbyterian colporteur, or, in his words, one who spreads the truth. He and the professor engage in an argument, with the latter claiming that the colporteur is engaged in an unchristian pursuit by condemning a historic Christian church. The colporteur responds that, while the Catholic Church was Christian, it was horribly corrupt, indeed harmful to the French Canadians, as they prayed to a Marian deity instead of God. In response, the businessman claimed that at least Catholicism allowed people to be content; the colporteur retorts that it caused the French Canadian to be poor, illiterate, and ignorant, and that their families were becoming so large they were moving to greener pastures in Vermont and Massachusetts, yet still living in poverty. The group proceeds to participate in a religious service for converted Catholics who have found the truth due to colportage. A converted old man concludes the story by repeating the oft-mentioned claim to the group that Catholicism was akin to slavery and perpetuated only darkness.[47]

The story reveals an important plot point of the anti-Catholic narratives of the time: the ignorant Catholic masses in Quebec and the almost unfettered dominance the hierarchy held over them. The businessman, who was quite skeptical of the young colporteur initially, and who acts as the voice of the entrepreneurial Protestant spirit throughout the story, responds in great alarm to these claims, stating, "If this young man is right, it's a serious business for Canada.

A million and a half Canadians kept in ignorance, kept poor paying taxes, bullied by their priests, kept from their rights as citizens."[48] Connor and like-minded English-Canadian nationalists in this period saw French Canadians as the remnants of a feudal past, unable to come to terms with the complexity of modernity. Only after overcoming these internal divisions could the "coming Canadian" appear.[49]

Murphy made a similar point in the opening of *Impressions Abroad*, characterizing Quebec City as consisting of simple, but charming, habitants. She paraphrased Henry Ward Beecher in a phrase that could serve as the mantra of the well-meaning Anglo-Protestant in French Canada: Quebec City was "a bit of medieaval Europe perched on a rock and dried for keeping," to be observed and cherished by visitors, yet representing a bygone age.[50] In Daniel Coleman's mind, this portrayal of the Other is used not to further understanding of these groups or individuals, or religions, but instead "to convey evidence of White, British, masculine civility." It is "they" who were the beneficiaries of the largesse of Anglo-Protestant Canadians and who needed to conform to superior standards of progress.[51] This distorted view of French Canada and the Catholic Church reinforced an English-Canadian nationalism that believed in an identity that was strengthened if shorn of the sort of regressive elements that stubbornly resided in the nation.

The passing of the infamous Regulation 17 in 1912 represented a more overtly political aspect of the concern with Quebec and the Church, designed in some minds to quell attempts by the French to create a bilingual and potentially clerical Canada. Regulation 17 was introduced by the Tory Ontario government of James Whitney in response to public criticism – including from the English-speaking Catholic Bishop of London, Ontario, Michael Fallon – of the quality of bilingual education in the province as "inefficient." The government was also responding to public concerns about the rising Franco-Ontarian population, particularly on its Eastern borders. Regulation 17 limited the use of French in bilingual schools to one hour per day and forbade its use in instruction after the second year of elementary school. Many French Canadians saw this measure as aimed not only at elimination of their language, but at funding for Catholic schools. To make matters worse, initially the Catholic inspectorate was put under the control of a more active Chief Inspector's office. These officials were Anglo-Protestant. The controversy was so heated that French Catholics in the Windsor region rioted in the tense year of 1917, and Pope Benedict XV had to officially intervene.[52] Sellar was typically blunt in his assessment: the opposition to Regulation 17 was part of the Catholic plot to create a papal state in North America. The controversy was not about language (many French Canadians agreed), but about whether the control of government-funded schools was to be through the elected legislature or by "French priests."[53]

C.B. Sissons, a relatively moderate commentator on bilingual education in the context of Sellar and the Tory provincial government, saw the initial regulation as designed explicitly to stem the "invasion" of French-Canadian Catholics into Ontario, although he was unclear as to whether this was a positive or negative.[54] Sissons, an educational activist, historian, Classicist, and cousin of Woodsworth, has curiously been described as both a passionate opponent of Regulation 17, involved as he was with the *Bonne Entente* movement, and as a champion of Protestantism.[55] Sissons was concerned with what he characterized as the misinformation and baseless accusations hurled between French-Catholic and English-Protestant Canadians and set out to rectify this with his slim volume *Bi-Lingual Schools in Canada*, released in 1917. It is clear from the start that Sissons's dream was a unified Canada, where mutual understanding and respect defined the relations between the variegated populations. Sissons condemned Orange Tories, while also chastising French "extremists," such as Henri Bourassa. Sissons wanted to revise Regulation 17 to allow for some French instruction, praising the concessions made by the Whitney Tories in 1913 to calm tempers. Yet he was convinced that "English must be the common solvent for us all."[56] Language was simply instrumental, a means of communication with little to no connection to culture.[57] This dream of unity, much like his cousin's, only begrudgingly accepted the very existence of separate schools, let alone French schools, as they perpetuated the isolation of populations from one another, inevitably exacerbating differences. Lost on Sissons was the hypocrisy of proclaiming the pure instrumentality of language while stressing that English served as a unifying force in Canada. Sissons maintained that separate schools were furthering the problem of segregation in Canadian society, acting as a model for a potential new separate system based on language and race within the already existing and fragmented Catholic system.[58]

Before the outbreak of war, Sissons was interested in the question of bilingualism in schools, and it is clear he could never disentangle religion from language. He investigated the condition of said schools in Manitoba for the *Globe* in 1912, when Regulation 17 was passed in Ontario, painting a bleak picture of the results of the Greenway-Laurier compromises of 1897 following the Manitoba Schools Crisis. According to Sissons, thousands of children were not only missing school, but fell into child labour because of shoddy bilingual schools that provided a terrible quality of education, essentially guaranteeing the failure of students in the modern world. He used the example of a Union Point school, where the local trustees had refused to implement bilingual reforms because they believed that a local man, Nolette, had simply moved into the district with his huge Catholic family to force their hand. Subtly referencing the alien nature of these "special interest" schools and an activist clergy, Sissons was indignant at the scene that unfolded at the courthouse, bizarre in a nation such as Canada. On one side were the trustees, and on the other were Nolette, his counsel, and "no less than twelve priests," reported Sissons, subtly condemning the involvement of these religious figures in a purely legal matter. As historian Barry Ferguson has noted, Sissons (and other Anglo-Protestants) of this period, were convinced that the clergy were a "manipulative interest" among immigrants and French Canadians preventing the overall goal of assimilation and national unity.[59] Clearly Sissons held these opinions toward clerical influence among the French Canadian population; he directly blamed the "mediaeval" ideas of Archbishop Langevin for the educational problems of the province, since he was for forcing Catholics to be loyal to the Church, nothing else. This was a dangerous view, as schools (and people) that placed religion above all else were bound to fail, as the "311,631 illiterates" in Quebec clearly proved. While Sissons admitted that separate schools were the law and therefore deserved an extent of protection, he saw this as an unfortunate reality in need of reform. Indeed, British Columbia, where there were no French or separate schools, served as the model of education in Sissons's mind. He painted British Columbia as an educational paradise, free from the compromises, patronage, and clerical machinations inherent in the Manitoba system.[60]

The future Ontario premier, Orangeman and Tory MPP Howard Ferguson, although he would end Regulation 17 in 1927, also explicitly linked the religious conflict in Ontario with language during the First World War, but went much further than Sissons. In an August 1916 speech, Ferguson claimed that French priests driven out of France due to anti-clericalism were leading all schools that were refusing to abide by the law. The French-Catholic clergy refused to allow their followers to learn English, according to Ferguson, as evidenced by the fact that, as soon as the priest left, or in schools not headed by a religious order, French Catholics prospered and learned English with enthusiasm. In a sentiment that would reverberate throughout the war years and moving beyond the national-unity, social-backwardness argument of Sissons, Ferguson believed this "clerical tyranny" was also behind the French Catholic resistance to military recruitment, because French priests taught students to avoid service or face excommunication and refusal of rites.[61]

As suggested above, the conscription crisis of the First World War exacerbated the existing animus between the French and English in Canada and encouraged a sharpening of anti-Catholic sentiment in the country. Newton Rowell, for example, the leading Liberal in the Unionist fold, was adamant about the negative influence the Quebec Catholic hierarchy had over the nation during the Unionist election of December 1917. In a speech in North Bay, which he delivered with Conservative Ontario premier William Hearst at his side, Rowell directly linked a dangerous Quebec nationalism and the hierarchy, explaining that most of the priests in Quebec agreed with Henri Bourassa's "Nationalist, clerical, and reactionary attitude." Rowell repeated Ferguson's claims, describing how disloyal members of religious orders in France found asylum in Canada and worked to dismantle the nation's unified war effort. Rowell concluded that this clerical-reactionary movement dominated the political situation in Quebec, and its secret plan was to use "this hour of grave national peril to dominate the political situation throughout the Dominion of Canada." The Union government was for Rowell the only alternative to clerical-nationalist government in Canada, and conscientious, intelligent Canadians needed to stop voting simply out of party loyalty. The political system was no longer the same, as an insidious clerical force now backed the Laurier Liberals, thus necessitating the obsolescence of partyism.[62]

John English, in his excellent study of the Borden Tories, *The Decline of Politics*, demonstrates that many supporters held Unionism to be the greatest manifestation of the progressive desire for an end to corrupt, inefficient partisan politics. Part of this was the belief that the Catholic Church represented the ultimate sectional interest in Canada.

English, however, does not discuss the prominence of Protestantism or anti-Catholicism in the Unionist fold in any detail, despite the clearly self-consciously Protestant nature of many thinkers. In *The New Era in Canada*, the text English views as the most prominent statement of English-Canadian intellectuals and activists in support of a progressive activist state, for example, the belief that Protestantism had unleashed the democratic forces of the world from the chains of Catholicism is self-evident.[63] Adelaide Plumptre, secretary of the Canadian Red Cross Society, secretary of the National Committee of Women for Patriotic Service in Canada, and a novelist of some note, added to this chorus when she contributed "Some Thoughts on the Suffrage in Canada." There is an excellent (and growing) scholarly literature detailing the connections between first-wave feminism, racism, and imperialism, although the anti-Catholicism of the elite, Anglo-Protestant feminists of the time is an underdeveloped topic.[64] In her essay, Plumptre advocated for a raft of progressive reforms (temperance, statism, bureaucratic efficiency), chief among them being women's suffrage. In justifying the granting of the franchise, Plumptre argued that the specific concerns and morality of women would serve to better the public sphere. She also, perhaps more radically, argued that the right to vote emanated from the self-government of all peoples, equally, in a democracy.

Plumptre appealed to her audience through the words of famed novelist H.G. Wells from his wartime novel *Mr. Britling Sees It Through*, who envisioned modern society transforming in distinctly racial-religious terms. For Wells, and for Plumptre, a "new culture" was forcing its way down from "the North," smothering the old culture of "the South": "Something is coming up in America and in England and the Scandinavian countries and Russia, an escape from the Levantine religion and the Catholic culture that came to us from the Mediterranean. We are Northerners," and this new Northern culture refused to allow women to remain "cloistered" in the home. "It minimizes instead of exaggerating the importance of sex ... It is just all this Northern tendency that this world struggle is going to release," finally freeing both women and men from the shackles of Catholic tradition. Plumptre endorsed this "new culture," seeing in it the growing sympathy for women's possession of a form of self-government.[65] Northern Protestants were embracing progress, moving away from an archaic understanding of women inherited from Western civilization's

Catholic heritage. Suffrage, in other words, was only the most recent manifestation of the triumph of Northern European progress over its own past.

The linking of geography, climate, race, and religion was central to the Anglo-Protestant understanding of Canada, history, and the shifting milieu around them. This vision valorized Protestant Northwestern Europe, seeing in it the home of democracy, individuality, and modern life, and denigrated Southern and Eastern Europe as corrupt, degenerate, and intrinsically authoritarian. This was staunch racial and cultural essentialism, summed up most succinctly by fellow suffragist, Emily Murphy, in her 1910 *Janey Canuck in the West*: "I think the proximity of the magnetic pole has something to do with the superiority of the Northmen. The best peoples of the world have come out of the north, and the longer they are away from boreal regions in such proportion do they degenerate."[66]

Unionism prompted other less-philosophical, but similarly ethnocentric, denunciations of the Catholic Church by supporters (and even members). As previously discussed, a young Watson Kirkconnell was adamant that Union government meant the trumping of the harmful influence that the Catholic Church had on politics and the nation. He urged his mother and sister to take advantage of the Wartime Elections Act (WEA) to vote in the upcoming election "against Frenchmen, Catholicism, and the abandonment of all national honour."[67] S.D. Chown, general superintendent of the Methodist Church, counselled his followers in an open letter to vote Union to transcend partyism, preventing Quebec and Catholicism from dominating the nation, much as Rowell warned. Chown went even further in a private letter to a K. Kingston, accusing French-Canadian Quebeckers of plotting to physically take over the nation by opposing conscription and Union. He asked his correspondent if it was "fair to leave the province of Quebec to retain its strength in numbers ... ready for any political or military aggression in the future, while our Protestants go forth to slaughter and decimation?"[68] This was an early and slightly modified version of the "revenge of the cradles" narrative that would soon emerge in both elite *nationaliste* circles of French Canadians determined to preserve their distinctiveness in an Anglo-Protestant North America *and* among Anglo-Protestants fearful of the consequences of a high Catholic birth rate (see Table 1.1).[69]

Sellar, a staunch proponent of the war effort and Unionism, used a study of Father of Confederation George Brown,[70] written at the

Table 1.1
French population of Canada

1901	1,649,371
1911	2,061,719
1921	2,452,743
1931	2,832,298

Series A125-163, A185-237, *Historical Statistics in Canada*, 2nd ed. Note: Referring specifically to the population's mother tongue as of 1931.

height of the conscription crisis, to voice his anger at the infiltration of French Catholicism into public affairs. For Sellar, the sinister influence of the Church had manifested itself most clearly in the cowardly behaviour of French Catholics who had heeded the urging of their priests that they refuse to go to war, allowing good British Protestants to die in a just cause. Sellar believed that the Catholic Church wanted to extend control over Canadian politics, but that the British nature of Canadian society, which promoted liberty (something that French Catholics could never understand) challenged the Church. The loss of Anglo-Protestant lives threatened this arrangement. Sellar ridiculed the *Bonne Entente* group who wanted to promote mutual understanding, believing that there were two governments in Canada: a papal one in Quebec and a democratic one for the rest of Canada. He concluded with a rhetorical question that embodies much of the liberal and progressive anti-Catholicism detailed thus far: "Is it not a degrading thought, that the future of this great country should be menaced by a priesthood?" he asked. "Is there not patriotism enough among us to rise above all petty issues and devote our political efforts to bringing about complete separation of Church and State – that Canada shall be ruled by and in the interests of her people, and not by and for the advantage of any church?"[71]

Some within the Unionist government itself did not accept Catholics as part of their vision for the nation. The Church was simply an obstruction in the way of the noble goals of winning the war and constructing a new progressive state. Borden himself, as English notes, even instructed some of the members of his government to link Catholic *nationaliste* Bourassa with Laurier during the election in December 1917 to expose them as traitors. He also sighed with relief at the election victory in a letter to imperialist author and lawyer George T. Denison, noting that the election was a triumph for "Canadian democracy," despite the tensions of wartime and "more than forty per cent of the population of non-British origin."[72] In other words, this foreign population was neither Canadian nor British, essentially equated in this formula, and could not be trusted to defend the form of democracy won through the election. In another revealing letter, Borden had to assure the Catholic Bishop of Antigonish, James Morrison, a few months before the 1917 election, that he was vigorously attempting to include Catholics in his new Unionist cabinet. Morrison was calling for better representation of Irish Catholics, the largest English-speaking Catholic group in the nation. The problem was not Unionism, according to Borden. The reason behind Catholic under-representation was Catholics themselves: there were too few Catholic men of ability in the House to promote, and, of course, one had to be "tried out and tested" to receive any form of cabinet representation. Canadian politics was itself neutral and meritocratic; prominent Catholics were simply not joining public life and attending to their responsibilities. Borden also made sure to refer to the all-consuming issue of conscription in this letter, again assuring the bishop that, while the Catholics of eastern Nova Scotia were undoubtedly patriotic men, demonstrated by their enlistment, "To my great regret I cannot truthfully bear the same testimony to the attitude of Roman Catholics in some other parts of the Country." He concluded by counselling Morrison to encourage his flock to be more concerned with national matters and politics.[73]

Another notable manifestation of anti-Catholicism during the war was the so-called Guelph Raid, which occurred in 1918 at the St Stanislaus Jesuit Novitiate, just outside Guelph, Ontario. There had been rumours circulating concerning the novices of this institution for weeks,[74] and authorities decided on an inquiry to investigate whether there were men in the novitiate avoiding enlistment. Avoidance of service was already a common charge against many French Canadians and Catholics, as demonstrated by Kirkconnell's earlier statements and a press report claiming that more French Canadians were hiding in forests to avoid conscription than were serving, with as much as two years' provisions to sustain them.[75] One of the three men initially arrested, on charges eventually revealed as specious, was the son of the federal justice minister and one of a very small number of Catholics in the Borden cabinet, Charles Doherty.[76] As scholar

Brian Hogan has described, this raid took place in a particularly tense atmosphere, as Orange politicians had mistakenly believed that a recent protest by Montreal students was perpetrated by Catholic seminarians. Influential and angry Orangemen had subsequently convinced Borden to drop divinity students from the exclusion clause in the Military Service Act (MSA) (which facilitated conscription). Doherty realized that this would inflame Catholic passions further against the Act and convinced Borden to make some concessions. However, these partial concessions allowed for the exemption of Catholic seminarians, as they received tonsure after only a few months and were considered members of a religious order at an earlier stage than most Protestants. Due to the continuing controversy, the reforms did not go far enough and did not include Protestant divinity students, as they were not ministers until graduation, a situation that Doherty had wanted to avoid in the first place.[77] When Marcus Doherty was arrested, he phoned his father, who in consultation with other officials concluded that Captain Macauley, the arresting officer, and the assistant provost marshal did not adequately understand the exemption clause. In addition, the minister of militia and defence, General S.C. Mewburn, had acted impatiently by quickly sending an initial message to the provost marshal that the novitiate was potentially harbouring at least two deserters.[78] Following this, a subordinate official improperly forwarded this memo to the assistant provost marshal with an attachment stating that the novitiate needed to be "cleaned out" of deserters.[79] The elder Doherty and Mewburn thus agreed that a press ban needed to be enforced, as many figures had made mistakes and, more importantly, to prevent religious and racial tensions from exploding at a national level.[80]

Anti-Catholic and anti-French sentiment was at a fever pitch due to the recent Unionist election and the battles over conscription.[81] Much of Ontario was pro-Union and pro-conscription, and Guelph was no different.[82] According to rumours circulating in Guelph, the novices were actively opposing the war effort in pursuit of their own selfish interests; yet St Stanislaus was not a French-Canadian institution, nor did it involve mostly French-Canadian Catholics. Catholicism was so often associated with French Canadianness that the facts about the novitiate were not important. It was simply a symbol of alleged Catholic power, influence, shirking of responsibility, and, most ominously, secrecy. The press ban was broken by Rev. W.D. Spence, who went to the offices of the *Toronto Star* and told reporters about deserters hiding out in the novitiate.[83] Spence, president of the Guelph Ministerial Association (GMA), the organization that had long suspected the novitiate of wrongdoing, publicly refuted a Protestant's ability to believe anything a Jesuit said, as Jesuits taught only lying and the defence of their Church.[84]

One particularly obstreperous individual was another member of the GMA, Rev. Kennedy Palmer, dubbed "a minister of the Gospel – of hate and bigotry" by the Catholic Unity League of Canada.[85] In a sermon to his congregation at St Paul's Presbyterian Church, Palmer repeated that the reason for his interest in the Guelph novitiate was his commitment to the men fighting overseas. Palmer outlined the danger in having Doherty, a Catholic, framing laws that were so flagrantly benefiting the Church. Catholics could not be trusted to hold positions of power, as they were unable to be neutral, unlike Protestants, especially in a time of national crisis. He concluded conspiratorially that the novitiate and other Catholic institutions had been planning a significant expansion in Canada; since the war had broken out, he continued, citing no evidence, Catholic colleges were full, while Protestant colleges were almost empty.[86] Without explicitly stating it, Palmer was repeating the charge of disloyalty, an insidious attempt at Catholic expansion at the expense of Protestant young men in an otherwise loyal, British nation, supported by powerful Catholic men in the government. In the subsequent royal commission that investigated the raid, which Palmer was instrumental in instigating, he and his representation even attempted to argue that the Jesuits were not a legal religious order in Ontario and that all the members of the order were liable for service immediately.[87]

A revealing example of attitudes toward Jesuits, and Catholics in general, occurred when one of the policemen from the raid was quoted by a witness at the novitiate as asking where the chains were for manacling the residents.[88] This sounds like the lurid and popular nineteenth-century tales of Maria Monk and Rebecca Reed, in which escaped nuns told of convents brimming with Gothic horrors and abuses.[89] In reminiscences from two of the arrested novices, Doherty and George Nunan, prepared in the early 1960s, both men remembered the police acting hesitantly, as if expecting Jesuitical deviousness, to the extent that residents began goading them. The police officer who waited for Nunan outside his dormitory while he changed, for example, was extremely nervous, and finally asked Nunan where the chains were in his room. Doherty recalled that when Father William

Hingston, a military chaplain who had just returned from overseas service and who appeared in full uniform, called for the serving of cookies and cocoa, the officers looked suspicious. This motivated one Brother Chabot to call for the trap doors to finally be opened, revealing their Jesuit treachery. This jocularity caused the officers to wait for the novices to drink the cocoa first, for fear of being poisoned.[90] More seriously, the rector, Rev. Father Bourque (who had demanded written authority for entry, as per the law, which Macauley could not produce), wrote Mewburn relating how insulted the novitiate was, along with all Canadian Catholics. Bourque confronted Mewburn with the fact that Macauley had later apologized for the number of men he used to search the premises, in full uniform and armed, by claiming he did not know what type of violence he would face. Bourque was furious, as this simply demonstrated that Macauley was no better than the officers who searched the building looking for "startling mysteries" but finding "only bareness and simplicity." The raid had accomplished nothing but had given credibility to those in Canada who saw Catholics as "double-dealing, dangerous men, who could be made to obey the just law of the land only at the point of a bayonet."[91]

Rev. Spence vigorously denied that the GMA was propagating intolerance. For Spence, he and his colleagues were doing nothing less than protecting the British Empire against the yoke of Rome. According to this logic, the Vatican had become a political force by preventing the efficient prosecution of the war effort in Canada and in Ireland, where the hierarchy allegedly had openly excommunicated enlisters. Spence asked a rhetorical question that summarizes the perception of Catholics during this tense period by many Anglo-Protestants: "Are the Roman Catholics with us in this war? ... I would regret very much to think that the Church of Rome was against us. Still, what do we see?"[92] This was not evidence of intolerance or illiberality to these southwestern Ontario Protestants.[93] They were convinced that what they were fighting for was the British principle of fair play and equality embodied in conscription. The official proclamations of even the distant Calgary chapter of the Protestant fraternal order the Royal Black Preceptory echoed this sentiment: it claimed solidarity with the GMA and its pursuit of "Equal Rights for all, special privileges for none."[94]

Canada certainly survived the war intact, but the trust between Anglo-Protestants and French Catholics was clearly injured. In their magisterial study of the "khaki election" of 1917, Dutil and MacKenzie detail a shocking example of the severity of anti-Catholicism, occurring right in front of King George V himself. The king was dining with some Canadian soldiers at Windsor Castle when the issue of conscription was raised; the soldiers were quoted as saying, "When we get back we will shoot Laurier and every d–d [sic] French Canadian – cowards and traitors. We will have Civil War and exterminate the whole lot. Especially the R.C. Bishops and Priests." Feelings such as these would not easily subside, even with victory.[95] Public figures could vilify the Catholic Church internationally and in Canada by appealing to idealized universal civic values, positioning the Church as the enemy of said values and of the war effort itself. Anglo-Protestants aghast at the Church were operating within a pre-existing anti-Catholic tradition. They adapted and adjusted the specifics of the discourse to fit their own interests. What did not change was the threat that Catholicism represented to the peaceful progress of Canada.

It was not only Quebec and French-Canadian Catholics that threatened the unity and progress of Canada, but immigrants, particularly Old World Catholics. Woodsworth's popular textbook, *My Neighbour*, was funded by the head of the Young People's Forward Movement for Missions, F.C. Stephenson, and commissioned to provide a Canadian perspective on important issues in the Western world.[96] Woodsworth, while mostly focused on the need to help those living in urban areas through social service and reform, repeated his concern with Western Canada from *Strangers* by using Winnipeg as the central example. The concept of Catholic immigrants being unable to help themselves and thus threatening the fundamental fabric of the nation also remained throughout. For Woodsworth, the bedrock of the nation consisted of self-realized citizens who had internalized the British traditions of freedom and liberty. Woodsworth expressed concern over the poor ghettos of foreigners that had emerged due to the rapid shift of the population from the countryside to the cities in Western and Eastern Canada. While in his opinion, as in the opinion of many other reformers in this period, the city was a site of spiritual alienation,[97] for the immigrant such alienation was even more severe because the only churches in these areas were often English-speaking Protestant congregations who did not understand the new arrivals. As a solution Woodsworth advocated more intensive Protestant missions, which would further their understanding of "these people" and their traditions, which included Catholics, Jews, and ethnic Protestants.[98]

Woodsworth's prejudices were not far from the surface of his concerns, however, as, while the foreign-born Lutherans and even the Mennonites were assimilating into Canadian society, the Catholic Church remained obstinate and jealously guarded its influence over an ignorant people. In Woodsworth's opinion, most Catholic immigrants secretly resented and hated their Church:

> The Church has a strong hold on the immigrant peoples as they arrive in this country. They fear it and they love it. Its power has been almost absolute in the lands from which they come. It, more than anything else, unites them with the old land and all that they once held dear. The church is a home, a meeting-place, an entrance into the larger world of music and art and emotion. But as time goes on better education and frequent intercourse with English-speaking Protestants and the prevailing spirit of the new world tend inevitably to weaken the power of the church. The men especially refuse to be guided by those whom they regard as their exploiters. In their revolt against the church they are called and call themselves Atheists and Socialists – which simply means that they are against the established order as they know it.[99]

Historians have noted that the Roman Catholic Church in Canada in this period, although often split along linguistic lines, was dedicated not only to strengthening its hold over its followers as immigration increased but also to spreading its influence throughout Western Canada, even attempting to subsume "rival" forms of Catholicism, such as the Ukrainian Church, into the Latin rite.[100] Terence Fay, in his survey of Canadian Catholicism, characterizes this aggressive policy as a "messianic myth," in which God had chosen Roman Catholicism over a materialistic Protestantism as the true faith for the nation.[101] Woodsworth was thus expressing a genuine fear among Anglo-Protestants of the decline of the importance of Protestantism when challenged by a Catholic Church pursuing control of Canada's immigrant population. It is in Woodsworth's language, couched in vast oversimplifications of a shallow Church dedicated only to its numbers and power, influenced by what Kenneth McNaught details as Woodsworth's hatred of dogma of any form, that his anti-Catholicism is apparent.[102] His overarching narrative of the inevitability of the decline of the Church's authority in the face of the enlightenment of Protestant freedom is fundamentally anti-Catholic, positing a stark binary between light and darkness, authenticity and superficiality of belief. The Church inherently fomented harmful sentiments, according to Woodsworth, encouraging the loss of faith among immigrant men. Among women, the Church maintained its influence, but even then, only superficially. It used its associations to perpetuate the immigrants' native languages and customs and to prevent assimilation and maintain control. In Woodsworth's opinion, "the Church often retains its hold upon the people long after it has ceased to nourish them."[103] It could not fulfill the true spiritual needs of the people.

The West was of interest to many concerned about immigration, with the arrival of thousands of immigrants from varying backgrounds in the first several decades of the century (see Table 1.2). The West in general embodied the optimism for a prosperous future, a chance to move beyond the crass politics, scandals, and recessions of the late-nineteenth century. It could also serve to revitalize a decadent Anglo-Saxon race, reinvigorated by the climate and hardiness of the land. Emily Murphy embodied this spirit of settlement in a trilogy of Janey Canuck books released between 1910 and 1914.[104] Along with her paeans for the rejuvenating powers of the Northwest,[105] she also made many observations about the foreign populations on the Prairies. In *Seeds of Pine*, Murphy attended a Uniat service in a Ruthenian community in Mundare, Alberta. She repeated the familiar litany of sensual experiences (opulent vestments, massive candles, golden, shining chalices), adding that she was assured by the nuns present that their veneration of the crucifix was not idolatry, as these were only symbols. She was impressed by the Ruthenians' and Galicians' expressions when they received "the mysterious sacrifice known as the 'elevation of the host,'" pointing out that they might be "sullen folk of unstable and misanthropical temper; they may be uncouth of manner, and uncleanly of morals," but here, at least, they had a song and energy (and maybe even God) inside them, if not knowledge. Yet Murphy was convinced that this Finding of the Holy Cross, which re-enacted the crucifixion, was morbid and fruitless, "sing[ing] to a dead god in a dead world."[106]

Murphy opened her tale by warning that it would take "some years to manipulate the crude European immigrant" into a true Britisher,

Table 1.2
Overall population of the western provinces

Year	Manitoba	Saskatchewan	Alberta	British Columbia
1901	255,211	91,279	73,002	178,657
1911	461,394	492,432	374,295	392,480
1921	610,118	757,510	588,454	524,582

Series A2-14, *Historical Statistics in Canada*, 2nd ed.

especially with "equally high political standards." Anglo-Protestants may have ignored the easy corruption of foreign communities by political opportunists thus far, but only at their peril. She asked what would happen in the next election, when "the preponderance of the foreign vote in educational and moral matters" outweighed the thoughtful Anglo-Protestant? Could those attendees at such a religious service be trusted with the morals of a British nation? For Murphy, these communities needed to be helped and saved to participate in a British democracy but should not be "over-civilized" and sapped of their latent energy. There is an ambivalence here that was missing from Murphy's earlier accounts of Catholicism/ritualism: the Ruthenians, Galicians, and French Canadians were the ethnic Other, potentially unable to adapt to Canadian civic culture without help, particularly while wrapped in the cloaks of an arcane faith. But help was possible, and she was optimistic for the future of these fundamentally good people, if baffled as to the function of what for her was a joyless religion.[107] Murphy, along with many other Anglo-Protestants, viewed the polyglot masses of the Prairie provinces and the increasingly depopulated and impoverished rural areas with a mixture of optimism and dread, a land full of potential yet increasingly disordered and un-British.

Woodsworth believed that Protestantism could amplify its "cultural prestige" by becoming active in these areas and engaging in social-scientific analysis of serious social issues. If the West was where Canada would achieve its greatness materially and nationally, then in the minds of many it had to be intellectually and spiritually pure, with the population espousing an ideology of development and assimilated into the modern, Anglo-Saxon-Protestant value of progress.[108] The Reverend Charles Gordon (Ralph Connor) proclaimed at the Presbyterian Pre-Assembly Congress for 1913, while discussing the level of need for Protestant evangelization in the West, that the population had to be forged into true, loyal Canadians with a "Canadian ... fear of God." For Gordon, and perhaps his audience, it was clear that a Canadian conception of the "fear of God" and Canadian ideals were tied inextricably to Protestantism, as he continued: "the Roman Catholic problem ... is a problem for us all."[109]

This was the Western concomitant to what French-Canadian evangelizer Rev. C.E. Amaron referred to as the "Eastern problem" in Canada at the same congress, namely the clerical nationalism and political corruption of the Quebec hierarchy.[110] Canada was and was always to be a British, Protestant nation, founded on principles descending directly from the Reformation, particularly the English Reformation, such as liberty, self-realization, and freedom of conscience. "The Catholic" had to be reformed to exist under these universal values. This narrative would continue throughout the twentieth century in Canada, with various Anglo-Protestant Canadians continuing to use the same rhetorical devices to describe the nation and the place of Catholics within it. These values continued to be loaded with connotations of Britishness and Protestantism for decades.

Saskatchewan was of special concern to many Anglo-Protestants worried about non-Protestant religious communities forming in the West. Saskatchewan grew from approximately 100,000 people nestled in the southeast corner of the province in 1910 to 648,000 by 1916, spread out across the province and made up of an enormous variety of ethnicities and religious groups.[111] One of the most influential figures who focused on the province was Dr J.T.M. Anderson, educator and controversial Conservative premier. The story of Anderson's 1929 electoral victory and the prominence of the viciously anti-Catholic Ku Klux Klan in his victory has been detailed elsewhere.[112] Yet Anderson contributed his own perspective on the Catholic Church and its influence among immigrants to Western Canada before he even became the leader of the provincial Conservatives. Anderson was from Ontario, and later became involved in the Manitoba educational system, which is when he wrote *The Education of the New Canadian: A Treatise on Canada's Greatest Education Problem*, before transferring to Saskatoon and getting involved with the dormant provincial Tories.[113]

In his 1918 book, Anderson expressed his fear of and indignation at immigrant communities in isolated bloc settlements. According to

Anderson, the only bulwark against this isolation, made worse by the presence of radicals, nationalists, and an obstinate clergy, was the public school. Anderson was not concerned with Scandinavian immigrants, as "these people" were hardy, thrifty, intelligent, and Protestant. Repeating the racial-religious framework of other figures profiled here, Anderson feared immigrants from Eastern and Southern Europe, where settlers had been exposed to tyranny their entire life and did not understand the obligations of a democratic nation. Engaging in a wide historical analysis, Anderson used the tragic example of the Czechs, who had formed the Hussite movement to escape from Catholic tyranny to Protestant liberty centuries ago, only to be crushed under clericalism, defining Protestantism as "independence" and Catholicism as inevitably meaning "political subjection." An aggressive hierarchy, perhaps embodying these ideas of "political subjection," controlled the parochial school and prevented the creation of the progressive Canada that Anderson envisioned. The government had to monitor religious schools rigorously, if they continued to exist, as they were remnants of the "ancient reign of ecclesiastical despotism" and prevented the formation of a democratic citizenry.[114]

While Anderson claimed that he did not want religious dogma taught in schools, he did support the teaching of Christian values as necessary for a modern society. The equation was simple: dogma was Catholic, modern democratic Christianity was Protestant. Anderson specifically mentioned the betterment of those "chaotic" Slavic settlements in Northern Alberta that had received and accepted the hard-evangelizing work of the Presbyterian and Methodist churches. These churches allowed Slavs to escape from their history of oppression and subjugation at the hands of the Church hierarchy, Catholic or Orthodox. For Anderson, the seriousness of these issues could not be underestimated, and he attacked politicians pandering to these communities for their political opportunism. Anderson charged politicians with "prostitut[ing]" ideals of citizenship for purely partisan gains, catering to the foreign vote and "making us the laughing-stock of all enlightened peoples" by not forcing children to learn the English language properly and thus undermining any chance of national unity.[115] He was convinced that decisive action was necessary to prevent the dominance of irrationality and the sacrifice of Canadian unity at the hands of a foreign master.

Anderson was also instrumental in a 1929 survey focused mostly on northern Saskatchewan compiled by Robert England. England was an Ulsterman who had fought with the Canadian forces at Vimy Ridge; when he returned, he became involved in education, and Anderson's book greatly influenced him. In fact, Anderson convinced England and his wife, Amy, to take over a school in a Ukrainian-dominated district to help integrate immigrant populations.[116] At the time of the report, he was the Continental Superintendent of the Canadian National Railways' Colonization Department.[117] A Masonic scholarship funded this survey, designed to aid in understanding the core issues of immigrant communities in order to further assimilation, and Anderson was the representative from the Provincial Department of Education in Saskatchewan.[118] The resulting report, entitled *The Central European Immigrant in Canada*, reflected the input of a number of teachers across the province, who were given surveys designed to reveal the nature of immigrant communities. Each survey focused on an aspect of the community, such as agriculture. Despite genuine concern for the practice of certain agricultural and economic customs, it was the implications for the health of the nation that concerned the surveyors. It also reflected the intersections of race, nationality, ethnicity, and religion so common at the time. In the section "General Topics" of Report II, for example, the survey asked the teacher, "Are the traditions, habits, customs and temperaments of non-English settlers in your district such as to conduce to the stability of democratic government and to make Canada a virile nation?"[119]

England viewed the Slav and other Central European immigrants, referred to in the report as dominated by their religion, whether Catholic or Orthodox, as being trapped in a medieval world of superstitions, ignorance, and unbridled passion. England was clear that these indisputable facts should have compelled the government to limit the immigration of Slavs. Single Slavic men in particular were uncontrollable in their passions, and those already in Canada needed to be properly acclimated to a modern democratic nation – if, that is, they were not already in prisons or asylums.[120] The survey questions were steeped in this language: Question 1 of Psychological Topics, for example, asked, "To what extent does *superstition* govern the lives of the people?"[121] England and Anderson, along with many others discussed so far, were dedicated to the liberal dream of education leading to the assimilation of these immigrants, and England believed that, in the areas most heavily non-Protestant, it was the "teacher's heavy task ... [to] moderniz[e] ... medieval communities."[122]

Anti-Catholicism certainly informed *The Central European Immigrant in Canada*, as did an essentialist idea of race. This represents the close connections in this discourse between racist attitudes toward ethnic minorities and prejudicial opinions of religion. Often it is impossible to separate these sentiments from each other, as they were part of a matrix of discriminatory thought, much like the perceived intrinsic connection between "Frenchness" and Catholicism. While anti-Catholicism cannot be, and should not be, conflated with racism, a series of stereotypes and tropes regarding Catholicism was central to the intellectual framework of some Anglo-Protestants who were convinced of the inability of Catholic European immigrants to "fit" into a democratic society.

For example, climate determined evolution, in England's mind, and, following the orthodoxy of many other racial theorists of the day, he divided the races of Europe into the Nordic, the Alpine, and the Mediterranean races. The latter reached sexual maturity earlier due to their exposure to warm weather, which explained their hyper-emotional culture. Region A of immigration to Canada came from the "North German Plain" and Scandinavia, as Nordic people were easily assimilable, while Region B contained Croats, Magyars, and Slovaks. Again, revealing the intersections between anti-Catholicism and racism, the latter groups were more difficult to assimilate due to their minimal exposure to the Protestant Reformation.[123] To England, the Reformation was *the* singular historical/cultural event that discerned the character of entire peoples, part of the superstructure built on the deterministic base of climate and geography. This Protestant way of imagining the historical place of the Reformation was common; Michael Gauvreau has described how many evangelicals saw the Reformation as the beginning of the "universal struggle between truth and error," a struggle in which the "true faith" would have to triumph to ensure social progress.[124] According to England, the Germanic people were able to resist the centuries of Roman ecclesiasticism due to their evolutionary superiority, as the Romanization of these peoples was only superficial and formal, while in the other people of Europe not privy to this evolutionary advantage the dominance of Rome and its stifling medievalism was almost absolute. England used the Ulster-Scot, a community to which he belonged, as a worthy model for Canadian values, as they were scrupulous, thrifty, and firmly opposed to indolence. He advocated for the inculcation of the values of this hardy group into the Central European, as this process would prevent the spread of crime in Canada. England concluded his work by directly linking Protestant Christianity and Canada's British heritage with the desire for measured progress.[125] Apparently, outside of this tradition, only emotionalism and backwardness was possible. Anderson, who contributed to the operation of this project, would have agreed.

As alluded to earlier, the Klan was prominent in the election of 1929 when Anderson's Tories, in an alliance with provincial Progressives, united to defeat the provincial Liberal machine of Premier Jimmy Gardiner. One of the major figures espousing anti-Catholic vitriol in the province was the Anglican bishop of Saskatchewan, George Exton Lloyd, who was never a member of the Klan, but expressed similar sentiments.[126] Lloyd, referred to as a "professional Anglo-Saxon" by journalist James Gray, founded the National Association of Canada (NAC) to lobby for the limitation of immigration and to protect the Anglo-Saxon values he so cherished. He saw the passing of the Railways Agreement in 1925, which allowed major railway companies to recruit directly from continental Europe, as proof that the federal government was undermining the British nature of the region.[127] Lloyd and the NAC were not alone in their opposition to the agreement; historian Rebecca Mancuso details the various women's groups and immigration officials that opposed the deal based on its facilitation of racial "impurity."[128] Historian William Katerberg has identified Lloyd, however, as the embodiment of a strain of racialist thinking in Canada in the early- to mid-twentieth century termed "Anglo-Saxonism." This perspective linked the concerns of many Canadian Protestants regarding immigration to an intense pride in British traditions and institutions.[129]

Lloyd, who was a member of a British emigrant party often known as the Barr Colonists dedicated to spreading British values to Western Canada, participated in the founding of Lloydminster, Alberta, in 1903. After the failure of the initial leader of the Barr Colony, Anglican minister Rev. Isaac Barr, Lloyd led the settlement and was successful by 1910, gaining notoriety and respect from many Canadians as he successfully entrenched British settlers and traditions in the West. The Barr Colony was a unique example of a concerted effort at a British bloc settlement in the Canadian West.[130] When he recruited for the excursion, Lloyd asked Anglicans to ensure that those who came would make good English Canadians.[131] In a recent republishing of

Lloyd's account of the founding of the Barr Colony, the editor notes that Lloyd was dedicated throughout his life to spreading English values throughout the world, founding the Fellowship of the Maple Leaf during the First World War in order to recruit Britons and British teachers to come to Western Canada and prevent subversion by foreigners.[132]

In a speech to the Grand Orange Lodge in Edmonton in 1928, entitled "The Building of a Nation," Lloyd was frank about why he formed the NAC. At a meeting of representatives from the Masons, the Orangemen, and the Sons of England, Lloyd had decided that one single organization was needed to pool resources to stop "the foreignization [sic] of Canada and the increasing aggression of the Church of Rome" and to preserve "the supremacy of British ... traditions, blood, characteristics and loyalty to the crown as the king pin of the British Empire."[133] Lloyd more explicitly equated British values with Protestant values here, something that was threatened by the "Mongrel nation" that would inevitably emerge from an open-door policy of immigration. This sentiment was present throughout Anglo-Protestant society. These intruders into the nation from Southern, Central, and Eastern Europe would not assimilate to the "normal" English Canadian framework, much like the troublesome French Canadian in Quebec, and would destroy any sense of unity of purpose and devotion to the British motherland.[134]

The NAC engaged in a massive letter-writing campaign from 1928 to 1929, directed largely at Prime Minister King and the Department of Immigration and Colonization. Most of the letters reiterated Lloyd's concern about the Railways Agreement and the "Mongrelization" of Canada. Much of the language used also demonstrates the constant slippage between the upholding of the ethnic Britishness of Canada and its Protestantism. In a letter from Copeau, Saskatchewan, for example, the author stressed that, because of the foolish immigration policies of the federal government, Canada was quickly dividing into two broad camps. On the one side was the "invisible enemy of ... British migration," the Catholic Church and its supporters among French Canadians and "foreign peoples," and on the other, Anglo-Protestants. One of the consistent allegations, repeated by this correspondent, was that the department was employing a huge number of French-Canadian Catholic priests to cater to Catholic interests. In one letter, the writer expressed his displeasure with the alleged employment of twenty-nine priests in the immigration department, allowing Southern Europeans to proliferate in the West and, through the encouragement of their clergy, refuse to assimilate into mainstream Canadian society.[135]

The department was concerned enough about the NAC and the sheer volume of letters they received from its supporters that the minister, Robert Forke, and his deputy ministers responded at length to dispel these accusations. Forke and his staff repeatedly corrected the NAC correspondents by pointing out that the department employed only two French-Canadian Catholic priests, and solely for repatriation purposes. In a revealing bout of frustration, the acting deputy minister responded to the local NAC leader in Copeau by bemoaning the fact that these charges of Catholic dominance and favouritism had bedevilled every government agency responsible for immigration since the Laurier Liberals opened the door. The minister thus felt the need to assure the anonymous correspondent that most of the staff was in fact Protestant, a fact that Forke repeated in another letter, in which he informed one A.P. Bigelow that, of the five immigration commissioners, only one was Catholic. These defensive measures continued until at least 1930, when an immigration official responded to queries about the religious makeup of the department by listing all of the individuals he knew and if they were Catholic or non-Catholic, concluding that the department was Protestant by a three-to-one ratio.[136]

What these responses reveal is not only the seriousness with which at least some immigration officials took the NAC, but that they felt the need to outline the religious makeup of the department both to disprove the charges of Catholic dominance and to prove the department's dedication to preserving Canada's Anglo-Protestant heritage. In one response to the NAC, Forke explicitly reassured the correspondent that the department was trying everything it could to coax "Britishers" to Canada.[137] The assumption that the settlement of "Britishers" was the goal was not questioned in this correspondence. Instead the focus of the message was that the NAC was wrong in assuming that the Department of Immigration and Colonization was controlled by Catholic priests and privileged non-Britons. In addition, the government pledged to increase British immigration in 1928 in the face of public pressure and had to admit by 1930 that the Railways Agreement had been a failure.[138] While the NAC's language was perhaps more aggressive than other commentators, its sentiments were by no means isolated.

As Katerberg has cogently written, nativism and racism were not the sole preserve of reactionary conservatives struggling with identity in a changing world. They were also part of progressive and liberal ideology of the early-twentieth century. Through reform and restriction, these figures and activists postulated, the control of immigration was possible, along with the modification and assimilation of these same immigrants.[139] One of the major aspects of English-Canadian identity and improving Canadian society was Protestantism and the liberties that it was assumed to entail. It is therefore unsurprising that the NAC was relatively successful in its campaign and that, when Anderson became premier of Saskatchewan and minister of education in 1929, his initial focus was regulating Catholics, foreigners, and religious schools. Indeed, the educational situation in Saskatchewan was complex. French was allowed as the language of instruction until the first grade, and subsequently for one hour per day, along with half an hour of religious instruction. Additionally, in the tiny number of areas where Protestants were a minority, Catholic trustees controlled the school boards where Protestant children would attend public schools and where nuns were teachers and crucifixes were displayed.[140] Anderson immediately legislated against religious education, the presence of religious emblems of any kind, and the teaching and speaking of French in schools.[141] The Depression *did* ostensibly destroy the Tories in Saskatchewan for decades to come, yet this does not mitigate Anderson's own anti-Catholic beliefs. His successful informal alliance with the Klan militate against a benign interpretation of his campaign and premiership.[142]

The Klan saw itself as protecting Canada against the organized machinations of the Catholic Church. Protestantism and patriotism were equivalent. The Klan viewed itself as "unafraid soldiers who dare to serve against all the secret, subtle enemies who strive to undermine the state." [143] This language was more than rhetoric. Several Klansmen attempted to bomb St Mary's Catholic Church in Barrie, Ontario, on 10 June 1926. Police arrested William Skelly, an Irish immigrant, along with two other men claiming to be Klansmen. They confessed to the crime of planting dynamite in the church; Skelly claimed that the Klan instructed him to do so as an initiation.[144] The case became even more sensational when the Klan denied all connection to the bombing, blaming them on Skelly's intense hatred of Catholicism inspired by the killing of his wife by Sinn Fein in Ireland. The various branches of the Klan defended themselves as part of a law-abiding, patriotic organization.[145] Indeed the attorney general of Ontario, W.F. Nickle, was convinced by a meeting he had with the "respectable" elements of the Klan, namely J.S. Lord, MLA in the New Brunswick legislature and chief of staff for the Fredericton Klan, and O.B. Neeley, Klan solicitor, that the Klan would punish any member engaged in these lawless affairs and would cooperate with authorities.[146] The Klan no longer refuted the membership of the three men; it simply upheld that the organization did not support the action. The Klan was an organization not necessarily accepted within the mainstream of Canadian society, yet espoused rhetoric and values that closely resembled many English Canadians' own ideas regarding the centrality of Protestantism in Canadian identity. Indeed, as late as 1935, the superintendent of the Protestant Home in Alberta admitted in his "Protestant Home News Letter" that he had accepted donations from the Orange Order and the Klan to stay afloat.[147] In the most recent analysis of the Klan in Saskatchewan, Pitsula has concluded that historians cannot dismiss the organization as an aberration in the Canadian narrative of multiculturalism and tolerance. The Klan was in fact using a language of Britishness to gain support, particularly when expounding a theme so entrenched in the public discourse as anti-Catholicism.[148]

The point on which figures and organizations differed regarding the ethnicities and religions populating Western Canada (and Eastern Canada) was that some saw in Catholics the ability to change and become truly Canadian; others, like the Klan and Lloyd, saw in these foreign hordes an interminable racial, political, and religious threat to the nation. Kate Foster certainly fits into the former category, as do her contemporaries Connor and Woodsworth. Her short work, *Our Canadian Mosaic*, offers another superficially inclusive solution to the "immigrant problem" in Canada. Foster, who was the national field secretary of the Dominion YWCA, was perhaps the first Canadian to use the mosaic metaphor to describe the nation's contemporary and desired makeup. She was praised for this by John Murray Gibbon in his seminal *Canadian Mosaic: The Making of a Northern Nation*.[149] Foster engaged in a wide survey of immigrants in Canada at the behest of the Dominion Council of the YWCA. She wanted to promote a better understanding between the peoples of Canada and preserve some aspects of the older culture of immigrants. Foster rhapsodized optimistically that, for "some minds, Canadianization is confused with a narrow nationalism that necessitates a ruthless severing of all ties with the Old World and its associations." In direct reference to Woodsworth,

Foster criticized this as prejudicial, suggesting instead that we should "concern ourselves with encouraging the 'strangers within our gates' ... to help build up a Canada worthy to take her place side by side with the progressive nations of the world."[150]

Despite her optimistic early-twentieth-century liberalism, Foster was clear in her desire for some types of immigrants over others. Foster agreed with the author of the foreword to her book, president of the Royal Society of Canada, James H. Coyne, about emphasizing quality over quantity, defining quality as the ability of the ethnic group to assimilate into the traditions of Canada. Coyne and Foster feared the lack of British and Northern European immigrants arriving and the "swamping" of the nation with Eastern and Southern Europeans, who were enthusiastic to emigrate due to their universally destitute and oppressed lives. For example, Foster characterized Poles through a lens of Catholic Orientalism, as intensely – even bizarrely – religious, embodied in a superstitious Mariology that led them to worship at the feet of Marian shrines to cure illnesses. This almost paganistic portrayal of Polish Catholics was contrasted by Foster with the sturdy, hard-working, and easily assimilable Protestants from Northern Europe. Coyne in fact explicitly stated that immigration should be restricted only to Anglo-Saxons, Teutons, and Scandinavians.[151]

In Foster's view, Catholics were to be tolerated, but the public school and the (Protestant) church were to act as the major institutions in the successful assimilation of foreign elements. This excluded any form of separate school, as this restricted children's exposure to Canadian values. Foster used the New Brunswick school system as the example of an ideal liberal, non-sectarian system, which created an equal playing field for all newcomers. She also privileged the recently formed United Church as the ultimate expression of Christian "tolerance and friendliness"; the United Church for Foster was nothing less than the "melting pot of God."[152] She advocated for the missions set up by the United Church to Italians in Hamilton and Montreal specifically, as Italians were hot-headed and prone to crime and violence. Foster repeated common ethnic stereotypes of the passionate and uncontrollable Italian who was only nominally Roman Catholic, allowing the United Church an entry point to change their minds, and repeating Woodsworth's earlier theory of the secretly uncommitted Catholic. These missionary initiatives were ensured success by the conversion of Eastern and Southern European Catholics (and Orthodox) to the "true" worship of Jesus. The true worship of

Jesus broke down barriers and allowed for the ordering of "these people's" lives, something clearly lacking from Foster's point of view in their previous world.[153] Foster was suggesting here that those arriving from the Old World, while bringing ancient customs and culture, were largely arriving in poverty, both economic and spiritual, in need of saving. The religion they practised was either superficial or almost paganistic and overwhelmingly unfulfilling. Foster did not advocate the complete assimilation of all aspects of immigrant culture, but wanted only the positive aspects, which did not, presumably, include Catholicism.

Foster also shared the racial theories mentioned earlier in Anderson's and England's works. These often confusing and inconsistent ideas of race again intersected with pre-existing assumptions about the superiority of Protestant Northwestern Europe. According to Foster, the people of Europe could be divided into several races: the Caucasian race contained the vaguely defined "Pre-Aryan" and "Semitic" peoples; the Mongolian race contained the Finns, Lapps, Turks, and Magyars; and the Indo-European, or Aryan, race, which could be subdivided into Latin, Slavic, and Nordic peoples.[154] It was clear which of these was the most desirable (Nordic), and it was certainly no coincidence that these groups were the most thoroughly Protestant and light-skinned. The Slavs and Latins simply accepted a lower standard of living and were bringing this poverty to Canada, undermining the nation's initiative and prosperity. Foster and many of her fellow Canadians concerned with immigration created a mutually constitutive racial-religious framework for understanding Others: climate, geography, and biology defined the nature of peoples and what forms of government they accepted, but these types of peoples embraced archaic and oppressive religious forms and practices that furthered their impoverishment. Foster represented this most clearly near the end of her book, where she provided a list of countries that had immigrants in Canada and added a brief profile of each country, listing religion, form of government, and primary settlement location in their host country.[155] Certainly, this typology was useful for those concerned with the "foreignization" of Canada and how to reform those arriving.

One of Ralph Connor's most famous fictional works, *The Foreigner: A Tale of Saskatchewan*, released in 1909, clearly demonstrates this approach to non-Protestant immigration. It is a tale of the immigrant communities of Western Canada and how the penetration of Canadian ideals, such as democracy and liberty, themselves both underlaid with Protestantism, could "save" some of the ignorant Catholics from a life of violence and degradation. For example, Margaret Ketzel, a character in the novel, "saves" her father, Simon, by teaching him English and providing him with Methodist literature.[156] Thus, her father's spiritual rebirth sacralized the importance of reaching the youth of these immigrants, an approach Woodsworth outlined in his work as being integral to the edification of immigrants about truly Canadian values.[157] Connor is exuberant in his detailing of the results of this conversion, believing that "as time went on it came to pass that from the Ketzel home, clean, orderly, and Canadian, there went out into the foul waste about streams of healing and cleansing that did their beneficent work where they went."[158]

In addition, the novel presents the consequences of rejecting the word of Protestant Christianity. When the doctor and Sergeant Cameron find a dead foreigner, the doctor expresses sadness for these "rough characters": "[A]n ignorant and superstitious Church has kept them in fear of purgatory and hellfire for the next [life]. They have never had a chance."[159] Connor was convinced that Protestantism was the answer to the issues in the West, most clearly embodied in his Mr Brown and Kalman Kalmar characters. Brown is the definition of the sturdy Western Protestant, unshakable in the veracity and utility of his faith in shaping Canada. Brown expresses the difficulties he has encountered in his establishment of a Presbyterian mission, because foreigners are convinced that it is simply a scheme to extract their meagre income. Brown understands this fear, as the only church they had ever known was constantly fleecing them. This fear also caused a secret hatred and resentment of churches in general, repeating Woodsworth's concern of a superficial faith, an even more prodigious crime resulting from Catholic greed. In addition, many of them were not even sure if the mission was a church at all, because Brown refused to take money or to have ritualistic externalities present. Once Brown exposes Kalmar to these ideas, he boldly denies another aspect of Catholicism, responding to a priest who wanted him to confess, "I make my confession to God." The priest is shocked, accusing Kalmar of apostasy; Kalmar calmly responds that he is in fact the opposite, that he has been reading his Bible and finally understands the true word of Jesus.[160]

Canadian national identity in this era was viewed through a prism of British values, with one of the key components being Protestantism. Any alternative was either unwelcome or at best to be tolerated but transformed into an appropriate value system for a citizen of a modern progressive nation. For some Anglo-Protestants, Catholics had the potential, if they refuted their Church and its traditions, to become good citizens. The Church itself, however, was inherently corrupt and authoritarian, violating the "British-Whiggish" historical narrative of a progressively increasing liberty protected under British traditions and institutions. Anti-Catholicism in early-twentieth-century Canada, as an analytical category, demonstrates the roots of the slippage between civic and ethnic nationalism. Civic nationalism is presumably based only on universal values, such as human rights, the liberty and equality of all, and participation in the socio-political fabric of the nation. The hostility toward continental European immigrants and French Canada based on religion, however, demonstrates that a progressive, liberal civic nationalism was also based on stereotypes, albeit at an early stage of potentially civic English-Canadian nationalist discourse. This constant slippage between civic and ethnic nationalism would continue throughout the twentieth century.

This discourse would also continue into the harsh years of the Depression. During this period, anti-Catholicism manifested itself in the expected places. Yet new political ideals and parties challenged the status quo in Canada. Some left-wing intellectuals and activists inherited an ideological framework that included a vigorous distrust of Catholicism and the Church. Anti-Catholicism, while remaining important in liberal and conservative circles, also became an important aspect of much left-wing discourse in Canada in its generalized war against fascism.

2

Fascism and "The Revenge of the Cradle": Anti-Catholicism and the Great Depression

> The authoritarian character of the Catholic Church makes it more lenient to the doctrine of fascism than the Protestant churches would be.[1]
>
> F.R. Scott (1938)

In June 1938, a minor scandal erupted when the publication of reformist Anglican clergyman and staunch birth-control advocate Alfred Henry Tyrer's successful and controversial guidebook, *Sex, Marriage, and Birth Control: A Guide-book to Sex Health and a Satisfactory Sex Life in Marriage*, was cancelled by Macmillan and Company. Tyrer was publicly furious and issued "To the Protestant Ministers of Canada," an aptly titled open letter. In this letter Tyrer fulminated against the Catholic Church, which he blamed for influencing Macmillan and Company to cancel his book, due to Macmillan's extensive separate-school textbook contract. Tyrer focused on the Catholic Church's view of contraception and its "fascist tendencies": "That Rome, by some sort of threat ... should be able to do this should surely be sufficient evidence to all Protestants of what the future may soon bring forth – the early dominance of Roman Catholicism in Canada." This would be achieved by expanding throughout the country the "'padlock' laws in Quebec; an index librorum prohibitorum ... telling the people what they may read ... the prohibition of free assembly; and the resuscitation, in a Fascist Canada, of the inquisitorial methods of the Dark Ages." Indeed, according to Tyrer, "[n]o intelligent Protestant knowing anything of the history of Roman Catholicism can look on this menace with equanimity. No British Protestant is going to bow his neck to a French-Canadian Fascist." In an interview Tyrer gave at the time of the release of this letter, he was even more alarmist in his position on the suppression of birth-control information by the Catholic Church and its implications for Canada as a nation: "The French nationalists and Roman Catholics ... are increasing due to the suppression of birth control. Sooner or later they will be in the majority here. We're headed for a civil war."[2]

Contained within this vitriolic letter by a progressive Protestant clergyman are many of the anti-Catholic themes that emerged during the Great Depression in Canada.[3] In this period of widespread social unrest, shifting politics, and international chaos, anti-Catholicism remained a central pillar upon which public figures, intellectuals, politicians, and members of the public built English-Canadian national identity. Many Anglo-Protestants still viewed French Canada as backward and medieval, for example, but this rhetoric grew to include an exaggerated fear of the growing international fascist movement that was allegedly taking root in Quebec and drawing upon specifically Catholic corporatist ideology. In the eyes of the Anglo-Protestants detailed here, this was represented not only by the extremist Adrien Arcand, but also by Catholic corporatist thought in general and by the success of Maurice Duplessis, believed to be driven by the powers of the Church (particularly Cardinal Villeneuve). Many Anglo-Protestants, especially on the left, characterized these men as clerical-fascists, representing an ideological system widely supported by Catholic French Canadians due to their "totalitarian inclinations." There had been concern in Canada about intersections between Catholicism and fascism with the rise of Mussolini in the 1920s,[4] but the worsening international situation, signalled by the rise of Hitler, the Italian invasion of Ethiopia, and especially the Spanish Civil War, combined with the deteriorating socio-economic status of Canada to breed a panic over Catholic totalitarianism distinct from earlier periods. In summary, Catholicism was "conducive" to these ideologies, unlike an inherently democratic Protestantism, which formed the basis of liberal nations.

These claims ignored the important debates occurring between Catholics dedicated to the "rechristianizing" of the population (the serious, academic study of social problems and hostility to fascist alternatives), such as Georges-Henri Lévesque and the great Catholic philosopher Jacques Maritain, and conservative Catholic nationalists who advocated the "refrancization" of Quebec, or even separatism. In fact, as Michael Gauvreau has demonstrated, personalist Catholicism was explicit about its determination to stop the spread of fascism and Marxism. It planned to do this through the regeneration of Catholicism by emphasizing the accountability of the clergy to the laity, the integrity of every person, and the formation of strong community ties to democratize social relations.[5] Some influential figures did indeed emphasize corporatism, a specifically Catholic organicist "third way" between capitalism and socialism that emphasized industrial and social cooperation between producers, owners, and, to an extent, government to solve the socio-economic crises. Corporatism as an ideology was dedicated to alleviating the suffering of modern industrial society by countering laissez-faire individualism *and* Marxist socialism through the organization of cooperative guilds, not necessarily industrial unions, and treating the family as the primary unit of society, not the individual or class. This form of organic social organization, according to corporatists, would allow for the spiritual life to once again take pre-eminence, even amid the excesses of industrial capitalism.[6] Corporatists did not always model their theories solely on Mussolini's Italy or Salazar's Portugal, however, states that did officially embrace a form of corporatism. Instead, many Catholics looked directly to the teachings of the Vatican for inspiration, especially Pope Pius XI's 1931 encyclical *Quadragesimo Anno*. Fascism certainly did not have a monopoly on corporatist ideology, even though the terms became synonymous in the eyes of many.[7] In fact, by the mid-1930s, Quebec's bishops were becoming wary of the extreme nationalism dominant in Italy, Portugal, and Franco's Spain and the associations made between these nations and corporatism. Thus, the Church began emphasizing the social and spiritual aspects of corporatism, as opposed to the nationalist prerogatives of priest-historian Abbé Lionel Groulx and his followers.[8] While it is also true that a hard-line anti-Communism was prominent in Quebec in this period, represented most infamously by Duplessis' draconian Padlock Law, this was true of English Canada as well.[9] In other words, Catholicism in Quebec was a complex aspect of French-Canadian identity in this period, irreducible to simple ideological labels such as fascism/corporatism. Yet this very reductionism was central to the casting of Catholic Quebec as the potentially fascist Other to the democratic haven of Protestant English Canada.[10]

Fear of fascism in French Canada was an important component of anti-Catholicism, but the foreign (read non-Anglo) population of Canada was certainly still a concern during the Depression.[11] The fear of the Protestant Anglo-Saxon element of Canada being outbred emerged as a major component of Anglo-Protestant anti-Catholic discourse during the decade. Unlike in the period from 1910 to 1929, birth control and the perceived monolithic Catholic hostility to contraception became *the* central issue in the ongoing debate over "the revenge of the cradle" narrative in Canada. This focus on the salvific nature of contraception, including eugenics, by many public figures and intellectuals clearly delineates Depression-era anti-Catholicism from that of the previous period, even among those progressives of that era who strove to reform society. A birth-control and eugenics movement did exist in Canada before the Depression, but the ravages of the decade added a certain amount of currency to the birth-control activists' arguments that being able to limit family size would benefit families and social stability.[12] The curtailment of most immigration during the Depression, while alleviating some fears over the nation's increasingly polyglot nature, focused the anxiety of many Protestant public figures into fear of the Anglo-Protestant inability to combat a prodigious Catholic birth rate, replicating the way race, ethnicity, and religion mutually reinforced such anxieties in the earlier period.[13] Catholicism was a foil for the feared "devitalization" of Canadian Protestantism and its potential shift from the centre of the Canadian identity, a concern that carried far into the post–Second World War era.

Anglo-Saxons were believed to embody the democratic values of Canada, bred as they were in British Protestant traditions and institutions. The stakes were also higher, as the debate was no longer only about the proper development of the nation but about the survival of democracy itself, something achieved only through a "fit" population. The Depression saw major debates, and one major trial, concerning birth control and its availability. The Anglo-Protestants detailed here saw the Catholic Church as opposing contraception solely to enhance its position in the world through numbers and, by inevitably keeping its people in poverty and ignorance through this policy, maintaining a slavishly devoted following of people foreign to a British nation like Canada, not just in ethnicity, race, and religion, but in values. The discourse concerning birth control, immigration, and the fear of fascism in French Canada were all interrelated, creating a unique brew of Canadian anti-Catholicism during the "dirty thirties."

What also differentiates the 1930s from the previous era is the prominence of a group of self-consciously left-wing (and progressive) intellectuals, churchmen, and public figures who participated in perpetuating this concept of the Catholic Church. This chapter will thus analyze not only the resort to anti-Catholic bigotry by the Ontario Tories in the heavily Orange riding of East Hastings, but also the negative characterization of the Church by such Co-operative Commonwealth Federation (CCF) and League for Social Reconstruction (LSR) luminaries as Eugene Forsey and F.R. Scott. Tyrer and C.E. Silcox symbolize progressive ministers who protested the power of an archaic and reactionary institution like the Catholic Church. These figures painted the Church as singularly responsible for the censorship and prosecution of fiery Protestants and open anti-Catholics, such as Rev. Morris Zeidman, once again demonstrating the reactionary and totalitarian nature of the Church.[14] Yet these figures simultaneously denied they were anti-Catholic or bigoted. This paradoxical attitude reflects what John Wolffe has outlined in his study of nineteenth-century British evangelical anti-Catholicism. Wolffe concluded that those he studied did not perceive hostility toward Catholicism as illiberal, but in fact the exact opposite. Anti-Catholicism was a defence *against* intolerance, not intolerance itself.[15] These Depression-era leftists often consciously strove to avoid propagating prejudice or stereotypes against the Catholic Church or other racial, religious, and cultural groups. They simply could not accept the influence and "inherently" intolerant nature of this institution.

According to historian Lara Campbell, identification as a British subject allowed Anglo-Protestants during the Depression (at least in Ontario) to condemn those who did not profess as fervent a loyalty to the intrinsic greatness of the British Empire. Britishness, in Campbell's mind, was a signifier of respectability and belonging, representing an organic link to Canada's past.[16] While Campbell does not explicitly mention anti-Catholicism, her analysis of Britishness is cogent. It continued to form the bedrock for the use of anti-Catholic traditions by Anglo-Protestants fearful of a world riven with conflict and hostile to democratic freedoms.

J.V. McAree, influential editorialist for the *Globe and Mail*, was supportive of Tyrer in his protests against the influence of Catholicism. McAree based his argument on the importance of self-realization and free choice, and argued that the suppression of any information, especially with regard to such an important issue as birth control, was unconscionable, and violated not only the law of Canada but also the natural rights of people.[17] Yet McAree made the problematic assertion that the efforts of Protestantism had already *won* the "birth control debate," with the only institution preventing its integration into respectable society and the law being the Catholic Church. According to McAree, this case was vital, as the banning of Tyrer's book impeded the progress of Canada. "It is an invasion of our liberties which cannot go unchallenged," said McAree angrily, and if upheld would set a dangerous precedent for a Catholic Church always poised to exercise its political influence. According to McAree, even the free distribution of the Bible was illegal in Quebec. He reassured his readers, though, that "news of the Gospels does manage to seep down into the minds of the French-Canadians,"[18] positing the typical French Canadian as mostly subservient to clerical elites but still Christian. This public denunciation of Macmillan forced Hugh Eayrs, the president of the company, to publish a retort, denying that the Catholic hierarchy was involved in the cancelling of Tyrer's contract. Eayrs instead blamed Tyrer's violation of the original publishing contract, which made explicit mention of the sensitive nature of the material and thus limited its distribution. With Tyrer continually demanding the spread of his book into all areas of society, and thus violating the agreement, Eayrs claimed he was motivated to cancel Tyrer's publishing contract legally.[19] McAree never admitted that Tyrer was wrong, but later responded that, while he had no problem with Catholicism as a religion, he still could not countenance the prevention of something that would "lighten their [Catholics'] ignorance" with regard to birth control.[20]

Another scandal revolving around the alleged influence of the Church involved Rev. Morris Zeidman, a prominent figure in the staunchly Protestant Toronto religious scene. An eccentric character, he was a convert from Judaism to Presbyterianism, the founder of the Scott Mission in Toronto, an Orangeman, the host of the Protestant Radio League's controversial Sunday broadcasts in the 1930s, and a central figure in the short-lived Canadian Protestant Association (CPA), formed to oppose Ontario Premier Mitchell Hepburn's divisive separate-school legislation (discussed in detail later).[21] Zeidman was no stranger to controversy: he claimed radio station CFRB fired him in March 1936 because of the influence of the Catholic Church, as it was hostile to his thoroughly Protestant message. He continued to give broadcasts, albeit with the caveat that he now had to submit his scripts to censors beforehand.[22] A year later, a broadcast on CFRB concerning birth control by Zeidman was restricted. He stated publicly that the CBC had told Harry Sedgwick, managing director of CFRB, to ban Zeidman's broadcast. The CBC and Sedgwick officially denied this, stating that they told Zeidman his broadcast was inflammatory and violated the CBC's recently adopted policy prohibiting "abusive" language against religion. Sedgwick claimed he had pointed this out to Zeidman and that he had privately cooperated by writing and presenting an alternative broadcast.[23] Zeidman, for his part, vehemently denied this cooperation, insisting that he was simply presenting the Protestant position on women's rights to contraception, not attacking a religion or an institution. To make matters more complex, Zeidman mentioned the ongoing Dorothea Palmer trial, in which he was a witness for the defence, in his broadcast, and therefore his script was potentially *sub judice*. Zeidman again defended himself by stating that birth control itself was not on trial, so that his references were perfectly acceptable.[24] Future Toronto mayor Leslie Saunders of the Orange Order and editor of the militant periodical *Protestant Action* immediately sent a protest to Prime Minister King, leader of the opposition R.B. Bennett, and Gladstone Murray of the CBC. Saunders decried that "[t]he hand of Rome is clearly seen in this unfair treatment, and we declare that such a condition should not be allowed to obtain in a free country." Saunders concluded conspiratorially that these censorship problems had emerged only since one Rev. Father Vachon had joined the CBC Radio Commission.[25]

During the controversy, the *Globe and Mail* decided to provide extracts from Zeidman's proposed broadcast that demonstrated his position on the Catholic Church and birth control in general. Zeidman referred to the ongoing problem of intermarriage, which in Canada was a problem only because of "the two widely divergent faiths, namely, Protestantism and Catholicism." "Meddling ecclesiastics" prevented happiness among couples and, relatedly, prevented women from using birth control. In Zeidman's mind, science had progressed to such a level in Canada that any woman who did not take advantage of it "sins against her own body and against her own children, who are entitled to all the love, care and upbringing which are a child's birthright; and she sins against the nation," adding, in a eugenically tinged phrase, "which expects quality rather than quantity." For

Zeidman, the Catholic Church's opposition to all forms of birth control was thus preventing Canada from being "a modern, civilized and Christian community" and would result in the swamping of the nation with people of lower quality.[26]

C.E. Silcox became involved in this controversy after Zeidman visited him, regaling Silcox with stories of CBC censorship. Silcox was an important public intellectual and United Churchman and was a major figure in ecumenical efforts to promote understanding between Catholics, Protestants, and Jews in North America, perhaps explaining his contact with Zeidman.[27] Zeidman indeed continued to have problems with censorship when the CBC demanded that he had to have specific denominational backing for his Protestant Radio League Sunday broadcasts. When he refused, he was banned for weeks from the air, causing Rev. William E. Long of the Evangel Temple in Toronto to give an advertised sermon provocatively entitled "Will Protestants Awaken?" stressing Zeidman's rights.[28] All this impelled Silcox to write a letter to CBC General Manager Gladstone Murray. Silcox condemned Murray and the CBC for trying to force Protestants to present only the positive aspects of their faith "for Protestantism is, in its very nature, *a protest* against certain assumptions made by the Roman Catholic Church, and to state what Protestants *deny* may be essential to the clarification of what they *affirm*." Silcox affirmed the British Protestant character of Canada's constitution as well, referring to the prohibition of Catholics from exercising regal power by the Oath of Supremacy and the privileging of certain aspects of Anglicanism in the British tradition.[29]

While placing Canada within this British Protestant context, he warned against the inevitable political aspirations and internationalist nature of the Catholic Church, particularly since Mussolini had restored the Vatican to its temporal power with the Lateran Accords in 1929. Silcox positioned these two camps, British democracy and Latin fascism, as binaries between which Canadians (indeed all people) needed to choose. He explicitly listed for Murray the three antecedents for modern democracy: "(i) The Protestant Reformation with its insistence on private judgement; (ii) The enlightenment which led to the French Revolution; (iii) Modern socialism (not Marxism) which is the child of liberalism." Catholicism did not fit into this world view or historical narrative. It was an undemocratic doctrine, truly alien to the British, Protestant nature of Canada. Silcox viewed this censorship by the Church as "subversive of the foundations of our democracy or however repugnant to the Protestant faith which is an integral part of the common law of England." He identified the major locus of this reactionary Catholicism as the province of Quebec: "The issue raised by the censorship is one therefore that concerns not alone *Protestants as Protestants* but *Protestants as protagonists of democracy*, and hence the decision of the Canadian Broadcasting Corporation is ... intensified by the present efforts to stifle freedom of discussion everywhere in French Canada."[30]

The belief that Protestants were special "protagonists of democracy" would be influential throughout the decade, even if not enunciated in such stark terms by other Anglo-Protestants. Nevertheless, despite Silcox's efforts, Zeidman would finally agree to a compromise in late 1937 to stay on the air, now in Hamilton instead of Toronto. He would refrain from openly discussing politics, focus on purely ecclesiastical matters, and carefully monitor his "abusive" language.[31] The entire controversy went beyond strong words, becoming violent according to the *Globe and Mail*. Following Long's sermon, Evangel Temple was partially burned, fulfilling threats that "it would be next" after the burning of Jarvis Street Baptist Church, home of noted anti-Catholic T.T. Shields.[32]

Tensions were also high in Quebec, the "fortress" of Catholicism in Canada. F.R. Scott and others on the left were very concerned with the continued movement of Quebec to the far right.[33] Scott was working at McGill as a scholar in constitutional and federal law (from 1928 onwards), but he was also known as an accomplished poet. The son of Canon Frederick George Scott, he had thus been born into the elite circles of Anglo-Quebec, attending Oxford on a Rhodes Scholarship along with many of the accomplished young Canadians of his day. Scott played a central role in the founding of the LSR and the CCF, becoming an eminent legal scholar and passionate advocate for civil rights in the ensuing decades.[34] Under the pseudonym "S," however, Scott contributed an article to the American periodical *Foreign Affairs* entitled "Embryo Fascism in Quebec" in 1938, describing the rise of Duplessis, the Union Nationale (UN), and the influence of the reactionary Catholic Church. Scott saw Quebec as the hub of fascism in Canada. In Scott's estimation, the passing of the infamous Padlock Law occurred without protest because of the overwhelming sanction of the clergy, a clergy dedicated to preaching what he believed was the fascist philosophy of corporatism in their schools as the only solution to modern social problems. Scott was unequivocal in his condemnation of the repressive legislation, fascist movements, and anti-Semitic violence he witnessed in Quebec at the time. He admitted, confusingly, that while the term "fascist" may have been unrepresentative, since none of the members of the Quebec legislature identified themselves as fascists, "[t]he great majority were simply obedient Catholics carrying out the request of their spiritual leaders." It was these respected luminaries of Church and state, not open fascists, who encouraged the anti-Semitic and anti-Communist violence that was taking place in Montreal. This statement exemplifies the common anti-Catholic motif of the "obedient Catholic," in a more literal sense here, simply blindly following the dictates of their authoritarian, enrobed masters. Even more troubling is his apparent conflation of fascists with "obedient Catholics." Scott goes even further, warning that the hierarchy in Quebec was advocating that Catholics openly break the law, as they needed to follow only "natural law," interpreted in Catholicism to mean Canon Law. The clergy, therefore, were exploiting their mindless followers and directing them to attack individuals and groups they did not agree with, paving the way for the introduction of pure fascism. "As in all *primitive* societies," Scott added disdainfully, "the 'outlaw' has no rights. In such an atmosphere Fascism takes ready root, and the practice of democratic toleration appears definitely sinful."[35] Quebec was, in this framework, a "primitive" religious enclave in an otherwise modern nation.

This is not to suggest there were no anti-Semitic Catholics in Quebec or Canada, or Catholics sympathetic to fascism. An historic Catholic anti-Semitism was apparent in Quebec, and proclamations of French-Canadian nationalism could be xenophobic. Some figures, such as Paul Bouchard, Arcand, and Italian-Canadian Montreal priests Father Manfriani and Maltempi closely identified Catholicism with fascism and even National Socialism. Historian Alexandre Dumas also notes that some fiercely *nationaliste* clergy, namely Pierre Gravel and Edouard-Valmore Lavergne, were openly anti-Semitic, with the upper clergy, such as Cardinal Villeneuve, responding in an inconsistent fashion. These concerns with anti-Semitism, violence, and authoritarian politics from segments of the population, therefore, were not baseless.[36] Scott's perspective, however, along with that of others detailed in this chapter, reiterated a caricatured vision of the Catholic Church as authoritarian and power hungry. As historian Sean Mills details, these figures, almost entirely English-speaking and largely unfamiliar with much of French-Canadian culture, invented an enemy by conflating Quebec nationalism, fascism, and Catholicism in their quest to confront the "Quebec problem." The "problem" for them was the inability of the CCF to break into the province, to convince Quebeckers that it was not just a party of materialistic Anglo-Protestants.[37] Yet Scott and others perceived the Church's very nature and history to be antithetical to freedom and progress, hindering their ability to communicate constructively with many Francophones and doing nothing to alleviate French Catholic concerns with these "radicals."

Sandra Djwa, Scott's biographer, believes that his 1930s articles about Quebec and its alleged predilections toward fascism simply represent the "double bind" of being a liberal in Quebec in this period, as he was highly critical of the repressive actions of the Catholic Church, but was completely dedicated to freedom of religion.[38] Scott, while often courageous in denouncing violence, restrictions against religious minorities, and the repressive Padlock Law of the Duplessis government, nevertheless portrayed a "priest-ridden" province full of obedient Catholics unable to attain individual self-realization. In Quebec, according to Scott, the Church had aligned itself publicly with the nationalist movement, creating a synonymy between *la survivance* and Catholicism. However, it was selfishly guarding its own power and maintaining its absolute control over the French-Canadian populace, constantly opposing any potentially beneficial influences throughout the years, such as Laurier Liberalism, modern secular France, or the radicalism of Papineau. Catholic control of education instead continued to promote obscurantist theories such as Thomism, preventing the full integration of French Canadians into the modern economy and society of North America. French Canadians constantly complained about not receiving equal treatment in Canada, but for Scott "boys and girls who are taught always to obey their superiors without question are likely to find themselves in this position." Near the end of this article, Scott savaged the Catholic Church for inculcating "a degree of backwardness, judged by modern social standards" that continued to result in a high infant-mortality rate, poverty, ignorance, and enormous families unable to support themselves.[39] For Scott, the Catholic Church and Catholicism was an anachronism, supporting a crumbling society in a Quebec unable to understand its need to integrate into the modern world. Instead, the province was retreating into the dangerous world of fascism, dictated by the absolute control of a totalitarian clergy.

In Scott's mind, there was an idealized "good Catholicism" and a caricatured "bad Catholicism." Laurier, as mentioned above, was a "good Catholic," exposed as he was to English liberalism and eschewing the ultramontanism of the clerical elites. Scott suggested that thoughtful Canadians meet Quebec nationalism with understanding and discussion, not the crass bigotry of the Orange Order, as French Canadians had legitimate grievances with the Canadian state. In his article "French Canadian Nationalism," written under the pseudonym "Quebecer," Scott warned, however, that while Catholics and French Canadians had been subjected to prejudices in Canada's past, "a feudal Catholicism is not the only nor the best Catholicism ... The trouble is that the Quebec branch of the Catholic Church has become inbred and unprogressive. Its reactionary outlook exceeds the bounds of what the faith requires." In other words, Catholicism in Quebec had become ultrareactionary, insular, and regressive. It had become dangerously linked to an irrational nationalist anger, and Scott laid the blame for this at the Church's feet:

> these nationalists fail to see ... that one principal reason why French Canadians have seldom advanced to positions of general importance in the economic life of Quebec is not due to the fact that they are constitutionally incapable of adapting themselves to modern industry, nor is it due simply to English unwillingness to give them jobs; it is due in great part to the fact that their schools and colleges, every one of which is in the grip of the Church, are giving them an education that is totally inadequate to the needs of today. It may train them to become good Catholics, but it certainly does not train them to become good scientists or businessmen.[40]

It was thus specifically Catholicism that prevented French Canada from progressing and becoming part of the modern economy and society of Canada, rather than the racial characteristics of the French Canadian or the narrow, prejudicial practices of the Anglo elite in Montreal.

Much of this was couched in expressions of admiration for what were believed to be exclusively British Protestant traditions, such as freedom, liberty, and the rule of law, causes which the Catholic Church in Quebec treated with contempt. Scott, for example, saw in the potential population shift, which favoured Catholics due to a lack of

Anglo-Saxon immigration and the higher Catholic birth rate, a threat to the ability of progressive political causes based within the traditions of British liberty to make headway in Canada. Indeed, Scott referred in two different articles to the fact that Canada's political scene and role in international affairs was negatively defined by the country being 41 per cent Catholic, in comparison to the 6 per cent of Catholics composing Britain[41] (see Table 0.1 for Catholic population; see Table 2.1 for French-speaking population). In one of these articles, "Canada's Future in the British Commonwealth," appearing in *Foreign Affairs* in 1937, Scott noted that Canada's massive Catholic population, consisting mostly of French Canadians and non-Anglo immigrants, as well as the country's proximity to the United States, had pulled Canada away from the collective security of the Commonwealth and into a naive isolationism. While in general this article is about how the "Americanization" as opposed to "Anglicization" of new Canadians hindered allegiance to the ideals of the Commonwealth, Scott did not hide his disdain for the role of the Church in worsening these conditions and preventing its followers from understanding the gravity of the international situation. "[I]t must be remembered that the French-Canadian is first of all a Catholic," Scott posited, "and will always support a *Vatican foreign policy*." This foreign policy was not necessarily isolationist, as Scott recalled the contingent of Zouaves Quebec sent to defend the Vatican in 1870. It instead was premised on defeating the enemies of Catholicism; Scott concluded, therefore, that French Canadians would support a war effort if "Great Britain joined the Fascist powers in an attack on the Soviet Union," as the Communist nation represented the ultimate enemy to Catholics worldwide.[42] French Canadians could not be trusted to be "on side" in any war with the fascist powers.

Scott was subtly insinuating a conspiratorial understanding of the role of Catholicism and the institutional Church in determining Canadian foreign policy, which, for him, was the overarching explanation why this segment of the nation was pulling back from international obligations and allowing Italy and Germany to run rampant. Yet Scott did not accept any accusation of intolerance; he was crusading against a major (perhaps even *the* major) progenitor of intolerance (and fascism) in Canadian society, the Roman Catholic Church. This also contradicts slightly his above rejection of racial/ethnic explanations for the state of French Canadian democracy. The mutually constitutive "foreignness" of Catholics, whether

Table 2.1
Population of Canada with French as mother tongue

| 1931 | 2,832,298 |
| 1941 | 3,354,753 |

Series A185-237, *Historical Statistics in Canada*, 2nd ed.

ethnically or in their religious traditions, was never far from the surface of these critiques.

One of the most volatile events that took place in Quebec in this period, which involved Scott and other leftist Anglo-Protestants, occurred in 1936 when a delegation from Republican Spain came to Canada to drum up support for their cause in the ongoing and ideologically polarizing Spanish Civil War. Within Canada, Catholics tended to support the Nationalists under Franco, hearing stories of grotesque massacres of clergy by the Loyalists, and they viewed the Civil War as a contest between materialism and Christian civilization. The non-Catholic Anglo community in Canada, on the other hand, mostly sympathized with the Loyalists, viewing the Civil War as a battle between liberal democracy and the totalitarianism of Fascist Italy and Nazi Germany. Various left-wing groups sponsored the delegation in their trip across Canada; in Montreal, this was the Committee for Medical Aid for Spain, chaired by Scott himself.[43] Hundreds of Université de Montreal students opposed the delegation's visit, occupying City Hall and pressuring the local authorities to prevent the delegation from giving its speeches. Police director Fernand Dufresne, who had promised Scott that the municipal authorities would protect the official delegation from any disruption, told Scott that Montreal was a thoroughly Catholic city, and that he and his cohort were wrong to hold any meeting of liberals, Communists, and other materialists there.[44] Later in the week, a rally of a hundred thousand was organized in Montreal, protesting Communism and the Loyalist side in the Civil War and making the ideological proclivities of the city clear to all. A highlight of the rally was a fiercely anti-Communist speech by Archbishop Gauthier.[45] This display sickened Scott, as did the cooperation of the Francophone authorities.

Two years later, Scott reiterated his distaste in a review prepared for the British Commonwealth Relations Conference, entitled *Canada*

Today: A Study of Her National Interests and National Policy. According to Scott, the Catholic Church in Canada supported both the Nationalists in the Spanish Civil War and the Italian invasion of Ethiopia because Rome, and not France, maintained a strong influence in Quebec. He added a conspiratorial tenor to his commentary, claiming that the Catholic Church "has interests in North America far wider than the aspirations of French-Canadian nationalism" because of this influence of the Vatican. This was due, clearly, to the "authoritarian character" of the Catholic Church, which made it more "lenient to the doctrine of fascism than the Protestant churches would be, and is teaching a form of 'corporatism' in Quebec." Scott added that, since "66 per cent of the Catholics in Canada are French Canadian," the Church tended also to be isolationist.[46] The Catholic Church was therefore supporting the militarily aggressive powers in the world by inculcating an intense isolationism in Quebec, making them doubly harmful to a democratic, British nation faced with international totalitarian postures.

Anglo-Protestant intellectuals such as Scott viewed corporatism and the periodic outbursts of fascist sympathy and suspension of civil rights in Quebec as an endemic problem within Quebec Catholicism and Catholicism in general. In a refutation of Scott's article, "Is Quebec Going Fascist?" Dr Rosaire Cauchon critiqued Scott not only for his simplistic understanding of corporatism at an intellectual level but also for exaggerating its popularity in Quebec, particularly among the Catholic hierarchy. Leslie Roberts added to this chorus in a letter to *Saturday Night,* drawing the uncomfortable conclusion that support for anti-communist legislation was strong throughout Canada and especially within the Anglo-Quebec community, which was thoroughly conservative.[47] Scott, nevertheless, was convinced of the popularity of fascism and corporatism within the clergy and in French-speaking Quebec, and he invoked not only the threat to Canadian democracy but to the integrity of a British nation in his official response to the protest against the Spanish delegation.[48] Scott was steeped in an Anglo-Protestant culture and an intellectual milieu that made it difficult to interpret the actions of the Catholic Church and its devout followers as anything other than a modern example of the Church's historic desire for power and control. This interpretation lends itself to conspiracy theory, as the Church was dedicated to hindering progress at all costs and in using its international power to achieve its ends.

The visit of the Spanish delegation was also important to another Anglophone progressive in Quebec, Eugene Forsey, motivating him to become involved in the newly formed Canadian Civil Liberties Union.[49] In addition to his activities in the Canadian left and Christian socialist organizations throughout the Depression, Forsey was a lecturer in economics and political science at McGill, while working on his PhD. For Forsey, the banning of the Spaniards reminded him of Nazi tactics he had witnessed on a trip to Berlin in 1932, right before Hitler took power. Forsey warned several correspondents that this violation of the right of freedom of speech in Canada would lead to the same fascist tactics that were present in Italy, Austria, and Germany. Forsey was also adamant in a letter to the Honourable C.H. Cahan that "[t]his is not a question of 'French' versus 'English,' Catholic versus Protestant. God forbid! It is a simple issue of freedom and justice and opinions."[50] However, generalizations concerning the nature of the Church in Canada undermined these potentially sincere sentiments. As a hallmark rhetorical strategy of the mainstream Canadian left in this period, such generalizations also served to further legitimize anti-Catholicism as a valid – and, importantly, progressive – intellectual framework.

Forsey and Scott were convinced that a form of "racial fascism" was emerging in Quebec, largely motivated by the Catholic Church. Forsey began to work his legendarily prolific pen in public protest of the abuses of the Catholic Church and the Padlock Law in the pages of his friend Graham Spry's *Canadian Forum*.[51] In the provocatively titled "Clerical Fascism in Quebec," Forsey posited an allegedly long-standing, secret plot to transform Quebec into a "clerical-fascist state" based on the doctrines of corporatism. The Vatican itself was directing this plot, according to Forsey. He believed the major avenue of creating this new state was through the Catholic domination of the labour movement, as Catholic unions were preventing the introduction of "real" labour unions dedicated to the interests of the workers. The pope guided these unions, instructing them to cooperate with their employers, oppose materialism, and slowly work toward organizing society along corporatist lines. Forsey even outlined this structure, taking the presence of corporatist rhetoric in public life at face value: a hierarchy of committee, directors, and centurions, each composed of a hundred families, would be the new structure of Quebec society. Therefore, in Forsey's mind the fight for international unionism in

Quebec was paramount, as it would determine the survival or death of democracy in this Catholic province.[52]

Cardinal Villeneuve, a prominent conservative Catholic figure in Quebec, was a major villain for Forsey and Scott.[53] Some of Villeneuve's statements in the 1920s were very provocative in their open support of Groulx's vision of the founding of a Catholic and French state along the St Lawrence. In the 1930s, he was often strident in his criticism of liberalism, and especially communism.[54] Despite this, even scholar Esther Delisle, who is extraordinarily critical of French-Canadian nationalists for their fascist leanings, notes that contemporaries saw him as ultimately loyal to the Commonwealth and Britain.[55] Dumas has revised the traditional interpretation of Villeneuve. He did oppose secular liberalism and Communism. His overall concern in Quebec politics, however, was opposing corruption, not the creation of a clerical fascist state with Duplessis as his willing puppet. After Liberal complaints of clerical interference during the 1935 election, Villeneuve, in fact, counselled the Quebec clergy not to get too involved in public politics, or at least to avoid partisanship and focus on moral questions. In fact, Villeneuve was not simply a sycophantic supporter of Duplessis, nor vice versa. Villeneuve did support the Padlock Act, but Dumas challenges the assumption of many Anglophones, then and now, that Villeneuve had dictated this policy to Duplessis, reinforcing their image of Quebec as priest-ridden. Villeneuve also saw in Duplessis a wasted opportunity to reform the patronage and corruption of almost forty years of Liberal rule in the province.[56]

Forsey, for his part, saw Villeneuve as the real power behind the throne of Duplessis, a perception Dumas notes was common among the left-leaning Anglo population in Quebec (and outside of it), and which has become the contemporary historical narrative. Villeneuve's dominance in the provincial legislature was the defining component of Quebec's move toward fascism. He dramatically stated in his article "Quebec on the Road to Fascism" that "[i]t seems likely, therefore that we are indeed only at the beginning of a reign of terror in which everyone who happens to incur the displeasure of M. Duplessis or his august Superior [Villeneuve] may expect to have his home or office ransacked and perhaps padlocked in the approved Nazi manner." He added, "Sinclair Lewis had better come to Quebec and write a new version of 'It Can't Happen Here,'" referring to that author's famous book warning of the importation of fascism to the United

States. Forsey concluded ominously that French Catholics needed to be careful, as Canada was still a country ruled by Protestants, and that the more they pushed their clerical-fascism in Quebec, the more likely was an Orange reaction in Ontario restricting the rights of the Catholic Church and the French language in that province. As was the case with their lower socio-economic position, French Canadians would only have themselves to blame.[57]

Yet Protestants in Quebec had plenty to fear as well, according to Forsey. Indeed, Duplessis's Quebec treated religious minorities abysmally, including not only the small group of Jehovah's Witnesses, but also various Protestant groups and figures, not to mention the anti-Semitism Jewish Quebeckers faced. It is how Forsey presented these concerns that reflect a deeper anti-Catholic framework, linking the various objectionable components of Duplessis's Quebec to a Catholic proclivity to accept arbitrary authority and the Church's desire for total control over society. This is a perfect example of Pincus's "popery" discussed earlier. In Forsey's words, Protestants were being targeted by the Padlock Law and the Duplessis regime in general because the Catholic Church could not abide the spread of Reformed ideas. Forsey used the example of the Grand Ligne mission, a French Baptist mission dedicated to spreading the "true gospel" to French Canadian Catholics,[58] which was prevented from distributing Bibles through missionary efforts as a demonstration of the determination of the authorities in Quebec to eradicate Protestantism. For Forsey it was a question of differing philosophies: both wings of Christianity believed in worshipping the Lord freely, but the Catholic Church was dedicated to "winning" the contest between Mother Church and the Reformed heresy by any means.[59] In an article denouncing the censorship and protests against the Spanish delegation, Forsey linked these events to a wider program of social control emanating from the Church, with Gauthier at its centre this time. Clearly, the Quebec authorities had already castigated communists, socialists, and Masons, but these activities were only a precursor to the specific targeting of liberals, democrats, Protestants, and the general English population of Quebec.[60] Forsey revealingly saw these categories as entangled, positing a binary of an English Protestant Canada, at least in Quebec, defending its values of democracy against the machinations of a politically aggressive Catholic Church.

Scott and Forsey were thus not immune to the conspiratorial thinking often associated with the "lunatic fringe." In fact, they were progenitors of it. Their writings during this tense period reveal the depth of the anti-Catholic tradition in the Canadian Anglo-Protestant milieu, shaping how these two eminent thinkers interpreted the events around them and pushed them into reductionist caricatures of the Church and French-Canadian Catholics. Certainly, the Catholic Church was not without fault in this era (or any era). It is the (historical) equation of Catholicism with "popery" and foreignness and of Protestantism with democracy and Britishness that these Anglo-Protestants perpetuated that represents their anti-Catholicism.

The divide between Protestant and Catholic was not just part of an abstract intellectual world view. Premier Mitch Hepburn's attempt to reform the funding system for separate schools in 1936–37 elicited just the vitriolic response Forsey feared from Anglo-Protestant Ontario, becoming the defining issue in a vicious provincial by-election in 1937. Catholic lobbyists convinced Hepburn and members of his Liberal government of the need to reform the educational system, something that Hepburn had promised Catholic voters earlier in his career. He proposed redressing the limitations on corporations choosing to pay rates for separate schools and the fact that public schools received all revenue from public utilities (in addition to having a much-larger residential tax base).[61] After lengthy stalling, Hepburn finally outlined legislation similar to that in the Quebec educational system in February 1936 at caucus, calling for the altering of the language of the law so that corporations "shall," not "may," contribute taxes to separate schools in proportion to the amount of Catholic shareholders of the corporation, leaving public utilities still entirely in public-school coffers. Organized Protestantism and Protestants received the proposal with widespread condemnation. The Toronto Board of Education, for example, had recently denied the distribution of free textbooks to schoolchildren in separate schools on relief and immediately organized a meeting after the legislation was announced voting fifteen to zero to hold a provincial referendum on the matter.[62] Martin Quinn, head of the influential Catholic Taxpayers' Association, made matters worse by his very public pro-Hepburn campaign in the by-election, fulfilling the Anglo-Protestant nightmare of Catholic dominance of politics.[63] The short-lived Canadian Protestant Association seemed to be concerned almost solely with the issue of separate-school reform, meeting at Cooke's Presbyterian Church in Toronto on 3 March 1936. The *Toronto*

Telegram quoted Rev. J.B. Thomson of Dufferin Presbyterian Church as appealing to a Protestant British past: "We are going to be worthy of those who shed their blood for us and we are going to tell the Roman Catholic Church that we are going to stand to the last man and maintain the freedom that is ours." Morris Zeidman, during his speech, continued his advocacy for the Protestant Radio League, again blaming the Catholic Church for his constant censorship: this was due solely to the fact that his league stood adamantly for the thoroughly British principles of "one Faith, one Flag, one Empire, one Language, one School, and one King."[64]

When Tory MPP James Hill, East Hastings, died in October 1936, Hepburn decided, against the advice of his inner circle, to hold a by-election to test his school legislation amendment, confident that, despite the intensely Orange nature of the riding, he could convince the majority that his school policy made economic and moral sense. This, coupled with Earl Rowe's recent victory as Tory leader and his concomitant desire to oppose Hepburn's amendment immediately, transformed a seemingly routine by-election into a religiously charged battle between Hepburn, Rowe, anti-Catholic agitator Rev. T.T. Shields, and Rowe's main challenger for the leadership, now turned adviser, George Drew.[65] Shields, the patriarch of Jarvis Street Baptist Church in Toronto and a major player in Canada's fundamentalist community, invoked the imagery of the Reformation, stating that he would oppose the intersection of religion and politics caused by Hepburn's attempt to amend separate-school legislation if he had to "die at the stake." Shields increased his vitriol during an open debate about the school issue with Liberal Deputy Speaker Major J.H. Clark, where Clark defended the influence of Catholic Senator Frank O'Connor[66] and castigated the Tories and Shields for degenerating into religious bigotry. Many opponents of separate schools believed that the influential senator – the founder of Laura Secord chocolates – was essentially responsible for Hepburn's legislation and was the spokesman for the Church in Hepburn's government. Shields responded angrily, alluding to the fact that George McCullagh, a wealthy Hepburn supporter, had recently purchased the *Globe* and the former *Mail and Empire*. Shields claimed, in colourful and inflammatory language, that McCullagh was attempting to silence any protest against Hepburn's machinations by creating a mouthpiece for the Liberal party and the Catholic Church: "The *Globe* and *Mail* have been killed and their blood-stained garments found in the possession of the protagonists of Hepburn, O'Connor, and the Roman Catholic hierarchy."[67] This was a charge made in the Tory campaign literature as well, with one such document comparing the opinion of the *Globe* before its purchase by "millionaire interests" as being more concerned with the province and nation in general, not serving "sectarian interests," referring to the Catholic Church.[68] The issue became serious enough that McCullagh felt the need to defend himself, stating in an editorial that he did not plan on silencing the *Mail and Empire*, assuring his readers that he was a Protestant and that no separate-school supporters were involved at all with the transaction. McCullagh thus framed his answer in terms that would prove his "objectivity" because of his Protestant credentials. Catholics, by implication, were a special interest, incapable of such clear-mindedness and fairness.

McCullagh simultaneously denigrated Tory tactics, most importantly Drew's infamous statement that French Canadians were a "defeated race."[69] This statement haunted George Drew for his entire career (although he did move into the provincial Tory leadership in 1938 and eventually into the leadership of the federal Progressive Conservatives), confirming for many that he represented the bigoted Anglophone wing of the Tories.[70] Historian John Saywell has characterized the young journalist who reported this statement in the *Toronto Star* in November 1936 at a meeting in Plainfield, Ontario, as taking liberties with the facts, but it is clear that Drew spoke about the Conquest as a historical event at this meeting.[71] Farley Faulkner, who was at Plainfield, corroborated the *Star* story in the *Kingston Whig-Standard*, reporting that Drew said, "It is not unfair to remind the French that they are a defeated race and that their rights are rights only because of the tolerance of the English majority, who with all respects to the minority must be regarded as the dominant race."[72] Drew denied this forcefully, clarifying that it was common to teach every child in Canada about the British domination of the country and that the largesse of the British had created the present nation. In this same speech, denying that he was prejudiced against French Catholics, Drew reiterated an Anglo-Protestant conception of Canadian history in which a beneficent British imperialism permitted diversity to exist. He accused Hepburn of reaching a "secret agreement" with elements of the Catholic hierarchy to maintain and expand separate schools, institutions that in Drew's mind existed nowhere else in the entire Empire. He concluded his defence by noting that separate schools and the Hepburn government's favouritism toward the Catholic Church violated the foundations of the nation, namely the Canadian constitution and British principles.[73]

Drew's actions were not limited to this one speech and the aftermath. He was extremely active in this by-election as an organizer, giving numerous speeches, which often referred to religious issues. Much of the campaign literature also revolved around religious divisions: for example, one piece of Tory campaign literature, simply entitled "Education," explicitly equated being Conservative with being Protestant. The pamphlet attacked Hepburn's educational policy, and concluded by asking, "What are we, as Protestants, going to do about it?"[74] Drew even utilized fascism and Mussolini as symbols for Hepburn and his allegedly Catholic-influenced government. He charged in a speech in Bancroft that Hepburn was violating British principles through the separate-school amendment, since he was circumventing the system of courts. Drew's was a strange charge, as Hepburn had certainly submitted the legislation to the courts, as the Ontario Court of Appeal ruled in January 1937 that no corporation with Ontario headquarters could distribute taxes to separate schools. This proved to be a shattering blow to Hepburn's legislation.[75] Yet Drew became almost hysterical in his denunciations of the "Hepburn-O'Connor dictatorship," going far beyond the campaign literature in equating a vote for the Liberals to a vote for O'Connor. Drew portrayed Hepburn as "O'Connor's puppet Mussolini" (was O'Connor presumably the pope in this equation?) and as "a traitor to the British flag and all it stands for. He has no right to continue as premier of this province ... We may have been slow in seeing the growth of a form of lawless Fascism in our own province, but the voters of East Hastings will show" that they would not be manipulated any further.[76] At this same meeting, Drew stated that, if Catholics were telling Protestants that they would be mixing religion and politics, then "[t]he war is on."[77] Drew warned the citizens of East Hastings that if they did not stop Hepburn and his cronies in this by-election then an actual Fascist government, with fasces for its symbol, would emerge in Toronto, destroying all traditions of British liberty. Drew concluded:

> Let us say to our Roman Catholic friends; we do want to live with them in utmost harmony so long as they recognize that Roman Catholicism is a branch of Christianity and not a form of politics. There is not a country in the world where Roman

Catholicism has become a political unit where the Catholic Church has not got into difficulties. In country after country there has been bloodshed resulting from its attempt to rule by political action. We will support the right of Roman Catholics to worship as they please without interference from us of any kind, but we as Protestants do not recognize their right to organize on a political basis and say to a government, "You do this or out you go."[78]

Drew's vitriol is astounding, particularly for a political figure who would one day be premier of Ontario, the epitome of mainstream Canadian politics, inaugurating forty-two consecutive years of Tory rule in that province.

The Tories won this by-election by an enormous margin,[79] undermining Hepburn's belief that through his own personal charisma he could transcend religious sectarianism. In the case of East Hastings, he was wrong. Commentators looking back at the legacy of Shields see him and his anti-Catholic diatribes as central to the Liberal defeat.[80] Beyond the anti-Catholic rhetoric of Shields, Drew, and other Tories, wild accusations circulated during the by-election and shortly after, such as a report that the pope himself was planning on coming to Ontario to take up residence in Casa Loma if the Liberals won, replacing the crown on all highway signs with crucifixes.[81] While Saywell believes that rumours such as these siphoned the respectability from the anti-separate-school movement, Hepburn's amendment *did* fail. The legislation failed partially because of the impracticality of having every widely owned corporation deciding on the allocation of its taxes to separate or public schools and partially because of the vehement campaign by separate-school opponents and professional anti-Catholics.[82] The Anglo-Protestant narrative surrounding Catholic education, at least in political circles, was that separate schools were harmful to national unity and violated British principles. Catholic education would remain a contentious subject for Protestants in Canada, particularly Ontario, for many years to come.

The East Hastings by-election reflects another anti-Catholic narrative in this period: the so-called "revenge of the cradles," which held that a burgeoning Catholic birth rate, which had always been suspect, would allow further Catholic dominance of the nation. Numerous times in the election, Hepburn's opponents referred to the adoption of the famous Dionne quintuplets as wards of the state by the Hepburn government. Drew dubbed the "Liberal elite" of the province "O'Connor's Quints," linking the Catholic Senator to Hepburn's Liberals and to the large, Catholic Franco-Ontarian family.[83] This connection was made even more explicit in a political cartoon used during the by-election representing the most influential members of the Liberal government as the famous quintuplets, with Senator O'Connor acting as their supervisor (see Figure 2.1). As soon as these five babies were born, and it was clear they were all going to live, the *Globe* advocated state aid to the family. Yet it felt the need to say, "True, these latest arrivals will arouse fresh apprehensions regarding French-Canadian ascendency in Northern Ontario," but by ensuring the health of the quintuplets, Canada would have "an exhibit which no other country in the world can equal."[84] Present here is a certain tension regarding the quintuplets: they were sure to be a commodity in a province ravaged by the Depression, yet they also represented the great fear of Catholic ascendancy.

C.E. Silcox addressed this sentiment at a meeting of the Institute of Human Relations in Williamstown, Massachusetts, in August 1935. Silcox, who at the time was the secretary of the Social Service Council of Canada (SSCC), gave a presentation on the general relations between English-Protestants and French-Catholics in Canada. He concluded in his talk that, while issues of language and race were of more import than religion, the Dionne Quintuplets represented "to many English-speaking Canadians, the 'symbol of a great fear.'" Underlying this fear, Silcox continued, was not only the "extraordinary fecundity of the French-Canadian," but the belief that this was purposeful, a striving to outbreed the English in Canada, even if it lowered the standard of living for everyone in the nation, in order to control public affairs.[85] Silcox was convinced that the Catholic Church as an institution, particularly in Quebec, was promoting mass population growth in order to protect and expand its own influence over the Catholic population. For Silcox "the French Canadians are a very loveable people – simple, contented, frugal," but the provincialism and authoritarian control of the Church had prevented Quebec from becoming integrated into modern Canada and halted French Canadians from being a useful intellectual force in the nation.[86] For many, the quintuplets were a symbol of the guiding hand of the Catholic clergy encouraging their docile flock to outbreed Protestant English Canada and gain control of the levers of power. This older anti-Catholic

Anti-Catholicism and the Great Depression

Figure 2.1 This cartoon compares the famous Dionne Quintuplets, who represented for many Anglo-Protestants the "revenge of the cradles" of Catholic French Canadians, to Hepburn's Liberal government, kept in power only by Catholic Senator Frank O'Connor. O'Connor presumably represents Dr Allan Roy Dafoe, credited with keeping the Quints alive (the caption reads "Not one of them would have survived if it hadn't been for me!") and the Quints themselves are (right to left): Hepburn; Peter Heenan, minister of lands and forests; Attorney General Arthur Roebuck; David Croll, minister of labour, municipal affairs, and public welfare; and Duncan Marshall, minister of agriculture.

perspective intersected with what historian Michiel Horn has characterized as the central characteristic of the Depression in Canada: fear. In the case of the persistence of anti-Catholicism, the fear was of the numerical and political domination of a foreign religion.[87]

All the components of anti-Catholicism in this period came together in "The Great Birth Control Trial"[88] of Dorothea Palmer in 1936–37. The 1930s saw the initial stages of a concerted lobby to make birth control not only respectable but legal. It was illegal under the section of the criminal code dealing with obscenity until 1969, with the significant and vague caveat that dissemination and advertising of birth control was acceptable if it promoted the "public good." In 1935, A.R. Kaufman founded the Parents' Information Bureau (PIB), located in Kitchener, Ontario, as a national organization designed to not only raise awareness of the importance of birth control but also to distribute birth-control information, along with the provision of contraceptives at a reduced price and a sterilization referral service. When one of Kaufman's nurses, Dorothea Palmer, who was not a trained nurse but a social worker, was arrested for distributing birth-control information in Eastview, Ontario, a small French-Catholic town located near Ottawa, Kaufman decided he wanted to test the "public good" clause of the law. He paid Palmer's bail and refused to allow the police to drop the charges after they found out she belonged to Kaufman's organization.[89] Yet Kaufman went beyond advocating for contraception: he lobbied for eugenics in Canada, praised Nazi sterilization laws in the early 1930s, and condemned Catholic opposition to contraception as motivated by an anti-modern world view and a desire to "swamp" the Canadian population with Catholics. Kaufman used his PIB to spread the gospel of eugenics in Canada, even explicitly comparing eugenics to Christianity, as both were about bettering the community. Modern eugenics was a science for the preservation of the quality of the race, not the castration of the pagan era, which, Kaufman noted, twentieth-century Rome still practised to produce soprano singers.[90] A scrawled note to himself regarding the Italian invasion of Ethiopia is one particularly vicious statement, revealing his contempt for Catholic hypocrisy. Kaufman asked, "I wonder how the R.C. Church (who are so opposed to 'murder' [referring to its opposition to abortion]) justifies the wholesale slaughter of the Ethiopians by Mussolini."[91] This rhetorical strategy linked two of the major anti-Catholic themes of this period: Catholic support for an aggressive fascism and the Church's hostility to abortion and/or contraception. Kaufman's disdain for Catholics was even clearer in a pamphlet in which he concluded that the attitude of the Catholic clergy revealed "the fanatical and bigoted attitude of those who oppose birth control, the cruelty of condemning an innocent child to *life* for the sake of a religious doctrine."[92] This discourse would seep into the trial.

Indeed, the larger debate subsumed Palmer in the subsequent trial, carried out mostly among male experts. Palmer did not testify for the defence, and Kaufman fired her after the trial. The organization that she had worked for and brought into the public eye ostracized her.[93] Nevertheless, the trial was widely reported and very significant for a birth-control movement that reflected wider middle-class fears in Canada about the fertility of the lower classes, particularly foreigners and Catholics (often viewed as synonymous). In this vision, contraception, including sterilization, was a means to alleviate the social and economic chaos of the Depression and to better balance the "racial tensions" within Canada.[94] Early in the trial, the defence, which was led by Francis Wegenast, a lawyer and registered member of the Eugenics Society of Canada (ESC),[95] gained a ruling expanding the number and type of witnesses they could present to the court, allowing them to assemble a battery of experts on contraception.[96] Present within this large group were Zeidman, Silcox, and Mary Hawkins, the wealthy head of the pioneering birth-control clinic in Hamilton, Ontario, and the Birth Control Society of Hamilton (BCSH).[97] According to the various scholarly studies of the trial, Wegenast and the defence used these experts and the "public good clause" to construct an argument which accused the prosecution and legal authorities in Eastview of attempting to legislate through Catholic doctrine.[98] W.A. Beament added to this conceptualization of the trial by arguing for the defence that Canada's birth-control law stood alone in the Anglo-Saxon world, suggesting that Canada did not fit into the wider British Empire.[99] This discursive strain is suggestive, and not just for its success in the legal decision. By demonstrating that, since Catholicism was the reason for the deficiency in Canada's birth-control legislation and its repressive prevention of women's free access to contraception, this caused Canada to lose a sense of belonging in the Empire. Clearly, Catholicism was *the* alien force in the nation.

Hawkins's testimony in support of Palmer was notable, as she explicitly stated that Catholic women, above all others, needed to be given information on birth control, because the Catholic Church disallowed abortion even in the case of fatal consequences to the mother during childbirth. Hawkins, admittedly, based her testimony partially on hearsay, along with quotations from the Jesuit scholar Henry Davis's *Moral and Pastoral Theology*. When Raoul Mercier, the prosecution lawyer, challenged her on her qualifications to evaluate theological texts (Davis's work does indeed deny the morality of aborting a fetus even to save the mother's life), Hawkins responded that it was her opinion that this was Catholic doctrine and therefore

Catholic women needed to be made aware of the very real risks of childbirth, which included death.[100] Her claims elicited a response from a young Catholic woman, using the pseudonym "Truth (A Child of Mary)," in the *Toronto Star*. "Truth" resented Hawkins's assumption that Catholic women were ignorant of the Church's position on abortion and birth control. For her, interfering in the birth of any child was the same as murder, and Catholics did not need "Mrs. Hawkins" to lecture them on Catholic theology and morality. "Truth's" letter in turn inspired Gladys Brandt, a trained nurse, former director of the Windsor Birth Control Clinic under Kaufman, and the current director of the Toronto Birth Control Clinic, who also testified for Palmer, to write to Hawkins expressing sarcastic sympathy with this poor, deluded Catholic. Brandt encouraged Hawkins to respond, signing as "Mary (with some common sense)."[101]

This was not the first time that Hawkins had run afoul of Catholic opinion. The bishop of Hamilton, J.T. McNally, vociferously opposed the activities of Hawkins and her clinic, especially after a visit from famed American birth-control activist Margaret Sanger in 1933.[102] However, Hawkins was careful not to descend into anti-Catholic caricatures, unlike her more extreme correspondent and ally, Brandt. During the trial, Brandt sent Hawkins a letter poking fun at Mercier for speaking Latin during the trial, even though he did not understand the language. More seriously, she drew Hawkins's attention to the fining of Ottawa paper *Le Droit* for contempt of court for publishing an editorial crassly alleging that the trial was about destroying the French Catholic birth rate "at the womb."[103] According to Brandt, the editorial stance undoubtedly came in the name of "Hierarchy." Brandt's creation of a proper noun is revealing: for her, the Catholic Church stood in the way of progress in its hostility to birth control, embodied in the undemocratic connotations of "Hierarchy." The term suggested an ominous unified enemy (or "unifying Other" as scholars Werner and Harvard have termed it) not even worthy of its proper title, distilling it to its bare essentials. She continued in her letter to characterize this as part of a larger, "carefully planned" Catholic plot, with Ottawa being determined by "Hierarchy" to be the "weakest spot to strike" in Canada against birth control. Brandt reiterated this conspiratorial sentiment in two other letters, pointing out that that there was only "one Protestant" on the Board of Health in Windsor and blaming that for the fact that no real birth-control movement was possible in the border cities; no one was willing to express their true opinions on the matter. She also claimed that an article in a Windsor-based Catholic paper opposing the Toronto-based League for Race Betterment was certainly "Supervised by an R.C. priest."[104] Clearly areas with a large French-Catholic population were "weak spots" being slyly targeted by the Catholic Church.

Despite Hawkins's caution, however, she and her BCSH were not without a problematic vision of Catholicism, the Church, and foreigners in Canadian society. A pamphlet outlining the aims of the organization stated that 1) the Catholic Church was opposed to clinical means of birth control, but 2) "since many Protestant Christians are in favour of Birth Control and since we are living in a Protestant Community," it was the right of all citizens to have access to this information. The BCSH was not trying to reject the rights of any religion, as it valued tolerance as a signifier of civilization: in fact, this was truly Christian work, as it represented the compassion at the heart of Christ's message. Hamilton was, however, a self-identified Protestant community that accepted the necessity of contraception as well as the free circulation of ideas.[105] Hawkins herself also repeated Brandt's confidential assertion that opponents of birth control were largely either socialists/Communists or Catholics, and thus easy to dismiss, at the fourth meeting of the Birth Control Society in early 1936. Like other female proponents of birth control at the time, identifying as feminist or not, Hawkins linked these issues to racial/ethnic tensions, seeing in birth control not only the opportunity for women to have more control over their sexuality but the striving for general population quality and an intelligent citizenship. This would be achieved through properly-scaled "Anglo-Saxon immigration," with Canada learning from the mistakes of the polyglot United States by "limit[ing] her welcome to people of sound mind, good physical condition and similar ideas to our own" after prosperity returned.[106] Hawkins had good reason to see the Catholic Church as opposed to scientific contraception. She and her allies did not imagine Catholic hostility. She and her organization were also routinely attacked by Bishop McNally. Her testimony concerning the special ignorance of Catholic women as to the dire consequences of unrestricted childbirth is revealing, however, of the conviction that Canada was, or at least should be, a fundamentally Anglo-Protestant society. This form of society would inevitably accept the inherent reasonableness of science and progress, at least regarding contraception, and would no longer be hindered by an excess population.

For his part, Silcox framed his testimony in the language of an expert sociologist. He quickly veered into Brandt's conspiratorial territory, however, referring to how a "well-organized minority" often hindered progressive action in a democracy. He immediately linked the Church with "those people in Canada who are flirting with the idea of a fascist state." Silcox ominously reminded these forces that Catholic hostility to sterilization and contraception in general may backfire if their ideal of fascism did overthrow the government in Canada, since in Nazi Germany compulsory sterilization had been implemented. Silcox noted, as did Tyrer and McAree earlier, that Protestants had already accepted the necessity for birth control in an industrializing and depressed world economy to prevent further socio-economic depredations along with the "over-breeding" of the lower classes and the ignorant. Silcox concluded apocalyptically that if Canadians did not accept contraception due to the whims of the Catholic Church, the only two options would be the drastic increase of taxation for relief rolls or, perhaps reflecting Silcox's growing conservatism, "the development of a socialist or communist state where all wealth is increasingly owned and managed cooperatively."[107]

Silcox was adamant in his support for birth control, but careful in his language regarding the "revenge of the cradles." He referred to the fear of a growing French population in Canada as a "disturbing influence in Canadian national life," quickly adding that "he himself thought it might be a thing to be welcomed, rather than feared" as it would encourage frank conversations between the two sides.[108] While answering a question from Crown Prosecutor Mercier about the speech he gave in Williamstown, however, Silcox added that, even if the breeding of French Canadians was not a deliberate policy on the part of the French Catholic Church, many in Canada would even question the "empire's security" if the French population overtook the English, since French Canadians were not as loyal to Britain. This was a particularly serious charge in the context of international events in the 1930s, with war becoming increasingly likely.[109]

Silcox certainly did not see himself as an anti-Catholic in any sense of the word. In correspondence with Scott, Silcox refuted charges by concerned Francophone lawyer Roger Ouimet that were related to him by Scott. Ouimet alleged Silcox was admitting in his testimony that his organization, the SSCC, had been disseminating contraception to French Catholics in order to maintain the Anglo-Protestant character of Ontario.[110] Silcox viewed all of this as absurd, guiding Scott to an issue of Saunders's militantly anti-Catholic *Protestant Action* from January 1937, which accused Silcox of being too admiring of French Catholics.[111] In another letter, Silcox defended himself by pointing out that he was an objective sociologist and that the dominance of one race or another did not matter to him; in fact his first name, Claris, was French, as was his mother's maiden name, paradoxically attempting to demonstrate his Francophone "credibility" while maintaining objectivity. He was merely describing aspects of Canadian society that caused cultural friction, "and if he recognized the existence of a national stork derby" dedicated to having as many children as possible, he had to elaborate upon this crisis.[112] Scott clearly accepted Silcox's explanation, responding that his "guess is that the Roman Church uses this kind of argument as an additional reason to persuade people to oppose the practice."[113] This also motivated Scott to write to Ouimet, correcting his interpretation of Silcox's testimony and accusing him of irresponsibility by publicly stating falsehoods about an already flammable trial. Scott admitted that there were English Canadians who wanted to limit the French-Canadian birth rate, and vice versa. The real cause of friction between the "two races" in Canada, however, was that French Canadians "are content with a much lower standard of living." Scott added, in language steeped in the racial essentialism and ethno-religiosity profiled in the previous chapter, that French communities paid very little attention to education, hygiene, and social services in general, "and therefore that when they form large groups in any province they tend to obstruct what the English Canadians believe to be progressive developments."[114] Thus, they had only themselves to blame for their position in Canadian society.

After Palmer's acquittal, Kaufman wrote to Wegenast that he hoped this would end the domination of "Quebec priests" in Canada.[115] Wegenast and Kaufman also gave an inflammatory speech at an Orange Lodge, praising their triumph over the Catholic Church.[116] In this speech, Wegenast repeated his defence: that the trial was simply an attempt to enforce canon law in Canada. Wegenast concluded by claiming love and tolerance for Catholics, calling for increased understanding between Anglo-Protestants and French Catholics in Canada.

To achieve this, however, Protestants had to accept a *biological* difference, "That the mind of a Roman Catholic does not work as *our* minds do. The process is not the same." The Church taught Catholics to accept only its dictates, which had resulted in a stunted mind steeped in medievalism and casuistry. The only solution to this problem, already occurring, was that Catholics themselves were finally beginning to realize their sordid situation, coming into the modern world. Those staunch Catholics who remained devoted to their Church were hopeless according to Wegenast: "They simply don't fit in, either in the rest of Canada or in the rest of the world."[117] Wegenast was barely straddling the line between those Anglo-Protestants who saw in Catholics an irredeemable foreign bloc perpetuating alien tradition and those who saw in Catholics the potential for conversion to "reasonable" civil society.

For those involved in the trial, the major issue was their fundamental belief that birth control was central to bettering society. Support for birth control was a sincere cause, and birth-control activism did not only involve pro-eugenics arguments or prejudice against Catholics and immigrants.[118] The official Church was opposed to contraception, although there was some confusion, as some Catholic clergy (particularly in the United States) began to support the rhythm method in the 1930s. Activists did not invent these facts, and it could understandably lead to tensions between groups, particularly feminists and/or women dedicated to the achievement of control over reproductive rights.[119] Myrtle Rogers embodied this frustration. She was an outspoken birth-control advocate in Winnipeg, who appears to have been involved with the Winnipeg Humanist Society and sent Wegenast numerous supportive letters during the trial.[120] She warned him that "it is not birth control you are fighting, so much as the Catholic church." She encouraged him, recommended books by British anti-Catholic freethinking author Joseph McCabe, and sent Wegenast viciously anti-Catholic lectures by Manitoba freethinker Marshall Gauvin. She even drew Wegenast's attention to an especially egregious accusation by McCabe that the Church was opposed to birth control because the pope wanted to help Mussolini build larger armies.[121] Rogers ridiculed the popularity of the rhythm method of contraception among American Catholics as 1) hypocritical, and 2) part of the clergy bilking their deluded and often poverty-stricken followers of income (as they had done for centuries) through the purchase of costly guides to the rhythm method. Rogers also told Wegenast that she had been in contact with Kaufman's nurses and given them material on the Catholic Church, hoping that the PIB could distribute these works to the women of Eastview and "enlighten[n] feminine opinion." Whether it would help was another matter, since "the Catholic mind is impervious to truth," a phrase that posited an irredeemable Catholic. Rogers's overall point in these letters, like Brandt's, is that birth control was only one component of the Church's centuries-long struggle for total power, to the detriment of free thought and civilizational progress. For Rogers, the war against scientific contraception was simply another salvo in the Church's attempt to destroy thriving cultures (temporarily) outside of its influence, such as the United States, as they did in Moorish and Loyalist Spain.[122] Underlying many of the arguments detailed here, though perhaps not stated in such extreme language as Rogers used, was a view of the Catholic Church nurtured in an anti-Catholic atmosphere, believing it to be helplessly regressive, anti-modern, inherently political, and harmful to the welfare of Canada as a progressive member of the British Empire.

Silcox's reputation has not held up to contemporary scrutiny. For example, the "stork derby" comment above was referring to the Millar Stork Derby, created by rich eccentric Charles Millar, who left his fortune to be spent on jokes. One was to give $500,000 to the Toronto mother who had the most children in the ten years after his 1926 death. Unsurprisingly, this elicited a concerned response from social elites and "moral arbiters" who feared the swamping of polite Canadian society with the children of the poor and/or of immigrants.[123] In 2002, Mario Azzopardi directed a television movie about the Millar derby, aptly titled *The Stork Derby*, based on Elizabeth Wilton's book *Bearing the Burden: The Great Toronto Stork Derby, 1926–1938*. The film contains a thinly veiled version of Silcox in the character of Rev. Claris Sinclair (played by Joel Miller). Sinclair represents the contradictions within Silcox's thought and that of other eugenicists: when Sinclair comes to see intrepid feminist reporter Kate Harrington (played by Megan Follows) about the stork derby, Harrington is initially very excited by Sinclair's apparent sympathy to her pro-birth-control and anti-poverty stance. She is soon disappointed when Sinclair reveals his true motivations. Sinclair is supportive only of selective sterilization to prevent the reproduction of "society's undesirables," namely "the French and the immigrants," as they would overrun "the English educated classes." The stork derby only encouraged the reproduction of "these decrepit women." Harrington recoils in disgust, bravely condemning Sinclair's views as "vulgar" and "repulsive" before storming out of the press room. The scene is designed to demonstrate Harrington's virtue, while denigrating the crass racism and terrifying eugenics of Sinclair. Yet Silcox was one of many progressive activists fighting for the rights of women and the betterment of Canadian society. The film easily signals Sinclair/Silcox as a cartoonish villain, equipped with arched eyebrows, garish self-righteousness, and virulent racism, and not as a mainstream aspect of intellectual culture. The reality was much more complicated, as it often is, than the fictional version, yet it is significant that the filmmakers chose Sinclair/Silcox as the epitome of these sentiments during the Depression.

Some feminists and female birth-control advocates of this era have not withstood contemporary scrutiny either, in contradistinction to the clear morality of Follows's Harrington. Emily Murphy has perhaps faced the most extreme revision of her reputation, particularly due to her endorsement of sexual sterilization for the "unfit" and her stark racism, and there is now a large scholarly literature dealing with the Anglo-Saxonism and support of eugenics among many of the major early Canadian feminists. The anti-Catholicism of said figures remains less of a focus.[124] Murphy, like Plumptre, Hawkins, and Brandt, was indeed concerned about the influence of the Catholic Church on Canadian society. In a series of now-infamous articles she wrote as Janey Canuck for the *Vancouver Sun* in 1932, not long before her death, she made it clear that she supported contraception, including state-sanctioned sterilization, to prevent abortions (which she viewed as "murder in embryo") and to limit the "human wreckage which has been dumped from foreign lands" from reproducing. According to Murphy, the Catholic Church was facilitating one-quarter of the institutionalized population of Canada to reside in Quebec, because "theologians" opposed birth control. In other words, the Church was one of the major forces allowing "the race" to degenerate and civilization to be threatened. The Church looked to the Edenic authority of thousands of years ago to "be fruitful and multiply" as justification for its opposition to the bettering of society and for allowing the breeding of "human offal." The Anglo-Catholic faction within the Church of England, of which Murphy was no adherent, had also opposed scientific contraception at the Lambeth Conference of the Anglican Church, to which Murphy responded as unsurprised but disappointed. She quoted Margaret Sanger, in this context, that a civilization worshipping mother and baby ignored the "waste" that emerged from said fecundity. For Murphy, contraception was truly Christian, as it was humane, and it was progressive because it recognized that morals changed. Western civilization no longer burned witches and society should not allow false "religions" to convince it of the "irreligious" now. Sterilization would *restore* individual freedoms, because it would avoid the mass institutionalization present in Quebec, salve the overburdened Canadian taxpayer, and result in the betterment of the race by limiting people who inherently bred too quickly.[125] It was the Church as unredeemable enemy of progress, allowing the swamping of the "fit" Anglo-Protestant population, and yet again linking race, ethnicity, and religion.

A close analysis of anti-Catholicism reveals that the fear of Catholic dominance of the nation was not a prejudicial aberration within an otherwise tolerant Anglo-Protestant intellectual and cultural milieu. Respected demographer and political economist William Burton Hurd of Brandon College and McMaster University, for example, couched these fears of Catholic dominance in more detached, academic language during the Depression. Hurd, along with Forsey, believed in the "displacement theory" of immigration, which posited that the large amount of immigration from foreign countries was forcing intelligent "native Canadians" to immigrate to the United States in search of better opportunities.[126] In a speech before the Canadian Club in 1937, Hurd addressed the "Immigrant Problem."[127] He stated that Canada could have provided its own acceptable level of population without the immigration policies of the Laurier-Borden years, which were continuing to this day, especially in Western Canada. He saw this as being *the* central reason behind large numbers of "real" Canadians flowing into the United States. Yet the rise of economic nationalism and the decline in people moving across the Canada-US border due to the Depression had now caused an enormous population and labour problem in Canada, forcing Canadians to analyze rationally the country's "absorptive capacity" for immigrants. To make matters worse, in Hurd's opinion, most of these immigrants were trapped in the peasant-agricultural stage of development of their repressed homelands, creating an enormous surplus of poor agricultural settlers in Canada who were not able to assimilate and were hindering the modern economy of Canada. "[A] peasant economy is inconsistent with the practice of democracy of the British sort," according to Hurd, and "[i]t was no mere historical coincidence that in the Motherland the decline of peasant farming paralleled the extension of the franchise and the rise of constitutional government." Hurd referenced the tense international situation as well, subtly suggesting that this form of agriculture and backward immigration policy facilitated the rise of dictatorships. Hurd concluded that Britain could provide Canada with all its needed immigration.[128]

In an academic article from 1937, Hurd presented his data after analyzing numerous censuses in Canada, viewing the high immigration years of 1901 to 1911 as distorting his data due to the preponderance of "high fertility peoples from Central and Eastern Europe." He described how the Canadian birth rate had been declining steadily since the 1880s, despite heavy immigration, due to emigration of Canadians to the United States. He identified two additional causes: 1) the delaying of marriage due to economic fluctuations, and 2) the rise of birth control in all provinces *except* Quebec and New Brunswick, which contained large French-Catholic populations. Hurd was cautious in his evaluation, noting that birth control was not yet widespread enough to significantly influence the birth rate. Yet what was significant was that birth control seemed to be concentrated only in the areas of the country where it was "religiously permissible," potentially dramatically shifting the population balance of Catholics and Protestants in the future.[129]

Hurd quickly altered his position on the efficacy of relying on British immigration to supplement the "natural" Canadian population and changed his academic tone. In a particularly alarmist article for *Maclean's*, provocatively entitled "Decline of the Anglo-Saxon Canadian," Hurd fully embraced an ethno-religious vision of Canada that privileged Anglo-Protestants as the sole possible defenders of British democratic traditions. By the end of the calendar year, Hurd declared, the numerical superiority of Anglo-Saxons would be gone, by 1971, French Canadians would make up 40 per cent of the Canadian population, and by the end of the twentieth century, Anglo-Saxons would be outnumbered two-to-one. The reasons behind this drastic change in population were foreign immigration, emigration to the United States, and low fertility among Anglo-Saxons. Hurd focused mostly on the latter issue, theorizing that the only real way for Anglo-Saxons to maintain numerical dominance in Canada would be for them to increase their birth rate. Hurd was pessimistic, refuting the sentiment that eventually years of living together would produce a "Canadian race" out of the disparate elements of the country through intermarriage. Hurd used the example of English and French Canadians who had been living beside each other for centuries and yet apparently did not engage in cross-marriages. For Hurd, this was a distinctly religious phenomenon, with Catholics marrying Catholics and Protestants "forced" to marry Protestants. The only statistically significant intermarrying among "native Canadians" and immigrant groups in Hurd's studies occurred between English Protestant Canadians and Protestant Northern Europeans. Catholics were synonymous with "high fertility stocks," and they married into only other "high fertility stocks," resulting in "[d]ifference in fertility and religion ... tend[ing] to perpetuate themselves."[130] These processes would transform Canada, therefore, both racially and religiously, particularly if large amounts of immigration from Catholic or Orthodox Central, Eastern, and Southern Europe continued unabated, with the nation being 60 per cent Catholic in a scant thirty-five years.

Hurd did not limit himself only to dry statistical analysis, believing that these changes would have a negative effect on the ties of Confederation, already rent asunder over the decades. Canada was always in flux, due to its racial and religious diversity and, of course, its varied rate of fecundity. In Hurd's understanding, Canada's various populations were central to preserving the peace in Canada and formulating what truly united its citizens. He spoke in explicitly Anglophilic language:

> If our young nation is to be welded into a unified whole, occasions for division must be avoided and attention focused on that which unifies. Probably the greatest unifying force in our national life is loyalty to the ideals of freedom, tolerance, and fair play, and to the democratic institutions and forms of government to which these ideals gave rise. Such being the case the measure of our national solidarity in the years to come will be determined, in a very large degree, by our success in applying those ideals toward using those institutions in solving the internal problems and making the inevitable readjustments with which we will be faced.[131]

Despite Hurd's detached nature, he clearly believed that years of Catholic immigration, differing birth rates, and the refusal to intermarry with "low fertility stocks," was not only changing Canada but altering its integrity as a unified, modern nation.[132] He felt the need to defend the ethno-religious purity of Canada, believing fervently in the inherently progressive/British nature of the nation in the face of a feared "Catholicization," which suggested dictatorship, passivity, and popery.

In 1938, John Murray Gibbon released a seminal work addressing the emerging multicultural nature of Canada, *Canadian Mosaic: The Making of a Northern Nation*. Where Hurd was pessimistic, Gibbon analyzed the composition of the nation from a decidedly optimistic liberal perspective. The book was a collection of radio addresses by Gibbon made earlier in that year at the request of the CBC, focusing on the folk music of the various cultures present in Canada. Gibbon was indeed an authority on folk music and musical traditions in Canada, organizing folk festivals in his work as the director of propaganda for the Canadian Pacific Railway.[133] Gibbon promoted greater understanding between the peoples of Canada, not the simple obliterating of cultural differences prominent among Anglo-Saxonists such as Lloyd and the Klan. He saw culture (especially music) and certain Old World traditions as providing "cement" for the mosaic, much like Kate Foster, Woodsworth, and Connor before him. Like these figures, however, Gibbon presented a patronizing and caricatured view of various ethnic groups and subscribed to racial theories that ascribed static characteristics to identifiable groups.[134] As John Herd Thompson has stated, the mosaic metaphor of the 1920s and 1930s allowed for the inclusion of a diverse population within the British Empire, reflecting the so-called "Third British Empire" concept of a free association of various peoples. While space was made within the Anglo-Protestant "imagined community" for these various peoples, the mosaic metaphor did not signify a strict obliteration of earlier identifications with Britain.[135] Instead, an acceptable amount of diversity reinforced and legitimized the superiority of this new Britishness, demonstrating its strength and adaptability in the modern world.

Gibbon reserved perhaps his most egregious stereotypes for Catholics in Canada, particularly French Canadians, Poles, Italians, and the Irish. Gibbon referred to the Irish as a "prolific breed," immediately reaching astronomical birth rates upon arrival in the New World. Gibbon's focus on population is also present in his description of Italians. Apparently the reason they began emigrating was the end of territorial wars and vendettas in mid-nineteenth-century Italy, along with the "racial tendency of the Italians to have large families," which forced surplus population to find a new home. This, and of course the Italian proclivity for manual labour, brought them to Canada and made them good workers.[136]

One fascinating tale told in the book has Gibbon attending a Polish dance routine at the New Canadian Folk-Song and Handicraft Festival in Winnipeg in 1928. Gibbon was confronted by attendees who were angry that "these people" were allowed to keep their traditions, citing Connor's famous *The Foreigner* as evidence against them. Gibbon, who was friends with Connor, was greatly disturbed and asked Connor to attend a dance and talk with the Polish crowd afterwards, and he happily obliged. Connor admitted later that he was wrong in his earlier assessment and presentation of Poles as "dirty labourers," and asked Gibbon what he could do in penance. Gibbon optimistically suggested that Connor rally his friends to attend these festivals so that they could be exposed to the simple traditions of non-Anglo cultures. Connor concluded, to Gibbon's satisfaction, that Poles were "as simple as they were charming."[137] This passage illustrates Gibbon's shared belief with Connor that the ethnic Other was not always subversive, but simply in need of the help and understanding of the hegemonic group to improve and achieve full acceptance.

The clearest example of this mindset in *Canadian Mosaic* is Gibbon's constant attempt to subsume difference within the ethno-religious framework of Britishness, no matter how ludicrous his comparisons may seem. He stated, for example, that the Swedish and English were similar (assumedly racially and religiously), contributing favourably to the easier assimilation of Swedes into Canada. Gibbon added, however, that since many Finns still spoke Swedish after decades of political rule, they, by proxy, also assimilated easily into Canada. He also linked the Greek community in Canada with mainstream culture by pointing out that since the Greek translation of the Bible, not the Roman, was used by the dominant Protestant population, Greeks were therefore not overly foreign. What perhaps hindered the Greeks in Gibbon's estimation, much like the Italians, was their racial inability to adapt to the harsh Canadian winters, unlike the Scandinavians.[138]

Gibbon's subsuming of ethnic and religious differences under the comforting umbrella of British traditions also occurs in his discussion of the Czechs. Gibbon presented a narrative common among Protestants critical of Catholicism and its historical role in Europe, namely that Jan Hus was the father of the Reformation and that the Englishman John Wycliffe, promoting liberty, tolerance, and Christianity until he was crushed by the authoritarian forces of Catholicism, directly influenced him.[139] Watson Kirkconnell, by now an English and Classics professor at Wesley College, who later served on the wartime Committee on Cooperation in Canadian Citizenship (CCCC) with Gibbon,[140] presented this argument in his 1930 study, *The European Heritage: A Synopsis of European Cultural Achievement*. Kirkconnell, who was proficient in many languages and acted as a translator for numerous European sources in the ensuing decades, claimed that Hus presaged Luther in his emphasis on direct loyalty to Christ and in speaking against the corruption of the Catholic Church, owing much of his thought to Wycliffe. Kirkconnell described a teleological binary within European history, in which freedom and progress, represented by Protestantism, fought against medieval regression and authoritarianism, represented by Catholicism. Kirkconnell concluded this interpretation of the European tradition by portraying the Anglo-Saxon Protestant, influenced by the eminent figures of Luther and Calvin, as alone furthering the progress of individual liberty, freedom, responsible government, and pioneering industrial capitalism.[141] Hus and Wycliffe thus served as proof that the countering and defeat of Catholicism in Catholic nations was possible, making certain immigrants and religious groups more acceptable to Anglo-Protestant-Canadian norms.[142]

Gibbon was essentially attempting to present to a Canadian audience a more acceptable and familiar face of a Catholic immigrant group, showing that, in Czech history, there was *potential* for the traditions of the Reformation. This historical understanding of the role of Catholicism and the Catholic Church in world history (read: European history) influenced Gibbon's characterization of French Canadians. For example, Gibbon defined the French Canadian by their respect for tradition, as "[t]he Church ... encourag[ed] him to be a believer in authority, and his instinct is to be conservative and thrifty."[143] The French Canadian was a humble, agriculturally inclined race with undivided loyalty to their Church. They had rejected the radicalism and republicanism of the United States and their own mother country. Gibbon repeated another common stereotype of French Catholics, namely that women essentially served only to birth huge families, a tradition dating back to Old France. The French Canadian especially promoted the arts, such as music and singing, not the crass materialistic world that existed outside of Quebec, again serving the interests of the omnipresent Catholic Church. Gibbon concluded his section on the French Canadian happily, believing that "Contentment with his lot, devotion to his job ... and a happy disposition made the French-Canadian the best kind of citizen that Canada could desire."[144] In Gibbon's formulation, Catholics were acceptable members of our society if they continued to fit into this romantic, patronizing ideal of the simple-minded Catholic habitant who was not interested in the serious business of politics and business in Canada.

Anti-Catholicism served to elaborate one's identity, especially in a period of great disorder like the Depression. It provided an existing, flexible tradition through which to communicate this identity. For the Anglo-Protestants detailed here, democracy and Protestantism were synonymous, as was Britishness. Catholicism was, at the least, problematic within this matrix of identity and, at the worst, to be eliminated. While the discourse varied in this period, in that there were moderate attempts at rapprochement by some left-wing and liberal intellectuals, Catholicism was still positioned firmly on the margins of respectability and belonging by many Anglo-Protestants. Even progressive figures embraced the conspiracy theorizing and caricatures of anti-Catholicism, fearing a nation dominated politically and numerically by an alien, undemocratic force. The diversity of anti-Catholicism(s) in this period reveals the depth and strength of this old Protestant tradition in English-Canadian culture decades into the twentieth century, as well as the continued importance of the ethno-religious matrix of Britishness as a pillar of English-Canadian nationalism, even when apparently shorn of explicit ethnic references.

Kirkconnell provides the clearest transition from the Depression-era concern with Catholicism to wartime. In an analysis of the world during the "Phony War," Kirkconnell praised French Canada for dispelling its "Duplessis infection" by electing the Liberal provincial government of Adélard Godbout immediately upon the declaration of war. This election was perceived by many Anglo-Protestants as evidence that Quebec had rejected the dangerous clerical-fascism of the latter Depression years.[145] Kirkconnell was still concerned about the slow progress of French Canadians to the obvious realization that 1) Duplessis was a thug, and 2) Francophone Quebeckers were ignorant in international affairs, signified by Catholic sympathy for Franco and Mussolini. This, for Kirkconnell, was due to both the control of an active clergy and the people's static nature, remaining centuries behind the rest of the modern world. Kirkconnell concluded his study ominously, stating that the steadily declining Anglo birth rate put the British heritage of Canada in danger. If this war was to be fought properly, Canadians had to escape complacency and materialism, as in Kirkconnell's mind, "*la revanche du berceau* [sic] will speedily submerge us in both East and West – and that deservedly, when the potential mothers of our race mistake comfort for civilization."[146] As in the previous Great War, Roman Catholics and Catholicism were a distorting influence on the Canadian body politic in a time of crisis.

3

Conscription and the "Omnicompetent State": The Second World War and Anti-Catholicism

> It is the Catholic countries of Europe that have succumbed to the fascist delusion that a counter-revolution against historic progress is possible.[1]
>
> Gregory Vlastos (1945)

While visiting family in Cambridge, Massachusetts, in 1942 with his wife, Harriet, Eugene Forsey penned a letter to his mother, noting that the child of a family friend had told Harriet that in their school the Irish children were openly supporting Hitler in the war. "It's a pity they and the same type of French-Canadians couldn't have a taste of Hitler's rule," Forsey commented, "they'd see then how much consideration their precious susceptibilities would get." Forsey was unequivocal regarding where the responsibility lay for these traitorous attitudes: "Of course the Vatican is behind a good deal of this; and, in the case of the Irish there is the poor excuse that in aeons gone by the British government of Ireland was very oppressive." Forsey finished his discussion of Catholics by referring to them as "goops" for not understanding "what century they're living in."[2] This letter is characteristic of the attitude of prominent Anglo-Protestant figures and intellectuals toward Catholicism and the Catholic Church during the Second World War. The Catholic Church, assumedly, was not fully supportive of the Allied war effort, a perception influenced by concerns during the Depression that the Vatican, certain elements in Quebec, and Catholics in general held fascist sympathies. These sympathies would inevitably hinder the war effort and caused the questioning of the loyalty, and thus Canadianness, of Catholics.

The concerns about Catholicism during the Depression were heightened during wartime as the world became engulfed in a brutal war. Along with the increase in the fierceness of anti-Catholicism came its politicization, perpetuated most publicly by various members of the federal Progressive Conservative Party (PC) and some of its provincial branches. Historian Linda Colley posits that Protestantism remained central to British identity, especially in times of crises, including the Second World War, as it bestowed a divine plan upon the nation to meet adversity. In this case the adversary was totalitarianism, represented not only by the Axis powers but also by the Catholic Church, an institution long viewed as alien to the fundamentally Protestant, British values of freedom and democracy. As Colley explains, this Protestant world view was entrenched within the mentality of Britons,[3] and many Anglo-Protestant Canadians shared it. The fervent Anglo-Protestant identity reinvigorated by war served to reinforce a sense of authenticity; Canada was truly British, loyal, and devoted to the values perhaps no longer supported even by the imperial metropolis. Canada was to represent an "untarnished" version of Britain, one that had not relented in the face of sectional interests, loyal to Britain but distinctly Canadian.[4] In this atmosphere, the Catholic Church and Catholicism were, yet again, inherently sectional, divisive, totalitarian, medieval, or perhaps even a "fourth Axis power," in the words of T.T. Shields.[5] The Church was a hindrance to the achievement of this idealized vision of the nation and Canadian identity.

The intensification and politicization of anti-Catholicism during the Second World War differentiates Canada from its American cousin, as many historians have concluded that public declarations of anti-Catholicism faded in America during the war.[6] A segment of Tories surrounding Ontario leader George Drew enthusiastically accepted its role as the political representative of the Protestant nation, embracing a fully British-Protestant Canadian nationalism and framing its opposition to family allowances and support of conscription in explicitly anti-Catholic, anti-French contexts. The Tories became *more* Protestant and British in this period, not less. Evidence of support from many English Canadians, along with the public pronouncements of influential members, reveals that this was not simply a cynical ploy to gain votes but reflected a tangible sentiment in Canada during the war that believed in and strove to revive the nation's Britishness.

With so much at stake, intellectuals, leading Protestant figures, mainline denominations, Tory politicians, and fundamentalist preachers all moved against the Catholic threat to national unity. The clearest manifestation of anti-Catholicism came during the debates over conscription and the alleged disloyalty of Catholic French Canadians. Anti-Catholic rhetoric blamed this directly on the Church: for some the Church was *the* special interest that controlled a King government, perceived, confusingly, as both weak and authoritarian. Compounding this sentiment was the common belief that the international Catholic Church, along with its counterpart in Quebec, was reactionary, bred a dual allegiance in its followers, and supported the various fascist and Nazi regimes throughout Europe, as evidenced by the initial support some French Canadians expressed toward the Pétain regime in Vichy France. Debates over civil liberties, and their very real suspension during the war under the controversial Defence of Canada Regulations (DCR), sometimes contained references to the authoritarian nature of the Catholic Church and its expanding control over civil government leading to totalitarianism. Many of these concerns became entangled with the older issue of "the revenge of the cradles" when family allowances were passed by the King government in 1944. There was an outcry among commentators, who often accompanied their denouncements of family allowances as an encroachment on provincial and individual jurisdiction with the claim that it was a "political bribe"[7] to Quebec. These commentators were convinced that family allowances were a means of rewarding prolific Catholic families and leading inevitably to the "swamping" of the Anglo-Protestant population. As historian Nancy Christie has noted, what emerged from the Second World War was a reinforced conviction among many Anglo-Protestants of various ideological positions that the Catholic Church was inherently incapable of existing within a democratic nation.[8]

Shields embodied anti-Catholicism in wartime Canada at its most bitter, and scholars have noted that his constant attacks on Roman Catholicism had been central to his fundamentalist crusade since the conscription crisis of the First World War.[9] Shields's role in the development of Canadian fundamentalism, his taste for the sensational, and the almost constant controversy swirling around him and his beloved Jarvis Street Baptist Church have caused him to be the subject of numerous studies.[10] During the Second World War, Shields quickly moved from his early support of King in the election of 1940, explained later by his refusal to vote for Tory leader R.J. Manion because he was Catholic,[11] to organizing the Canadian Protestant

League (CPL) as a protest against Catholic influence over the government. As Brent Reilly has noted, the impetus for the CPL emerged from a misunderstanding during the Week for National Reconsecration, organized in September 1941 on Parliament Hill to raise national morale. Through a series of scheduling errors, the joint Protestant-Catholic service was not held at the Peace Tower; advertisements instead only mentioned a Catholic mass, although Protestant services were held later in the week.[12] This seeming favouritism toward the Catholic Church angered some Protestants and motivated Shields to organize a meeting at Jarvis Street, which resulted in the eventual formation of the CPL in late 1941. At this meeting, Shields denounced the Catholic Church as "the enemy of the home, the enemy of the church, the enemy of all free men, and of all free institutions; that it is a totalitarian system which fastens upon its victims a yoke more deadly than that of Hitler, because it is a yoke which stretches beyond the bounds of time."[13]

The CPL was never the influential organization Shields and his close supporters hoped it would be (never reaching more than six thousand members), remaining largely centred in Toronto.[14] However, the language it used to define itself is revealing of the linkages Shields and his supporters forged between anti-Catholicism and their British-Canadian identity. This rhetoric emphasized a dedication to the preservation of British civil and religious liberties in Canada, linking these liberties to the doctrines of the Reformation and the need for Protestants to defend them constantly against the "supreme authority falsely claimed by the Roman Catholic Church."[15] In Shields's world view, the CPL was the protector of national unity, while Roman Catholicism, which was in essence Antichrist, was the prime disturber, insidiously pursuing its own goal of international political and spiritual domination. Shields compared Catholicism to a tumour that demanded removal from the body politic to prevent its spread. His CPL would stop the spread of these diseased Catholic fifth columnists in Canada to preserve its existence as a British nation.[16]

Shields's stature was perhaps never as nationally prominent as it was during the Second World War, when the House of Commons debated censuring his inflammatory periodical, *The Gospel Witness and Protestant Advocate*, and even discussed interning Shields. Wallace McDonald, Liberal MP for Pontiac, Quebec, called on Justice Minister Ernest Lapointe in March 1941 to prevent Shields's publication from being circulated, as it was subversive of national unity and offensive to Catholics. Later that year, Liguori Lacombe, Independent Liberal MP, Laval-Deux Montagnes, claimed that Shields was an enemy of national unity and had placed Christendom itself in contempt with his literature.[17] Wilfrid Lacroix, Liberal MP, Quebec-Montmorency, asked Minister of Justice Louis St Laurent to intern Shields on the basis of hindering national unity. Lacroix drew attention to one of Shields's many inflammatory claims, namely that "The Roman Catholic Church has done everything possible to discourage enlistments."[18] In 1943, a former Tory from Gaspé, J. Sasseville Roy, called for a sub-amendment to Pierre Cardin's recently proposed amendment to legislation concerning the conscription of men for overseas service under the National Resources Mobilization Act (the NRMA allowed the government to requisition the services of Canadians for home defence; in 1942 King amended the NRMA, allowing NRMA men to be sent overseas, causing Cardin to resign in protest, believing King had betrayed his promise to not implement conscription). The sub-amendment would prevent the publication of "anti-Catholic propaganda and prevent the circulation of some abusive publications conflicting with the purposes enunciated at the time of our war declarations."[19] Roy's sub-amendment connected the conscription question to a hostile Anglophone nationalism, a connection perhaps too inflammatory for the Liberals to endorse. King responded that persecuting Shields would transform him into a martyr, particularly since the new minister of justice, Louis St Laurent, was a French Catholic (Lapointe had unfortunately passed away), and suggested that Roy retract his amendment. King ended his response by expressing himself with uncharacteristic emotion: "as a member of a Protestant church, I wish to say that I have utter contempt for Mr. Shields and his unworthy utterances."[20] Roy's amendment was nevertheless annihilated 194–8, with all the yeas coming from Quebec.[21]

Not everyone in the House reacted negatively to Shields. Tory MP for Yukon, George Black, mentioned the *Gospel Witness* in the House briefly in May 1943, when condemning the public accounts committee of the Wartime Information Board (WIB). According to Black, the WIB was not limiting itself to publishing defence-related material, but was engaging in pro-Liberal politics. Black added, using Shields's periodical as evidence, that the board had released a French-Catholic pamphlet entitled "Nouvelles Catholiques," demonstrating favouritism toward the Catholic Church. Black was essentially shouted down by the laughter of the other members of the House for introducing such an inflammatory periodical in the House, as well as being denied standing by the speaker on a procedural matter. Yet he clearly took the issue seriously, and before he was forced to sit down he stated that this issue was of importance to all members of the House, "no matter what their religious beliefs may be or what their political adherence may be."[22]

The response to these debates over Shields from outside the House is also revealing of the temper in English Canada toward him and his claims regarding the Catholic Church. Shields was unsurprisingly incensed at the 1943 charges, responding from his pulpit on Jarvis Street that it was his right as a British subject to reject a system he believed was dangerous and false. For Shields, Catholicism was anti-Christian and blasphemous; while he vigorously opposed racism or hostility to individual Catholics, this evil institution was controlling them. It was a barrier not only to national unity, but it also created a province of "slackers" in Quebec who were not assuming their responsibility in the war effort against the Axis powers.[23] Editorialist J.V. McAree of the *Globe and Mail* expressed tacit support of Shields. The *Globe* had earlier stated that the very mention of Shields in the House was a waste of precious parliamentary time,[24] to which Shields characteristically responded that the newspaper was under the control of the Catholic hierarchy.[25] McAree now called attention to the more-pressing fact that French Canadians should be curtailing the spread of the sinister Order of Jacques Cartier, an extreme separatist movement that had allegedly infiltrated the major governmental and educational ranks of the province and was dedicated to creating an independent Catholic state, "Laurentia."[26] In McAree's view, this organization was much more significant than Shields, and represented a concerted attempt to implant fascism in Canada; it was "the naked Hitler idea with a religious slick."[27] In a subsequent editorial, McAree was even more supportive of Shields, stating that he had the right to make certain statements he believed were true about the Catholic Church, as he was a minister of the Gospel. McAree claimed that most Protestants did not mention these beliefs, "not because they ought not to be said, but because it does not happen to be our business to say them." Shields had taken an oath to defend Protestantism against incursions from faiths he sincerely believed to be in error. He saw Shields as having the total right to freedom of religion and speech, and the only major difference between Shields and King's critics, who castigated the prime minister for relying on the support of Quebec, was that the former traced this dependency directly to the Catholic

Church. Others, including presumably McAree himself, saw King as manipulating simple-minded French Canadians.[28]

Although McAree does not comment on this aspect of his reasoning, in both cases the authors represent French Canadians as ignorant of the actual events and issues circulating around them and being under the control of some external force. For McAree, Shields simply represented "Fundamentalism," which should have been no stranger to French Canada, since "that is what Rome has always represented. It does not change with changing fashions or scientific discoveries." McAree ended his editorial by admitting that, while most Protestants did not believe that the pope was Antichrist, as Shields did, in Toronto "which is supposed to be a very stronghold of Protestantism and Orange intolerance, Dr Shields is about the only voice to uphold a faith that once all Protestant ministers proclaimed. He is left naked to his enemies."[29] Shields was to be applauded for courage, in this rationale, due to his willingness to fight the fundamentalist enemy (Catholicism) with a fervent fundamentalist Protestantism.

It was not just conservative fundamentalist Baptists or hard line Anglophiles who were questioning Catholicism in wartime and suspicious of the Church's attempts to control the nation. An editorial from the official organ of the United Church, the *United Church Observer*, casually referred to such a fact when examining Louis St Laurent's recent 1943 speech on the redistribution of seats in the House. St Laurent opposed any motion to redistribute seats during the war, believing that it would create conflict, because Quebec would gain in seats, due to an increase in population (see Table 3.1). St Laurent condemned those who charged that the French and Roman Catholic people of Canada were engaged in a "sinister plan ... to get control of the government," shirking their military duties and allowing English Canadians to die, giving this as the reason why redistribution should be postponed until after the war, when controversies could be dealt with more easily. When St Laurent stated that some believed Quebec's population increase "is the result of a dark conspiracy of 'that man' in the vatican [*sic*] and 'that cardinal' in Quebec to get control of the country," Opposition House leader Gordon Graydon asked, "Who ever suggested that?" St Laurent wryly answered his colleague, "If my hon. friend has never heard it suggested, then he has not full knowledge of what has been going on in this country for the last quarter of a century."[30]

Table 3.1
Population of Canada with French as mother tongue

1941	3,354,753
1951	4,068,850

Series A-185-237, *Historical Statistics in Canada*, 2nd ed.

The *Observer* did not appreciate St Laurent's appeal to national unity or his confrontational tone toward Anglo-Protestants, who in the author's opinion had been *too generous* toward Roman Catholicism and Quebec. Long-time *Observer* editor A.J. Wilson (1939–55),[31] the presumed author of the editorial, stated that Anglo-Protestants in Canada had in fact been extraordinarily tolerant of French Catholics, despite their low enlistment numbers and periodic hostility to the war effort in general. St Laurent was simply lying when he claimed that there was widespread French enlistment.[32] In addition, Wilson claimed, it was common knowledge that Quebec was currently attempting to dominate the Canadian government, referring to William Burton Hurd's widely referenced census predictions of the French outnumbering Anglo-Protestants by 1971. Quoting a recent inflammatory article in the nationalist *Le Devoir*, Wilson warned that this represented not just the revenge but also the "victory of the cradles."[33] In Wilson's mind, Protestant Canada had gone beyond tolerance and entered the territory of appeasement, a word loaded with meaning during the Second World War, due to its association with Neville Chamberlain's appeasing of Hitler in the infamous Munich Agreement.[34] He referred to a recent message delivered to the Maritime Conference of the United Church by Dr E.M. Whidden of Acadia University, in which Whidden denied that Catholics recognized the inherent rights of the appeasers, but instead cynically accepted appeasement, while waiting until they had numerical and political dominance in order to facilitate their own control of Protestants. Whidden's tortured thinking regarding Catholics had impressed Wilson, and he concluded that St Laurent, in his militant attitude, was in fact hurting national unity by provoking Protestants who were patiently tolerating an inherently aggressive Church.[35]

Wilson's attitude was perhaps not surprising. Donald Wicks and historian Phyllis Airhart both note that Wilson included many articles hostile to Catholicism in this period in the *Observer*, with Wicks adding that he was supportive of Shields's CPL, writing him in 1943 that "I am all for a united front against the present unprecedented Roman Catholic propaganda."[36] This was the organ of the largest Protestant church in Canada, indeed a church that envisioned itself as at the core of the Canadian nation, revealing slippage between the "fanatical" anti-Catholicism of Shields and a mainline denomination. While the *Observer* and Wilson may not have descended to the violent language of Shields, these writings suggest a wider Protestant concern with Catholicism than previously understood.[37]

Another United Churchman, C.E. Silcox, joined in these wartime diatribes against Catholicism. The stakes were high for Silcox, since he believed that if the major branches of Christendom could not achieve true unity, then Christians throughout the world were playing into the hands of Hitler himself.[38] Silcox was in fact the subject of condemnation in the House during St Laurent's maiden speech, in which he discussed the results of the 1942 plebiscite on conscription. King and the Liberals had decided to hold a national plebiscite in April 1942, asking Canadians if they released the government from its promise not to implement conscription. King was convinced that national unity depended on avoiding the mistakes of the First World War, especially the reckless enforcing of conscription. His government therefore only very cautiously moved toward conscription, using the polarized results of the plebiscite, which predictably saw English Canada heavily support conscription and Quebec oppose it, to amend the NRMA and try and salve the anger on both sides of the debate.[39] The amended NRMA now allowed men enlisted in home defence, known as Zombies, to be sent overseas; yet King still did not actually send any of them, continuing his delicate balancing act.[40]

St Laurent attacked extremists on all sides, from his radical anti-conscriptionist opponent in the Quebec East by-election, Paul Bouchard, to "the Shieldses and the Silcoxes, and even the *Globe and Mail*," who were happy to blame the lack of full conscription on "French-Canada's stranglehold on this dominion."[41] Silcox was not shy about advocating for full conscription and dismissing Liberal claims that they were attempting to preserve national unity as politics at its worst.[42] In an article that appeared in *Saturday Night* weeks before the plebiscite, Silcox expressed a mixture of fatalism and anger at the French-Canadian population: he called on English Canadians to wait for their answer to the plebiscite before judgment, but he warned that, if they voted "non," the very country could collapse and be swallowed by the United States. Perhaps worse (other than an Axis victory), if French Canadians voted "non" and the Allies won the war, English Canadians would rightfully reject the French-Canadian desire to maintain their "way of life." French Canadians, locked in their "futile isolationism," were committing "hari kiri" on a continent controlled by Anglo-Saxons.[43] It was perhaps this sentiment that St Laurent was referring to in his House speech, comparing Silcox to Shields.

Silcox took public offence at St Laurent's comparison and wrote an open letter to him in Judith Robinson's conservative paper, *News*. Silcox was furious in these letters: in the first part, he attacked St Laurent for not understanding English Protestants at all by accusing them of being "imperialists." Silcox retorted that they were not being colonial or imperial, but that the English peoples had decided that this war was between civilization and destruction. English Canadians indeed had close ties to Britain, but were just as Canadian as French Canadians. In a particularly vicious section, which bordered on a repetition of his eugenical theories of the 1930s, he retorted that this population had simply intermarried into other communities more than the French-Canadian population, which claimed a foolish form of ethnic purity. This "inbreeding" among French Canadians had resulted in biological problems, although he is vague as to what these problems were. He also condemned St Laurent for expressing sympathy with those Francophones who did not enlist, and even called on St Laurent to be interned for such rhetoric. In the second part of the letter, Silcox attacked St Laurent for playing politics and not calling on his people to reject the isolationism that had allowed Hitler to prepare for war in the first place. Silcox labelled French Canadians hypocrites, who denied the importance of the Commonwealth while benefiting from the freedoms it guaranteed its people. He also specifically denied that he was an anti-Catholic, pointing out that he had personally attacked Shields's CPL and worked toward ecumenical relations between Catholics and Protestants. He admitted to talking about the fear of the "revenge of the cradles," but denied that he shared it with other Anglo-Protestants. He had only described it in hopes of bettering understanding in the nation, a claim that ignores much of his public and private utterances during the Depression.[44]

His anger at being accused of prejudice is palpable. Silcox saw himself as a healer of national unity, simply outlining the reality of the consequences of French-Canadian obfuscation in a world torn apart by war. Forsey agreed with Silcox's self-evaluation. Forsey told Arthur Meighen, his friend, arch-conscriptionist, and briefly leader of the Tories (again) from 1941 to 1942 when he was recruited from the Senate to try and force the conscription issue, that St Laurent had fumbled badly by attacking Silcox. "I know Silcox well," said Forsey, "and he is the mildest, most moderate, most conciliatory of men, and notably on this very question of English and French." According to Forsey, "St Laurent could not have chosen a worse representative of intolerance if he'd gone over the province with a fine-tooth comb," concluding that St Laurent had made "a contemptuous jackass of himself." Meighen agreed, stating that Silcox's *News* letters resembled his own thinking, including the distaste for St Laurent's attempt to defend Francophones.[45] What is striking here is that a prominent Tory and a self-described progressive shared an opinion of Silcox and defended his credentials as a representative of national unity. This was a man who, throughout the 1930s and into the war, had drawn attention to the regressive nature of French-Canadian society and who warned that the refusal to participate equally in the war effort would lead English Canadians to no longer tolerate French Canada's claim to a particular "way of life." Apocalyptically, Silcox also warned at one point that, in the postwar world of Allied victory, the inevitable global religious revival would reform all religious institutions into a truly "catholic church." Were French Canadians thus willing to sacrifice this grand objective and allow the "narrow bonds" of the past Church to dictate their actions?[46]

If one document can be said to represent a significant change in Silcox's tone, it is his pamphlet *Must Canada Split?* written during the tense year of 1944 and focusing on the conscription crisis. Silcox revealed his temperament in a letter to George Drew, congratulating him on his 9 August broadcast condemning family allowances (discussed in detail later). Silcox boldly proclaimed, "I believe that the time has come for a showdown with Quebec," adding that, if Quebec wanted to remain in Canada, "they must play the game fairly; if they do not wish to play with us, they should go off by themselves. Any other solution along the lines suggested by Mr King is fatal to both and to Canada."[47] He pursued this thought process into his pamphlet, questioning the idea that Canada needed to preserve unity at all costs, since not all ethnic groups had pulled their weight militarily. Toleration was for Silcox now not only impossible but a sign of disloyalty. This pamphlet is Silcox at his most vitriolic, dedicated as it was to those who protected "moral freedom" and "freedom of conscience" in this war, as opposed to the "ideological regimentation" upheld in Ireland, Vichy France, Italy, and Quebec. Silcox believed that to preserve true freedom in the postwar world, Canada needed true peace, and because Quebec did not support the war effort to its best ability, the country could avoid a full-fledged civil war only by completely severing the province from Canada. Silcox is clear that this was not a racial matter, as he viewed the French and British as quite close racially; instead, he specified that it was a matter of religion. For Silcox the Catholic Church was *the* cause of all the conflicts in Canadian history through its political machinations. It promoted only its own interests in Canada, as it had around the world through the centuries. Most importantly, the Catholic Church was simply not adaptable to a modern world or a modern country such as Canada, fundamentally based on the Protestant conception of freedom:

> French-Canadian Catholicism, so far as it is corporatist and anti-democratic, is absolutely incompatible with Anglo-Canadian Protestantism, essentially democratic and insistent on the priesthood of the believer, on the direct and authentic appeal of the voice of God to the individual heart of man ... No, if the liberally-minded wish freedom of conscience and the liberal view of God and His will to prevail, they must be prepared to fight for it. They must organize themselves according to their underlying faith in freedom – religious and political; they must protect themselves against such open plotting and spiritual sabotage.[48]

Silcox was thus convinced that Catholicism was by its very nature untenable in his vision of the future of the world.

This is Silcox at his most extreme, as there is no evidence that he ever again openly supported the separation of Quebec from Canada. By the end of the war, he became mostly concerned with the passing of family-allowance legislation and the incursions of the "omnicompetent" welfare state into Canadian life.[49] This did not exclude, however, discussions of Catholicism. In fact, Silcox's critique of the managerial state was inextricable from his belief that Catholic interests had overrun the government. As Nancy Christie has described, some Protestants saw in this legislation the invasion by Catholicism of that most sacred of institutions, the family itself.[50] If the family was the model for authority in society, then the attempt by Catholicism to influence this institution was particularly insidious. For Silcox, the increasingly "Catholic" nature of the government was concomitant to the increasingly totalitarian nature of the state. Once again, Silcox positioned the Church as an institution hostile to individualism and freedom. In a letter to Major Gladstone Murray, for example, he described his interest in Friedrich Hayek's recently released *Road to Serfdom*. Hayek's book was a landmark refutation of the welfare state and the ubiquitous concept of planning that emerged in the mid-forties. Hayek feared that the new statism would lead to the success of totalitarianism in Western nations, akin to the Nazi nightmare of Germany.[51] Silcox agreed with Hayek in his defence of classical liberalism, but questioned why Hayek did not analyze the most consistent enemy of liberalism over the past century: the Vatican. Silcox concluded his letter to Murray by expressing his interest in understanding the different motives behind fascists, socialists, and Catholics for attacking liberalism, rhetorically linking these totalitarian forces. Murray, who had recently founded the anti-Communist Responsible Enterprise Movement, agreed with Silcox, particularly mentioning his reference to the anti-liberal agenda of the Vatican through the ages.[52]

Unlike Silcox, the views United Churchman and prominent historian Arthur Lower presented in public were very different from the private concerns he expressed about Catholicism. Lower was asked to revise the ninth draft of the Report of the Commission on the Church, Nation, and World Order (CCNWO), compiled by the United Church in 1944. This draft of the report contained a savage criticism of the political ambitions of the Catholic Church. The draft stated in section 153 that religion, nationalism, and language had merged into a potent and inflammatory mix in French Canada, causing tensions between Catholics and Protestants. According to the report, Catholics caused this tension due to their intransigent hypocrisy in demanding full freedom in Protestant nations but denying it to Protestants in Catholic countries. The Church had "religio-political" ambitions. It was the inheritor of the Roman Empire, striving to create an "ecclesiastical imperialism based on Latin tendencies ... authoritarian in its nature, distrustful of democracy except when it exists in a democracy ... determining its 'politique' less by the law of nature than by the ultimate ends of institutional power and aggrandizement and avid to use the power of censorship."[53] In the opinion of the report, a welcome schism within Catholicism would prevent the conservative faction centred in French Canada from dominating. This group "threatens the fabric of Canadian unity, and ... may even destroy confederation unless the people of French Canada ... themselves shake off the yoke of bondage and demand to the full, in church as well as in state, government of the people, by the people and for the people." Only a truly catholic church, universal in nature, could stand up to the "demonic forces" of the modern world.[54]

Lower counselled moderation when he read this report. Even though he saw the sections concerning the Catholic Church as important, since they defined the position of one Christian Church to another, the language was essentially "declaring war on the Roman Catholic Church." Lower stressed the need for discussion in the true Christian spirit of understanding, elaborating commonalities between denominations instead of divisions. He admitted "[m]ost Protestants will agree only too heartily with everything that is said in [section] 153, but the question is, is it politic to say it? The [United] church will have to make up its mind whether it wishes to open all the old sores and carry on a religious quarrel." In his mind, the cause of unity in the postwar world was more important overall, and worth cooperating with even the Catholic Church.[55]

In a letter to Lower, Rev. Gordon Sisco, who was a founding member of the Inter-Church Committee on Protestant–Roman Catholic Relations (ICC) and secretary of the CCNWO, agreed with Lower that all explicit mention of the Catholic Church in Canada should be eliminated from the final report, due to the tensions it would create. Sisco concluded, however, not that they were inaccurate, but in fact the complete opposite. If the United Church made these statements, all Protestant churches should also make them, creating a united front against a monolithic Catholicism.[56] Indeed, in the final document, presented to the 11th General Council of the United Church of Canada in 1944, all the possibly offensive references to Roman Catholics have been excised, much as Lower advised. Instead, the report briefly addressed the positive aspects of the ecumenical movement, including the projected World Council of Churches (WCC).[57] Despite the ecumenical olive branch that the United Church officially extended in the face of modern materialism, the ninth draft of this report, the involvement of commission members in the anti-Catholic ICC and of Silcox and Lower in its preparation reveal that the leadership of the United Church was, at best, highly suspicious of Catholicism.[58]

Lower was much franker about his perception of Catholicism during the Second World War in a letter to historian M. Seraphin Marion, a representative of La Société canadienne d'histoire de l'Eglise catholique. Lower responded angrily to prejudicial charges by Marion that Protestants were more materialistic than Catholics because they had fully embraced modernity. He stated that, while modernity had thoroughly infiltrated Protestant ranks, Protestantism would be able to defend itself against the total domination of the acquisitive spirit despite the fact that it did not contain the "authoritarian" defences of the Catholic Church. This was due to its focus on the integrity of the individual. Lower questioned whether Catholics would be ready to prosecute the war effort in the face of the actual decline of Anglo-Saxons, answering this query in the negative: "Your people are still too parochial for that and even another century will hardly suffice for the training in initiative necessary to rule a continent." Lower continued that he admired the Catholic focus on community – as this was how they maintained their "biological urges" to perpetuate their culture through large families. Yet the Protestant ideal of the community did not eschew the burden of individual responsibility. This was one of the major problems with Catholicism for Lower, for Catholic contentment resembled the "attribute of irresponsibility, as in children, whereas the very essence of Protestantism is responsibility." This attitude toward modern life is what prevented French Canadians from achieving their potential in Canadian society, not prejudice against them in employment or governmental positions. Catholic French Canadians themselves were to blame for their status.[59]

Lower's lifelong determination to preserve national unity in Canada through the compromise inherent in liberalism and liberal institutions propelled him to discuss Catholicism and French Canada in public often. Despite not being quite as openly critical of Catholicism as he was in his private correspondence, these public statements reflect an understanding of history as the unfolding of liberty since the English Reformation, embodied now in British institutions. One of Lower's most important intellectual statements was his presidential address at the Canadian Historical Association meeting in 1943, entitled "Two Ways of Life: The Primary Antithesis of Canadian History." Lower made his address in a tense atmosphere, attempting to promote an understanding of Quebec in English Canada as opposed to the prejudicial statements coming from other camps.[60] He outlined his belief that the French-English divide was the defining characteristic of

Canada, but that reason and compromise could resolve the inevitable conflicts between these "ways of life."⁶¹ Religion was one of the defining features of both societies, determining their character and history. He presented the Catholic Church specifically as creating and preserving a static, agrarian society, as opposed to the dynamic, capitalistic one that emerged out of Protestant English Canada, labelling the French-Canadian Catholic "way of life" the "peasant-spiritual ... the primitive outlook on life." Lower admired the lack of materialism in French Canada and condemned the overwhelming materialism of Protestant society, but this caused him to paint a familiar portrait of a simplistic habitant and Catholic society opposed to the natural progression of history.⁶² Lower concluded his "Two Ways of Life" address with a call for compromise between modern, urban acquisition and French Canada. Yet he asked a revealing rhetorical question: "'Who has created the French race in America?' I make bold to say that the English industrialist has created about three-quarters of it." The "Protestant man of business" had brought modern civilization into existence, reaching out to his otherwise hapless French-Catholic compatriots and succeeding in convincing some that modernization was necessary to benefit the overall populace in both economy and size. Some clearly resisted this effort.⁶³

Lower's brand of anti-Catholicism revolved around his anxiety about the power of a homogeneous Catholicism to infiltrate and undermine liberal-democratic life, ultimately hastening the demise of a "de-vitalized" Protestantism as a spiritual and political force. In Lower's words, the religiously based homogeneity in Quebec was so extreme that all "French Canadians are, as it were, the same French Canadians" as the original settlers of New France, resulting in a harmful insularity.⁶⁴ He did not oppose the idea of national homogeneity per se; in fact, he consistently opposed immigration into English Canada lest it undermine the Anglo-Protestant ability to construct a suitable identity.⁶⁵ In French Canada he believed that the trauma of the Conquest and protection from the outside world by the Church created the same kind of inferiority and claustrophobia that was "the motive power behind Nazi-ism, Fascism, and 'Japanese-ism.'" Writing in the context of the fear of fascism within Quebec, Lower attempted to explain the presence of these ideas to English Canada. Without the opportunity for "free expansion," meaning the inability or unwillingness of French Canadians to move beyond their "French island" in North America or to pursue an education that promoted action and industry instead of contemplation, extremist nationalism, and racialism were inevitable. The resentment felt by any Latin Catholic people cut off from their religious and cultural centre (Rome) and forced to accept a British culture only exacerbated this attitude. Along with English-Canadian chauvinism, this explained the fervent opposition to conscription among French Canadians in the Second World War.[66] To preserve unity, good Canadians clearly needed to be patient with such a people, not attack them.

Lower's discussion of the vitality of Protestant Canada so concerned Gregory Vlastos that he was motivated to write Lower and express his displeasure with the pessimism of "Two Ways of Life." Vlastos, philosopher and co-editor of the left-wing Fellowship for a Christian Social Order (FCSO) tome *Towards the Christian Revolution*, saw even a materialistic English Canada as adjusting better to the modern world than Catholic French Canada. It was "the Catholic countries of Europe that have succumbed to the fascist delusion that a counter-revolution against historic progress is possible." This would inevitably lead to doom for these countries. Lower, while not sure about Vlastos's conclusion that materialistic Anglo-Protestants would still thrive relative to "fascist" Catholics, concurred with Vlastos's suggested teleological historical framework, as the engine at the core of Lower's own teleology was also English Protestantism. Even with his ambivalence toward materialism, Lower was convinced that the solution was not for citizens to turn their backs on the modern world or for modern nations to counter the tide of historical development, as these Catholics often had, and to succumb to a conflict between "Protestant commercial capitalism and Catholic ecclesiastical capitalism." Lower also rejected the apparently "natural" progress of Western societies toward collectivism.[67] The solution was to moderate the devotion to materialism with attention to preserving the core aspects of true Christianity; this would result in the triumph of liberal democracy and individualism.

Lower believed that the loss of vitality within Protestantism was the result of the necessary-but-problematic synonymy of Protestantism with individualism and liberalism. In correspondence with Gordon Sisco, Lower was convinced that the excessive materialism of the current period was due to a possible ending of the cycle of increasing liberalism and individualism that began with the Renaissance, leading to the "rawest kind of selfishness" of modern society. Protestantism was "painlessly extinguish[ing] [it]self" through its low birth rate, allowing the dynamic of Roman Catholicism, which Lower did "not profess to understand," to continue unabated, as it had for centuries. His Protestant notion of history again becomes apparent when Lower warned that this Catholic dynamic was causing Catholics "at the moment [to] confidently look [...] forward to the end at no great distance of time of the great Reformation heresy." He ominously added that this would be disastrous for a modern society based upon Protestantism: "Unless we can discover a way of life for our people that will be genuinely spiritual, as I suppose theirs is, they will have their hopes fulfilled." Sisco, for his part, expressed fear of a world where "liberal Protestantism" was threatened from all sides by fascism and communism, with the separate phenomenon of "Catholic fascism taking us in the flank."[68] The decline of Protestantism was not just about maintaining numbers, but about preserving the political, cultural, and spiritual basis of liberal democracy as developed throughout the ages. Sisco and Lower, while representing in their own minds the liberal wing of Canadian Protestantism, thus saw a future in which their faith was not hegemonic demographically, ideologically, or spiritually as a future blockaded against postwar reconstruction and the reinforcement of Western democracy. Catholicism, once again, was the foil against which they compared their own "de-vitalized" faith tradition.

Vlastos's co-editor of *Towards the Christian Revolution*, R.B.Y. Scott, contributed to a document, "English-French Relations," released by the CCNWO, that *did* contain anti-Catholic rhetoric during the Second World War. Scott was research director for the CCNWO, while his co-author, Rev. Claude de Mestral, was the minister at Bethanie Church in Montreal and a leading French-Canadian United Church evangelizer. De Mestral was a problematic choice by the CCNWO, as he had labelled Catholicism "a sad deformation of Biblical Christianity" in the pages of Wilson's *Observer* and maintained that the "Roman Church" needed to reform itself by recognizing Jesus, not the hierarchy. This reform would occur only if Catholics and the hierarchy embraced the tenets of the Reformation, finally achieving true Christianity by "Protestantizing," as opposed to relying on "dictatorship and a reactionary power."[69] De Mestral's presence as an author in this document demonstrates the paucity of options – or perhaps the lack of concern – of the CCNWO and the United Church with actual French-Catholic opinion when analyzing a central issue in Canadian society during wartime.

De Mestral's viewpoint certainly colours the report. De Mestral and Scott note that behind much of the tension in Canada was the Anglo-Protestant concern surrounding the demographic shift, once again referencing Hurd's 1941 census.[70] The report made plain that this tension was at its core a religious struggle. The English in Canada would not be as vigorous in their condemnations of French-Canadian interests and nationalism in the war if it were not for the "Roman Catholic Church stand[ing] in the shadow behind the French, controlling and ultimately determining every move." The local priest did not worry Protestants; instead they were concerned about an international Church composed of a wealthy, disciplined hierarchy that dominated backward countries like Spain and Poland. The Catholic Church for Scott and de Mestral threatened the basis of Canadian society, namely "British institutions," which protected liberty and freedom for all citizens. The Church was an alien force that distorted the composition of the nation and threatened its stability, with the authors painting a nightmare scenario of a Catholic Canada:

> What would this great Church, with its arrogant claims, and which imposes its strong will upon the minds and hearts of its people and allows so little place for freedom of thought or action – what would it do if it should come to a place of dominant influence in Canada? Is it likely that this powerful institution, so definitely opposed in its structure, its methods and its philosophy to all that is truly free and democratic, so bitterly antagonistic to the great truths for which Protestantism has bravely struggled for four centuries, – is it to be expected that it, once having gained a controlling voice, would exert a different influence in Canada than it has in other countries under similar circumstances?[71]

The religious solution for national unity during an international crisis was to promote the French-Protestant churches as a means of reaching those Catholics who wanted a new spiritual experience and to further the reformation of the Catholic Church. This solution is perhaps unsurprising, given that de Mestral co-authored the work, yet it is characteristic of the type of understanding and ecumenism at the end of the war. In this scenario, Canadians should tolerate the Catholic

Church, perhaps even engage with it at a practical level, to achieve a victory over the forces of materialism and conflict; but it was not a "truly" Christian institution. Instead, it was an authoritarian rival, a divisive force in Canadian national life. "Democracy and the Roman Catholic Church, as it functions today, appear to be entirely incompatible," the authors boldly proclaimed, adding ominously but without comment that the "Roman Catholic hierarchy has recently set up its national headquarters in Ottawa, the national capital," suggesting that the Church was becoming even more committed to controlling the affairs of the nation. Amidst this rhetoric, the authors did acknowledge that organizations such as the Orange Order were hindering national unity due to their extremism. The Order in fact fostered a *more* ardent French nationalism. Tolerance and understanding were necessary to counter the six major barriers to national unity: language, separate schools, divided loyalties – "the English to the Motherland, the French to the Papacy" – the "political ambitions of the Roman Catholic Church," racial snobbery, and the low wages in Quebec.[72] It is clear from this list which institution was primarily to blame for Canadian problems in wartime.

The United Church was certainly not the only mainline Protestant denomination to profess anti-Catholic statements during the war. As author Brent Reilly has shown, there were many prominent Baptists outside Shields's fundamentalist orbit, such as public intellectual Watson Kirkconnell, who promulgated the idea that Protestantism as a force in Canadian life was declining in the face of both Catholic fecundity and Protestant apathy.[73] Kirkconnell voiced these sentiments in an article entitled "The Twilight of Canadian Protestantism," in which he condemned Protestants in Canada for sacrificing their racial survival for material comforts. He also stressed the need for Anglo-Protestants, especially in Ontario, to relent in their constant belligerence toward those of different origins, as they were quickly becoming a minority themselves.[74] Kirkconnell was involved in the Committee on Cooperation in Canadian Citizenship (CCCC) and other wartime propaganda efforts such as the Nationalities Branch and its successor, the Citizens' Bureau. The CCCC was dedicated to preserving the distinct cultural traditions of the various groups in Canada, while still emphasizing a belief in the ultimate but future need for assimilation into a larger Canadian framework. Scholar Ivana Caccia characterizes this approach as supporting unity but not uniformity.[75] Yet Kirkconnell's position on Catholicism and ethnic minorities was not a simple promotion of multiculturalism in the face of prejudice, as some scholars have posited.[76] Instead, he expressed his belief in a unified nation built on a paternalistic understanding and acceptance of certain aspects of folk cultures. In this article, Kirkconnell singled out the Protestant clergy as being silent partners in "race suicide" by not addressing the issue and revising the Protestant conception of the family; he concluded by boldly stating that, if there was to be any hope of Protestant recovery, a "wistful hope" at best, these facts needed to be directly faced.[77]

Kirkconnell was arguing for a Canada in which the various groups expressed understanding and tolerance toward each other, these being fundamentally British values, to preserve at least a modicum of the Anglo-Saxon presence upon which Canada was built. Kirkconnell identified the major problem as the "catastrophically low Anglo-Saxon birthdate [sic]," yet quickly amended this statement by pointing out that, while the Protestant birthrate was dwindling, immigrant groups from traditionally Catholic countries were exploding in numbers, particularly on the Prairies. This demographic shift led to a Western frontier populated by empty former mission buildings and Baptist churches, because the Catholic Church had effectively inculcated in its followers a "virtually impregnable" shell against "the appeal of other creeds."[78]

Despite the language of mutual understanding and tolerance, this article is an example of the wartime concern not only with Catholic dominance but also with Protestant decline. Protestantism was the essence of historical democracy in this formulation, and it had served for centuries as the basis of British identity; Canadians could not allow it to disappear. Also apparent in this article are the consistent anti-Catholic tropes of uncontrollable reproduction, unmatchable indoctrination, and the insatiable expansionism of the Catholic population. Kirkconnell predicted gloomily that the "future trend is towards pronounced Catholic predominance ... Standing as we Protestant Anglo-Saxons do on a steep slope down into obscurity, we shall be wise to take to heart the lessons implicit in such a situation."[79]

The fear of an emerging totalitarian state due to the crumbling of democracy was tangible in wartime Canada in the face of unprecedented government involvement in the economy, the slow but palpable formation of a state-controlled social-security system, and the very real excesses of the Defence of Canada Regulations.[80] Central to this transformation, for some, was the influence of the Catholic Church over specific government policy, such as family allowances, King's refusal to institute full conscription, and even the interning of "Catholic enemies." During a debate initiated by CCF MP T.C. Douglas, which protested the raid of a Jehovah's Witnesses meeting by the RCMP, the discussion broadened into a debate concerning whether the Witnesses should be considered subversive (the Witnesses had been banned under the DCR in 1940).[81] It was widely believed by Witnesses and others that the banning occurred because of the group's explicit and vicious anti-Catholicism and King's need to keep support in Quebec, although the government maintained it was because the Witnesses saw laws and politics as "devil's tools" and refused to salute the flag. A 1941 letter complaining about the ban on Witnesses and signed "Christian," which was sent to King, the attorney general of BC, Gordon Wismer, and various MPs, stated that it was the Catholic Church that was the real fifth column in Canada and that the nation was being fooled by then justice minister Ernest Lapointe. The author also boldly attacked English-Canadian pride by writing, "Evidently the whole of Canada has yielded to a pompous son of the church of Rome [Lapointe]."[82]

In the House, Alberta Social Credit MP George Ernest Hansell asked now-justice minister St Laurent directly whether it was illegal or subversive to state that one's church was the true church, as in the case of the Witnesses. In addition, Hansell queried St Laurent about the stance of the Catholic Church, which allegedly believed all other denominations were "satanic." While Hansell offended St Laurent by his challenge, St Laurent allowed Liberal MP Arthur Slaght to attack Hansell instead. According to Slaght, the true reason behind the internment of Witnesses was the group's rejection of the primacy of human law over them.[83] Another Alberta Social Credit MP, Victor Quelch, asked why the government had not interned Doukhobors, given the periodic violent outbursts of their Freedomite wing, adding that there was a difference between religious controvery and subversion.[84] Quelch admitted that anti-Catholic tirades were regrettable, yet the law "does make one wonder whether the action against Jehovah's Witnesses is largely on account of their attitude toward the Roman Catholics, instead of their attitude of a subversive nature." Quelch and Hansell were convinced that the Catholic Church had enough influence over the government to persuade them to outlaw and arrest members of a religious organization that was unapologetically anti-Catholic. When Liberal MP Léo Richer La Fleche called Quelch's statement "a shame," Quelch answered that it was a sincere question, asked by Canadian citizens across the nation. Minister of Mines and Resources Thomas Crerar denigrated Quelch and his colleagues for raising unfounded suspicions that would fundamentally hurt national unity. Quelch concluded his remarks with the comment "suspicion is there. I am not planting it."[85]

The suspicion of French Catholic fascist tendencies and the Church's ability to decide government policy was not present only in Canada. In a lengthy article in *Life* magazine in May 1941, New Dealer Eliot Janeway accused Canada of failing to uphold the American diplomatic plan of spreading democracy and the New Deal throughout the world, even though America would not join the actual conflict for several months. This was due entirely to the "timid, unimaginative Mackenzie King Government," which "continues to be blackmailed by the crudely pro-Axis French Canadian minority (an ideal Nazi Fifth Column)."[86] Lapointe condemned this article in the House when he responded to charges by *nationaliste* Maxime Raymond that Canada had joined the war only because it was subservient to Britain. Lapointe believed that extreme statements like Raymond's allowed ignorant anti-French articles, like Janeway's, to exist.[87]

Elizabeth Armstrong contributed to this discourse when she published her sympathetic *French Canadian Opinion on the War: January 1940–June 1941* for Ryerson Press's Contemporary Affairs series in 1942. Armstrong specifically addressed the issue of Vichy-Canada relations. She stated that while some elements within French Canada did support Pétain's Vichy government in France, the majority did not, and even those who supported it saw it as a puppet of the Nazi government and eventually reversed their position. Referring specifically to Janeway's article, she denied that French Canadians had descended into acting as fifth columnists due to the patient attitude of the King government, which privileged sincere national unity as opposed to aggressive jingoism in its cautious attitude toward conscription.[88] Historian Paul M. Couture, in his study of the Vichy–Free France propaganda war in Quebec, characterizes the province in general as profoundly ambivalent regarding the status of France. While many Quebeckers were elated at the success of the war hero and staunch Catholic Marshal Pétain ruling the "decadent" republic, the undeniable presence of Nazism prevented most from unrestrained enthusiasm.[89]

In a more recent study, Olivier Courteaux painstakingly examines the complexities of Canada-Vichy relations, with King placing national unity at the forefront, fearing the reaction from Quebec if the government unilaterally broke with the legal regime in France. He was assailed both by ardent Tory conscriptionists, who wished him to break relations (Vichy had broken official relations with Britain in 1940), and by hardline French-Canadian nationalists, who believed that Vichy was a symbol of resistance to a British imperialist war. In fact, Britain and America both pressured King and his colleagues to maintain relations with Vichy, King's "Vichy gamble," in order to preserve communication with the collaborationist regime in the dark times of the war following the fall of France.[90] In addition, thirty-three countries had recognized Vichy France, including the United States and the Vatican, which convinced many in Quebec that it was a valid nation, if a troubled one.[91] Dr Louis Phillipe Roy, a frequent contributor to *L'Action Catholique*, epitomized this cautious acceptance of Pétain in a reprinted and translated article in *Saturday Night*, in which he opposed the Nazi influence in France but accepted Pétain as its legitimate leader and a possible "restorer" of the greatness of the nation.[92] This sentiment for Roy did not mean that he was against the Allied cause; the author strove to hold both opinions simultaneously.

Wartime did not lend itself to nuance, and many English Canadians perceived Quebec to be a province full of fascist/Vichy support and sympathy, pointing to D'Augustin Frigon, the head of the French-language CBC, who *did* use his position to broadcast Vichy propaganda more prominently than Free French polemics.[93] T.T. Shields characteristically declared that relations with Vichy represented nothing less than the influence of the "Fourth Axis Power," the Vatican, in Canada.[94] McAree for his part believed that Vichy sympathy was widespread in Quebec, emanating yet again from the apparently omnipotent Order of Jacques Cartier.[95] McAree's Anglophile *Globe and Mail* made Vichy the subject of over one hundred editorials between 1940 and 1942.[96] While these editorials covered a range of topics, Catholicism and the Church was certainly a main subject of interest. In one, the editorialist pleaded with French Canadians that, despite their understandable sympathy for the mother country and Pétain's revival of traditional Catholicism, they must realize that Vichy France was simply a vassal state of that great enemy of Christendom, Nazism. The goal for a "Latin Catholic bloc" of Vichy France, Italy, and Spain, which was apparently the real reason for Vichy support, was simply a "very distant dream."⁹⁷ The paper did present some nuanced analysis: one editorial drew an important distinction between Vichy's representatives in Canada, Archbishop Charbonneau of Montreal, who had controversially called Pétain "his country's Good Samaritan," and the majority of Catholics in Canada, especially Cardinal Villeneuve, who was adamantly supportive of the war effort.⁹⁸ Yet the *Globe and Mail* just as often countered this type of thinking. For example, in its coverage of the transition of the Soviet Union to ally, two editorials expressed anger at the maintaining of relations with Vichy but the unleashing of propaganda against Russia, blaming the isolationism in the United States and anti-Communism in Canada directly on the Catholic population and the institutional Church. Canada could be a great model for the world, especially the isolationist United States, as it had a 40-per-cent Catholic population, yet was still involved in world affairs. Instead, maintaining ties with a puppet of the Nazis and foolishly banning the Communist Party at the behest of the French Catholic population in Quebec had mired the nation in an embarrassing situation.⁹⁹

When trying to explain the apparent "situation" in Quebec to English Canadians, the *Globe* oversimplified matters and, yet again, was patronizing. Anti-Catholicism crept into even what appeared to be a positive report on the potential for a clergyman to wean Quebeckers off their support of Vichy. The *Globe* claimed that Capt. George d'Argenlieu was a successful spokesman for the Free French forces in Quebec because he was a Superior of the Carmelite Order. French Canadians needed this to dispel the facade, indeed the "halo," which Pétain, with his "mystic idealism" and "religious fervor," had gained in their eyes. English Canadians had to be patient with their French-Canadian brethren in this slow transition to enlightenment: French Canadians, due to the numerical dominance and "technical superiority or greater commercial aptitude" of Anglo-Saxons, had turned to a sentimental connection with their motherland, even in the face of collaborationism.¹⁰⁰ D'Argenlieu represented hope, in other words, that French Canadians could shake off the baggage of this inferiority complex and join the community of nations. Yet even this hope was portrayed as almost pathetic, necessary only for an ethno-religious group that was clearly not at the same level of development as Anglo-Protestants.

Many on the left also castigated Quebec's attitude toward Vichy, viewing it as simply another example of the fascist inclinations of the

Catholic province. In a pamphlet for the *America Looks Ahead* series, Frank Scott warned Americans that, with the advent of the Vichy government, and its corollary revival of Catholicism, French Canada had re-established long-atrophied sympathies for France. This affected America, due to the vast French-Canadian emigration there (mostly to New England) over the past several decades, which allowed for the expansion of Catholic influence over American policy. This Catholic bloc was believed to be a great supporter of the "Pan-American" policy of non-intervention in Europe, thus allowing the authoritarian powers to engage in war against the democratic world, and form closer relations to the "Latin and Catholic peoples to the south."[101] Forsey, for his part, wrote a letter to his mother describing a gregarious gathering at the Catholic students' club at Oxford (his hosts were a "Nice crowd; too nice for the Church!"), noting that the French-Canadian elite in Canada were very pro-Pétain *"under the usual guidance,"* clearly referring to the Catholic hierarchy.[102] In the same letter to his mother quoted at the beginning of this chapter, Forsey stated that the House should formally censure King for his crass opportunism in maintaining ties with Vichy solely to placate Quebec *nationalistes*, a group he should never have allowed a voice in the first place.[103]

In a pamphlet for the leftist FCSO entitled *Inside Quebec*, Helen C. Howes echoed McAree when she claimed that the Order of Jacques Cartier was the reason Canada had not closed the legation to Vichy France in Ottawa. Howes, an English-speaking Quebecker and former national secretary of the League for Social Reconstruction, presented the familiar portrait of a province where people were controlled and kept in ignorance by the clergy.[104] Fascists, like the Order, had taken advantage of the disenfranchisement of the average French Canadian, who, due to clericalism, was poorly educated, illiterate, and raised in families too large for the modern world. French Canadians were embracing corporatism and fascism because they were being told by their leaders that it was the only alternative to Bolshevism; in other words, it was the political ambitions of the clergy and the Church that explained why Hitler's fifth column in Canada was emanating from Quebec.[105]

Howes even questioned Cardinal Villeneuve's motives for explicitly supporting the war effort but not sufficiently opposing domestic fascism in French Canada. She believed that only three explanations sufficed, although she never stated which one she believed: 1) that

Villeneuve was himself sympathetic to a corporatist state; 2) that he feared the powers he was against, or 3) that he did not have much control over the bishops in his province. Yet she was optimistic, however, that the workers of Quebec were slowly realizing the exploitation and oppression they faced and, if encouraged by a government that refused to kowtow to the isolationist-clerical-fascist element of the province, the true Quebecker would even support overseas conscription.[106] This leftist sentiment both resembled and differentiated itself from liberal or conservative visions of French Canada. Certainly, the authoritarian Catholic Church was a major harbinger of fascism within Quebec, yet this was in addition to the exploitative capitalist system, which worked in tandem with the Church to keep the average French Canadian disenfranchised and ignorant.

The left was not monolithic in its opinions, however. When Scott dared to posit that the clear majority of French Canadians voted no in the 1942 plebiscite because they desired democracy at home and more influence in the nation's decision-making, he was savaged by Forsey in the pages of the *Canadian Forum*. Forsey was increasingly tying himself to conscriptionist-Tory circles, corresponding as he was with Meighen and hardline conscriptionist Toronto MP Herbert Bruce. He rejected the idea of Scott's article as a salve to the wounds between French and English Canada. Instead it would simply embolden the irresponsible *nationalistes*. He denied that French Canadians had been "left out" of Canadian history: Who ran the CBC? Were there not French-Canadian ministers in the government? Did English Canadians want continued relations with Vichy? Did English Canadians really want the plebiscite? French Canadians instead had as much democracy as – if not more than – English Canadians, as demonstrated by the existence of the Zombies, which Forsey saw as being mostly French Canadians.[107] Daniel Byers provides a nuanced analysis demonstrating that, while more Zombies were from Quebec than other provinces, the percentages were not dramatically divergent. Yet stereotypes emerged almost immediately that portrayed French Canadians as not "pulling their weight." In general, the Zombies reflected the population of Canada in racial, religious, and linguistic composition, while the armed forces themselves were not equipped to provide extensive French facilities or services. This caused feelings of isolation and further resentment among French troops that went beyond the periodic prejudice of a colleague or officer.[108] None of this mattered to those pushing for conscription. The argument was not about facts; it was about the "disloyal nature" of French-Canadian Catholics in Canada.

Indeed, Forsey told Meighen that opponents of conscription's implementation were distorting history by referring to alleged conflicts caused by conscription in the First World War, and were in fact perpetuating "anti-Britishness." He often mentioned conscription to Meighen, praising Jean-Charles Harvey's anticlerical *La Jour*, while attacking the French-Canadian "delusion" of isolationism as "crazy." Forsey also echoed George Drew when he stated that King was presiding over a crisis in national unity, not the preservation of it, condemning even Churchill for expressing his confidence in the Canadian prime minister. Conscription was a simple matter of a "barbarian war between nationalism and patriotic service," with French Canadians on the wrong side of history.[109] Forsey most vehemently denied any legitimacy to Catholic or French-Canadian grievances in a rejoinder to V. Soucisse's letter to *Saturday Night*. Soucisse's letter was a condemnation of English-Canadian hypocrisy, praising the liberation of minorities elsewhere but denying the rights of French Canadians at home. Soucisse, who was the nephew of the late Senator Laurent-Olivier David, drew attention to the lack of French-Canadian officers and military leaders, which made the armed forces less than attractive for French-speakers. He also concluded that, if Anglophones wanted a separation from their "shotgun marriage," French Canadians were happy to oblige.[110] In his response, Forsey demanded that Soucisse prove where persecution of Catholics had ever occurred in Canada. Some "hatred" may exist in English Canada, but Forsey denied that it was widespread, or more widespread and significant than hatred of Protestants within French Canada. For Forsey, these claims of persecution were simply a delusion of a sick mind, noting that English Canadians had never intervened in the French proclivity to fly the tricolour, "the special flag" (perhaps referring to the *fleur de lis*), or "the papal flag" and minimizing the historical examples Soucisse provided, such as the Manitoba Schools Crisis.[111] It was this type of total rejection of French-Canadian concerns that characterized, and polarized, so much of the pro-conscriptionist Anglo-Protestant opinion of the time, right or left.

Although this view of the Catholic Church and its special place in French Canada was present in parts of the progressive circles in Canada, these groups were for the most part quieter in their denunciations of the Church during the war. Many saw the international

Church as harbouring sympathies toward Italian fascism and being fanatically anti-Communist, but these same figures often also saw the Church as a dedicated enemy of Nazi "paganism." This fact, coupled with the vigorous efforts of the CCF leadership to gain support in Quebec, served to mute public criticism of the Church from left-wing circles during the war, unlike the case during the Depression.[112] In addition, public attacks on French Canada and Catholicism increasingly became the purview of the PC party, who embraced an aggressive Anglo-Protestant identity for themselves, an association many in the various leftist organizations would surely be quick to avoid if only for partisan reasons.

The fear of Catholic control of the Canadian government, whether from conservative, liberal, or progressive sources, was not limited to concerns over Vichy or the persecution of Jehovah's Witnesses and reached its apotheosis with the infamous claims of T.-D. Bouchard in his maiden speech to the Senate in June 1944. Bouchard represented for many the anti-clerical, business-oriented wing of the provincial Quebec Liberal party, dedicated to undermining the influence of the Church in Quebec society and opposing traditionalist nationalism.[113] He used a Senate discussion on implementing uniform history textbooks to launch into an anti-clerical diatribe. Bouchard positioned that Anglophone bogey, the Order of Jacques Cartier, as an insidious group dedicated solely to the revolutionary overthrow of liberalism and the founding of a corporative Catholic state in Canada, possibly even annexing some of Ontario due to its insatiable hunger for power and land. His speech contained numerous references to the medieval nature of the Catholic Church in Quebec, its static ultramontane proclivities, and *Castor* (ultraconservative Catholic) political ideology. Bouchard believed that the Catholic Church and its associated, often secret, organizations, which included Duplessis' Union Nationale, were determined to cause Quebec to regress into "the social and economic status of the Middle Ages," wrecking the multinational, modern, and liberal nation of Canada, which was formed through conciliation and Confederation. These enemies of liberalism exploited the emotional French-Canadian attachment to their language to promote this vicious, narrow, European form of clerical nationalism. Bouchard believed that the future of Canada itself as a united, modern nation was at stake. The solution, in his mind, was to expose French Canadians more to English Canada to easily prove that Anglophones were not the callous architects of French-Catholic disenfranchisement.[114] In an article summarizing his views for *Maclean's*, Bouchard counselled English Canadians that most of French Canadians and most Catholics did not agree with this plot to control the country. The majority simply wanted to live in harmony with their neighbours. Bouchard warned good, moderate English Canadians that an aggressive and influential Catholic minority did exist, however, and explicitly desired the founding of a state resembling Portugal, Ireland, and Spain in Canada.[115]

Bouchard's charges reverberated throughout Canada, eliciting a diversity of responses from Anglo-Protestants often united by a single underlying theme: Bouchard was an insider, representative of an idealized "good French Canadian," valiantly attempting to warn Canadians about the real dangers within Quebec.[116] McAree dubbed Bouchard the contemporary Laurier for standing up to the dictates of the reactionary clergy and protecting the core principles of liberalism from within his own people. McAree ominously added that recent events in Canada proved that Laurier's earlier victory over the forces of reaction was only a "skirmish," as the overarching battle against clerical dominance had continued for decades.[117] When Bouchard was fired from his recently appointed post of president of Hydro-Québec by order-in-council, due to his inflammatory statements, the controversy was exacerbated. The *Globe and Mail* portrayed Bouchard's silencing as the initial steps toward fascism, which Canadians needed to take seriously as there were "French" and "clerical" schools throughout the nation, unhesitatingly linking the rise of fascism with Catholic schools. The *Orangeville Banner* provided the most explicitly anti-Catholic commentary. It noted that English Canada had "borne with the ill-considered attempts of the French Roman Catholic Church to make canon law superior to the civil law," adding that, unless Quebec stemmed the spread of this organization, English Canada would halt its tolerance of French-Canadian disloyalty in the war effort, although the author left vague what actions English Canadians would take.[118]

Corolyn Cox, the chairwoman of the Canadian Women's Committee on International Affairs, added her perspective in an article for *Saturday Night*. Cox was a major figure in the war-support activities of coalescing American and Canadian womens' groups, and saw in the clericalism of Quebec a barrier to a full-fledged war effort. In her passionate defence of Bouchard, she repeated the idea that he was a "good Catholic," again directly comparing him to Laurier, as he was a staunchly religious man but opposed to "pomp, supernatural manifestation or assumption of infallibility in temporal matters, wherever he has found it among the clerics of his Province." Bouchard was a "true Quebecker," who saw his nation as the whole of Canada. He was simply trying to "unclog" the dust from within his province for it to progress with the rest of the world, fighting the "Corporative State" of Catholic Quebec ever since his entry into public life in the early-twentieth century. Cox repeated Bouchard's conspiracism as well, claiming that the "Jacques Cartier Society of Quebec" was only a local manifestation of a global movement, what she dubbed "Christus Rex," dedicated to the resumption of clerical authority over temporal affairs, undoubtedly emanating from the Vatican. Canadians should look to Bouchard's message as a warning against this movement and as a voice of "broad Catholicism" that was increasingly entering South America, Mexico, the United States, "and in Rome."[119] It was only this broad version of Catholicism that could be trusted to fully support Canada's war effort.

Bouchard's charges seemed to play into Duplessis's hands. Dumas details how the dominant narrative that the Godbout government (1939–44) was an enlightened interregnum between the clerical authoritarianism of Duplessis's two periods in power is quite false. In fact, this was the very narrative that Duplessis himself manufactured, particularly after Bouchard's speech. He could paint himself as the defender of Catholic tradition and the Liberals as radical anticlericals, even if his previous government had been unevenly supported by the clergy and even though Godbout himself had relatively cordial relations with Villeneuve, especially over the war effort. Bouchard obfuscated these realities, as the passions of a country at war and divided between French and English continued to rise. Duplessis's re-election was thus interpreted as the culmination of Bouchard's fears of a clerical government, not the result of other political currents and concerns (for example, increased centralization under the Godbout and King governments).[120] Nuance and mutual understanding did not fit the narrative.

Throughout many of the discussions of Roman Catholic Quebec there is a clear theme: this is a problem in need of fixing. The solutions varied from person to person, but overall, improvement through "liberalization," industrialization, and/or "de-Catholicization" could perhaps lead to an idealized Quebec, and even Canada. Shields wanted the eradication of Catholicism from the nation, perhaps even the world; Silcox eventually advocated for the separation of Quebec to dampen the power of the Church over Canada. Others, like Scott and Forsey, saw a province with great potential, but also one that reactionary forces could easily overrun if Canadians were not vigilant. The war magnified these issues, and the introduction of family allowances in 1944 only worsened the situation, dredging up older concerns of *revanche des berceaux*.

The introduction of family allowances in Canada exacerbated fears of Catholic political dominance in the years 1944–45, intersecting with the ongoing conscription crisis. Scholars, such as Raymond Blake and Nancy Christie, note that the granting of allowances to families on a universal basis represented a major component of the desire of the Liberal government to restabilize the nuclear, male-breadwinner family structure, as well as a political outmanoeuvring of the left by the Liberals. While much of the hostility toward family allowances revolved around concerns of federal overreach, scholars have also noted a significant discourse denouncing family allowances due to its alleged support of large Catholic families, even though it incorporated a sliding scale of rates after the fourth child.[121]

Dr Herbert A. Bruce, Tory MP for Parkdale and former lieutenant-governor of Ontario, for example, adamantly opposed the plan, posing as its staunchest enemy in the House. In a speech in the House, Bruce agreed with PC leader John Bracken that it was a crass political bribe to Quebec caused by the upcoming provincial election, as it would benefit Quebec more than other provinces, due to the tendency of Catholic Quebeckers to have larger families.[122] Bruce had written to Drew, a friend, days before the speech, since he knew Drew felt similarly about family allowances. Bruce noted that he would speak against this legislation, as it was a foolish means of supporting children and would force the taxpayers of Ontario to "support [the] large families in Quebec."[123] During his speech, Bruce went much further, however, basing his opposition firmly in the context of his support for eugenics.[124] Bruce stated, "If we are to encourage large families, I think care should be taken that they are eugenically of the kind that will be most likely to improve our race. He added that "I believe it that it is a fact" that most of the families with more than ten children were Quebec families, especially compared to that of British Columbia, again posited as the model non-Catholic province, where families were manageable. Bruce even compared King's policies to those of the Nazis, who created a system in which it was more profitable to have children than to go to work. Bruce added the refusal of French Canadians to support the war effort adequately to his rejection of family allowances, claiming that "This bill will result in bonusing [sic] families who have been unwilling to defend their country." These issues, conscription and the "revenge of the cradles," constantly intersected during wartime and were fuelled by the ever-present fears of Catholic numerical dominance and the challenging of Catholic loyalty to the nation and the war effort. Nevertheless, the House voted unanimously to pass the family allowances bill, as Bruce (and many others) was absent during the vote; he had been suspended from the House for replying to King that the bill was "a bribe of the most brazen character."[125] Despite this overwhelming result in favour of the legislation, and the refusal of the Tories in the House to oppose the act, the Tory press portrayed Bruce as a manly hero, standing up for his principles and not bowing to political expediency. These opinions implicitly accepted Bruce's eugenically tinged speech, castigating Quebec's role in the nation and perpetuating an effeminate, corrupt Liberal elite.[126]

In addition, Bruce received several letters of support, which he copied and sent to George Drew, who had been elected premier of Ontario almost one year earlier. There was ubiquitous agreement that family allowances were a bribe for Quebec in these letters. One A.L. Bailey was even more explicitly anti-Catholic and anti-French than Bruce, referring to Quebec as the "fascist province." This was a familiar attack, but Bailey added that the true enemy of the British Empire was the Vatican: "I really believe this is so and the world picture of fascist nations being largely R.C. ... supports this idea." He advocated for Bruce to continue in his stand, keeping Canada "as English and free as possible." Historian Edwin C. Guillet agreed, praising Bruce for maintaining his opinion despite his party's cowardice and for clearly supporting Senator Bouchard's revelations. Guillet ended his letter by comparing the current situation, including Bouchard's charges that there was a clerical separatist conspiracy in Quebec, to the Red River Rebellion of 1870, and warning of the consequences.[127] Without doubt, for at least these conservative Canadians, family allowances represented the worst of the King government: corrupt, crass, and depending on the support of a clerical province that refused to fight for a democracy it did not truly believe in.

Bruce was admittedly a hardline opponent of the King Liberals: he had called for King's resignation in 1940 in favour of minister of national defence and pro-conscriptionist James Ralston. But he was also a paragon of respectability, particularly in Ontario, as a former surgeon, military man, and lieutenant-governor. He was undeniably dedicated to the prosecution of a successful war effort: the creation of a National Government and a total war effort were the only reasons that he even stood for election that year, according to his autobiography. His opinions were not those of a fringe extremist. He believed for the rest of his life that this call for King's resignation was the real reason that he was suspended from the House. In his autobiography, *Varied Operations*, which was released in 1958 and in which he thanked his "good friend" Silcox in his acknowledgments, Bruce maintained not only his dedication to sterilization but his belief that King had sacrificed the nation at the altar of a false national unity and selfishness during the war. Bruce counselled good Canadians to ignore those who warned against returning to these matters for fear of sparking another unity crisis. Canadians instead must never be allowed to forget the conscription crisis nor the fracture over family allowances, as they revealed the true nature of the Liberal Party and of King: beholden to an isolationist French Canada.[128]

Drew continued Bruce's condemnations of family allowances, filling the role that House Tories were either unable or unwilling to play due to the acceptance of social security by some and the desire of party luminaries not to appear as the old, reactionary, imperialist Tory party.[129] At a PC rally in Richmond Hill, Drew repeated Bruce and Bracken's charge that the family-allowances bill was a political bribe to Quebec.[130] He ominously added that it was simply one component in the overarching plan of the King Liberals to dissolve the British connection, inevitably resulting in the predominance of Quebec over English Canada, which was footing the majority of the cost of the bill.[131] For Drew, the British connection was the guarantor of democracy; this British form of democracy was inextricably religious, or Protestant, as it was the "age-long attempt of British people to interpret in temporal law applicable to our daily life the ethical standards of Christianity."[132] This concept of democracy was under threat by the purposeful creation of a French-Catholic majority within Canada.

Drew boldly broadcast his views on 9 August 1944 in a controversial address entitled "Where Ontario Stands," in which Conservative ideological opposition to federal intrusion into the provinces dovetailed with Drew's caricatured portrait of French Canada and his promotion of conscription. Drew prefaced his discussion by positioning himself and his province behind the ideal of family allowances, but he made clear that he resented the fact that the federal government passed the legislation with no consultation with the provinces, solely for the political benefits it would accrue in Quebec.[133] Drew dubbed this policy, and the silence that had accompanied it from most of the nation, appeasement, warning that Canada would pay for this policy "just as the people of the world are paying the penalty of appeasement in the international field." It would result in a nation based on the violation of mutual obligation and equality of advantage.[134] Drew famously asked his audience, in a question that would hurt his career in French Canada and nationally,[135] "Are we going to permit one isolationist province to dominate the destiny of a divided Canada?" For Drew the answer was simple and obvious: eliminate any sense of special privilege for Quebec and stop the implementation of family allowances to save national unity. The vision of the Fathers of Confederation would never be realized, in Drew's opinion, if this "arrogant usurpation of power" was carried out unabated. Echoing Bruce, Drew questioned the loyalty of Francophones, denying them any privileges, since they "denie[d] an equal share of the obligation to protect their country in its hour of peril."[136]

Drew received support from correspondents who saw in family allowances yet another threat to the integrity of the nation from the French Catholic Church. "Standing up for Fair Play" sent him a poem entitled "Family Allowance," which opened with the stanza "Oh its [sic] great to be French/and to be so prolific/The money we'll make/Will be *something* terrific." The poem closed with a verse rebuking the French Canadian for his sloth and fecundity: "We won't have to work/What a heavenly life!/Its so easy on us/If hard on my wife."[137] Birth-control activist A.R. Kaufman congratulated Drew for standing up against the "Quebec Parasites" who were benefiting from the sacrifice and taxation of the rest of the nation. He asked, like Silcox, whether forced secession from the Dominion might not solve the "Quebec problem."[138] Some were much more openly anti-Catholic in their viewpoints. Colin S. Macdonald epitomized this when he praised Drew because Canadians had to prevent Quebec from controlling the nation, adding, "when we say Quebec, we say 'The Roman Catholic Church.'"[139] One particularly venomous correspondent cited experience with French Canada. G. Scott of Montreal believed that the design of the legislation was to drain Canada of millions of tax dollars for "the super-breeders in this Province ... who are still living in the 'Dark Ages.'" The ignorant French Catholic and the hierarchy cared nothing for the Allied war effort, according to Scott, but instead only wanted the perpetuation of their race and the inevitable creation of a fascist province in Quebec.[140]

What makes the reaction to Drew's speech revealing is that those supporting Drew were not limited to those with "vulgar" conspiracy theories, easily dismissed as marginal bigots. The former mayor of Galt, Ontario, sent him congratulations,[141] as did the federal PC candidate for Huron-Perth.[142] The publisher of the *Banff Crag and Canyon* thanked Drew for his statements, as did Gladstone Murray,[143] while a representative of the Toronto Weekly News organization believed Drew had opened up a discussion that could prevent civil war in Canada.[144] The Conservative *Ottawa Journal* supported Drew's charges, noting that the average number of children per French Canadian family was 4.23, while the average in English Canada was a dismal 2.86, citing no sources. This editorial in fact countered statistics Drew had in his own files that stated French families averaged 2.85 children, while English averaged 1.66.[145] The Orange Order, unsurprisingly, expressed similar sentiments at a large meeting at High Park, days before Drew broadcast his speech but after Bruce made his stand in the House, adding that one-tenth of the "baby bonus" would go directly into the coffers of the Catholic hierarchy, acting as a form of government-sponsored tithe.[146] Significantly, Tory MP and former mayor of Toronto T.L. Church was present at the meeting, exploiting his audience's temperament by discussing apparently related issues: calling for immediate conscription and denouncing St Laurent for violating the traditions of the Magna Carta through the DCR. Church, in language that was rife with symbolism at an Orange meeting regarding a French Catholic minister, concluded that, under St Laurent and Liberal policies, "we are approaching ... authoritarian State tyranny."[147]

The controversy surrounding the speech forced Drew into damage control. He claimed that he had always supported family allowances and denied that he was an old, imperialist, Tory bigot. Yet even in his denials and attempts to deflect the issue into one solely about provincial jurisdiction, he never wavered on his condemnation of Quebec's war effort, maintaining that he refused to funnel millions of Ontario tax dollars to the "benefit of a Province whose Legislature representatives had gone on record opposing the effective use of military reinforcements. That was the simple and fundamental issue."[148] Drew was determined in his construction of a simplistic binary in which Canada was either to be Quebec-dominated or fervently loyal to the British connection. He expressed this to friend and fellow Anglophile Hugh Farthing in an August 1944 letter denying the benefits of a "Quebec-dominated country": "I would much rather see my children grow up as citizens of the United States than to be citizens of a Canada which was reduced to the low ethical and moral standard of the people of Quebec." This was a striking admission from a man so firmly attached to the British connection. It was this very connection he saw at threat from the "isolationists" in French Canada, and if the King government continued to "appease" them, any chance at unity in not only the war effort but in the nation in general would be undermined. In this environment, with one segment of the nation fully behind the British ideal of full service and the other segment embracing "anti-British" notions, Drew envisioned a decline into "civil war."[149] The ruling Liberals, according to this world view, were an effete dictatorship controlled by Quebec and the spoiled Catholic *nationalistes* that resided within. In the face of the "low ethical ... standard" of Quebec, segments of the party thus became *more* anti-French and anti-Catholic during the war, particularly in its latter stages. This was despite the earlier efforts of some within the party to shed this image, efforts embodied in the selection of the Catholic Manion as leader in 1938.[150]

The most explicitly anti-Catholic opposition to family allowances came from the increasingly conservative Silcox (he was in contact with Drew and Bruce), however, who released a pamphlet for Ryerson Press's *Canada Must Choose* series, fittingly entitled *The Revenge of the Cradles*. Silcox was alarmist in tone, repeating the familiar charge that it was a bribe for the large families of Quebec, but also that the bill was "the most precipitate and indefensible piece of legislation which a civilized government has ever ventured to pass in wartime."[151] Silcox saw family allowances as more than just the poorly planned result of the unchecked growth of the technocratic state.[152] It was part of a plot: The Catholic hierarchy for decades specifically forbade birth control of any form. Coupled with the constant pressure from Catholic Quebec to stem any immigration from Britain, the plan was to ensure French dominance in Canada as early as 1961. In a particularly vulgar phrase, Silcox savaged French Canadians for expecting benefits when they were unwilling to share in the equal burdens of wartime: "they breed while we bleed."[153] Even with great effort, modern industrialism had failed to undermine the desire of the Catholic Church to perpetuate large families and, paraphrasing Senator Bouchard approvingly, a system of "medieval fascism."[154] The hierarchy demanded, through their political influence, that the federal government subsidize large families at the expense of small Protestant ones, thus ensuring that "morons shall inherit the earth" and paving the path for a French, Roman Catholic Canada.[155]

Silcox was proud of this pamphlet, along with Charlotte Whitton's companion pamphlet, *Baby Bonuses: Dollars or Sense?* released at roughly the same time and attacking family allowances with equal vehemence. Due to the almost simultaneous release of their pamphlets for Ryerson Press, the public linked Charlotte Whitton to Silcox, which her biographers believe displaced her forever from the mainstream of social-policy thinking.[156] Yet Whitton had long been one of the most vocal opponents of federal social security, who had been compelled to write a study denouncing the Liberal plan by Tory leader Bracken in 1943, often basing her opposition on a conservative (and Conservative, as she was a partisan Tory) antipathy to the bureaucratic state usurping the responsibility of the individual citizen.[157] In *Baby Bonuses: Dollars or Sense?* Whitton shared Silcox's anger, portraying family allowances as destroying the notions of "intelligent maternity, responsible paternity and wholesome family life in this Dominion."[158] Perhaps more importantly, it would also subsidize the "mentally deficient," creating a "moronic" population prone to fascist manipulation. She agreed as well that the act was a bribe designed to placate the political demands of Quebec, placing the blame specifically at the feet of the French Catholic minister of justice, St Laurent, who by this time symbolized for so many Anglo-Protestants the epitome of French Catholic power.[159]

Whitton was a bit subtler about her discussion of Catholicism, writing that most "New Canadians" had proved their loyalty to Canada during the two world wars, except those of "particular religious attitudes" and French Canada, equating French Catholics with either ethnic pacifist groups or simply their non-French co-religionists. These groups had benefited however from the sacrifices that good, brave Canadians had made who had fought in these wars, and they were continuing to benefit from their cowardice. In fact, French Catholics had swamped Ontario and New Brunswick in the interwar years due to the expansion of the French population and the collapse of the Anglo-Protestant population caused by war. Whitton's anxiety thus not only revolved around the nascent totalitarianism she saw in legislation being "forced" upon the citizenry, but in the creation of a docile population composed of the lowest classes.[160] Whitton essentially claimed in *Baby Bonuses* that French Canada had opposed the war effort (both now and in the First World War) to benefit from the deaths of thousands of true Canadians by breeding and gaining employment. Family allowances were simply the culmination, literally rewarding them for birthing an inferior, disloyal population.

Whitton presented Catholic French Canada as being outside not only the nation but also the Empire, undeserving of any aid, benefit, or sympathy.[161] Her work was conspiratorial, drawing attention to pro-family-allowance statements by Quebec officials in 1943, when the province passed the Quebec Collective Agreement Act. For Whitton, this was the basis of the current act being debated: it was thought out in Quebec and prescribed for the rest of the nation by a King government both vacillating and bordering on totalitarianism. Family allowances, as constructed by its Quebec masters, not only flew in the face of sound policy and democracy, but rejected the British traditions of careful statesmanship and fair play. According to Whitton, if this policy had any genealogy in the world, it belonged to Central and Southern Europe, not to the Anglo-Saxon nations. Near the end of her discussion, Whitton made the link between these various strains of thought clear to all readers:

> However, the family allowances measure is so designed ... as to effect the reallocation of revenue predominantly from the people of those areas within each of the provinces whose social philosophies and attitudes plan family responsibility to fit within anticipated income limits while the overwhelming number of recipients will be those who hold contrary views. Moreover, in frank facing of the facts most of the latter are opposed to the former, also in their fundamental attitudes towards the purpose, direction, and primary allegiance of the Canadian state and the correlative obligations of its development, defence, inter-Empire and international relations.[162]

Whitton, again, was subtler in her language, but this paragraph was immediately preceded by a discussion of the higher living standards of small Anglo-Protestant families compared to the fecund realities of rural Quebec, "where the mode and standard of life is of the Province's own preference." All of this, for Whitton, was leading down the road to a crisis in national unity and the possible collapse of democracy in the nation.[163]

For the third pamphlet in this series, Ryerson employed Margaret Gould, the executive secretary of the Child Welfare Council of Toronto and a colleague of Whitton's fierce rival, Harry Cassidy, director of the University of Toronto School of Social Science. Gould defended family allowances as allowing children to finally truly share in the surplus of Canada, and attacked those, like Whitton, who saw in the legislation a strain on national unity and the funding of excessive breeding of deficient people. Gould openly refuted the anti-Catholicism and Francophobia of these figures, believing that the ingrained prejudices of some prominent English Canadians was what was truly hurting national unity.[164] Cassidy was quoted by family-allowance advocate and author Dorothy Stepler in another defence of family allowances, this time for the Canadian Institute of International Affairs. While defending allowances, she condemned those who opposed the plan on the basis that money "will go to half-starved Quebec babies." These people were, in their obstinacy, "at the same time keeping the food from the mouths of other Canadian children."[165] Whitton was furious, denying that any of Gould's or Cassidy's criticisms were legitimate and instead seeing in them only ad hominem attacks based in long-standing personal grudges.[166]

Drew was nevertheless forceful on the same points as Whitton, denigrating the King government as a dictatorship hiding behind platitudes of national unity to placate those "elements" in Canada unwilling to sacrifice themselves for the nation.[167] In a remarkable letter to a lawyer friend, William O. Langdon, reacting to King's recently announced plebiscite in 1942, Drew expressed his utter distaste with the vacillating politics of the Liberals. Drew believed that the time had come for a "showdown" between those who believed in an open partnership with the British Empire and those who clearly did not. Drew framed the French-Canadian refusal to enlist in the war effort in the wider context of a totalitarian government appeasing a callous group that hoped to benefit from the war: "I do not think the anti-conscription in Quebec is anything more than a symptom of a much more deeply rooted disease. I have no doubt whatever that with a few exceptions they are strongly anti-British and propose to follow a course which will result in an actual voting majority in Canada within a comparatively few years."[168] Drew was thus convinced that French-Canadian Catholics were engaged in a purposeful plan to take control of the nation through either refusing to enlist, by influencing the government, and/or, with regard to family allowances, by increasing their numbers naturally. When Langdon responded to Drew, he was more explicitly anti-Catholic. He counselled that the most effective way to promote real national unity was the abolition of separate schools, as this institution was a hindrance to the achievement of a homogeneous population loyal to Canada and the British Empire. Langdon was suspicious that famed Catholic philosopher Jacques Maritain, "The chief publicity officer of the Catholics in the Western World," had been in Toronto for a long period. This fact, along with stories of French-Catholic desertion in the army, the boisterous rhetoric of French-Canadian nationalists in the House, and the continued presence of the ambassador from Vichy France in Ottawa caused Langdon to suspect fifth-column activities among the French-Catholic population in Canada.[169]

The PC party tried to take advantage of this type of sentiment throughout the war, no matter where in society it was located. French Canada and the authoritarian, medieval Church that was presumed to be supreme were disloyal, and "true" Canadians had to guard against its incursions, even though some Catholic leaders were viewed as so pro-war they were being denigrated as pawns of "les Anglais" by *nationaliste* segments of French-Canadian society. Villeneuve, for example, was forced to redraft a letter he read publicly supporting the war effort in June 1942 (after the plebiscite), because the clergy found it too pro-war. Others saw him as supporting the "blissful submission" of the French-Canadian people. The periodic anti-imperialist diatribes of MPs, MLAs, public figures, or clergymen, or even simple opposition to conscription, were seized upon as evidence of the "spoiled child" that was Quebec, prone to emotionalism and perhaps fascist sympathies.[170]

A perfect example of the Tories' embrace of conscription and the subtle (or sometimes not so subtle) interconnection of anti-Catholic and anti-French-Canadian themes was an important by-election held in North Grey, Ontario, in February 1945. In late 1944, another conscription crisis was sparked when Ralston returned from Europe and told King that the Zombies had to be sent overseas immediately, dividing King's cabinet. King still believed that conscription would destroy national unity. He forced Ralston's resignation and brought in General Andrew McNaughton, who still believed in voluntary service. King, for his part, believed that Ralston and the generals had betrayed him and were even plotting to remove him in a coup, and he used this essentially as justification for his one-time concession of releasing sixteen thousand NRMA men for overseas service. This move placated the pro-conscriptionists in his cabinet and was moderate enough to maintain much of the Liberal support in Quebec, although Quebec cabinet minister Chubby Power did resign in protest.[171] Amid all this, McNaughton needed a seat in the House. Some commentators referred to this by-election as historic, signalling a possible sea change in Canada's manpower policy.[172] King and the Liberals ran a strange campaign, relying on the desire of the electors in this rural Orange riding to agree with them that the sole issue in the by-election was that McNaughton needed a seat to prosecute the war effort.[173] The Tories, however, wanted to ensure that the by-election was about conscription; they focused their energies on lambasting the Liberals for their controversial policy, constantly appealing to anti-French and anti-Catholic themes. *Saturday Night* and even *Time* magazine noted this fact in January 1945, causing a simple by-election to become a barometer of English Canada's opinion on King's manpower policy.[174]

The Tory candidate, mayor of Owen Sound, Garfield Case, told a crowd in Oxenden that King was asking the "most British riding in Canada" to cover for his mistakes. He added that while the residents of North Grey were "under the British flag" they would not allow the Liberals to dictate their beliefs: "A vote for me ... is a vote for the boy in the front line – a boy who comes from North Grey."[175] Case exploited his insider status in the riding, portraying McNaughton as a villainous anti-British outsider promulgating an alien policy of manpower recruitment amicable only to Quebec. This was an insult to North Grey, as Quebec was "lacking in courage, loyalty and resolve, a community which has deteriorated till we find them paying tribute to those who would hamper the war effort," as he told an audience in Shallow Lake. One John Diefenbaker, an up-and-coming Tory MP, reiterated Case's anti-French sentiment when he rhetorically asked an audience in Meaford what province deserters or those refusing to go overseas were from, concluding that the electors of this constituency needed to vote against McNaughton and Quebec.[176] John Bracken himself came to the riding and made claims about Zombies throwing their rifles overboard to protest serving overseas in order to pillory McNaughton's manpower policy, claims later found to be specious.[177] Bracken repeated the Tory line of "equality of service," a phrase historian J.L. Granatstein believes had been discredited by Borden's government, thus "dipping into the same barrel of vituperation as that of men such as Rev. Shields."[178] When Bracken was in Britain in late 1944 and early 1945, former Conservative PM R.B. Bennett told him to "Make the keynote of campaign British connection," as the "reputation of Ontario" was at stake.[179] This is exactly what Bracken and the Tories did throughout the by-election, painting Liberal policies as borderline traitorous and certainly "un-British."

T.T. Shields, unsurprisingly, expressed anti-Catholic sentiment most viciously when he travelled to the riding. Shields attacked McNaughton personally in a speech he delivered under the auspices of the CPL at the Owen Sound City Hall, drawing attention to the fact that McNaughton had a Catholic wife and claiming that the Catholic Church often exercised its sinister influence through women. Shields linked this marital fact directly to McNaughton's support of the voluntary manpower policy. It would allow Catholics to stay in Canada, breed, and force good Protestant Canadians to go overseas and die for the cause of democracy.[180] For Shields, very simply, "a vote for McNaughton is a vote for the Roman Catholic hierarchy and for the further enslavement of Canada."[181] Shields's incendiary speech garnered much opposition, both within the riding and from outside of it, most sensationally from Alderman Joseph Matte of the Quebec City Council, who called for Shields's internment (once again).[182] Privately, King confided to his diary that Shields's statements were "cruel" and reflected the "unpatriotic" machinations of the Tories to inflame racial and religious hatred. By 5 February 1945, the day of the election, even King had become convinced that the combination of Tory patronage, corruption, and anti-Catholicism was a serious challenge to McNaughton's success.[183]

Many commentators, then and now, have concluded that religious prejudice was central to Case's victory, and that Shields represented only the extreme wing of pre-existing Protestant opinion.[184] Wilfrid Eggleston, journalist and former chief censor for the government, believed that McNaughton's Catholic wife was central to Case's victory in a staunchly Protestant riding, despite this being a "deplorable factor ... in a country like Canada, but nobody denies [it is] often influential."[185] Journalist John Marshall characterized North Grey as a "typically Old Ontario" area, intensely Protestant and fervently devoted to the British connection.[186] What is important here is the assumption by many authors that an important government minister with a Catholic wife, running in a Protestant Ontario riding, was doomed. McNaughton himself was convinced that his wife's religion decided the election, perhaps ignoring the additional factor of poor Liberal organization.[187] Whatever the overall cause of the Tory victory, anti-Catholicism along with its corollary during wartime, anti-French-Canadian sentiment, was a major factor. Catholics were perceived by many in Canada as disloyal to the full prosecution of the war effort, and the King government was understood to be hopelessly beholden to this "bloc." Indeed, when the by-election was over, and preparations for the upcoming federal election began, King noted in his diary that North Grey had proven to him that the campaign would revolve largely around "my friendship with Quebec and attacks on the Catholic influence."[188]

King and the Liberals would win the 1945 election, campaigning on an optimistic platform of reconstruction, social services, a cautious approach to conscription, and victory over totalitarianism.[189] Herbert Bruce wrote Forsey that the Liberal victory ratified King's dictatorship, which relied almost solely on the dictates of Quebec.[190] Yet it quickly became apparent that a new, powerful totalitarian threat loomed over the horizon, one perhaps even more threatening than Nazi Germany: the USSR. In the Cold War world that followed the Second World War, virulent tensions between political, ideological, and religious groups flared up once again. Resentment toward French Quebec's alleged denigration of the war effort would linger for decades, heavily influencing postwar attitudes toward French Canadians and Catholicism. It also influenced the maintenance within the PC party of a fervent Britishness, embodied in the representation of Canada as a Protestant nation. Drew's selection as the leader of the federal party in 1948 signalled the party's postwar identification as the defender of the Canadian Protestant tradition for some years.

In the Cold War, however, the almost exclusive focus on French-Canadian Catholicism declined, replaced by a wider concern with the role of the authoritarian Catholic Church in a world now polarized between two superpowers. Catholic loyalty was still suspect, as were the totalitarian inclinations of the religion, as English Canadians strove to reconstruct Canada as a modern nation firmly on the side of democracy.

4

What It Means to Be (Truly) Canadian: Cold War Anti-Catholicism and the Transformation of Britishness in Canada, 1945–1965

> It was not to be the privilege of the Roman Catholic Church to show the modern world the way to liberty ... [as the] spirit of Roman Catholicism must be authoritarian.[1]
>
> Arthur Lower (1954)

In a letter dated 14 June 1956 to Jack Pickersgill, minister of citizenship and immigration and an old colleague, Arthur Lower outlined what he thought of French-Canadian nationalist historians. "[Guy] Frégault, etc., are members of that restless intellectual proletariat to be found in all Catholic countries, and most Asiatic, who feel defeated and would like to remake the world closer to their heart's desire," he wrote, adding that "They are not far off from Mussolini and indeed Hitler." The nationalism of these figures was too narrow, not based on the higher principles of freedom and tolerance Lower so cherished, as "Freedom and tolerance, unfortunately, are not prominent articles of Catholic practice."[2] His anti-Catholicism was also tinged with specifically Cold War rhetoric, demonstrating the connections he made between the Catholic Church, French Canada, and the new totalitarian threat, the Soviet Union. Angry at the recent barring by Pickersgill's department of known Communist musician Paul Robeson from entering Canada, Lower continued, "It is no mere coincidence that Communism has not flourished in Protestant countries and that [Joseph] McCarthy is a Catholic. I could almost surmise ... that some such influence has been at work in the Department of Immigration.

I trust not."³ Present here is the old bogey of the Church controlling the immigration process, deciding in a secretive fashion who could enter Canada and who was excluded (in this case the very real prohibition of Communists). The Catholic Church's fervent anti-Communism, according to Lower, violated the principles of liberal democracy that he upheld, much like Soviet Communism. The Church's authoritarian nature in fact paved the way for the emergence of other forms of authoritarianism, creating the paradoxical situation of the alleged great enemy of international Communism, the Vatican, instead facilitating Communism's spread.

For intellectuals like Lower, who identified themselves as progressive and liberal, the Catholic Church in Canada was an anachronism; yet this was not simply the old imperialist, "Orange Ontario" English-Canadian nationalism that criticized French Canada and Roman Catholicism at every turn. Lower caustically attacked George Drew for these very reasons.⁴ Instead, the intellectual trajectory of liberal nationalists such as Lower represents the continued prominence but flexibility of anti-Catholicism as an organizing mental framework and cultural reference point. This included intellectuals, politicians, social activists, and Protestant cultural leaders from across the political and religious spectrum who sought to delineate their vision for Canada in the modern world and to construct a new English-Canadian national identity.⁵ Unlike the case in wartime, however, anti-Catholicism was not only devoted to criticism of a specific ethnic or linguistic group. Anti-Catholicism in the Cold War became "universalized," as it was partially – and slowly – detached from this past ethno-linguistic-racial framework and characterized by the comparison of Catholicism and the institutional Catholic Church (particularly the Vatican) with the various Communist regimes in Europe, due to its totalitarian, and thus alien, nature in a democratic country.

As is subtly present even here in Lower's letter, the Anglo-Protestant ethno-religiosity of anti-Catholicism did not totally disappear, however. Lower lays at the feet of the Church not only a distorting influence on the immigration department but the reason for French Canadian dogmatism and/or potential fascism. It became less publicly respectable to overtly attack the race-ethnicity-religion of immigrants or French Canadians particularly by the 1960s. Yet a residue of ethnocentric anti-Catholicism *did* remain in the postwar period because of 1) the deeply intertwined and mutually constitutive nature of race, ethnicity, and religion in the Otherness of Catholics in the

Anglo-Protestant world view, and 2) the increase in the number of immigrants from Catholic countries, especially from Eastern, Central, and Southern Europe (see Table 4.1). In other words, ethnocentric anti-Catholicism became increasingly coded in the language of "universal" values, such as self-reliance and individualism, but Britishness was still at the core of these definitions. Several Anglo-Protestants detailed here saw Catholic immigration from Europe as evidence of a changing country and, for some, a continuation of the old Church plot to take over the nation itself. As immigration changed with the relative decline of immigration from continental European Catholic nations and the rise of non-white and/or non-Christian immigration from Southeast Asia, Africa, and the Caribbean (see Table 4.2), so too did the discourse and the universalization and solidification of these values. In addition, as Gauvreau and Christie note, the early postwar decades saw the gradual and uneven dechristianization of segments of Canadian society amidst postwar affluence and the widespread embrace of personal choice and individualism.[6] Ironically, perhaps, these were the very values that many Anglo-Protestants saw as their sole jurisdiction, and thus helped ensure that anti-Catholicism remained a means of explanation in the Cold War world, even if the role of public sectarian Protestantism shifted in the public's mind. The early Cold War was thus a transitional period, which saw older anxieties about Catholic foreignness and demographic dominance intermingle with fears of potential Catholic totalitarianism and/or illiberalism.

This vision rested upon a familiar definition of the Catholic Church as trapped in a stagnant medievalism. Yet, to critics, Catholicism was not solely a medieval delusion. It was also a threatening form of counter-modernity or, along with Soviet Communism, a rival/alternative form of modernity. In Cold War Canada, the Catholic Church represented a highly organized, systematic, and authoritarian alternative to liberal democracy, the latter held as synonymous with Protestantism. This rival-(counter) modernity was especially harmful when paired with the concern that Protestantism was declining in influence. The causes of this decline ranged beyond an increase in material comforts, to the growth of the state and a general complacency among the population. This furthered the anxieties of Silcox and Lower, for example, about what the world (and Canada) would look like without the traditions Protestantism represented. In addition, the Catholic Church itself seemed to have shifted, increasingly

Table 4.1
Immigration from predominantly Catholic and/or Communist continental Europe

Year	Austria and Hungary	Czechoslovakia	Italy	Poland	USSR
1951	70,527	29,546	57,789	164,474	188,292
1961	143,092	35,743	258,071	171,467	186,653
1971	108,945	43,100	385,755	160,040	160,120

Series A297-326, *Historical Statistics in Canada*, 2nd ed.

Table 4.2
Religious composition of immigration to Canada, by percentage

Religion	Before 1961	1961–70
Roman Catholic	39.2	43.4
Protestant	39.2	26.9
Christian Orthodox	3.8	6.3
Jewish	2.7	2
Sikh	.1	1.1
Muslim	.2	1.3
Hindu	–	1.4
No religion	11	13.5

2001 Census: Analysis Series, Religions in Canada (Statistics Canada: 2003), 19.

resembling a mainstream North American church, particularly with the advent of Vatican II. For those concerned with Catholic influence, this was not occurring because the Church was finally "protestantizing" after centuries of resistance, but to allow the Church to gain more influence in a divided and confused world. This plot was also the true reason behind its role as primary antagonist to Soviet Communism. In this tense atmosphere, which system "won" was vital.[7]

A separate intellectual thread was also present, expressing concern with how the Catholic Church would exacerbate tensions due to its inherently reactionary nature. Among many mainstream Protestant clergy and laity, the new ecumenical movement had gained currency; it was an important facet in the attempt to promote world peace and to curb the power of international Soviet materialism. Many Anglo-Protestants, however, feared the inevitable dominance and bullying of the Catholic Church in any ecumenical effort. Will Herberg found this sentiment in his influential sociological survey of American religion, *Protestant-Catholic-Jew: An Essay in American Religious Sociology*. Protestant (and Jewish) suspicion of the Catholic Church's involvement in ecumenical relations was in fact a defining characteristic of American interfaith cooperation.[8] Canadian counterparts agreed, critiquing the very real refusal of the Catholic Church to participate in some ecumenical efforts through an anti-Catholic framework. These views all represented the Catholic Church as a monolithic and internationally powerful organization, particularly in Southern and Central Europe and in the global south, which threatened the freedom and stability of the Cold War order, yet again "ethnicizing" the threat the Church represented.

The Anglo-Protestants discussed here often based proclamations of inclusivity and ecumenicity on "universal" British Protestant values, making the transformation of Canadian identity in this period a messy process. The universality attached to Britishness by these Anglo-Protestants was thus inherently contingent. As English-Canadian nationalism started to disentangle from the strict ethnic chauvinism of earlier decades, the formation of this more-inclusive identity in the postwar era did not empty it of exclusionary tendencies or prejudicial opinions about those groups that still did not "fit," including ethnic Others and recently arrived immigrants. Residual anger at Quebec's "shirking" of its duty and the continued belief that the Church controlled civil society in the province ensured that anti-Catholicism would remain interconnected with the shifting discourse surrounding Quebec and ethno-religious identity in general (see Table 4.3). The contingent universality of English Canadian values defined the first twenty-five years of the postwar era in terms of national identity, particularly in its relation to anti-Catholicism.

The comparison of Catholicism with socialism and fascism noted earlier by C.E. Silcox would continue through the postwar segment of his career, being a central point in a lecture he gave to the St Andrew's Young People in 1948, entitled "Why Are We Protestants?" and a two-part series he wrote for the *United Church Observer*, provocatively entitled "Paganism and Papalism." In the lecture, Silcox emphasized that religious indifference, which he defined as the acceptance of the theologically untenable, was a threat to the integrity of Protestantism. For him, the weakness of Protestantism lay in its "sentimental and invertebrate liberalism and its bumptious and inadequate fundamentalism," neither of which paid enough attention to the

Table 4.3
Population of Canada with French as mother tongue

1951	4,068,850
1961	5,123,151
1971	5,793,650

Series A185-237, *Historical Statistics in Canada*, 2nd ed.

Christological foundations of the faith. Silcox claimed that this foundation is what represented the superiority of Protestantism, as it did not rely on idolatry, sacerdotalism, papal infallibility, or the Immaculate Conception of Mary. It was better prepared to meet modern challenges by promoting true cooperation, as opposed to divisive doctrines and practices. Indeed, in answering the eponymous question, "Why are we Protestants?" Silcox outlined a broadly liberal view that placed Protestantism at the centre of democratic culture. Historic Protestant societies represented the principles of the Reformation, located mostly in Western and Northern Europe, the most important principle being the Christian doctrine of man, which emphasized the individual. If removed, "the house is swept clean for occupation by the totalitarian, statist, devils." He asked his audience rhetorically, "Can democracy and Catholicism really flourish side by side?" He answered characteristically and updated the ethno-religiosity of previous decades into the Cold War world: "[f]or the most part, fascism and communism which the Church fears flourish in countries which have largely been informed by its authoritarian spirit. They are not so menacing in countries which have retained the Protestant respect for the individual and insistence on democratic techniques."[9] There was thus a direct connection between the Catholicism of certain nations/nationalities and their democratic "abilities."

In his articles, Silcox clearly desired that Protestants work with Catholics in a united front against the evils of communism. The problem was that Protestants expected their allies to conform to democratic principles, something Catholics rejected due to their acceptance of papal authority and infallibility. For Silcox, the Vatican supported only a superficial democracy of numbers, designed to overwhelm liberal democratic societies in a sea of Catholics. In the second part of this series, Silcox confusingly pleaded with the Russians to act reasonably and not push Protestants into a distasteful alliance with an ecclesiastical power that Protestants knew had a distorted conception of freedom. Silcox added that at the core of these problems, of a world splintered among the false absolutism of papalism, the tyranny of Russian Communism, and the freedom of Western Protestantism, was that "the East" had never had a Reformation, the event that liberated the spirit of the individual and led to all the most developed countries in the world being Protestant. Silcox's plea for unity was thus intrinsically impossible, as it was the Others that had to conform to Western Protestantism's values. An alliance with either "Internationale," openly equating the Soviet Union and the Catholic Church, was problematic for Protestants, as both violated the conditions of freedom and liberty he so cherished. He concluded his first article in the same vein: "We refuse to take our marching orders either from Rome or from Moscow," warning that the current world conflict could transform into one solely between the Vatican and the Soviet Union if Protestants were not vigilant, leaving them and their heritage of democracy behind. He added, "so long as real Protestants suspect that an effort is being made to regiment them either under the papal flag or under the hammer and sickle, they will prove adamant."[10] Protestants had to act intelligently, but they could not be expected to sacrifice their values, even in such an important conflict. It was these democratic Protestant values, these concepts being synonymous here, that had to be defended in the first place.

From the mid-forties through to the late fifties, Silcox often returned to this characterization of Catholicism as authoritarian in spirit. Implicit within this discourse, however, was the related anxiety that Catholicism was in fact insincerely "protestantizing" by shedding its old ultramontanism, consciously making itself appear more politically acceptable in a liberal-democratic society. The Church was attempting to hoodwink the public into believing that the Church was now "normal," not a totalitarian aberration in the modern world, like the Soviet Union. Silcox's anxiety over the potential Catholic dominance of Canadian society in this period is palpable, particularly in a lecture series he gave, "Protestantism and Roman Catholicism: Their Similarities and Differences," at the Yonge Street United Church in early 1955. Silcox, in this series, pointed to the fact that Hitler was a Catholic, that Mussolini was raised Catholic, that Yugoslavian strongman Tito was a Catholic, as were the horrifying Croatian fascists the Ustaše, and that Stalin had been raised in an Orthodox seminary. Silcox asked a rhetorical question to explain this trend: "Does not an authoritarian religion of the Catholic type, *unless it is adequately challenged and continually modified by a religion of the Protestant type*, inevitably tend to produce a state of mind which, when it finally rebels ... carries over the authoritarian emphasis and seeks to secure its revolution by a new form of totalitarianism?" It was thus the role of Protestantism to prevent political or economic totalitarianism from replacing spiritual totalitarianism, or even vice versa. While Protestants had to work with Catholics, they did not have to respect Catholicism. The stakes were too high. He closed his lecture by attacking the Archbishop of Chicago's refusal to allow Catholics to attend the meeting of the World Council of Churches (WCC): "this refusal seemed ... in the light of the world crisis ... short-sighted, and it may prove calamitous for the Church itself as was the policy of the hierarchy which, in the first half of the sixteenth century, hastened the Protestant Reformation. To the Protestant mind, it resembles too much the technique practiced by the Kremlin."[11]

Silcox's concern with Catholicism went deeper than just theological differences, ethnic Otherness, and proclivity for authoritarianism, however. It reflected an idiosyncratic reading of Western history. In a letter to the famous historian and communications theorist Harold Innis, Silcox detailed the perceived connection between the shallow Protestantism of the modern day and Catholicism. Silcox agreed with Innis's sentiment from his lecture "The Church in Canada" that Protestant churches in recent years were completely bereft of ideas or philosophy, instead focusing on planning and becoming another arm of the technocratic state.[12] For Silcox, the major problem of Western Christianity and its trouble with dealing with the new postwar world dated as far back as Constantine, when the religion he founded, Roman Catholicism, became obsessed with comprehensiveness, instead of just spiritual salvation. This resulted in a Christianity reduced to superficial social action as opposed to dealing with the fundamental problems of a hedonistic and divided world.[13] Silcox's ability to causally link his distaste for the social Christianity of modern Protestantism with Catholicism is breath-taking in its historical scope and demonstrated the depth of his antipathy to the doctrines and structure of the Catholic Church.

Arthur Lower represents another strain of anti-Catholicism in Canada in the Cold War age, emphasizing liberalism and individualism in the face of the Soviet threat. He was explicit about how this depended on preserving the liberal democratic tradition of Britain. Lower's complex, seemingly contradictory, world view and his prolific pen make him a difficult figure to pin down. The same man who wrote the letter to Pickersgill that opened this chapter could also write a letter to *The Native Son* of Winnipeg in 1944 condemning the authors for using a source from the Orange Lodge, "the most anti-Canadian and one of the most illiberal organizations existing on Canadian soil." Lower continued by almost summarizing his intellectual world view, noting "As you know, I am a staunch supporter of anything that will forward the cause of Canadian nationalism, but that nationalism must be liberal in its outlook ... True liberalism, which comes close to true Christianity, must rank above nationalism."[14]

What is therefore necessary to comprehend Lower's position on Catholicism is an analysis of his liberalism. Lower most comprehensively detailed his Cold War liberalism in the 1954 book *This Most Famous Stream: The Liberal Democratic Way of Life*.[15] In this book, Lower stated that liberalism was a deeply human phenomenon, equivalent to the "eternal spirit of man," transcending history and alone being able to appreciate the value of the individual, not simply as a means but as an end. Lower's conception of liberalism was very specific, based on the English tradition and English institutions from centuries ago. It was this tradition that had protected the world from tyranny throughout the ages and was doing so now against Soviet communism. The reason Lower wrote the book was to respond to the charges by the communist world that the West did not have an ideological basis or believe in anything fundamental. The choice given to the reader was to believe in the liberal/Christian conception of man as worthwhile, or to accept the reverse, which had resulted in the gas chambers.[16]

Protestantism was central to this world view. He boldly proclaimed "[t]ake out English-speaking Protestantism and its derivatives from the modern world and the major creative force left is Russian Communism." At the root of the Protestant advantage was the balance between authority and freedom. Freedom for the Catholic Church throughout the centuries had meant only an increase in its power.[17] This corruption of true liberty resulted in conflict over who had authority in the Christian Church, a dispute that contributed to the Reformation, since the papacy refused to accept any undermining of its authority. If various reform movements had succeeded, Lower speculated,

> [the Catholic Church] might have found it possible in time to put itself clearly on the side of freedom, as Protestant churches have little difficulty in doing, and to have avoided many of those dubious and damaging associations which have always caused Protestants to think of it as an agency of illiberalism, reaction and despotism. But the constituted Church made its choice. Despite the fine, wide sweep of the philosophy which had been developed for it, it steadily pursued its way to the quasi-totalitarian structure which it has since achieved.[18]

The Church quashed all forms of liberty and retreated further into authoritarianism with the proclamation of papal infallibility in the nineteenth century. "It was not to be the privilege of the Roman Catholic Church to show the modern world the way to liberty," Lower added. Instead, obedience and power became the sole concerns of the Church, forcing him to conclude that the "spirit of Roman Catholicism must be authoritarian."[19]

Lower did temper his condemnation of the Catholic Church, mentioning in passing that Catholicism was not always authoritarian, since the Magna Carta did emerge from Catholic bishops. Yet this was in England, a country that avoided the coming absolutism of the continent through its institutions, paradoxically emerging from the very tradition Lower castigated. Perhaps implicit here is the ethnocentricity so common within anti-Catholicism, seeing in English-speaking peoples some inherent ability to combat excesses. Lower also allowed that in many traditionally Catholic societies, including Quebec, Catholicism had provided a bulwark against unrestricted capitalism, a bulwark Lower valued. By the late-eighteenth and nineteenth century, however, Protestantism became obsessed with humanitarianism and eschewed much of the focus on material accumulation that once characterized it. A plethora of sects emerged in the English-speaking world, particularly Methodism, which in his mind finally represented what was truly liberal in the world, while the Catholic Church was building totalitarian barriers. Present here again is Lower's attempt to link liberalism to Christianity, specifically the English Protestant tradition, as the only true alternative in the modern world to Soviet communism, as it guarded both the dignity of the individual and could stand against the excesses of the capitalist system.[20]

Lower's theorizing about the broad historical nature of Catholicism in contradistinction to his cherished liberalism underpinned his continued patronizing view of French-Canadian society from earlier years, particularly in his acceptance of the Tawney-Weber thesis. This thesis linked progress and the acquisitive ethic to Protestantism, especially Calvinism. The French Canadian was impervious to the excesses of capitalism, due to the fact that he was medieval and simplistic; Catholicism did not lead to capitalism or progress, just stasis.[21] He even explicitly mentioned the Tawney-Weber thesis in perhaps his most-lasting statement of the postwar era, the Governor General's Award–winning and often-used university textbook *Colony to Nation: A History of Canada*.[22] Lower himself noted that this book was explicitly nationalist, designed to inspire Canadians to embrace a united nation with a unique role in the world after a divisive war.[23] He repeated his "two ways of life" thesis almost verbatim, painting a well-worn picture of Canadian history as defined by the conflict between the Calvinist Protestant work ethic of English Canada and the simplistic and "careless" nature of Catholic French Canada. One manifestation of the carelessness and simplicity of Catholics was the willingness of French Canadians and Catholics in general to have huge families, repeating the fear of *revanche des berceaux*. In a footnote, Lower articulated perhaps his darkest vision of the potential consequences of the decline of Protestantism, to go along with the collapse of liberalism and thus democracy: a nation swamped by the "mis-shapen [sic]." Harkening back to the racial-eugenic language of "quality over quantity" in populations, he noted that in 1941, 43 per cent of the "deaf-mutes" in Canada were French Canadian, while 56 per cent of them were Catholic. Lower concluded that these "figures represent a whole economic, social and philosophical complex," not just poverty rates among Catholics. Protestants, on the other hand, were "decaying at the bottom," as they were obsessed with material advancement, attending to responsibilities and using birth control to regulate family size, an only slightly altered version of the fears of race suicide.[24]

It was not just the physical consequences of a large Catholic population that concerned him. Every aspect of the "national structure" of French Canada (again equating it with Catholicism) was the result of a pre-Reformation people. French Canada was acquiescent in the face of hardship, and yet jealous of protecting its way of life against the incursions of a more-energetic people. This went beyond just the antithesis of French and English Canada for Lower: to "the Catholic everywhere, but especially to the rural Catholic, life is more than livelihood. It is a series of ritual acts ... There is little need for striving, little occasion for the notion of progress." Within this world, "the Catholic," particularly in rural areas, was almost pagan, suggesting that, unlike the strong individual conscience it took to be Protestant, it was easy to accept Catholicism. Catholicism was a superficial faith, which explained its greater success in converting Indigenous peoples than Protestantism. Protestantism demanded total conversion, not just the performance of easy rites.[25] Lower (like Murphy in earlier decades) portrayed Catholicism as resting on externalities, some of which were dangerously authoritarian, as opposed to the constant internal struggle and striving for progress that defined Protestantism and a modern nation.

In an article for the *Star Weekly Magazine* in 1959, left-wing journalist Richard Lunn criticized Lower's *Canadians in the Making* and *This Most Famous Stream* as pulling Canada apart at the seams, as Lower overemphasized the contribution and greatness of the "Englishman." Lower allowed only this ideal to be the bearer of liberty and democracy. Lunn theorized that Lower gained his specific views of liberty and democracy from his Protestant Ontario roots and his English-born father, and that these views embodied the expected prejudices of someone from Ontario. This infuriated Lower, who always rejected charges of prejudice and ethnocentricity.[26] He believed that "vulgar" organizations such as the Orange Lodge were tearing Canada apart. He, on the other hand, was the purveyor of liberalism, not bigotry, which was to be the saviour of Canada. Lower was convinced that anti-Catholicism, along with unfettered ultramontane Catholicism, was intolerable in Canada, as it undermined the balance necessary for the nation's functioning.[27]

Alan Mendelson's study of anti-Semitism among the Canadian elite can help explain Lower's seemingly inexplicable blindness to the similarity of his views to those of the very people he abhorred. Mendelson attempts to revise the existing analytical divide between so-called vulgar and genteel anti-Semitism. The elite figures he examines believed that Jews shared characteristics that differentiated them from the rest of humanity and that their overall influence on society tended to be harmful and dangerous. They could justify their anti-Semitism because they theorized their views through "intellectual rigour."[28] Lower and many of the other figures in this story were therefore able to understand themselves as the upholders of modern values of tolerance and liberty, and yet simultaneously view the

Catholic Church as an inherently insidious influence on Canadian society, much like extremists such as Shields and Saunders. In his self-evaluation, Lower was not anti-Catholic, because he was a liberal. It was *the Church* threatening this liberty.

Lower often stated his opinion of Catholicism more explicitly in his private correspondence. For example, in one letter Lower denied his correspondent's claim that Quebec was closer to socialism than the other provinces. This was *unless* the correspondent was referring to communism, due to the tyrannical nature of entrenched premier Maurice Duplessis, who had an open alliance with the Church. "[B]ecause of the authoritarian nature of the Roman Catholic church," Lower continued, "I always contend that communism cannot get too far in Protestant countries because debate always blunts its points. Senator [Joseph] McCarthy, an Irish Roman Catholic, would not have debate. Neither does Quebec understand debate in the sense in which I use the word."[29] In other words, Catholic Quebec facilitated the rise of that which it persecuted: totalitarian communism. While he was dedicated to national unity through liberalism, he could not help but fear and loathe the influence of such an authoritarian institution over one of the two major national communities in Canada. Lower's anti-Catholicism was quite genteel, in the sense that he was grudgingly and publicly able to tolerate Catholicism if it aided in maintaining the unity and progress of Canada. Yet he saw connections between it and Soviet communism, that other major creative force in the Cold War world, rivalling the necessary superiority of liberalism. In another letter, Lower was perhaps more frank, refuting Sister Mary Jean's belief that he was a Catholic. Sister Mary Jean, who wrote to Lower praising *Colony to Nation* and stating she wanted to use it in an upcoming history course she was teaching, was met with a clear summary of his understanding of Catholicism: "I am on the contrary ... the very essence of a Protestant, in that the right of personal decision means everything to me."[30]

These narratives also existed in the pages of the official organ of the United Church, the *United Church Observer*, into the 1960s. Added to traditional narratives, however, was the hope that there was genuine potential for change within the Church. This is represented most clearly in the denominational coverage of Vatican II by the United Church. What emerged, at least in the *Observer*, was a profound ambivalence toward closer relations with a modernizing Catholic

Church.³¹ An editorial from 1 October 1962, authored presumably by editor A.C. Forrest, was aptly entitled "Let's Wait and See – And Pray." Here Forrest notes that, while many Protestants were excited about the possibilities of this historic council, the Catholic Church defined ecumenical and Catholic in a much different way than Protestants or the United Church.³² Even this apparent cautious optimism did not prepare many in the United Church for the *Observer's* following issue, which had a picture of the popular Pope John XXIII on the cover. It elicited a mixed response: some letter writers were furious, even demanding the cancellation of their subscription, while the hostility of their co-religionists embarrassed others, viewing the entire Vatican II experience as a prime opportunity for improving true Christian unity.³³ The *Observer* itself noted in an editorial that it had received several types of letters about the controversial cover, some hard-line Protestant criticism, some thanks from Catholic allies. The author added, however, that, while the journal opposed "the old-fashioned Protestant who can see no good in Roman Catholics," the "so-called Protestant who is so overpowered by the new winds of reform from Rome, that he can't tolerate any forthright criticism whatsoever, is worse." The editor saw these latter figures as less than solidly Protestant or manly, equating the two, as they undoubtedly wore "panty-waists beneath their grey-flannel suits."³⁴ It seemed that to accept Catholic attempts at change at face value was foolish; any good Protestant always had to be wary of the intrigues of Rome. In an earlier editorial, Forrest noted the importance of papal infallibility as a hindrance to unity. At best, reinterpretation of this doctrine could occur. Without this, the most ardent Protestant defender of unity could not reasonably countenance closer relations. Forrest noted that Vatican II did not necessarily mean reform, as it was at Vatican I that the abhorrent doctrine of infallibility was proclaimed. To expect too much was "sentimental," again using a gendered term to describe enthusiasm for Vatican II, as the last council had resulted in a doctrine that was "unscriptural, unacceptable, and utterly impossible for Protestants."³⁵

In the official report from Forrest at Vatican II, this ambivalence is again at the forefront. Forrest reported that Protestants should be excited about the predominance of "liberal" Catholic opinion at the council, including many of the Canadian representatives, and even the pope himself. John XXIII spoke of religious liberty and condemned the linking of political oppression with the Church, something that garnered murmuring among the large contingent of clerical reactionaries in the audience. This should please Canadian Protestants, according to Forrest, as it directly targeted the excesses of "suppression of error" that occurred in Quebec over the showing of the film *Martin Luther* and the union of Church and state in that province. Forrest concluded that Protestants should pray for John XXIII, the "best pope Protestants ever had," but that in the end everything he was saying was pleasant but completely unrealistic.[36] Rome, in other words, would not – in fact could not – truly change. It would simply engage in cosmetic adjustments that would leave Protestants excited but unsatisfied. No true Protestant could accept the values that Rome upheld without a total revolution in its structure and theology.

This ambivalence, or perhaps fatalism, in the *Observer* represents what Phyllis Airhart has noted as a tension within the United Church in this period regarding Protestant-Catholic relations. The tension was between those who rejected any compromise with their historic enemy, those who emphasized only the most general of common beliefs, and those who endorsed working with other denominations to do good works on a global level, despite confessional divides. Within the latter group, many slowly abandoned pre–Vatican II assumptions and stereotypes about Catholics, at least publicly.[37] Yet this was a slow process, and there remained a strong old guard, unable to change its perceptions of an enemy that they had compared their church against for decades.

Hugh McLeod, moderator of the United Church, was a member of this old guard, and he remained unconvinced as to the possibilities of Vatican II. He voiced his concerns about Vatican II, along with the consequences of a predominantly Catholic Canada, at his retirement speech at the Twentieth General Council in September 1962. He distrusted the convening of Vatican II and the resulting enthusiasm from Protestants. Protestants "have no reason ... to conclude that the dominance of Rome in any nation" would mean anything other than the very subversion of the nation's democratic heritage, as it had throughout history. Democracy was fragile, embodied in a free press and political parties that were dependent on circulation numbers and crass majorities; an aggressive Church dedicated to control could easily manipulate these institutions. Protestantism, on the other hand, was sinking in a morass of materialism, echoing Lower's fear, and was divided against itself, with some denominations becoming overly organized and bureaucratic. He did defend the strength of Protestantism and the United Church in North America compared to the horrendous decline of the faith in Western Europe. Yet he quickly added that this strength required attention and effort. Without this, a weak Protestantism would be a perfect victim for a highly organized Catholicism, which, if given the chance, would abandon the concept of religious liberty and subject Protestants to the type of treatment they received in Salazar's Portugal or Franco's Spain, worse even than the atheism of the Soviet Union.[38]

Linking ethnicity and religion, McLeod saw immigration as the secret means through which Catholic dominance was presently building. For over a decade, according to McLeod, immigration into Canada had been overwhelmingly Catholic (see Table 4.2). While the individual Catholic was, according to McLeod, undoubtedly a good settler and "capable of enriching our nation," they were members of a Church that "everywhere favours the establishment of a monolithic infallible authority under Rome," and, perhaps unwittingly, "may herald and achieve the end of liberty as we have known it and as we deem it necessary for life."[39] These were the stakes according to McLeod, titular head of the largest Protestant denomination in Canada. The nation was to be either Protestant and free, maintaining its democratic heritage earned through the struggle of the Reformation, or become Catholic and authoritarian, spurning the progress of said heritage. Canada had to protect its borders against the infiltration of Catholics, allegedly streaming into the country to change its ethno-religious makeup and the democratic values that were inextricable from this makeup. Upon leaving the office of moderator and responding to criticisms of his speech, he sent a letter of thanks to supporters in the church, painting an even starker portrait of the conflict: "I trust that conditions will brighten in our fair country, and that freedom shall not languish or perish from the world."[40]

McLeod's speech elicited a flurry of responses. The mayor of London, Ontario, the location of the council, denounced McLeod's comments as "un-Christian." Others present at the meeting who spoke to the *Globe and Mail* were appalled at his statements in this time of ecumenism and threat from communism. Nonetheless, J.R. Mutchmor, the incoming moderator, agreed with McLeod's concern over Catholic immigration, as did the moderator of the Presbyterian Church of Canada, Dr Ross Cameron. Cameron added that a Canada in which Catholics were in the majority would see a threat to the liberty of all non-Catholics in the nation, transforming Canada into another Francoist Spain, that great symbol of modern Catholic dictatorship.[41]

The *Observer*, in the issue preceding the one with the pope on the cover, defended McLeod, claiming that the public had taken his statements out of context. In fact, the *Observer* had reported on Catholic immigration in the issue immediately predating McLeod's speech, noting that there had been many rumblings to the General Council accusing the Catholic Church of infiltrating the department of immigration.[42] The letters-to-the-editor section also represented the debate within the United Church over these issues. One anonymous author, anonymous because he was a civil servant, noted that it was a well-known fact in Ottawa that the department of immigration was under the control of the Church, with the Catholic St Laurent claiming no favouritism to lull the populace to sleep. R.H. Dowdell from Ottawa, on the other hand, dismissed these claims as prejudicial, representing a twentieth-century version of the mania over "popish plots" that belonged to the sixteenth century.[43] The *Observer* for its part reiterated after McLeod's speech that, while the overtures at Vatican II were signs of progress, McLeod was essentially correct. The United Church needed to convene official commissions to investigate the changing demographic nature of the nation through unfair immigration processes favouring Catholics and hindering the entrance of Britons, and the future of publicly funded Catholic education. If the number of Catholics continued rising, conflict was inevitable, as the Church would not stop trying to strengthen its influence over Canadian society – or, in fact, over the entire world.[44] Clearly, the ethno-religious nature of anti-Catholicism had not disappeared, even in the 1960s, remaining for many Anglo-Protestants a determining factor in the Otherness of postwar immigrants.

Anti-Catholic thinking and tropes were present among traditional conservatives as well. George Drew, who became federal leader of the Progressive Conservatives (PC) in 1948, represented for many the epitome of Anglo-Protestant Canada, despite his frequent alliances with Duplessis, that great enemy of Anglo-Protestant liberal democracy, designed to establish his status as a truly national political figure.[45] In the 1949 federal election, for example, Drew's attempt to cultivate a following in Quebec through Duplessis's Union Nationale (UN) machine backfired, epitomized by the *Toronto Star* running a front-page advertisement two days before the vote telling Canadians "Keep Canada British/Destroy Drew's Houde/Vote St Laurent" (despite the fact that Camillen Houde actually ran as an Independent in the election, decimating the PC candidate).⁴⁶ What is revealing is the paper's use of Britishness as a political wedge against a candidate viewed as "too close" to Duplessis, but promoting a candidate who was actually French Canadian.

Drew demonstrates the complexity (or opportunism) of anti-Catholicism, as he and his supporters were not averse to similar accusations about the inordinate political influence of Quebec and the Church in Canada. Drew responded moderately to a letter from a disappointed campaign worker from Vancouver South in the failed 1953 election, who concluded that Quebec simply voted for Louis St Laurent because he was French Catholic, and the province was in the grip of the Church. Drew agreed that there were many "discouraging features about the election," but that the Tories maintained their proportionate position "against tremendous odds."⁴⁷ The dominance of the Catholic Church in this election loss was a sentiment shared by one Mrs G.H. Dresser, who blamed it on the "swamping" of Canada with central European Catholic immigrants and concluded by recommending Blanshard's anti-Catholic classic *American Freedom and Catholic Power*.⁴⁸ Drew was non-committal, responding that whatever the causes of the Tory loss, "we must do everything within human power to keep alive the democratic system which is so greatly threatened today."⁴⁹ Drew thanked another long-time supporter and "dearest friend" for a letter of support in which the author blamed displaced persons (DPs) and the control of the Catholic Church for the electoral loss, demonstrating that, for at least these two correspondents, the relationship between foreign (read: non-Anglo) ethnicity and Catholicism was still strong. This "dearest friend" also feared the changing of the national anthem from "God Save the Queen" and the appointment of an ambassador to the Vatican, and even thought a religious war in Canada was looming.⁵⁰ Later in the 1950s, Drew agreed with another supporter that the Liberals were not paying attention to unemployment, carefully ignoring the fact that this writer blamed his lack of job on the favouritism given to Catholics by the Liberal government throughout the nation.⁵¹

However, in other correspondence, Drew revealed he was convinced that the Liberals won almost entirely because St Laurent was a French Canadian and that this would come back to haunt the Grits. The next leader, according to Drew, would have to be an Anglo-Protestant, as per the unofficial Liberal rule of alternating English and French leaders.⁵² An Anglo-Protestant leader would be open to criticism, unlike a French Catholic apparently, and, in the Cold War context, Drew believed that the leader would have to base their platform on a stand toward communism or autonomy on the international scene, which "is not palatable to the people of Quebec." What exactly he means here is not clear; he *is* clear, however, that only a "son of Quebec" like St Laurent could get away with countering the opinions of the province and, apparently, that an Anglophone would automatically embody values counter to Quebec and French Canadians.[53] Any self-respecting Anglo-Protestant leader of the Liberals would immediately poison the party in Quebec by embracing certain Anglo-Protestant values. Drew had expressed this belief in Quebec's control of the federal government often during the Second World War, and this continued into the postwar era. He wrote his friend Hugh Farthing near the end of the war that the major domestic question in Canada was "whether Quebec was going to march shoulder to shoulder with the rest of Canada" or whether the federal government was to continue "appeasing" that disloyal province.[54] Drew's hostility toward Quebec, as Marc Gotlieb has described, was linked to his opposition to government centralization, as the strengthening of the federal government would result in more power for Quebec over Ontario and over Canada in general because of the King Liberals toadying to *la belle province*. "[I]f we did not stimulate British immigration into this country," he told Farthing, harkening back to the "revenge of the cradles" theme, "then it would only be a ... few years before we had an actual French majority in Canada." This would destroy the British connection and therefore "the very thing for which so many of us have fought."[55] Discussing the upcoming Dominion-Provincial Conference, Drew restated his goals for the future of Ontario and for Canada: a less centralized federation, the "British partnership ... and the maintenance of British stock in this province at any rate."[56] It is unsurprising that, with ethno-religious views such as this, Drew would not reject the claims of more vicious anti-French and anti-Catholic supporters.

Drew was unable, or perhaps unwilling, to distance himself too far from this imperialist Tory core for fear of facing attacks by more hardline anti-Catholics and Orangemen. In a revealing instance, Drew had to engage in damage control when Léon Balcer, his Quebec lieutenant and president of the party, reportedly made comments supporting not only a new Canadian flag but also that ubiquitous Protestant fear of a diplomatic representative to the Vatican. Drew repeatedly responded to concerned Orange Lodges that any statement made by Balcer was purely opinion and "was certainly not a statement of the policy of our Party and has at no time been discussed."[57] An ambassador to the Vatican and/or a new flag were both beyond the pale for a Tory party wedded to the British connection, and Drew saw no advantages to adopting these policies, no matter what the support for them in Quebec. Revealingly, file 20, volume 228, of Drew's fonds is entitled "Roman Catholic Church" and is filled almost entirely with protests about Catholic influence, corruption, and cronyism, buttressed by a small number of cordial letters to and from Catholic bishops. Underpinning Drew's views, and those of many of his supporters, was an understanding of a Canada in which the Tories were the bulwark against the further encroachment of "alien" traditions, and the Liberals were the party of Catholic French Canada. The latter was an "interest group," determined to undermine sacrosanct values of Anglo-Protestantism.

John Farthing, although never a politician, was a thoroughly Tory intellectual, whose brother, Hugh, was often in contact with Drew bemoaning the collapse of the British connection. John was also deeply concerned with the influence of Quebec and Roman Catholicism in general on Canadian society and the concomitant decline of the British connection. Farthing belonged to the Anglo community in Quebec: he was the son of the Anglican bishop of Montreal, the Right Reverend John Cragg Farthing, and attended McGill under Stephen Leacock, along with Eugene Forsey in the 1920s. Forsey and Farthing became friends in the early fifties, after Forsey began publicly attacking the King–St Laurent governments for "betraying" Canada's British heritage. Farthing stressed the role of the Crown-in-Parliament above all other factors as central to the functioning of the Canadian state. His main concern with regard to Catholicism, however, was that it undermined Canada's relationship with Britain, particularly the institution of the Crown, and therefore made Canada vulnerable to alternative materialistic ideologies, including communism.[58]

Farthing expressed this strong monarchist sentiment in his only published full-length work, *Freedom Wears a Crown*, released posthumously and compiled from his notes by conservative journalist Judith Robinson. For Farthing, the monarchy ensured slow, organic development; this monarchical fact within Canada and the Commonwealth represented an option outside of the stark Cold War binary of American liberalism and Soviet communism. Farthing refuted the reduction of modern man by contemporary ideologies and government policy to purely materialistic components, what he dubbed "Newtonian man." Real freedom was "the basic idea underlying the Christian tradition, which is still [the] source and substance [of Western civilization]" and was represented in Canada by the unmaterialistic nature of the monarchy.[59] Farthing causally linked this Christian tradition to the Reformation, which he viewed as the progenitor of every significant political principle in the Western world. Instead of falling into the nihilism of the modern age due to the failure of Newtonian man and resorting to the solutions presented by Marxists, the Americans, or the "medievalists," Farthing advocated the return to the traditions of the Reformation expressed in England. The equation was a simple one for Farthing: the unity of the people under law and the monarch was the fruit of the Reformation and the realization of a Christian social order. The British tradition was the embodiment of Canada, and Farthing accused the "Kingsians" of the Liberal Party of degrading this and promoting a false Canadian unity.[60]

Farthing's idea of false unity is where his concern with French Canada and Catholicism became most apparent. He labelled men like Lower, optimistically seeing Canada as progressing from colony to nation, "pure Canada cultists," or those who presented Canada as just French Canada. Since it was feasible to reduce French Canada to a geographical certainty in Farthing's mind, these "pure Canada cultists" were trying to promote an idea of Canada that forced all Canadians to reflect only geography. This vision would dismiss any historical sense of the British connection.[61] Yet implicit within Farthing's work is a conspiratorial view of French-Canadian traditions, something so apparent that Davie Fulton, a Catholic Tory, had to address it in his introduction to the book.[62] Nevertheless, Farthing claimed that "since the pure Canadianism of French Canada consists precisely in traditions that have come to the French Canadian from France and from Rome ... we can never realize a pure-Canada unity until all English-speaking Canadians have accepted, as have the French, these traditions." Farthing continued, seemingly predicting the stunned reaction of his readers, that "[t]his is no fantasy but the only logical conclusion of the fallacious idea of unity on which we are now seeking to build our national life."[63] For Farthing, the Canadian government under the Liberals was therefore promoting an idea of Canadian unity in which the English-speaking component would have to renounce its traditions and instead accept those of French Canada.

Farthing revealed the central role of the Catholic Church in his world view in a letter sent to Forsey concerning the planned removal of the terms "Royal" and "Dominion" from the title of Canada and certain institutions in the early 1950s.[64] Here he expressed his fear that "The power behind, seeking to upset the Throne, is the R.C. Church, which knows that if it can destroy the British tradition in this country it can then readily dominate the flabby unprincipled mass or mess that is then left." The Catholic Church, as the largest and most powerful political pressure group in the nation, was striving to destroy the British heritage and replace it with that of pre-Revolutionary France. In fact, the Church was supporting a form of South American republic, in which there was no substantial separation of church and state. This was truly alien to Farthing's ethno-religious and monarchistic vision of the nation: Canada was to be an Anglo-Protestant haven from the crass materialism of the atheistic and Catholic world. Farthing railed against the "secret forces" in Canada that were demanding these changes. Secret forces were the only explanation, because there could not possibly be substantial enough public support for these reforms to explain them. These were crafty people, and any current decline in their rhetoric was simply a "tactical retreat," drawing a direct comparison to Stalinist methods of obfuscating true motivations.[65] Once again, Catholicism, like communism, was a Trojan horse in the body politic, cloaked in normality while still representing alien traditions. In his estimation, the hatred that Quebec and the Catholic Church held for Canada's British institutions would never abate, and thus English Canada needed to be vigilant, strenuously restoring the freedoms guaranteed by the constitutional monarchical system in this otherwise materialistic world.

Farthing reassured Forsey that their strong, shared position regarding the need for the monarchical tradition was based on their intellectual bravery, and savaged the Liberal government's position for its alleged vacuity: "it has all the garish attractiveness of a neon sign ... It is merely one of the manifestations of the dominant 'modern' mind of our times," continuing "which, where it is not the expression of a basic, all-poisoning hatred (which the Roman Church can generate fully as effectively as Marx and Lenin) expresses a state of mental bewilderment, drift, confusion, fog and emptiness." Farthing reiterated his anti-Catholicism in the closing paragraph of his letter, stressing the need to speak honestly, and temporarily suspending the ardent ethnocentricity of his pleas: "I have no dislike whatever of French

Canadians; but the absolute and absolutist imperialism of the Papacy and the Roman Church is something we can ignore only at the loss of everything that has ever been of value to the non-Roman world."⁶⁶ Canadians had to discuss openly the Catholic Church's plan of gradually eroding guarantees of freedom, most evident in the King-Lapointe ideal of unity: "At the centre of all is King-Lapointe unity – or the R.C. domination of this country. English Canada needs to be awakened to the danger."⁶⁷ The danger was nothing less than the survival of the British way of life. Canada needed to regain its true heritage of freedom, a heritage grounded and expressed perfectly in the Britain of the Reformation era.⁶⁸

Farthing and Forsey agreed on a great deal, despite their seeming ideological polarization. Forsey was a staunch proponent of British traditions in Canada, and increasingly found himself sympathizing with Tory sentiment regarding the importance of the Crown and British symbols in Canada during the High Liberal years of the 1940s and 1950s. He wrote to John's brother, Hugh, in 1957 that *Freedom Wears a Crown* was a masterpiece.⁶⁹ According to conservative historian Donald Creighton, Forsey and Farthing both shared an intense distaste for what they viewed as the undermining of the intellectual and moral basis of Canada and its demoralization under the King and St Laurent governments through the elimination of the British connection. Creighton, who shared these opinions, outlined how Forsey and Farthing planned to write a book together, along with Judith Robinson, a project not released but that seems to have metamorphosed into Farthing's posthumous *Freedom*.⁷⁰

Interestingly, Forsey explicitly disagreed with Farthing's anti-Catholicism. Despite his private and public statements about French Canadians, he claimed he never wanted to reduce conflicts in Canada to race and religion. He admitted that Farthing was undoubtedly right "about some forces in the Roman Church," but that in recent years his exposure to many different Catholics, such as conservative journalist Grattan O'Leary, had convinced him that there were "all sorts of cross-currents" in the Church. Frank argument based on reason with French Canadians was necessary, which some would inevitably misrepresent as "anti-French-Canadian feeling," but not the attack Farthing was advocating.⁷¹ After rereading his earlier letter, Farthing responded with surprise at how anti-Catholic it was, yet proceeded to continue in this vein anyway, though he agreed that he and Forsey should not raise the spectre of race and religion in public, as it was divisive. It was the Roman Church, however, that provided the organizational and ideological core for the anti-British forces in Canada. Farthing was convinced that the opinion of individual Catholics was immaterial, as the aim of the Papacy was political domination. If the British connection was severed in Canada, which the Church and other forces were attempting to facilitate, "the R.C. Church will move in bag and baggage."[72]

Although more cautious and measured in his language than Farthing, Forsey, as noted earlier, made his opinions toward the Catholic Church quite clear throughout his career. In a letter from Robinson discussing suggestions Forsey had made concerning Farthing's book, Robinson agreed with Forsey that "a frontal attack on that organization [the Roman Catholic Church] isn't going to serve our purpose now." For Forsey and Robinson, it would be better for Farthing to simply allow logic to make the inferences concerning the Catholic Church in Canada and not be explicit. Following this logic, however, did indeed make it difficult not to take "a poke at what he finds."[73] The suggestion in this correspondence is that broad public attacks on Catholicism and French Canada were pointless, not necessarily wrong. They would only result in false accusations of intolerance, even if the points made were accurate and important for the overall goal of preserving the British connection in Canada. While some of the positions of the Catholic Church in Canada, and especially Quebec, may be harmful, publicly engaging the Church would only lead to misrepresentation and paint the forces fighting Liberal domination with the brush of bigoted imperialism.

There are similarities between the views of these mainstream figures and of conservative evangelicals, fundamentalists, and "vulgar" anti-Catholic publications. The latter was embodied in the militant *Protestant Action*, spearheaded by Toronto mayor Leslie Saunders.[74] These "vulgar" forces were simply more willing to express their views in public, used much more vicious, theologically oriented, language when describing Catholicism, and tended to focus on Catholicism as *the* cause of national and international crises to the exclusion of most other forces. In *Protestant Action*, dubbed "a bastardy smear-sheet" by Watson Kirkconnell, Saunders exposed what he viewed as the insidious Catholic conspiracy to subvert civil liberties. The Church's public opposition to communism was simply a ruse; communism was in fact more successful in Catholic countries due to the Church's authoritarian nature. The Catholic Church had tricked the public, since at least its collusion with fascism, and the free world needed to ignore the claims that it was the bulwark against international communism.[75] Saunders's "Letters to the Editor" section was full of equations of the Catholic Church with Soviet Communism, with a Mrs Blake proclaiming that the militant Protestant would always oppose dictatorship, whether Papal or Soviet, and would thus not let the French language overtake Canada.[76] The language increased in vitriol with a letter from Lay Preacher, who took Saunders's advice for organized Protestantism to be militant and evangelical quite literally:

> McCarthyism is the stepping stone to a Roman Catholic America ... It is the Catholics' continual bid for power and we shouldn't fail to use every weapon at our command. Comparing the Catholic church [sic] to communism, I'd prefer communism one hundred times. It is time that Protestants made it clear that we know we are being sold down the river, and unless this is brought to an end, we shall use every means at our disposal to bring before the people the shameful record of this antichrist and enemy of mankind. Too long have we hesitated to speak the whole truth and I myself am afraid, but would be willing to do my part in a campaign to at least enlighten the Protestants of the danger of our tolerant attitudes towards the Roman Catholic church [sic].[77]

For conservative evangelicals and fundamentalists, as for many others, Quebec remained the indisputable fortress of an aggressive Catholicism in Canada. The treatment of religious minorities, in this case Protestants, in the province was a topic of concern for these groups, as religious discrimination represented the close connection between the autocratic rule of Duplessis and the Church. For example, L.E. Maxwell of the fundamentalist *Prairie Overcomer* (official organ of the Prairie Bible Institute in Three Hills, Alberta) was outraged about the abuse of the evangelical Christian Brethren in Shawinigan Falls, Quebec, in 1950.[78] In March 1950, Paul Boeda, the leader of the tiny community of Christian Brethren in Shawinigan Falls was kidnapped and forced onto a train to Montreal. When he returned to his post, the local community continued to threaten him. Some Catholics in the town had apparently confused the Brethren with the Jehovah's Witnesses, who had been distributing aggressively anti-Catholic material throughout the province for decades, causing seemingly endless controversy.[79] For two days before a Christian Brethren meeting on 12 April, the Witnesses handed out a particularly obstreperous pamphlet in Shawinigan Falls. When the Brethren threw a young Catholic man out of their meeting for causing a disruption, an angry mob attacked the small group of Protestants, pelting the chapel with eggs and rocks, forcing those inside to flee. A riot ensued, and the roughly fifteen hundred rioters stormed the chapel, destroying much of the property inside and forcing a group of the worshippers to take refuge in a room above the makeshift chapel.[80] The police made no arrests following these shocking events, convincing many that the local government and the general atmosphere in Quebec tacitly supported the persecution of non-Catholics. Maxwell, for his part, blamed the entire event solely on the political machinations of the Catholic Church; obviously, the Church controlled the government in Quebec, and Maxwell was convinced that no political party in Canada was willing to risk opposing this "secret fifth column" for fear of losing the next election.[81]

Former House leader of the Social Credit Party John H. Blackmore, MP (Lethbridge), did bring the events in Shawinigan Falls into Parliament. Blackmore was no stranger to making controversial statements in the House or in public, as he was an arch anti-communist and anti-Semitic conspiracy theorist, who represented the far right of the Canadian political spectrum.[82] Blackmore spent most of his speech reading into the record various newspaper accounts of the events in Shawinigan Falls. Blackmore, for his part, believed that this example of religious persecution threatened those Canadians dedicated to "peace, order and good government," as all citizens should be free to practise their own religion. Yet Blackmore, like Drew, claimed his true concern as being the potential for the increased centralization of federal power. He warned against those representatives attending the upcoming Dominion-Provincial meeting, thinking that this event meant religious freedom should become the purview of Ottawa. It must be a provincial jurisdiction or, better yet, an issue of individual conscience. Blackmore warned that the Shawinigan Falls affair was in fact an example of "what might happen if some single organization of religious worshippers were to attain dominant control at Ottawa, some organization that might not hesitate to use that power to the disadvantage of other religious organizations."[83] He did not mention any religious group in particular, but it was clear that he was referring to the Catholic Church, subtly equating governmental centralization and the entrenched power of the Church.

When discussing this speech privately, Blackmore assured some correspondents that he was not referring to any specific denomination. "Personally," Blackmore told a correspondent who feared he was engaging in the Catholic-baiting of Canada's past, "I have only the kindest feelings for Roman Catholics."[84] In other letters, however, it becomes clear that the Catholic Church was the true target of his speech. Blackmore responded to these other letters by attempting to rally the "freedom loving" forces of Canada against those hostile to religious liberty. In a letter to one M.O. Rollefson he noted, "the time has come for Protestants to organize for the protection of religious freedom in Canada," leaving no question as to who the enemy was.[85] Blackmore also wrote to the Canadian Protestant League (CPL), asking it to become the vanguard of this movement to unite the freedom-loving forces in Canada. Blackmore told the CPL that he had become aware of it when a friend sent him a copy of its viciously anti-Catholic *I Was a Priest*, written by former priest Lucien Vinet. Blackmore even asked CPL president, Rev. Edward Morris, to send him a list of all the different Protestant groups in Canada and those who were already associated with the CPL.[86] It was simple: The Catholic Church meant authoritarianism, and Protestantism equalled the love of freedom.

Blackmore's choice of the CPL as the leader of a movement guaranteeing religious liberty in Canada and his explicit calls for Protestants to unite against the forces of reaction reveal the depth of his anti-Catholicism. While such a Canada-wide organization dedicated to freedom never emerged, the CPL responded to Blackmore's requests by officially stating that "we are fully in accord with your expression of the seriousness of the situation developing across this Dominion through organized anti-British, Pro-Roman control of our Dominion politically, religiously, publicly, industrially, and in every department of our national life."[87] Yet again, being "pro-Roman Catholic" meant being anti-British; one could apparently not be a loyal Canadian and a Catholic – especially if one were a French Canadian.

Perhaps the most extreme reaction to the Shawinigan Falls affair came from an obscure Baptist minister from Northern Ireland, now located in Ottawa and associated with Shields's Jarvis Street Baptist Church, Rev. George Olley. In a letter forwarded to Blackmore by the CPL, Olley called for public commissions in the provinces to determine whether immigrants accepted religious liberty to better balance the numbers in the country. While Olley never explicitly mentioned the Catholic Church, he noted that the Shawinigan Falls affair demonstrated that "the leopard has not changed his spots," repeating the same violations of liberty perpetuated for "fourteen centuries of terrible history." Blackmore felt that Olley's suggestions were important enough to forward the letter to Ernest Manning, the patriarch of the Social Credit Party and premier of Alberta, and to clarify that, while Olley had only been in Canada a short while, his experience in Northern Ireland gave him more than enough experience with "the kind of thing under discussion." For his part, Manning rejected Olley's plan as utterly ridiculous. Yet he did conclude his letter by expressing sympathy for the overall concern of Blackmore and Olley about religious liberty. For Manning,

> It has always seemed to me that one of the great reasons for the situation that currently exists with respect to religious liberty is the indefensible apathy of so many Protestant people. If they were half as vigorous in the defence of what they believe to be true as are those of other groups, the problem would, to a large extent, be automatically solved. As long as so many people place so little value on their professed religious convictions and remain so apathetic to their propagation and their defence, the field is left wide open for those who are aggressive to manoeuvre to dominate their fellows to the ultimate loss of their religious liberties.[88]

For these men, the events in Shawinigan Falls clearly symbolized something more than an episode in religious conflict. It was symptomatic of a society and nation that was losing its spiritual moorings, and thus its dedication to freedom and democracy. In this familiar equation, a vigorous Protestantism was synonymous with the values and institutions of a democratic society, and all other traditions were outside this narrative. Catholicism represented a unified and aggressive rival, complete with an alternative system of values, as well as an ethnically foreign intrusion. If Protestants allowed themselves to become complacent in the context of an increasingly affluent society, Shawinigan Falls would be only the beginning.

Another group concerned with Catholicism, albeit much more mainstream and respectable than the CPL, was the Inter-Church Committee on Protestant–Roman Catholic Relations (ICC). The ICC, formed in late 1944 at Bloor Street United Church, was originally composed of churchmen dedicated to researching the encroachment of Catholicism into the wider life of Canada. Its objectives were threefold and contradictory: to attempt to work with Catholics, to engage in research into any potentially problematic issue undermining Protestant-Catholic relations, and "to work to protect Protestant rights and interests from any encroachment which appears to be prejudicial to such rights."[89] This organization was broad in its denominational sweep, but almost exclusively centred in Ontario, including official representatives from the United Church, the Presbyterian Church, the Anglican Church, the Canadian Baptist Federation, and the Salvation Army.[90] The membership included such influential church figures as George Pidgeon, moderator of the United Church of Canada and the initial chairman of the ICC, Gordon Sisco, secretary of the general council of the United Church, J.R. Mutchmor, and Rev. Canon W.W. Judd of the Anglican Church.[91] Prominent lay Protestants also populated the "general committee," supporting its initial efforts to limit separate schools. These included Tory luminary Donald Fleming, a leadership candidate in 1956 and Diefenbaker's minister of finance, prominent University of Toronto historian George W. Brown, and the dean of the Ontario College of Education at the University of Toronto, A.C. Lewis.[92] Despite this mainstream status and often "single-issue" focus (separate schools), the ICC embraced an intensely anti-Catholic mandate only slightly different from that of previously mentioned "extremists."

For example, in a December 1945 brief to the Hope Commission, which had been called to analyze the separate-school situation in Ontario, George Cornish of the University of Toronto presented for the ICC an elaboration of its conspiratorial vision of Catholic plans in Ontario. Cornish was adamant about restricting the spread of separate schools, embracing an "originalist" interpretation of Catholic educational rights by denying the validity of developments that had changed the religious landscape in the province. The ICC wanted to revert to the policies enacted in the 1860s, which outlined but also limited the right to Catholic education. Even these policies, in the ICC's perspective, had been forced upon Ontarians by "clerical authoritarianism and the solid French Catholic Block from Quebec."[93] For Cornish, the main issue was that Catholic separate schools were not a right, unlike public schools, which were the basis of democratic society. The 1937 legislation, the brief fumed, allowed the formation of separate schools without the presence of public schools. In reality, the design of the legislation tabled by the Mitchell Hepburn government in 1935 and defeated in 1937 by an intransigent Protestant Tory party was to reform corporate taxation policies to aid separate schools, but would have also led to a minor windfall for public schools.[94] Nevertheless, the ICC perceived this as an example of political pressure and crass opportunism by the Hepburn government of the time, crippling the public school system and feeding into the hands of the Catholic Church. To the ICC, this entire situation was nothing less than part of a sophisticated plot by the Catholic Church to create a papal state consisting of Quebec and eastern and northern Ontario. The alleged ease with which the government was building separate schools due to the failed 1937 legislation – a confusing proposition – was presented as evidence that northern Ontario was becoming a French state. In a vein resembling that of the racial and ethno-religious theories of the earlier decades of the century, Cornish also argued that these schools were being used to hinder all self-respecting Anglo- or Scandinavian Canadians from settling there. The ICC promoted these latter settler and immigrant groups as the appropriate and superior settlers, solidly Protestant, while the government of Ontario was allowing this fertile land to go into the hands of the Roman Catholic clergy, with the separate schools acting as "the most devastating instrument in their hands in achieving this revolution."[95]

The ICC maintained its opposition to separate schools throughout its existence, even if its ethno-religious language became somewhat tempered. It based its support for the Drew provincial government's controversial Hope Report, which reiterated the legality of separate schools in Ontario but suggested curbing their jurisdiction, on the fact that "unwarranted" spread of the schools had to stop.[96] The Hope Report became a *cause célèbre* for the ICC, despite the fact that the subsequent Leslie Frost government immediately disowned its impolitic and potentially disastrous assertions that separate schools should be limited to Grade 6 through engineering a restructuring of the grading system after Drew moved to federal politics. Frost received over one hundred letters from Protestants demanding that he implement the suggested changes, many of them couching their support in language about the pedagogical advantages of restructuring the grading system to eliminate separate schooling in intermediate grades. Frost was unmoved.[97] In the ICC's opinion, the danger was that the

Catholic clergy, who often agreed to compromises, were in actuality planning to subvert them, and this problematic ethical framework revealed to Protestants "the kind of people with whom we have to deal."[98] Once again, Catholics were viewed as deviously untruthful, prepared to hoodwink the naive Protestants, who were negotiating in good faith. The authors of another ICC report bemoaning the temporary collapse of the Hope Report warned, however, that if electors did not pay enough attention to legislation, "it becomes easier for 'any class of persons' to secure legislation to meet its special desires. A heckneyed [sic] expression may be worth repeating here, 'Eternal vigilance is the price of freedom.'"[99]

Watson Kirkconnell engaged in a passionate public debate with the ICC, rejecting its line of argument. This brief exchange signifies the complexity of Canadian anti-Catholicism, as Kirkconnell did not approve of the ICC, yet simultaneously engaged in some of the same discourse. Well known for his strident public anti-communism, Kirkconnell was not without his concerns about Protestant-Catholic relations. The way he and Silcox linked the issues was similar, in that they both stressed the need for Christian unity in the Cold War in the face of Soviet materialism. For Kirkconnell this great battle between Christianity and communism trumped any conflict between Catholicism and Protestantism; in fact, he warned that Stalin himself was trying to use anti-Catholicism to divide the great Christian traditions.[100] Kirkconnell used this strand of discourse to dismantle the arguments of the ICC, which he sneeringly described as "a Protestant 'Research Committee,'" in an article for *Saturday Night* in early 1947. He attacked the anti-Catholicism of the ICC as harmful to Canada and the Christian cause in the face of the "Red Crucifixion of Christian nations." For Kirkconnell "honest Protestantism" did not need this type of "research."[101] This article appears to have stemmed from an initial refusal by Kirkconnell of overtures from the ICC to engage in research for them concerning Catholic influence over foreign policy in Canada. He responded frankly that he was "unsympathetic towards the work of your committee," pointing to the need to stem "belligerent atheism" embodied in communism. This for Kirkconnell prevented him from "bit[ing] the Catholics in the leg," concluding dismissively that the ICC was "fifty years out of date."[102]

Despite his proclamations of Christian unity in the face of a supreme enemy, Kirkconnell simultaneously maintained many of the same stereotyped opinions of Catholics as his contemporaries, particularly with regard to their allegedly more-prolific breeding habits. For example, Kirkconnell told the ICC that it should concentrate more on what united Protestants and Catholics instead of "an anti-Catholic crusade," as Catholics composed most of the young people in this country and were growing in number. Old-fashioned bigotry would only result in "grief and humiliation" for Protestants in the face of a changing demographic reality.[103] However, in the same article in which he denounced the ICC for fanning the flames of religious bigotry in a polarized world, Kirkconnell repeated the "revenge of the cradle" fear. He pointed out that the ICC was not paying attention to the indisputable fact that the real conspiracy in our society lay in the Protestant home, not in the Catholic Church. In a manner resembling his wartime article, "The Twilight of Canadian Protestantism," Kirkconnell believed Protestants in Canada were committing "race suicide," while French Catholics were growing exponentially through their birth rate and the large number of Catholic immigrants arriving on Canada's shores. This forced Catholics in Quebec to expand and move into Ontario and New Brunswick to gain a better quality of life. Kirkconnell alarmingly estimated that by the end of the century Canada would be fully half French Catholic and by the year 2100 roughly 90 per cent.[104]

Kirkconnell believed that Christian unity was necessary in an increasingly tense and materialistic world, but not at the cost of sacrificing what he viewed as the central values of Canadian society based on a pure Protestantism. Protestantism could preserve democracy, and Kirkconnell did not want Protestants to lose sight of why there were valid disputes between Protestants and Catholics. It was not necessarily the hostility of the ICC toward Catholicism that offended Kirkconnell, but its ignoring of communism, its aggressive tone, and its apparent lack of concern about demographic issues. Kirkconnell noted in one letter to Rev. S.J. Farmer of Toronto that the current communist threat to annihilate all Christianity made religious conflict a "luxury," particularly if, like the ICC, it was based on dishonest "anti-Catholic propaganda, false thinking and emotional prejudice." Kirkconnell opened his letter, however, assuring Rev. Farmer that "I have no more enthusiasm than yourself for Catholic theology, Catholic practice and Catholic ecclesiastical organization."[105] It was simply not the time to debate these genuine contentions between the two branches of Christianity. In a letter to one Mr Brant, Kirkconnell, then president of Acadia University, speculated on the purpose of university education. He felt slighted by the recent suggestion of St Francis Xavier alumni Don Reily that Acadia should adopt the principles of the Catholic Antigonish Movement. Kirkconnell told Brant that, while principles of community involvement endorsed by the pope were important, what was more important to a university education was being able to think and act for oneself, without the interference of a priest. What Reily did not understand was that a "Protestant ... needs no intermediary between himself and God. God speaks directly to him so he knows what is right."[106] For Kirkconnell clearly the essence of Protestantism was self-possession. Catholicism served as the antithesis of this concept.

In the 1960s, Kirkconnell contributed an essay discussing the religious and philosophical gulf between French and English Canada to Mason Wade's edited volume for the Committee of the Social Science Research Council of Canada, *Canadian Dualism*.[107] Kirkconnell repeated his belief that the major disputes at the religious and philosophical level in Canada were due to differences in the growth of population, although he admitted that these differences may have been exaggerated over the last several decades. For true understanding to emerge between the populations in Canada, harmful rumours, such as the claims that Catholic immigrants outnumbered Protestant ones, or that illegitimacy was more prominent in Catholic communities than Protestant, needed to be contradicted. Instead, Kirkconnell identified three *more important* current issues separating the two religious groups in Canada: education, intermarriage, and Canadian representation at the Vatican. It is here that he revealed his broad sympathy to the ICC's opposition to separate schools in Ontario, although the ICC was too prone to "the excesses of anti-Catholic enthusiasts." Kirkconnell was clear that, while these excesses existed, it was the remnants of the ultramontane wing in the Vatican that closed the door on true conciliation in 1950 by proclaiming Mary's assumption, adding to the insult of the Catholic perspective on mixed marriages, which Protestants found unacceptable. Kirkconnell also viewed the desire to gain diplomatic recognition at the Vatican as a violation of one of the central tenets of Protestantism, the separation of church and state. Representation would possibly give political status and preferential treatment to the Catholic Church in Canada, a sentiment shared by many Protestants in Canada throughout the postwar era.[108]

It is here that Kirkconnell mentioned a conspiracy theory fuelled in the Cold War world. With the imminent destruction of Catholicism in Marxist Europe, "the Papacy may consider a transfer to Canada or the United States and may seek an even-fuller control over the political life of this continent – a control in which special political recognition of Catholicism would play a strategic part. Such rumours may be unfounded, but they influence Protestant thought."[109] Kirkconnell was not the first figure to posit this seemingly bizarre theory, as columnist and former Canadian correspondent for the London *Times* John Stevenson wrote an article in 1947 for *Saturday Night* on the very same issue. He saw the seat of the Vatican in Rome as under threat, due to the prominence of the Communist Party in Italy and the pressure from Stalin's Eastern bloc. Stevenson believed that Belgium and France were too anti-clerical for them to be valid candidates for a new Holy See, with Spain being an international pariah under the Franco regime. This left North America as the most logical choice for Papal relocation. Canada, with its huge Catholic population, which was only increasing with immigration, was thus the only nation with a realistic chance of harbouring the Papacy, an occurrence that would divide Canada and inflame relations between it and the USSR. Expressing residual anger at Quebec's war effort and subtly blaming the influx of Catholic immigrants, Stevenson concluded that at least there would be no opposition to conscription within Quebec, which would rally to protect their beloved religion. Kirkconnell utilized the very same type of rumour and conspiracy theory he had previously condemned as a forceful reason why he opposed representation at the Vatican, couching it in the context of preserving national unity. Canada's overwhelming Catholic population was the result of both Anglo-Protestant apathy as well as the potential to destabilize its traditions of democracy. Kirkconnell concluded, in language like Silcox's, that cooperation was central to defeating communism: "[y]et before that co-operation can be ... given there needs to be a[n] ... understanding by ... Protestants and Catholics ... of the true nature and spiritual nobility of genuine Protestantism and of its reasons for disliking a form of church government that is the negation of democracy."[110]

The ICC continued for many years beyond Kirkconnell's criticism, often struggling to stay afloat, but still engaging in the research Kirkconnell derided. Perhaps the most fascinating and revealing issue the ICC pursued during the 1950s in the context of the Cold War was the "Bossy Case." The "Bossy Case" reveals the continued intersections for many Anglo-Protestants between race, ethnicity, and religion, even if these overtly ethnocentric sentiments were slowly becoming subsumed in concern with "universalized" values of freedom and democracy in the Cold War. Walter J. Bossy was a naturalized Ukrainian Canadian who had authored a bizarre collection of articles in the 1930s that advocated what he termed "Classocracy," or the organic union of all classes in society under a Canadian and Christian "monarchy of toil."[111] Bossy worked for the Montreal Catholic School Commission (MCSC) for sixteen years and in 1948 founded the New Canadian Service Bureau (NCSB), which was designed to help new Canadians, mostly Catholic, to adjust to their host society. Bossy claimed that one Dr Joseph Saine donated a sum to the NCSB, asking Bossy if he could help the federal Liberals in their Western tour, as this area contained numerous new Canadians. Allegedly, Saine offered Bossy a Senate seat if he provided these votes for the Liberals in the 1949 election. The school board subsequently fired Bossy, as he was now engaged in overt political action, which was against official policy. After the Liberals handily won the election, the Grits told Bossy that they were washing their hands of the whole affair, causing his hospitalization due to stress.[112]

At the 15 December 1955 meeting of the ICC, Rev. Ralph Latimer and W.W. Judd presented information concerning the "immigration problem" in Canada. Latimer read a confidential report he had compiled concerning the Bossy case, as Bossy had requested financial aid from the ICC. Bossy also claimed to have left the MCSC because he disagreed with Catholic designs on Canada.[113] Latimer described how the Canadian Caritas, a French Catholic organization, had met and secretly decided that what was needed was not only a social agency for helping immigrants in Quebec but also that it had to "establish a provincial, political, organic council as the highest body, and a clearing station embracing all non-Anglo Saxons and non-French Christian Canadians in Canada." Latimer's major concern was a suspected plan by the Catholic Church and the Quebec government to use these various groups, which were already mostly Catholic, as a potential converted minority to further the goals of the *nationalistes* in Quebec. According to Latimer, the MCSC was specifically to address the immigrant problem in Quebec under the watch of Bossy, as was the subsequent NCSB.[114]

Latimer continued, simultaneously expressing Cold War anxieties over the arrival of politicized DPs and the fear of the swarming of

Canada by Catholic masses. In his opinion, what these organizations that Bossy once led were trying to accomplish was to gain the trust and allegiance of the new, educated, and politicized refugees and use them to convince the less-educated, already-settled immigrants of an earlier era to support the clerical nationalism of the Quebec clergy. The French-Canadian press, politicians, and clergy were thus moving "towards [the] cohesion of New Canadians in general with the Province of Quebec, the Roman Catholic Church, and national policies ... The Catholic hierarchy is behind these efforts and gives its moral and realistic support." Latimer feared their success, since the Church was highly organized and centralized in Canada, and most of the Catholic immigrants were without their own bishops and authority figures. This would result, in Latimer's mind, in the fracturing of Canada, the prevention of the integration of immigrants, and the expansion of power of the Catholic Church.[115]

Latimer's statements could have easily been pulled from the interwar immigration literature profiled in Chapter 1 that linked the religion, race, and ethnicity of continental European immigrants together into a web of Otherness. In this web were the suspect cultural practices, languages, "look," and potential politics of DPs and other immigrants.[116] Their Catholicism (whether that of Poles, Hungarians, Ukrainians, or others) was part of this, and part of the overarching concern about assimilation and integration. It was yet another problem to be solved, as in this Cold War battle between authoritarianism and democracy, the Catholic Church could not be counted on as a devoted friend of democracy. What is different here from previous years is the ICC's decision on whether to publicly pursue these conspiratorial, anti-Catholic, and ethnocentric charges.

Judd grounded his commentary on the Bossy case in an intellectual framework also fundamentally distrustful of Catholics, if more measured than that of Latimer. Judd went to Ottawa to interview people to prove the veracity of Latimer's report. These interviews caused him to largely refute the claims of a clandestine Catholic plot to dominate Canada, along with the fact that Bossy seemed to have been terminated solely because of the conflict of interest associated with his political involvement.[117] Judd admitted, however, that he, the unnamed figures he interviewed, and "most Anglo-Saxon non-Roman Canadians agree that there are always long range political views present in the policies of the Roman Catholic Church, whether French or other ethnic strains." Judd counselled that, because there was very little evidence to support Latimer's claims – though he himself "wish[es] they could be so proved" – instead of publicly releasing these statements the ICC should concentrate on integrating immigrants in a more-constructive way.[118] Another Anglican, Rev. James Craig, who shared the Bossy information with Bishop of Toronto, F.H. Wilkinson, echoed this sentiment. Both were unsurprised that Catholics might try to create a unified majority in Canada, but they also knew from experience that releasing any statements, no matter how moderate, was often "misconstrued" by the public as prejudicial. He and Wilkinson concluded that the promotion of British immigration, rather than public animosity toward the Catholic Church, was the solution to these very real problems.[119] Latimer responded to these sentiments by clarifying that he never wanted to present these schemes as clandestine, comparing the open activities of the various Catholic organizations to Hitler authoring *Mein Kampf*, in that the public was simply unobservant. Yet he agreed with Judd and Craig to make no full-frontal attack upon the Catholic Church, but that the ICC and Protestant churches in general simply needed to pay more attention to immigrants.[120]

Another demonstration of the ICC's, and perhaps the United Church's, problematic perspective on working with Catholics and ecumenism in general was that secretary of the General Council, Rev. Ernest Long, was not only a member of the ICC but was involved with many other ecumenical organizations, such as the Central Committee of the World Council of Churches (WCC).[121] According to United Churchman Rev. W.G. Berry, Rev. Long opposed the inclusion of the ICC in the WCC, not because it was an anti-Catholic organization, but because its involvement would dilute the work of the ICC.[122] The ICC also had a troubled relationship with the Canadian Council of Churches (CCC), the major example of respectable ecumenism in the Cold War. The CCC was formed in 1944 and included in its initial membership all the major Protestant denominations in Canada. Its two main objectives were to organize cooperative programs between the various member denominations and to engage Canada with the international ecumenical movement, which culminated in 1948 with the founding of the WCC.[123] The CCC rejected the ICC's formal integration into its structure, as the ICC was too adamant that the CCC recognize the third and most important aspect of its work, to "work to protect Protestant rights and interests from any encroachment which appears to be prejudicial to such rights."[124] Wilfred Butcher, the general secretary of the CCC, wrote to secretary of the ICC V.T. Mooney that the organization was going through restructuring and could not possibly absorb the ICC, ending his letter with the provocative statement that its inclusion would create "dangerous and mischievous [sic] confusion." Mooney's response was perplexed and hurt, as in his mind the ICC had proven itself as an assiduous watchdog of the constant pressure by the Catholic hierarchy to promote its own devious interests.[125] The ICC was unwilling to alter its program at all and, in fact, Chairman W.G. Berry gave a presentation to the Department of Ecumenical Affairs of the CCC in which he suggested that the ICC should perhaps become a standing committee within the CCC. He feared that, if the CCC took over its "controversial" agenda of opposing education and an envoy to the Vatican, these issues would be "'soft-pedalled' in the interests of ecumenicity."[126] R.M. Bennett, another member of the CCC, did not seem to have the same scruples concerning the ICC, as he was a member,[127] sending a collection of editorials to Mooney all of which discussed attempts by Catholics to expand their educational rights in Ontario. Mooney thanked Bennett for securing an American clergyman for the last ICC meeting. This meeting had addressed, yet again, movements for an increase in Catholic education, adding a characteristically ominous warning: "The movement here is just part of a North American campaign."[128]

Elements within the CCC undoubtedly shared these opinions of the Catholic Church, despite its proclamations of liberality and the thoughtful, sophisticated reports and theological discussion that often characterized the organization.[129] First, there are numerous copies of the minutes of the ICC contained in the papers of the CCC, and these demonstrate that some members saw the ICC as an organization of note concerning ecumenical affairs.[130] When the Vatican announced the doctrine of the Assumption of Mary, the CCC distributed copies of the statement of the Archbishops of Canterbury and York, who explicitly condemned the action and accused it of hindering ecumenical relations.[131] One Rev. H.E. Wintemute of a Toronto Baptist Church sent a letter to Rev. Dr W.J. Gallagher of the CCC ridiculing the doctrine and pointing out that even the Vatican was having difficulty persuading theologians as to its efficacy, "[o]f course, they do not admit having made any mistake."[132] In an undated and unsigned document contained in the CCC files, the authors explored the "Implications of Diplomatic Representation at the Vatican." The document addressed the fears that Catholics viewed the Church as a "society above all others" and that an envoy would officially recognize the fact of the Vatican state and its centrality within Christendom, using these relations to further its unchanging goal of recognition as the leader of nations. What truly concerned the author was the role that the Vatican had assumed as the defender of Christianity against communism; its staunch position and existence as a political as well as religious organization promoted tension where it was strong, "increas[ing] rather than decreas[ing] the danger of war." The report concluded that the Catholic Church was destabilizing an already tense world by contributing to the self-righteous anti-communism and intense embrace of capitalism of the West, which had prevented the West from constructively dealing with "social and economic evils." The answer must be "no" to official diplomatic relations, as spiritual forces, especially a militantly anti-communist organization such as the Catholic Church, should not be manipulated for political ends.[133]

One report within the CCC files regarding "Civil and Religious Liberty," presented to the United Church of Canada General Council, by the chairman Ernest E. Long, and secretary, Ivor D. Williams, passionately condemned the ludicrous and harmful stereotyping of each other by narrow nationalists from both the English and French communities. Long and Williams believed that this treatment of the "other" was part of the irrational mentality that had resulted in McCarthyism, and they opposed Protestant characterizations of Quebec as fascist and the Church as authoritarian.[134] When discussing the recent censorship of the film *Martin Luther* by Quebec authorities, however, they expressed the fear that these actions resembled those of the Catholic authorities in "countries like Spain," yet again the great symbol of unbridled Catholic authoritarianism. Indeed, tolerance had its limits in their minds, as in "a land like ours, where Roman Catholicism is an important element in the national life, our discussion of freedom must take account of the fact that the Roman Church has no clearly defined doctrine favouring liberty of thought or expression."[135] In this atmosphere, Protestants needed to be vigilant concerning their liberty, particularly when the Church was so concentrated in one definable and important component of the Canadian nation.

Running throughout much of this discourse was concern with the place of Quebec within a changing nation. By the mid-to-late 1960s, the debate over Quebec nationalism and separatism dominated public life. The predominance of Catholicism in the province – even an apparently liberalizing Catholicism – played a significant role in some Anglo-Protestants' interpretations. Mainstream discussion of French-Canadian Catholics was no longer as hampered by the theological anti-Catholicism of Shields as public declarations of sectarian Christianity declined, nor was there the stark nativism and anti-French-Canadian sentiment of the Depression or of the Second World War. In addition, as demonstrated, public utterances of blatant anti-Catholicism within mainstream society changed, at least in the sense that those who once spoke them feared the label of bigot. By the mid-to-late 1960s, the anti-Catholicism underlying some of the discourse regarding French-Canadian nationalism was even more coded, expressed largely through portrayals of the intellectually inferior and irrational French-Canadian Catholic unable, and/or unwilling, to grasp the obligations of democratic society due to their poor education.

An example of this is Forsey's 1962 article "Canada: Two Nations or One?" Forsey savaged the idea of separatism, the reconfiguration of Confederation, or a recognition that Canada was founded by two peoples.[136] Forsey admitted that while some French Canadians understood that Canada was one nation in a political, legal, and constitutional sense, they were also under the faulty impression that they were being "short-changed" in this technologically advanced society. Forsey elucidated a caricatured vision of the French Canadian by outlining how business and government were constantly looking for qualified French Canadians, but that their religiously dominated educational system did not provide enough education in technology and science.[137] Forsey blamed the French-Canadian religious education system for the underrepresentation of Québécois in positions of power and authority even in their own province, reminiscent of Canadian National Railway representative Donald Gordon's infamous claim in 1962 that the reason the company had so few French Canadians in leadership positions was that there were no qualified French Canadians to occupy these positions.[138] Forsey asserted that Catholic education was inherently inferior in a modern society, expressing his anti-Catholicism in a subtle-yet-still-familiar form. In Forsey's mind, Catholicism was simply a force dividing the nation by forging a mentality of victimization.

The respectable press more often condemned explicit pronouncements of anti-Catholicism, at least publicly, for tearing Canada apart in this period. Rev. Fred Ellis of Hamilton, Ontario, learned this lesson when in 1962 the United Churchman and long-time member of the board of education in the city vehemently opposed the introduction of French as a mandatory subject in Ontario elementary schools. If French Canadians had refused to learn English in three hundred years, why should English Canadians learn French? To make matters worse, for Ellis, this refusal to learn English stemmed from the fact that French Canadians in Quebec were subject to a "monolithic religious domination" that had isolated them from the rest of Canada. Ellis boldly proclaimed that he would never "kow-tow" to an alien culture, particularly the "clerical-fascist system of Quebec."[139] This latter comment elicited much of the commentary, both hostile and supportive, revealing a shift in public discourse from earlier years, as Forsey, Scott, and many other commentators had regularly referred to the "clerical-fascist" nature of Quebec without public reaction. This terminology was no longer acceptable, apparently, to many in the public.

Despite the outrage, Ellis remained unrepentant, claiming that, of the three hundred letters he had received regarding his statements, most professed support for his position. It was thus a fact: the "monolithic ecclesiastical system" in Quebec hindered its proper development through isolation, something he stated everyone in Canada knew but simply could not prove. He was explicit about what constituted proper development: exposure to the British tradition of Canada. "I claim the British tradition has done more in the last 100 years or even the last 400 years," Ellis confidently announced, "for the emancipation of human minds, human dignity and the freedom of women than any other culture."[140] Ellis's opposition to bilingualism and the teaching of French was not, therefore, simply about the wasting of tax dollars, as he later claimed.[141] It was a reflection of an ethno-religious understanding of the "British tradition," the value of which lay in its preservation of freedom, liberty, and democracy.

Hugh MacLennan, author of the seminal Canadian novel *Two Solitudes*, added his impressive voice to the chorus denouncing Ellis in an editorial in the *Toronto Star*. Yet even within his spirited attack on Ellis, there was a subtle narrative justifying past instances of anti-Catholicism. MacLennan is careful to state that "Quebec *today* is not a 'clerical-Fascist state,'" as under the Jean Lesage Liberal regime the province had embraced modern society and technology, and was attempting to improve its education, so that French Canadians could take their rightful place beside English Canadians as one of the two founding nations of Canada. MacLennan added that "[Quebec's] culture is exploding; it is not priest-ridden *anymore*." Implicit within MacLennan's argument is that what was once a fact, that the Québécois were subject to the unquestioned rule of the Church and its allies in government, had been quite recently discarded. English Canadians had to embrace their partners in the nation, as Lesage's enemies were simply "neurotics," who loved nothing more than statements such as Ellis's emanating from Ontario. Lesage and his colleagues thus represented a constructed "reasonable Quebecker," which, MacLennan explicitly noted, included almost all English Quebeckers and, presumably, himself.[142] MacLennan was essentially parroting the line of anticlerical editor Jean-Charles Harvey and of Pierre Trudeau (especially in his *Cité libre* days), a narrative that has become extremely influential in subsequent decades: Duplessis represented a union of Church and state dedicated to keeping Quebec in the dark ages, with all of the religious connotations of that phrase. The province, by voting in the enlightened Liberals, who allegedly rejected all clerical influence and sparked a Quiet Revolution, was now responsible enough to participate in national life.[143]

MacLennan's tone was more strident in his correspondence with friend Lower only two years later. In a 1964 letter, MacLennan reported to Lower that the Québécois students in his class at McGill, particularly those crying "libre," were "remarkably infantile." This was due to the Québécois inferiority complex, as they felt inadequate in the modern world.[144] Close to the surface in the lengthy correspondence between MacLennan and Lower is the belief that the French Canadian was simply too primitive to truly "fit" into the world, resulting in youthful anger. The familiar intersections of race, ethnicity, and religion had also not totally disappeared from the commentary of those concerned with the place of "primitive," "alien" peoples in public life, at least as demonstrated by MacLennan and Lower. This was most striking following the October Crisis, when Lower blamed the violence of the Front de libération du Québec (FLQ), and Quebec nationalism in general, on the Québécois' "authoritarian education ... unsympathetic to the 'mundane,' the practical, the empiric, the commonplace ... little related to reality." Lower added some racial essentialism when he told MacLennan he had been rereading French Anglophile Hippolyte Adolphe Taine's classic 1873 work *History of English Literature* and was struck by Taine's description of his own people. Taine portrayed the French as superficial, pedantic, a dead or dying culture, stagnant in their unwillingness or inability to challenge orthodoxy. In the English, on the other hand, the liberty of the mind appeared and the ability to embrace individual thought took hold. While condemning much of Taine's work as embodying the race theory of the nineteenth century, Lower concluded that Taine had indeed been "realistic," and his account "explains much about French people today."[145] In his response, MacLennan easily understood Lower's reference to "authoritarian education" as meaning that education in Quebec was "clericalized" in its focus. This, for MacLennan, coupled with the "fact" that most Québécois were of vague indigenous heritage, explained the FLQ. Here was the linking of race, evolutionary development, and cultural maturity at its most bare: It was not intellectual nationalism, but blind fury, "a furious drive of the Territorial Imperative always stronger in the primitive. At the moment this further divides the *soi-disant* nation."[146]

Lower remained concerned about the role of Catholicism in French Canada throughout the 1960s, which dovetailed with his increasing concern over separatism. In a draft brief for the recently appointed Royal Commission on Bilingualism and Biculturalism, Lower was adamant that the current separatists in Quebec were nothing more than an embodiment of Hitler's racialism. The current conflict between English and French Canada was still reflective of his old "Two Ways of Life" thesis: English Canada represented the pinnacle of "the materialistic, individualistic society," while French Canada was "the quintessence of the conservative society." Yet Lower altered his formulation in one major sense: Catholicism had largely lost its hold on the French-Canadian intellectuals, a major group supporting *la survivance* for decades. Now a "Latin-Catholic type of urban civilization" was emerging from the Quiet Revolution. Inevitably, according to Lower, this would result, as it did in Mussolini's Italy, in an explosion of nationalism/racialism. In other words, because Catholicism had hindered the development of a mature identity and society for so long, now that the Church was declining as a defining force in French Canada, the overall nation would suffer from attacks demanding the total subservience of English Canada to French-Canadian needs. Lower advocated for partnership and slow decentralization to counter this extremist trend in Quebec, but his analysis was still rooted in the idea that Catholicism somehow distorted French Canada, and that only through reason and compromise with a mature people could Canada finally resolve its tensions.[147]

One could not sever Catholicism from the problem of French-Canadian nationalism in the minds of some Anglo-Protestants who had come of age in the years of this story. Yet what these statements demonstrate is not simply the perpetuity of ethnically charged anti-Catholicism or its total disappearance. Instead it showcases the non-linear transformation of English-Canadian identity. Britishness was undoubtedly still an important component of English-Canadian identity, as was Protestantism. Increasingly, however, ethno-religious pronouncements of it were measured, implicit, private, or even rejected within mainstream public opinion. For many during the first two decades of the Cold War, including liberal Protestants, Orangemen, or dispassionate social scientists, the Catholic Church and its multitude of flaws was still an internationally influential organization prone to authoritarianism, and was thus a threat to the progress of the democratic world. This "universalized" sentiment, namely that the Church was inherently incapable of existing within the liberal-democratic world, did not disappear, but once again shifted, along with other manifestations of anti-Catholicism, into the present day, as the nation became increasingly, self-consciously multicultural and tolerant.

5

Anti-Catholicism, 1970s–1990s: The Strange Survival of an Old Prejudice

> We have now ... created a situation in which the religious and moral values of the Roman Catholic Church are to be official policy.[1]
>
> Richard J. Doyle (n.d.)

At the close of the 1970s, Arthur Lower, long retired but still active, released a tome designed to counter what he saw as the narrowing of professional history into microscopic studies. *The Pattern of History* was his attempt to recall the "universalist" histories of Toynbee and Spengler. Lower posited that all of history (although he only looks at Western history) could be explained through a "three-stage evolution from zeal to intellect to disorder." First, an impulse begins as emotion and total conviction, which is then toned down through intellectualization and eventually ratiocination. Yet the wider society is never totally separated from the freedom promised by the first impulse, and eventually chaos and anarchy emerge and battle against the staid, intellectualized elites. Finally, the cycle starts all over again, and order is returned. In his conclusion, Lower expressed his own grim vision of the time: it was a dark era, one in which revolution and anarchy were just around the corner. This was largely attributable to the dominance of science and technology in modern society, an issue that Lower had been concerned about for decades. He viewed it as sapping the vitality and spirituality from humanity, particularly in the Anglo-Saxon population. Lower pointed to "the pill" as the culprit of the "killing of the 'WASPs,'" at least in North America. While the pill had saved women from the burden of "Unlimited child-bearing," it had gone too far, and was undermining the very basis of North American society. Implicit here is Lower's long-held belief that it was the

Anglo-Saxon Protestant population that had built modern Western civilization, that had provided the industry, efficiency, and commitment to individual freedoms necessary to construct the great democracies of the world. By the end of the 1970s, Lower saw this as disappearing, to the delight of "non-WASPs." Undoubtedly, Lower was referring to the increasingly diverse population of Canada, but with overtones of his previous concerns with the French-Canadian and immigrant Catholic population.[2] Without Protestantism, literally extinguished by its own selfishness and scientific advances, Western civilization faced another revolution, perhaps one that could finally awaken Protestants from their technological slumber and force them to re-establish their commitment to the democracy they had created.

Anti-Catholicism persisted beyond the 1960s in Canada, taking several different forms. One was an ethnically charged anti-Catholicism, embodied by the "BMG group," which continued to castigate Quebec as a backward, aggressively priest-ridden province, no matter if the Quiet Revolution had pushed the Church out of the public sphere. Another form was the even older and more marginalized theological anti-Catholicism of the tiny Canadian Protestant League (CPL) and other militant Protestants, which had little influence in Canadian public affairs beyond periodic outbursts. Most revealing, however, is the continuation of anti-Catholicism as a tradition within which some Canadians still operate when discussing the Church, Catholics, and Catholicism, seemingly self-consciously disconnected from any overt theological or ethnic anchors. The population of Canada changed dramatically in this period, as immigration increased from non-white, non-European, and/or non-Christian countries (see Tables 5.1 and 5.2). The official narrative of the nation, or "personality" of Canada, began to revolve around multiculturalism, bilingualism, and tolerance, as opposed to explicit Britishness (although a residual Britishness still inflected commitment to "progressive" values).[3] Many Canadians also became increasingly uncomfortable with overt expressions of Christian faith in the public sphere. The issue of secularization is a complex process in any nation, and Canada is no different. Historian Gary Mediema has skilfully shown how public declarations of Canadian identity, beginning in the 1960s, gradually became religiously "neutral" (i.e., non-Christian) and eventually reflected a multifaith society by the 1970s. Unity through diversity became the mantra

Table 5.1
Foreign-born population, descending from non-European areas

Area	1971	1981	1991	2001	2011
Caribbean	68,100	173,200	232,500	294,100	351,400
Central/South America	36,000	106,800	219,400	304,700	442,700
Northern Africa	28,700	38,700	53,200	93,200	186,700
Sub-Saharan	10,700	63,000	113,000	189,500	305,300
Western Asia and Middle East	25,200	63,200	151,100	285,600	456,000
Eastern Asia	66,600	195,500	377,200	730,600	962,600
Southeast Asia	13,100	152,200	312,000	469,100	729,800
Southern Asia	46,300	130,000	228,800	503,900	892,800

Statistics Canada, Censuses of Canada, 1951–2001, National Household Survey, 2011, http://www.statcan.gc.ca/pub/11-630-x/11-630-x2016006-eng.htm

Table 5.2
Religious composition of immigration as percentage of immigration

Religion	1971–80	1981–90	1991–2001
Roman Catholic	33.9	32.9	23
Protestant	21	14.5	10.7
Christian Orthodox	3.8	3	6.3
Jewish	2.2	1.9	1.2
Muslim	5.4	7.5	15
Hindu	3.6	4.9	6.5
Sikh	3.9	4.3	4.7
No religion	16.5	17.3	21.3

2001 Census: Analysis Series, Religions in Canada (Statistics Canada, 2003), 19.

of the post-1960s state. For Mediema, and for my study, this transformation of the public role of religion was not a linear decline in the face of modernity and multiculturalism; instead it was an uneven process that many Canadians resisted (and continue to resist) and which left some forms of Anglo-Protestantism intact. For Mediema, the state and public life never became wholly secular, it became pluralistic.[4] However, it is undeniable that the role of Christianity in public life changed dramatically across Canada throughout this period, as acceptance of non-Protestant and non-Christian faiths became an important sign of national development and Protestantism became cautiously decoupled from at least elite expressions of national identity (outside of the monarchy, of course).[5]

Canadians who disagree(d) with or wholly reject(ed) these changes to "traditional" Canadian society, on the other hand, aim(ed) their anxiety at non-white, often also non-Christian communities, instead of Catholics, as seen in the rise of contemporary Islamophobia. In fact, many conservative evangelicals began to openly align with Roman Catholics and the Church on socio-moral issues in the so-called "permissive society" of the post-1960s. Older theological divides and fears of Catholic authoritarianism were put aside in the pursuit of a united front against the secularity and materialism of modern society, particularly over abortion and LGBTQ rights.[6] This left deeply fundamentalist Protestants as the standard-bearers of an older, theological anti-Catholicism. In the wake of these changes, and keeping in mind residual ethnocentric and theological strains, anti-Catholicism remains a means of communicating one's liberal and progressive bona fides in Canadian society. It comes through a now-ironic non-denominational Anglo-Protestant lens, ironic in the sense that contemporary progressives and liberals would find many of the past prejudices and attitudes of this Anglo-Protestant milieu anathema, even as the old bogeys of "the revenge of the cradles" and Catholic control of Canada fade into Canada's past. The desire to oppose intolerance through opposing Catholicism remains as present as ever.

The process of "universalization" of anti-Catholicism that began in the early postwar period continued here, as critics of the Church focused on its negative social and cultural influence. The resiliency of the raft of meanings, historical assumptions, and tropes produced by anti-Catholicism often inflected otherwise legitimate debates over the Church and faith on central issues in contemporary society, such as LGBTQ rights, women's rights, and abortion. The Catholic Church remained stubbornly involved in the public sphere, with Catholic schools continuing to receive public funding and Catholic officials consistently making public statements on social and moral issues. Staunch secularists and those who believe in the total privatization of faith as a sign of modernity have bristled at the Church's claims to comprehensiveness in moral affairs, even though, as Mark McGowan points out, many Catholic politicians in Canada agree that

Church and state should be completely separated. McGowan draws attention to a particular irony: most of the prime ministers since 1968, an era often characterized as liberalizing the moral strictures of society, have been Catholics who have stressed the secular, multicultural nature of Canadian society. He goes so far as to say that the "privatization of religion has been evident most clearly in the public behaviour of Catholic politicians."[7] As Philip Jenkins has noted in his study of contemporary American anti-Catholicism, newer anti-Catholicism resembles older attacks on the Church and faith, because anti-Catholicism is a "living tradition," remaining as a "subterranean stream" in the intellectual and cultural life of some nations and providing a language through which to speak about the Church and faith.[8] While any perpetuation of anti-Catholic discourse is harmful, it is particularly harmful in this case, because it can be used to dismiss calls for change from within and from outside the Church, and it masks the very real debates going on within the Church and among the faithful. It also extends the life of an old prejudice based in an ethno-religious milieu (Anglo-Protestantism) that most contemporary progressives would find archaic. Nevertheless, Catholicism was/is perceived by these same figures as an alien force, invading and challenging the modern public space made possible by the struggle for individual rights, liberties, and secularization. Anti-Catholicism, therefore, serves as a manifestation of the subtle continuation of the influence of Anglo-Protestantism in English Canadian society, even without denominational allegiance or reference.

Winnett Boyd, Kenneth McDonald, and Orville Gaines founded BMG Publishing in the 1970s as a voice for conservative reaction against Pierre Trudeau and separatism in Quebec. Boyd was active in Progressive Conservative politics (he was the unsuccessful PC candidate for York-Scarborough in the 1972 federal election), former president of Arthur D. Little of Canada Limited, and an engineer, notably at the Chalk River nuclear reactor. McDonald knew Boyd from his days in aviation technology, worked at Canadair, and became a full-time author in 1969. He was unable to get his ideas about an increasingly socialist and Francophone Canada accepted by a publisher. Gaines was a mutual friend and illustrator. Boyd saw in this publishing company an opportunity to protest the growing centralization and bureaucratization of Canadian life under Trudeau's Liberals.[9] Their publishing company released a series of conservative tracts during the contentious debates over official bilingualism in the mid-to-late 1970s and in reaction to the election of the separatist Parti Québécois (PQ) in 1976. These tracts directly linked the Catholic Church to the efforts of French-Canadian nationalists to undermine Canada's integrity, bemoaning the collapse of British traditions and institutions and positing wild Francophobic conspiracy theories. Boyd pointed specifically to French traditions as a source of anxiety, because of the French proclivity for authoritarianism and state control of industry, which "are alien to the British traditions on which the country was founded."[10] For the BMG authors, Britishness and Anglo-Protestantism were not just a residue from an earlier era; they were fundamental to their world view and anxiety regarding a country they claimed to no longer recognize.

Lieutenant Commander (Retired) Jock V. Andrew wrote the best known and most popular of these works, entitled *Bilingual Today, French Tomorrow*.[11] In this diatribe against official bilingualism, Andrew went even farther than Boyd, by claiming that Trudeau's policies were part of a conspiracy designed to create a unilingual French nation. Andrew's concerns with the "francization" of Canada intersected with his anxiety around the concomitant elimination of its British heritage through coercive bilingualism and the encouragement of French immigration. Andrew noted that Catholicism was inextricable from this alien tradition. According to him, Trudeau and his Francophone ministers had been secretly sending agents through all French communities to foment "militant racism" against Anglophones. In Andrew's account, these agents were predominantly French-Catholic priests, operating under the guise of an organization called the Richelieu Society. Andrew linked this activity directly to the clergy's past goal of "outbreeding" the English to gain control of the nation, through a "revenge of the cradles." This "breeding-project" was so successful that French Catholics had usurped Quebec and were now, through immigration, governmental influence, and bilingualism, ready to spread their dominance through the entire nation (although Andrew is unclear as to when French Canadians did not control Quebec). Andrew could not ignore the fact that the Church was declining in public influence in Quebec, stating that the French were no longer a "Church-controlled race." However, the absolutism of the Church was difficult to shed, according to Andrew, allowing Catholicism to linger in the province.[12] He also equated the planned expansion of French-language schools across Canada to existing separate schools, suggesting that the increasing need for Canadians to speak French in order to get jobs – a constant refrain within the gathering English-language-rights forces – resulted in more people attending Catholic schools, where French instruction was more readily available. Attendance at these schools inevitably caused Canadians to convert to Catholicism, a form of backdoor conversion. Andrew was convinced that language policy and language schools would result in "every last English-speaking Canadian ... marr[ying] a French-Canadian ... promis[ing] to bring the children up in the French language. Or am I now getting mixed up with religion? Maybe it's the same thing."[13]

Andrew maintained this hostility toward Trudeauvian language policies and the constitutional politics that characterized this era into the 1980s and beyond the existence of BMG, condemning all major Quebec political figures as part of the French-Catholic conspiracy. In fact, Andrew's vitriol only seemed to increase. He was convinced that the only hope to preserve the Canada that he and other Anglo-Protestants had fought and died for in two world wars – implying that French Canadians had not – was for all English Canadians to join the radical anti-bilingualism group, the Alliance for the Preservation of English in Canada (APEC). He hoped this would still be possible, "concentration camps and Mr. Trudeau's SS and Gestapo notwithstanding," once again comparing the increase in French-Canadian influence in Canada to authoritarian powers. Only APEC, a group that Andrew played no small part in inspiring and strengthening in Ontario, could stand against this aggressive minority fuelled solely by the "race-hatred" instilled in French Canadians for centuries by the Church and used by opportunistic politicians. Brian Mulroney, only posing as an Irish Canadian but truly a French Canadian, was simply continuing Trudeau's sinister policies of mobilizing French-Canadian support when needed by exploiting the inherently subservient, docile, and isolated French-speaking masses to further their overarching goals. Andrew, of course, laid the blame for said docile masses at the feet of the Church, an institution dedicated only to furthering its power in the nation through its influence in Quebec.[14]

Andrew was not alone. Sam Allison, another BMG contributor and Montreal high-school teacher, provided an even-more-radical anti-Catholic argument against bilingualism and French influence in Canada in his *French Power: The Francization of Canada*, released in 1978. Allison saw in the separatist dream for an independent

Quebec and in the Trudeau government's plot to create an entirely French country an underlying pre-Conquest ideology, steeped in authoritarianism, intolerance, and Catholicism: "In effect, the Parti Québecois [*sic*] seems to be returning to the spirit of Quebec's pre-Conquest past. Therefore, it can be argued that independence is not a prelude to a New Quebec, it is a resurrection of a Brave New France."[15] The "spiritual authoritarianism" that many *nationalistes* and French Canadians were raised in had seeped into civil society, causing Quebec to appear more "like South America than North America." While Allison attempted to moderate his viewpoints by pointing out that political "ultranationalism," operating through a politicized Church, not through Catholicism itself, caused Quebec to be backward and authoritarian, he quickly descended into the racial theories that had much in common with an earlier anti-Catholicism.[16] Allison referenced the familiar "revenge of the cradles" idea as the central socio-economic aspect of the "tyrannical" Catholic Church in Quebec. This produced an uneducated, unhealthy surplus population, which was not only easily exploited by Anglophone employers, because they made up a large pool of cheap labour, but that were also physically diminutive and inferior to other Canadians.[17] Allison thus blamed the Catholic Church for fostering an inferior race of French Canadians, born and raised to be bitter toward the natural Anglophone elite who simply embraced true Canadian – that is, British – values of free enterprise, democracy, and self-restraint. Andrew's bizarre ethno-religiosity, along with the constant slippage between race, ethnicity, and religion, that appears in the BMG works, represents at least in some quarters the continuing salience of staunchly ethnic anti-Catholicism and anti-French Canadianism. Politically the authors reflected the changing conservative landscape of the 1970s and 1980s; however, their fears of a unified French-Catholic force undermining/overwhelming the "Canada they knew," based in Anglo-Protestantism, resembles that of earlier years. What had changed were the faces of this plot (Trudeau, Lévesque, a less publicly powerful Catholic Church), not the goals.

While the conspiratorial diatribes of Andrew, Allison, and Boyd sold well and elicited support among some segments of a disillusioned Anglophone population, no longer was the aggressively ethnic Anglo-Protestant nationalism of the BMG authors considered intellectually respectable, as demonstrated by its relegation to a specialty-publishing firm largely dedicated to protesting Trudeau's "insidious vision."[18]

Norman Webster's book review of Andrew's *Bilingual Today* for the *Globe and Mail* is an excellent example of the tension between competing visions of the nation. Webster dismissed the book as the work of a "madman" dedicated to provoking civil war, going so far as to compare it to *Mein Kampf*, yet he expressed concern about its very existence and popularity. Webster recalled recently attending a meeting of school trustees who were trying to promote French-language education; they were met with vehement opposition on financial grounds. Webster notes that one man informed him that this opposition to French-language schools was actually because they were the "first step" to French Canadians colonizing the nation and "outbreeding" true Canadians.[19] Webster's fear that "nuts" were either gaining in influence, or had never been curtailed in the first place, is characteristic of mainstream Canadian sentiment in the 1970s, by which time elite nationalist discourse was becoming largely void of explicit references to Britishness or chauvinism. Those continued manifestations of the latter were attacked as regressive and divisive, the work of "nuts" unable to progress with the rest of the nation and not fit for a modern bilingual and multicultural country. In other words, Andrew and his coterie were largely dismissed as relics of a different time, along with the Orange Order or the "no popery" movements of the nineteenth century.

The ideas expressed by the BMG Group did not disappear. As Matthew Hayday has noted in his invaluable study of pro- and anti-bilingualism in Canada, Andrew and BMG may have catered to a niche audience, but they served to create an infrastructure for future radical anti-bilingualism activists and/or opponents of French-Canadian nationalism and separatism. In addition, Hayday discusses the constant slippage among these organizations and conspiracy theorists between anti-French and anti-Catholic sentiments, revealing the continuing conflation of Catholicism with Frenchness.[20] In fact, the intersections of anti-French-Canadian and anti-Catholic conspiracy theories appeared as recently as Diane Francis's 1996 anti-separatist polemic *Fighting for Canada*, a book that would sit comfortably on the shelf beside these earlier tracts. Francis, at the time editor of the *Financial Post*, used her platform to vigorously attack Quebec separatism, portraying the separatist movement and the razor-thin 1995 referendum as the result of the machinations of a concerted conspiracy of Jesuit-educated Francophone elites. For Francis, the constitutional wrangling that had dominated Canadian public affairs since Trudeau took power in 1968 and the alleged transformation of Ottawa into a Francophone debating society reflected the higher aptitude of this generation of French Canadians as politicians, as they were pushed into the professions, the priesthood, or politics by their Jesuit teachers. The best English Canadians, on the other hand, "naturally" gravitated toward pragmatic activities, such as business, leaving public affairs open to crafty Jesuitical Quebeckers who enthusiastically embraced their newfound control of the levers of political power. Francis was repeating the old English-Canadian bailiwick that Catholic education was obscurantist, lost in idealistic pursuits of classical knowledge. While in this case it prepared its students for some aspect of modern society, French-Canadian religious education was still, in the end, harmful to Canadian society and the future of the nation.[21]

Francis even explicitly repeated T.-D. Bouchard's sensationalistic wartime claims about the Order of Jacques Cartier provoking an extremist French-Canadian nationalism, adding all the prominent contemporary French-Canadian political class to the list of membership. Francis seems to borrow much of her information regarding the order from journalist and disgraced former Mulroney press secretary Michel Gratton's fuzzy reminiscences of his father's membership in his book *French Canadians*. In Gratton's mind, the order was a powerful francophone organization, controlling much of the politics of the time in French Canada.[22] For Francis, the order, which essentially created the PQ, was "racist and fascist" and determined the entire makeup of the separatist movement since at least the 1940s. She referred approvingly to a French journalist's 1941 description of the order as a French-language version of the KKK, as it embraced the populist dictatorship of Mussolini and Franco, yet again presenting the earlier fears of a coherent, internationalist Latin fascism percolating in the province.[23]

PQ leader Jacques Parizeau and his cronies, apparently, wanted the same: an "ethnocentric, biased, xenophobic, and corporatist new state, which ignores the constitution and some of the rights of minorities." According to Francis, the order was to blame not only for perpetuating the inherent racism of separatism and the separatist mythology of oppression, but for harbouring Vichy war criminals after the Second World War and, she bizarrely suggests, with being the true inspiration behind the Maple Leaf flag of the Pearson Liberals. Here Francis seems to revert to the old Tory argument that the Maple Leaf flag was a sellout to Quebec nationalists by a corrupt Liberal Party beholden to the province.[24] Repeating another mid-century Tory shibboleth, Francis also claimed that the order was behind the anti-conscription movement in Quebec during the Second World War and that this resulted in the polarizing 1942 conscription plebiscite, which, she alleges, exempted French Canadians from the draft. Like those wartime commentators profiled earlier, Francis extolled Bouchard's bravery in exposing this group and regretted that Canadians had not heeded the words of Senator Bouchard then, as he had accurately warned the nation that the "Catholic-propagated myths" of French-Canadian disenfranchisement and the need for separation truly threatened the integrity of the nation. "[H]e's still correct," Francis confidently added, as this narrow-minded elite had nothing less than the destruction of Canada and the creation of a racist, socialistic dictatorship planned for an independent Quebec.[25] Francis is clearly linked, at least in her attitudes toward Catholic French Canada and in her understanding of twentieth-century Canadian history, to those earlier English Canadians who denigrated the French-Canadian commitment to the war effort, and thus the nation, no matter what the truth was.

What these authors share is not only a proclivity to deny the validity of Quebec separatism, Trudeauvian language policies, or even French-Canadian claims of historical marginalization, but also a residual acceptance of equating "French Canadian-ness" with Roman Catholicism, no matter the secularization of Quebec society. These authors position these forces as alien, indeed harmful, to the foundation of the nation. In this framework, Catholicism bred a propensity for authoritarianism and collectivism, reflected in the allegedly totalitarian socialist nature of modern French-Canadian politics and society, especially the separatist segment. It did not matter *how* secular Quebec had become (or not become) or how ethnically diverse it was; what mattered, as MacLennan had claimed in the 1960s, was that Quebec *had* been priest-ridden. Francis repeatedly denounced the socialist goals of Parizeau and his gang and, in an interview with Radio-Canada, openly equated separatism with socialism, that great bogey of collectivism of the second half of the twentieth century.[26] She also responded to criticism of her book by one of her interviewees, Benoît Aubin, who refuted her claims that he was a disillusioned separatist but had to follow the party line to keep his job, by expressing sadness, since Aubin was the victim of "tyranny," as were all

Quebeckers trying to promote democratic Canadian values.[27] Explicit references to Britishness as the defining feature of Canadian identity may be lacking in Francis's polemic, and the anti-statism of the discourse of all of these authors certainly reflects the neo-liberal right in post-1960s Canada, yet still lurking closely beneath the discourse of Francis and the BMG Group are the anti-Catholic conspiracy theories of an earlier era. As Andrew ominously told Hayday when refusing to be interviewed for his study, the book would "be little more than the record of the conquest of a nation by a determined third of its population. I watched it happen and I do not wish to relive it again."[28]

These caricatured ideas of French Canada also remained important for one of the major Anglo-Protestant intellectuals of the twentieth century in Canada, Arthur Lower. In his *Pattern of History*, he yet again repeated his "two ways of life" thesis, so central to his earlier landmark works. He portrayed North America as "one huge monument to Calvinism," as it had embraced the freedom of individual choice that Protestantism fought for in Europe. Freedom, for Lower, was the "Trojan Horse that Protestantism carried into Troy," eventually destroying the dominance of the old faith, which he termed "mediaevalism," and allowing for two faiths to exist, one dedicated to freedom (perhaps too much freedom) and one dedicated to the unity of state and church and maintaining the residue of Paganism. When these visions of the world were carried over to North America, they battled for control, with Jesuit and Puritan resembling each other in their passion, separated only by the "spectral figures in the Vatican." The French-Catholic "way of life" inevitably lost to the English, as the former remained wedded to the "hesitancies of a still semi-mediaeval Catholicism," while the latter had fully embraced "individualism and initiative."

While Lower may have moderated his language, notably stating that "No one any longer believes that without qualification Calvinism was the parent of capitalism," a dearly held belief of his own in previous decades, it was still clear that Protestantism equated freedom and progress and Catholicism meant regression and authoritarianism in his intellectual universe. Many times Lower mentioned how conflicts between these "ways of life" represented attempts to "turn back the clock" of history, to stem the "march of the mind" that Protestantism represented to the world.[29] While he does not directly mention the

Canadian situation, beyond rehashing his interpretation of the battle between New France and New England, it is clear that, for Lower, the terms within which he understood Catholicism as a faith and the Church as an institution had changed very little since his early days as a historian and despite the changes in Canadian society. It remained mired in the anti-Catholicism of his earlier life.

The Inter-Church Committee on Protestant–Roman Catholic Relations (ICC), no stranger to these visions of Catholic French Canada, was also still active into the 1970s. While some of the rhetoric of the ICC was still steeped in Canada's British tradition, much of the public work of the ICC was designed to prevent any further encroachment of Catholic education at the expense of the public system. In this way, the ICC of this period can be viewed as a transitional group, representing an anti-Catholicism replete with references to Britishness, but also attempting to maintain credibility. Respectable establishment figures such as Bill Davis, minister of education and eventual premier, were meek in discouraging the support of the committee over such a controversial issue as education, as Davis was already opposed to extending publicly funded Catholic education up to Grade 13, at least in the late 1960s and early 1970s. Davis in fact accepted an invitation from V.T. Mooney to attend a meeting of the ICC in 1968, but was careful not to do this in any official capacity as the minister of education.[30] In another letter from Davis to Mooney, during Davis's ultimately successful leadership bid for the Ontario PCs before the 1971 provincial election, he thanked the ICC for their support over the years but expressed hope that separate schools would not become a divisive issue in the election. He was, however, vague and political in his comments, unwilling to alienate a potentially important Protestant voting group.[31]

Davis was being naive at best in his dealings with the ICC, as it had several meetings with, and submitted several briefs to, the Ontario government over the years harshly condemning Catholic schools; in one brief, the ICC stated that the problem was "an aggressive element within the Roman Catholic communion" dedicated to the religious segregation of children, preventing the government from creating an "inherently" tolerant unified school system.[32] It was also at this time circulating a pamphlet it had written in the late 1960s protesting Catholic separate secondary schools and provocatively entitled "A New Separatism for Ontario?" In this document, the ICC stressed its continuing desire for a united Canada, disparaging the Catholic Church in Ontario for spreading Catholic separatism in the province and repeating their old argument that Catholics were attempting to control the province and perhaps Canada in general. In addition, the title was clearly an allusion to the increasingly vocal and controversial Quebec separatist movement, linking in the minds of the ICC the Quebec movement (unpopular in English Canada) and separate schools. "If the young people of today are separated in schools," the ICC bemoaned, "the adults of tomorrow will have this disability to overcome."[33] Mooney sent a letter of congratulations to Davis on his victory in the 1971 provincial election, in which Davis opposed extension of full funding to Catholic high schools. Mooney in fact took credit for Davis's success; the ICC and the Tories were the only groups steadfastly opposing Catholic encroachment, as the other parties vacillated to gain Catholic votes. Davis politely thanked Mooney for the support from the ICC during the election and hoped for continuing dialogue with the group, but, once again, did not make any solid promises.[34]

Despite this dialogue with Davis, by the early 1970s even the members of the ICC knew that the group was finished, due to institutional and organizational problems. Within the correspondence of this dark period for the ICC there is bitterness toward Protestant Canada's inability to perceive the importance of its task throughout the decades.[35] Mooney admitted that the Anglicans were about to pull out of the ICC, along with the Presbyterians, but he tried to maintain its unity for the provincial election, revealing that "I think the Protestants will be pretty weak-kneed if they let the Catholic zealots, in the name of 'ecumenicity,' take more and more privileges in education."[36] It was not ecumenism per se that the ICC was opposed to, but the perceived sacrificing of Protestant values on the altar of Catholicism that this politically correct ecumenism truly represented. The new chairman, James Craig, wrote to Ralph Latimer, who was now a member of the General Commission of Church Union, that "*we are not opposing the extension of separate schools because we are anti-RC; we are opposing it because we believe in ecumenism.*"[37] Despite constantly proclaiming its tolerant nature and belief in true ecumenicity – not the ecumenicity of the Catholic Church, which was in fact a plot to force Protestants to accept Catholic doctrine – within ICC correspondence into the 1970s, members continued to discuss Catholics in prejudicial terms. For example, according to Mooney,

Catholics comprised a larger proportion of the criminal population of Canada, due to their authoritarian church and parochial education. For Mooney, this was proof that Catholic schools did not create good Christian citizens; they simply produced more "dedicated (or bigotted [sic]) Roman Catholics." The Anglican High Churchmen who had been fooled into ecumenicity, disowning the ICC to maintain a fraternity with Catholics and the young clergy, simply did not "consider how useless the kind of religious education given in most separate schools apparently is, for 60% of the penitentiary population is Roman Catholic." Catholics were an irredeemable population, impervious to progress and reason (represented by the ICC) due to the propaganda of the Church. The ecumenism of the ICC, in other words, was hollow, based almost entirely on its hostility toward Catholicism, which itself rested in a conspiratorial understanding of the influence and role of the Catholic Church in Canada and throughout the nation's history. Mooney concluded a 1972 letter gloomily, admitting that the ICC was, for all intents and purposes, finished in the face of this powerful foe and foolish Protestantism.[38] Nevertheless, while certainly not espousing the same ideas as the ICC, Davis would stand firmly against funding for Catholic secondary schools through Grade 13 in the election of 1971, gaining the support of the traditional anti-Catholic wing of the provincial Tories.[39]

The issue would not go away, however, and Davis decided to reverse his decision in 1984 to provide full funding to Catholic high schools through Grade 13, eliciting a violent reaction from some Anglo-Protestant quarters. Toronto Anglican Archbishop Lewis Garnsworthy, who long-time Tory Eddie Goodman recalled had been quite ecumenical during the 1971 provincial election and was a liberal clergyman, compared Davis's actions to those of Hitler. Garnsworthy believed Davis was being "authoritarian" by not, somehow, consulting with the people, but instead fundamentally changing the fabric of the province by decree, joining others in casting a suspicious glance at the close relationship between Davis and Cardinal Emmett Carter. The questions about Davis and Carter often replayed old anti-Catholic arguments of Catholic political intrigue and harmful special-interest-group politics.[40] Conservative columnist Claire Hoy certainly perpetuated the idea of a clergy-mandated policy change in his 1985 biography of Davis. Hoy, citing unnamed sources close to Davis, claimed that Davis's 1984 announcement was not just a matter of conscience, as

Davis contended, but was the result of a 1981 meeting he had with his close friend Cardinal Carter, in which he promised extension in exchange for official Catholic support within the life of the government, if re-elected. When 1984 arrived, and Davis told Carter that he could not now extend Catholic funding, because Pope John Paul II was arriving in two months and sectarian tensions were rising, Carter allegedly threatened to pull Catholic support from the Tories, forcing Davis to relent and extend funding. Davis and Carter denied this arrangement vehemently (Carter almost sued Hoy for his claims), always stating it was a change of conscience, as he had apparently regretted his 1971 decision to not fund Catholic high schools.[41]

Many of those pushing a conspiratorial vision of Davis's decision, which was made without even consulting the minister of education, Bette Stephenson (to her great embarrassment), overlook the importance of the Ontario Students' Association for Fair Funding's active court challenge to the 1928 Tiny Township case that had originally prevented separate-school funding from being extended to the end of high school. The advocacy group had retained the services of noted lawyer (and future Ontario Attorney-General) Ian Scott, great-grandson of Sir Richard Scott, a pioneer of separate-school education in Canada and the man after which the Scott Act of 1863 was named. It had delayed its filing of the case, guaranteeing it would be argued during Pope John Paul II's visit in September, to maximize the potential pressure on the government. This was a serious challenge to the consensus over separate schools Davis had tried to create in 1971 and he announced extension only a few days after his Attorney-General, Roy McMurtry, filed the government's statement of defence. This suit, along with Davis's change in conscience, certainly motivated him to alter his policy. *Toronto Star* journalist Rosemary Speirs, in her analysis of the fall of the big blue machine in Ontario, rejects Hoy's conspiratorial understanding of the Tory reform, admitting that, yes, Davis and Carter had a close relationship and almost certainly discussed the extension of full funding, but this was not the deciding factor in Davis's decision. Whatever the nature of the relationship between Carter and Davis, Garnsworthy and others saw in it a violation of the separation of church and state and the privileging of one group over all others in the province.[42] This evocation of the importance of a secular public sphere had great effect in the post-1960s era, as Canadians came to increasingly question the presence of sectarianism or religiosity in public. Orland French of the *Globe and*

Mail was forced to confront the conviction of some that this deal had been made when he questioned Hoy's conclusions, since, French claimed, Davis was a wily politician himself and could avoid being "snookered by the men who play politics on God's behalf." J. Wood wrote a letter in response, condemning the Church's recent picketing in front of Henry Morgenthaler's abortion clinic in Toronto (to be discussed later) as an example of Catholics forcing their opinions on all other Canadians and asking French, "Is there an Ontarian who really believes the William Davis–Emmet Cardinal Carter–Frank Miller conspiracy won't result in the Catholic domination of our public funded schools[?]"[43]

Davis may have seemed to some commentators like a curious friend to Catholics, as he had been lambasted only three years earlier, during the 1981 provincial election, for cozying up to the Orange Order and exploiting anti-French sentiment in the province by not adopting official bilingualism. Columnist Alan Fotheringham provided such commentary in *Maclean's*, invoking the issue of tolerance for minority populations and attacking Davis as "sleazy" and "expedient" for supporting Trudeau on his language policies but refusing to implement progressive language policies in his own backyard. Davis knew "he has the last remnants of the Orange bigots," that "Ontario is one of the last places where they still have King Bill parades," and that this was "demeaning" for the non-Anglo-Saxon population. In the accompanying cartoon, Davis's government was labelled the "Big Blue and Semi-Orange Machine," placing "King Billy" Davis himself on top of the white horse in place of Orange hero King William (Figure 5.1).[44] Despite past associations between Davis, the Tories, and the traditionalist Protestant element within the province, the reaction to his compromise in 1984 demonstrates it was viewed by some as a betrayal of traditional Protestant values and by others as a betrayal of progressive values. The synonymity of these values for some Anglo-Protestants is unmistakable. Yet the true violator of said values, no matter the political or socio-cultural perspective, remained the same: the Catholic Church.

Garnsworthy sent Davis a letter almost immediately upon the announcement of extended funding, promising Anglican support, but with the proviso that all religious traditions had to be treated equally. Otherwise, as currently constituted, Garnsworthy claimed that Davis's policy would force all citizens of Ontario to "finance the teachings of the Roman Catholic Church in the Separate School system."[45]

Figure 5.1 Bill Davis sits in place of William III on his white horse, as portrayed in Orange symbolism. On his standard is the phrase "Elect King Billy & The Big Blue and Semi-Orange Machine," attacking Davis's famous electoral machine as still dependent on the bigoted Orange Order.

Absent here is any recognition that the government already financed separate schools up to Grade 10 and that this legislation would simply extend the funding three years for Catholics who chose to send their children to these schools. Garnworthy also wrote an article for *The Anglican*, denying any claims that he was anti-Catholic in his opposition to full funding; his opposition to this matter was not religious, but political. Garnworthy was never clear as to what the consultation he demanded would comprise, however, as extension had the support of the three major parties in the legislature. There were some who were not wholly supportive (such as dissident Tory Norman Sterling), but overall, no major party figure opposed Davis's principle of extension.[46] As it became clearer that the Frank Miller government, which took over from Davis after he resigned only a few months after the announcement, was going to tentatively proceed with Davis's plan to extend Catholic funding – and right before the

1985 election – Garnsworthy held his infamous press conference in which he compared Davis to Hitler. Garnsworthy denied any form of bigotry, while simultaneously using coded language steeped in anti-Catholicism. For example, Garnsworthy coyly stated that perhaps he should have called these actions fascist instead of Hitlerian, as the latter was "too loaded," a notable statement given the history in Canada of labelling Catholicism clerical-fascism. He added that he was not speaking for all Anglicans, as "We are not a monochrome church. We are democratic and people can disagree," presumably unlike people in the Catholic Church.[47] The Catholic Church was thus condemned as a particularly hierarchical institution, currying "special privileges" in a democratic society. This was reminiscent of the old "equal rights for all, special privileges for none" calls of the late-nineteenth century.

Garnsworthy portrayed himself as a defender of progress against the archaic machinations of the Church, a cause to which he seemed genuinely dedicated. Before he made his Hitler comparison, Garnsworthy claimed that Davis, by extending Catholic education three years, had caused "the religious and moral values of the Roman Catholic Church ... to be official policy" in the province. "I do not agree with Roman Catholic teaching on planned parenthood, nor the negative attitude the Roman Catholic Church has towards contraception," Garnsworthy stated, continuing, "I do not agree with the Roman Catholic position on abortion, nor that the Roman Catholic Church is the sole arbiter of religious or moral truth." For Garnsworthy, separate schools violated the very existence of a secular, progressive civil society. His final quotation, however, demonstrates that "secular" and "progressive" could also be coded terms: "Can it be that we are simply left with a public school system which is to have no value system, religious or moral, and a separate school system which is to represent the moral and religious values of this province?"[48] It was not religious education that was the problem, nor was it simply the privileging of one denomination and/or religion over another. At the core of Garnsworthy's opposition were the values that the Catholic Church was believed to represent and the potential victory/threat separate schools posed to his own interpretation of a progressive democratic society.

Although there were no explicit references to Canada's fundamental Britishness or even Protestantism, the legacy of that Anglo-Protestantism was implicit throughout this discourse. It was the public school that would be emptied of any moral importance, giving the

Catholic Church a monopoly on societal morality. Garnsworthy was suggesting that the Catholic Church was using its peculiar political influence to gain special privileges that violated the very foundation of a modern democracy, especially the separation of church and state and the principle of "fair play." Even more explicit were the quotations that emerged upon his retirement in 1989 and his untimely death soon after. Garnsworthy told reporters that he resented having to pay any tax that supported "those damned separate school[s]" and that he opposed the "medieval" attitudes of the Church on abortion and sexuality, an issue that remains central to debates about the influence of the Catholic Church to this day.[49] Yet this language is not neutral; the claim that the Church is inherently medieval and that this is in itself a pejorative, is central to the anti-Catholic tradition(s) detailed thus far.

Garnsworthy often appeared in public with the former moderator of the United Church of Canada, Clarke MacDonald, to rail against Davis's actions. MacDonald, for his part, expressed the old fear of Catholic dominance and violation of the separation of church and state at a press conference. He claimed that the extension of separate schools would not only promote divisiveness in the province and the nation, but that it could also lead to the establishment of a state church. Later, MacDonald told the government's committee on social development that by extending Catholic education the government was opening the possibility of "fundamentalistic" groups gaining their own schools and using them to attack Catholics, along with the mainstream churches and Jews, "in a Keegstra fashion," referring to the then-breaking case of a rural Alberta high-school teacher, James Keegstra, who was found to be teaching his students anti-Semitic conspiracy theories and Holocaust denial.[50] MacDonald accompanied Garnsworthy and about five thousand demonstrators to Queen's Park in 1985 to demand that the new David Peterson–led Liberal government denounce the Davis-Miller plans to extend full funding.[51] Political scientist Reg Whitaker added his voice to this chorus in an April 1985 article for the *Globe and Mail*. For the most part, Whitaker's opposition to separate schools rested on the premise that the funding of any religious school was archaic and based in a historic agreement at Confederation that no longer applied to the contemporary situation, a common criticism of the existence of separate schools. Whitaker, however, added that this act of extending Catholic educational funding by three years would create an "established church" in the province, recalling that great fear of Catholic disregard for modern secular civil society. Whitaker was not alone in his hyperbole. Frank Jones, in a *Toronto Star* article responding to Cardinal Carter's anger at what he deemed the anti-Catholicism of opponents of extension, called separate schools a "mistake of history" that needed to be fixed, not expanded. He accused Carter of looking backward to the Ontario of his childhood, which was indeed rife with sectarian conflict between Catholics and Protestants. But, according to Jones, this time was over: The Orange Order was gone, society had progressed, and Carter and his cadre needed to move forward, not look back at past prejudices.[52]

Ron Seberras of Rexdale, Ontario, embodied this complex discourse in a letter to the editor of the *Toronto Star*, albeit less eloquently than many of these previous examples. Seberras called for the end of religious segregation, the need for justice for all religions, and his desire for "economic sanity" in the educational system. Yet he also noted that these schools did nothing to keep Quebec in Confederation, one of the original reasons behind separate schools, and, perhaps more ominously, this minority that Ontarians had attempted to protect in 1841 now composed roughly half of the province. Beyond the familiar suggestion of the consequences of Catholic numerical dominance, these schools were now pointless, as they were no longer even protecting a vulnerable minority or keeping the nation together. They were instead potentially serving an aggressive *majority*.[53] Clearly hostility toward separate schools was not limited only to Garnsworthy or MacDonald.

Most commentators, both contemporary and with hindsight, analyzing the fall of the Tories in 1985 (first as a small minority and eventually losing government completely through a historic pact between the Liberals and New Democratic Party), see Garnsworthy and his comments as an important component of these events. Donald MacDonald, the long-time leader of the provincial CCF/NDP, believed that it was the religious conflict sparked by Garnsworthy, along with the obvious disorganization of Davis's successor, Frank Miller, which ended the forty-two-year Tory dynasty in 1985 because his extension of Catholic education did not have the support of even his own party.[54] Tory MPP, David Rotenberg, who lost in 1985, told the press that Garnsworthy deserved the "Ian Paisley award," as he had made it "respectable to be anti-Catholic" in the province and had caused the collapse of the Tories.[55] The theory that Garnsworthy had personally destroyed the Tories by appealing to traditionalist Protestant anti-Catholicism remained for years, as even Garnsworthy's 1990 obituary was titled "Ex-archbishop's views on RC school funding helped topple Tories."[56] However, Rosemary Speirs, in her measured assessment of the collapse of the Tories, notes that Garnsworthy himself did not cause the end of the big blue machine. Speirs quotes pollsters of the day who believed the Tories remained relatively strong in their traditional rural Protestant strongholds, but lost big in urban centres populated by, perhaps ironically, Catholics who had a traditional distrust of the Tories. Anti-Catholicism was not *the* defining factor, in other words, of their loss. Instead it was, at least in part, the cavalier way Davis and his successor, Miller, handled the roll-out of the new separate-school legislation.[57] Separate schools were thus undoubtedly a central factor in these events, yet, as stated before, opposition to separate schools is not inherently anti-Catholic; these schools are often opposed on very reasonable grounds of cost, or religious favouritism in a changing world. What *was* anti-Catholic were the tropes that Garnsworthy and others used in communicating these ideas.

Whether Garnsworthy caused the fall of the Tories or not, what his language reveals is that anti-Catholicism – at least in Ontario – existed as an undercurrent in society, only waiting to be reignited by some major event, even by those dedicated to a progressive, multicultural, and tolerant society, as Garnsworthy claimed to be. It was not just the purview of ethno-religious bigots like the BMG Group, easily dismissed as far-right conspiratorial cranks. As historian John Wolffe has so eloquently stated, anti-Catholicism "is like the granite that underlies the peat moors of Southwest England but breaks through in isolated places to form stark formations of weathered rock." It is always there and, periodically, when it surfaces, anti-Catholicism "can provide valuable viewpoints for understanding the geography of the whole" of the society and culture at these times.[58]

More explicit manifestations of anti-Catholicism of a specifically theological bent – hinted at by Garnsworthy and others – occurred around this time as well, embodied by the Canadian Protestant League (CPL), an organization which continued to operate into at least 2012. Long after Shields was gone from its helm, the CPL became embroiled in a major controversy regarding the distribution of hate literature in 1980s Ontario, running afoul of Attorney-General Roy McMurtry. Nicknamed "Roy McHeadlines" for his outspoken pronouncements,[59] in the early 1980s McMurtry made several public statements decrying the ineffectiveness of existing laws to prosecute these crimes. The CPL office in Burlington, Ontario, was one of several locations where anti-Catholic literature could be found at this time, and it became the most ardent public defender of the right of Protestants to distribute and read this material. In late 1983, Tory MPP Robert Eaton of Middlesex received from a police officer in Strathroy a copy of the viciously anti-Catholic Alberto Rivera comic books released by Chick Publications. Eaton brought the comic books to the attention of McMurtry by tabling them in the Ontario legislature; McMurtry responded that, while the comics were clearly anti-Catholic, he was unsure of whether charges could be laid. These works had been the subject of scrutiny earlier in the decade, when it was found that Rev. Jim Neale was selling Jack Chick's comics from his Toronto store, Christ Is the Answer. Yet when Customs Canada banned the importation of these books as hate literature for seven months in 1982, the courts eventually lifted the ruling, greatly frustrating McMurtry. Neale personally responded to this "persecution" to *Maclean's*, before the actual ban, telling the magazine that he was not worried about anything, as "McMurtry, the popes, they'll all stand before God in the end."[60]

Chick Publications, named after the patriarch of the company and militant fundamentalist conspiracy theorist Jack Chick, has published hundreds of comics and small illustrated "Chick tracts," expounding Chick's views on a variety of theological and moral matters.[61] Prominent among many other conspiracy theories are anti-Catholic stories outlined by the alleged former Jesuit Alberto Rivera. Rivera and Chick claim that the Catholic Church is not only bent on world domination, but that Catholicism is sending millions of people directly to hell for worshipping a pagan faith. Among Chick's more grandiose claims is that the Vatican holds a database on all "real" Protestants and is plotting the assassinations of these evangelizers.[62] The CPL, for its part, continued to distribute Chick's works and challenged McMurtry, the courts, and the Church itself to sue them. In a 1983 letter to provincial attorneys-general and the federal justice minister, the CPL claimed that the material was not criminal, because it did not attack a specific group, even though it clearly attacked the entire Catholic Church. Instead, it stated that it was simply disseminating "truth": "evangelical Protestant Canadians," it added, had the right to "express our treasured freedom of religion ... and expos[e] everything we believe to be in serious error."[63] The CPL was instrumental in rescinding the ban on Chick's material in Canada, with the head of the CPL, Rev. Jonas E.C. Shepherd, acting as the appellant against the deputy minister of national revenue, customs and excise. Judge J. Kenneth concluded that, while these publications were clearly an "attack [on] the Roman Catholic church and its doctrines," they did not "go beyond what the contemporary Canadian community is prepared to tolerate," perhaps further justifying McMurtry's frustrations.[64]

The CPL was not alone in distributing Chick tracts and other anti-Catholic literature in the early-to-mid-1980s. McMurtry, Toronto police, and the Ontario Provincial Police all noted a spike in the spread of anti-Catholic works caused by Premier Davis's decision to extend funding for separate schools and the visit by Pope John Paul II in September 1984, the first such visit to Canada by a pontiff. These parties worked together in task forces targeting the dissemination of hate literature in general. This material spread across Canada, with accounts of anti-Catholic literature coming from Edmonton as well as Manitoba.[65] Confusingly, in the months leading to the pope's visit, the *Globe and Mail*, which often denounced the rise in anti-Catholicism, allowed Christ Is the Answer to place a full-page advertisement in its book supplement, touting Avro Manhattan's lurid anti-Catholic conspiracy books, with such titles as *The Vatican-Washington-Moscow Alliance* and *The Vatican Billions*. This latter inclusion is particularly surprising, since it was advertised in a Chick tract to which then-provincial Liberal leader David Peterson drew attention in the legislature in February. The books supplement elicited outrage from at least two readers offended by the inclusion of anti-Catholic literature, but the *Globe and Mail* itself did not respond to the criticism that it was advertising the very materials that the government of Ontario was trying to prohibit from circulation.[66]

McMurtry loudly declared that anyone caught distributing anti-Catholic material would face arrest during Pope John Paul II's September visit. He and the police got creative preceding the pope's visit, proclaiming that, since hate-speech laws were so ineffective at leading to conviction, officials would charge offenders for encouraging others to breach the peace. Four people were in fact arrested for such an act outside the Eaton Centre in Toronto during the pope's time in Canada, but it is unclear if they were convicted.[67] Frank McClelland of the Toronto Free Presbyterian Church, a recently founded Canadian branch of Ian Paisley's notoriously anti-Catholic

Northern Irish denomination, boldly proclaimed that he and his congregation were willing to be imprisoned to defend their right to protest the papacy, which was a fraudulent representative of Christianity.[68] Yet when, at the invitation of the Canadian Council of Churches (CCC), Pope John Paul II did meet with Protestant leaders in an advertised ecumenical conference at St. Paul's Anglican Church in Toronto, McClelland and his congregation were conspicuously absent from any protests, claiming that the crowds would have been too large to get "their message" out to enough people.[69]

The Free Presbyterian Church was simply the loudest and crudest of those opposed to attending the pope's meeting. Relatively mainline denominations and organizations, such as the Evangelical Fellowship of Canada (EFC) and the Baptist Convention of Ontario and Quebec, refused to attend what they interpreted to be a Catholic-dominated meeting in Toronto. President of the latter, Rev. William Wood, claimed that participation in the meeting was such a divisive subject that the council had to choose between unity in their church or unity with all other churches. Wood wanted to avoid the public image that Protestants, "even Baptists," might be returning to the Roman fold after centuries of preaching the faith of the Reformation. The papacy as an institution and "the political relationship" of the Roman Catholic Church with the civic authority in Canada (and really in any other country) frightened Baptists, along with the Church's potential power to harm Protestants, as it had in many other countries. For Wood, "some people's memories are rather long," making it difficult to overcome the historic tensions between Catholicism and the Baptist Convention.[70]

William Jones, editor of the *Canadian Baptist*, had to defend himself against charges of anti-Catholicism, claiming he had simply published a critique of religious commercialization of the pope's visit in an editorial in March. Yet, within this editorial, Jones makes reference to how the pope's wealth and position as a head of state violated the traditions of Jesus and, more significantly, compared the sale of merchandise to raise money for the visit to the sale of indulgences.[71] Brian Stiller, editor of the EFC's *Faith Alive*, repeated these concerns, warning against the danger of viewing this new charismatic pope as the means to achieve "world Christian organic unity," thus ignoring the fundamental theological differences that necessitated the Reformation centuries before. Stiller also focused on the selling of "pope junk" to help defer costs of the trip, demonstrating that Catholics themselves were unwilling to support their own leader. Stiller concluded by calling for an end to "anti-Catholic head bashing," referring to the recent spike in anti-Catholic literature, but noted that the "flashing of coins in the marketplace" by the Church was distasteful at best. "[W]e call all those who claim to be Christian to discover Biblical truth," Stiller stated, reiterating what he believed was a key difference between a "modestly" corrupt Catholicism and a pure Protestantism, and "encounter personally the living Christ."[72]

The Papal Visit Advisory Committee of the CCC, on the other hand, certainly no fringe group, represented the complexity for Protestants who did recognize the pope's visit and wanted to discuss matters of importance to the Christian world with John Paul II. In notes for the first committee meeting on 12 July 1983, Donald Anderson, general secretary of the CCC, questioned whether it was appropriate to ask the Protestant churches represented to pray *for* the pope's visit, as opposed to simply praying *with* Pope John Paul II. At the forefront in these documents is always a genuine commitment to ecumenism integrating the Catholic Church. Yet Anderson felt the need to remind those on the committee that "the papal visit will be pastoral and celebratory but *not* a triumphal progress to Roman Catholics. To ensure this, it is strongly felt that the visit should take place in a setting of prayer and sensitive meeting." Later in 1983, Clarke MacDonald, before he became involved with Garnsworthy's anti-separate-school cause, prepared a statement outlining what he thought the CCC should ask the pope to say upon arrival, an unusual document to prepare for an arriving religious leader. The first section contains what MacDonald wanted the pope to reaffirm, including his commitment to Jesus as the saviour of humanity. MacDonald's second section called for the pope to tie his message to the Canadian context, specifically recognizing the rights of various marginalized groups, and suggested the CCC explicitly include the right of women to serve in Church leadership positions in its statement to the pontiff. MacDonald concluded that he hoped people welcomed the pope with open arms and saw his visit as useful, but more important, in the end, was the message of the gospel for humanity, not the leader of any church.[73] The perhaps inevitable tensions within Protestant communities that were recognizing and preparing for the arrival of the head of the Catholic Church, a Church unarguably dedicated to a hierarchical and patriarchal structure, are tangible. Some assumptions of anti-Catholicism, however, namely that the pope would be less interested in recognizing the importance of Christ as saviour than in gaining glory for himself, seep through, as does a concern with the Church's policies in the modern world.

According to its website in 2012, the CPL was dedicated to the "defense and confirmation of the Gospel" in Canada. The Protestant Reformation gave the "real Gospel" to the modern world, and Protestants in Canada today must be encouraged to understand this heritage. "Canadians at large must not be allowed," the site continued, "to be taken in by the pretensions of the Roman Catholic religion to be the 'Church' in Canada; or to think there is no ... difference between Roman Catholicism and true Biblical Christianity."[74] The online bookstore also advertised infamous anti-Catholic tracts such as *The Priest, the Woman, and the Confessional* by Charles Chiniquy and produced a fiercely anti-Catholic periodical entitled *The Protestant Challenge*.[75] Even this strain of anti-Catholicism has changed with time, however; despite the focus on Roman Catholicism on the website and in the literature, the new alien religious threat of Islam was also present. The CPL moved easily between its historic concern with the encroachment of Catholicism on Anglo-Protestant Canada and the Islamic violation of "Canadian values," because Catholicism and Islam served as different but related threats: these systems (not religions according to the CPL and other Christian fundamentalists) were a direct threat to Christian Canada, or at least the traditionalist Christian vision the CPL held as defining the "true" nation.[76] Nevertheless, this organization and manifestation of anti-Catholicism, while distasteful, is no longer as influential within the mainstream intellectual or cultural firmament of Canadian society, and is mostly relegated to hardline fundamentalists, who continue to see Rome as embodying the error and blasphemy opposed in the Reformation. Revealingly, when the CPL's old domain name is now entered, the user is sent directly to the website of the Toronto Free Presbyterian Church. The small Free Presbyterian Church of North America, with only nine churches spread across Canada, continues to reject modernism and liberalism in theology. It also rejects ecumenism, viewing it as inevitably leading Protestants back into the arms of Roman Catholicism.[77] These sentiments may not be as mainstream as they once were, yet the discussion surrounding Pope John Paul II's visit in the early 1980s and the proliferation of anti-Catholic hate literature around the same time reveal that they are also not as far from the surface as Canadians have assumed.

Another example of the remaining existence of these older forms of anti-Catholicism, particularly in rural Ontario, took place earlier in the small township of Cavan, just outside of Peterborough. In 1977, the Canadian Cistercian Order, based in Oka, Quebec, applied to the Cavan Township Council to have farmland rezoned from rural to institutional to found a monastery. The application was unanimously denied, with Councillor Joe Thompson proudly announcing, "Cavan is a Protestant township and it shall stay like this." Councillor Alex Ruth added that this was an overwhelmingly popular decision judging by the phone calls the council had received protesting the religious order.[78] While Cavan and the surrounding region are noted as strongly Protestant, Tory and Orange in several accounts, this was a step too far for some residents.[79] Thomas Lord was outraged, recalling a town meeting he had attended which debated the building of a separate school in the area. In one discussion, a man reportedly said that, if the monastery were built, "perhaps the Cavan Blazers should ride again," referring to a Protestant vigilante group of the nineteenth century that operated in the area and forced Catholic settlers out by burning their properties.[80] Rev. Barry Day of Peterborough's Trinity United Church and Rev. W.L. Chatterton, a Pentecostal minister from nearby Millbrook, both also condemned the decision in the name of ecumenism and brotherhood.[81]

However, a revealing statement by another local reflected the continuing tension between French and English and its intersection with anti-Catholicism. Melville Morrison, a local farmer, told the *Toronto Star* that "Catholics are a bad mixture. French Catholics are the worst kind," ignoring the fact that the Cistercians applying were mostly English-speakers. Lloyd Hooton, township clerk, and Councilman Ruth attempted to explain the actions of the township council by repeating the mantra that they were simply acting in the interests of the township. "Catholics are just as good neighbours as anyone else," said lifelong resident Hooton, "But the majority of residents don't want their township turned over to them." Ruth agreed, as he was concerned that the founding of a monastery was simply the first step in the eventual creation of a separate school and even a Catholic Church (there were no Catholic Churches in the township).[82] Clearly, the threat of French Roman Catholic infiltration of this small southwestern Ontario community was taken seriously by the townspeople, sparked by something as innocuous as a rezoning application.

A major difference in this example from the past, however, is that press and public reaction was uniformly negative across the country in condemning the council for representing the bigotry in Canada that was supposedly gone. This form of bigotry appeared to be particularly embarrassing for some Canadians because 1) it was viewed as a holdover from a less-enlightened time, and 2) it represented an existential threat to the nation, providing grist for the separatist mill that claimed grievance with an Anglo-dominated Canada. All three major Toronto newspapers attacked the council, with editorials reading "Ontario's Shame" (*Toronto Star*) and "Only Bigots Need Apply" (*Globe and Mail*). The former editorial went so far as to portray Cavan residents as hurting the country, accusing them of doing the work of Quebec separatists.[83] The *Toronto Sun* ran a cartoon on 7 October representing the Cavan Township Council as Klansmen ready to lynch McMurtry for interfering (McMurtry stated in the Ontario legislature that the government was willing to overturn the zoning by-law in Cavan to allow the monks to build their monastery).[84] In fact, the Canadian Civil Liberties Association did file a protest and the Ontario Human Rights Commission investigated the ruling of the Cavan town council to ensure that prejudice was not the primary reason for refusing the application, as the council claimed it was purely a zoning issue.[85]

The Cavan Township Council was embarrassed, and in its public statement expressed regret for any "inferences" of racial and religious discrimination, assured all citizens that the township was not prejudiced, and appealed to the Ontario Municipal Board to allow the council to include a new anti-discrimination clause in its zoning by-laws. The council even invited the Cistercians to reapply to prove its dedication to equality.[86] Yet even in the personal apologies of the councillors they did not actually admit any fault. In the official records of the Cavan Township Council meetings, an undated but signed handwritten division slip notes that it would send an apology to the newspapers because "the press has misquoted some statements made by council members at a regular meeting of Cavan Council." This was at best disingenuous, given the fact that several councillors came out after the controversy erupted reiterating the township's opposition to a monastery based on the township's Protestant heritage. Joe Thompson, who was largely responsible for sparking the debate, even acknowledged in a bizarre apology that he had made derogatory comments about Catholics. Thompson told the *Examiner* that he regretted referring to Cavan as a "Protestant township," as it was inflammatory, but he passionately denied that he had ever said anything against French Canadians, or Catholics, a confusing claim since he had denied the founding of a monastery to preserve the township's Protestant nature and even admitted he had attacked Catholics. The Cistercians, saddened by the obvious anti-Catholicism, decided to build elsewhere anyway, in Georgetown, Ontario.[87]

While the public reaction to the "Cavan incident" was largely negative, anti-Catholicism in a less overtly ethno-religious guise is often not maligned. This strain of anti-Catholicism is largely emptied of ethnic, linguistic, or theological hostility. It is often representative of how, in an increasingly secular, pluralistic culture, one speaks about Catholicism, the irony being that this framework is steeped in the language of centuries ago, positioning the Catholic Church as an enemy of progress, or as harmful to the functioning of democracy. It is still present in the mainstream and often centres on the alleged socio-cultural and sexual backwardness and distortedness of the Church in the modern world. Mark Massa has best labelled this form as "social-scientific anti-Catholicism." Here non-Catholics (and some Catholics) emphasize their dedication to religion as thoroughly privatized, with Catholicism representing that which has consistently refused the rigid divide between public and private religion. Therefore, while public culture in North America has often attempted to become, or at least appear, fully secularized, the Catholic Church has stubbornly continued to assert its authority over moral matters, an authority that it sees as natural, raising the ire of many within this public culture.[88]

For example, during the increasingly fraught debate over abortion in the 1980s, in which the Catholic Church proved to be a staunch ally and prime mover in the pro-life movement, criticisms of the seeming obsession of the Church with reproductive rights would often move into anti-Catholic stereotypes. As mentioned earlier, Archbishop Garnsworthy used the Church's "medieval" attitude toward abortion as one of his reasons to oppose the public funding of separate schools, ostensibly because funding these schools would legitimize Catholic morality. Michael Cuneo, in his excellent analysis of the rise of the pro-life movement in Toronto in the 1980s, provides several examples of how complex this movement truly was and how in fact the more militant and activist pro-lifers viewed the Church as a weak ally, beholden to political interests that prevented it from engaging in the on-the-street battles with what were perceived as murderers. For Cuneo the pro-life movement, at least in the mid-1980s, represented a radical example of lay dissent and a "self-contained subculture" within Canadian Catholicism. Nevertheless, these nuances were often ignored, and Cuneo writes that during his research he was confronted by several people making broad anti-Catholic statements, believing abortion to be a particularly "Catholic issue."[89]

Much of this fury came in reaction to Cardinal Carter controversially calling on the faithful to protest in front of Henry Morgentaler's newly opened abortion clinic in Toronto in late February 1985, protests that even bused in students from various Catholic schools to participate. Carter's actions demonstrate that, while the Church may have not supported the more radical pro-lifers, it certainly was firmly on the pro-life side in the debate and willing to cross certain political lines.[90] During these protests, which contained not only Catholics but also conservative Protestants and Jews,[91] Cuneo was told by a policeman that "It's always the same with these papist bastards. They want to take over the fucking country. Do these pricks think they can run my life?" A student taking notes told Cuneo that the protest was full of "Catholic nazis who'll flush the country down the toilet if we give them the chance." Finally, Cuneo observed, a United Church minister was taking picketers aside to tell them how wrong they were by giving them a lecture rife with anti-Catholic allusions: "Don't you realize that the whole country's laughing at you? You think you're making a point, but we're all in stitches," the minister told them indelicately, adding, "You're worshipping the Roman fetus-god, but this isn't Rome. Abortion has nothing to do with true religion. Consider this an invitation to the twentieth century," essentially labelling Catholicism an archaic, pagan faith with little to do with actual Christianity.[92]

A small Catholic organization, modelled on the American Catholic League for Religious and Civil Rights, was formed in Toronto in 1985 by University of Guelph history professor, conservative Catholic, and pro-life activist Keith Cassidy.[93] The Catholic Civil Rights League (CCRL) was dedicated specifically to countering the increased anti-Catholicism circulating through southern Ontario, especially with Carter's controversial decision to support these protests, and received the support of the *Catholic Register*. Cassidy and those involved defended the right of Catholics and the Church to speak out on socio-political and moral issues, such as abortion, resenting what he believed was the assumption that Catholics had no right to the public sphere.[94] The founding of the league elicited some thoughtful commentary, which revealed that attitudes toward the Catholic Church and Catholicism *had* changed over the decades and become much more nuanced. A *Globe and Mail* editorial, for example, accepted the fact that Catholics, indeed any citizen, had the right to engage in public debate, but rejected the presumption by Cassidy and more militant pro-life Catholics that debate over the Catholic position equalled anti-Catholicism. To disagree was not discrimination. Hugh Reynolds from Guelph, Ontario, echoed these views in a letter to the editor in which he regretted that average Catholics felt the need for such an organization when it was only the activities of a small group of "dogmatic" anti-abortion activists that caused a problem. Judy Rebick, spokesperson for the Ontario Coalition for Abortion Clinics (OCAC), a staunch ally of Morgentaler and a legendary feminist activist, told the *Globe and Mail* that OCAC and other pro-choice groups self-consciously refused aid from anti-Catholic groups, recognizing that this was a sentiment that existed in some corners of the pro-choice movement; instead they tried to convince individual Catholics as to the justice of their cause.[95]

Yet just as often there was anger at the Church and Catholics for pushing their views on the population, for transgressing the "proper" boundaries between state and church and between the private and public spheres. It is here that the residue of anti-Catholicism becomes visible, acting as a means through which people understand the Church and Catholics. In a letter to the editor of the *Globe*, H.R. Hallman of Toronto rejected even the idea of a league, noting that it should stand for everyone's rights, not just Catholics, and that the Church was trying to get public funds to impose its own views about women and abortion on the wider population, presumably referring to separate-school extension.[96] *Globe* columnist Orland French detailed a conversation he had with Cecil Baldwin, a retired man from Ottawa, who had written to all seven female MPPs in Ontario. Linking separate schools and abortion, he asked them why they had not opposed extension of separate-school education, as "Women in many countries around the world have led the fight against the state imposing the will of one religious group on all citizens of the state and have led the fight for equality and rights of women." This was a foundational battle in the preservation of human rights, according to Baldwin, equating the extension of Catholic education three years in a single province with international battles against theocracies. Baldwin sincerely hoped that all female MPPs would stand against any attempt by a Catholic school trustee imposing a "Catholic lifestyle" on teachers or board employees.[97]

Even the existence of anti-Catholicism has been challenged, often by attacking the Church's conservative position on moral issues or assuming Canada had moved beyond the sectarianism of the past. One example is the response to an article by Ian Dowbiggin, an assistant professor of history at the University of Prince Edward Island. In an April 1995 article for the *Globe and Mail* with the provocative title "Why Is Anti-Catholicism Tolerated?" Dowbiggin specifically responded to a comment made by Stephen Lewis at the International Conference on Population and Development in September 1994 that accused the Vatican and conservative Islamic states of being misogynistic in their equating of the language of reproductive rights with abortion, the latter of which they simply could not support. This had caused a lot of controversy at the meeting in Cairo and hindered talks about how to manage global population growth and improve women's reproductive rights. Dowbiggin interpreted Lewis's comment as representative of a contemporary anti-Catholicism, as he would not have openly spoken of any other church in this way. For Dowbiggin, this newer anti-Catholicism, which had roots in Canada's Orange past, largely revolved around telling Catholics what they should and should not do and how they should "properly" be involved in the public sphere. He characterized it as a "hip discourse that tries to reduce a worldwide church with hundreds of millions of parishioners to a handful of trendy slogans of dismissive contempt." It violated what was allegedly Canada's pluralist framework, including most but excluding Catholics.[98]

While Dowbiggin's frustration is palpable, what he ignored is that Lewis did mention other faiths, namely conservative Islam, and that he was defending the right of a conference on population and development, which had shifted to revolve largely around women's rights and empowerment, to openly discuss all forms of family planning and reproductive rights, including – but not limited to – abortion. Nevertheless, the reaction to Dowbiggin is revealing, and the flurry of letters, both in support of and opposed to his claims, crystallize the complexities of recent anti-Catholic discourse. A.D. Brewer of Puslinch, Ontario, in the same letters column, countered that Dowbiggin was mistaking criticism of the extreme elements in the Church, namely those totally opposed to compromise on abortion and/or women's rights, with anti-Catholicism. The Church had the right to express its opinion "medieval or mistaken [as] most people believe it to be." The problem was, according to Brewer, that the Church did not stop at this and was constantly trying to enforce its own set of morals on society. Brewer compared the Church's position on contraception to its treatment of Galileo. Could the world, with its massive overpopulation, survive the interregnum before the Church was forced to apologize? It had taken hundreds of years to recognize Galileo's correctness.[99]

Brewer was moderate compared to others. One set of responses, aptly entitled "Seeing a problem where none exists," rejected either the existence of anti-Catholicism entirely or the victimization of the Church and faith as portrayed by Dowbiggin. Marc A. Schindler of Spruce Grove, Alberta, for example, called Dowbiggin disingenuous, claiming that, while some small Protestant-Catholic conflicts had existed in Canada's past, Catholics had contributed to these as much as, if not more than, Protestants. In the case of the Jehovah's Witnesses in Quebec, the state, following the orders of the priests "as with the Inquisition," persecuted a sect deemed intolerable in a Catholic society. The gothic figures of the Spanish Inquisition were referred to again in a letter from Frances Walsh of Waterloo, Ontario, who pointed to the irony of a "descendant of Torquemada" bemoaning persecution, especially in a country that funded Catholic education but did not tax the Church itself. Walsh concluded with a revealing literary flourish, quoting Henrik Ibsen's *Ghosts*, positioning Catholicism as the remnant of a long-ago society, poisoning the contemporary world: "It is not only what we have inherited from our fathers that exists again in us, but all sorts of old dead ideas and all sorts of old dead beliefs and things of that kind. They are not actually alive in us; but there they are, dormant, all the same, and we can never be rid of them."[100]

Michael Enright, at the time the host of CBC Radio's *As It Happens*, and a Catholic himself, was even blunter in his evaluation of the Church in the nineties when he told Michael Posner of the *Globe and Mail* in a lengthy interview in 1997 that he perceived the Catholic Church as "the greatest criminal organization outside the Mafia." While Enright did apologize publicly in a letter to the *Globe*, he never specified which crimes he was referring to, although in the context of the late 1990s one can speculate that Enright meant either the emerging sexual-assault crises (emerging in that it was becoming more publicly-known, not that these crimes had just occurred) or the corruption in the Vatican bank.[101] He defended himself by pointing out that he was just "joking" and had certainly not meant anything malicious. In fact, he claimed he had been attacked in the past as a "mouthpiece" for the Church, trying to insert his own faith into commentary.[102] This is revealing, speaking to the ability/inability of Catholics to be "objective" as public figures, being dominated and controlled by their faith. Enright was perhaps inadvertently pointing to another aspect of anti-Catholicism that had affected him: namely, the inability of Catholics to "think for themselves." In addition, Enright's statement elicited no commentary from the interviewer (at least that was printed), and any controversy passed quickly.

Even Rebick, a thoughtful proponent of women's rights and access to abortion, in more recent years provoked accusations of anti-Catholicism. One specific case revolved around a cartoon by Mike Constable that appeared on Rebick's rabble.ca in 2005. The image depicted Pope Benedict XVI delivering a Nazi salute to a statue of the Virgin Mary and exclaiming "Heil Mary!"; Constable told reporters that it was in response to the "hypocrisy" of a pope who was in the Hitler Youth as a child delivering a speech condemning the Holocaust. The cartoon was criticized, unsurprisingly, by the CCRL, but it also elicited a response from readers of the *Ottawa Citizen* after an article interviewing Constable and Rebick appeared on the front page of the paper, in which both defended the cartoon as embodying the tradition of satire in Canadian culture.[103] The letters were largely negative, seeing in Constable's cartoon itself the height of hypocrisy, coming instead from the progressive left.[104]

Rebick provided a different explanation to the *Saint John Telegraph-Journal*, namely that when hypocrisy arises in an institution like the Catholic Church, one had to "take shots," adding that, since rabble.ca had recently published an article from the *Catholic New Times*, no one could accuse her website of being anti-Catholic.[105] Yet this cartoon *does* exist within a historical tradition of anti-Catholicism, particularly in its progressive strain. As has been demonstrated, equating the Church – especially its high clergy – with totalitarian dictatorships is a hackneyed trope, appearing throughout the twentieth century from figures across the political spectrum. Rebick noted in an interview that she and most rabble.ca users opposed the Church's position on same-sex marriage and its systemic homophobia, although it is not clear how Constable's cartoon commented on this issue beyond simply ridiculing the pope.[106] While it is unclear what exactly Constable was satirizing (the Church's position on women's rights? Its veneration of Mary? Its historic anti-Semitism? Its hierarchical structure? Or just Ratzinger's past in the Hitler Youth?) the cartoon does suggest a corrupted, undemocratic institution run by a tyrannical leader incapable of stopping himself from saluting a (in this case, faceless) religious emblem. It fits comfortably with earlier accusations by Forsey and Scott that the Church was encouraging a form of clerical-fascism and with other, more theologically-oriented, figures, who ridiculed Catholicism's veneration of Mary. Jenkins has noted that hostility toward Mariology, portraying Catholics as worshipping an "idol-godesss," has been a characteristic of the "new anti-Catholicism" that has emerged within liberal American circles since the 1970s. It represents for critics the superstition of Catholic practice and its arbitrariness, beholden to the whims of papal emotion, as the Assumption of Mary was dogmatically defined by Pius XII in the early 1950s.[107] Constable was, perhaps unintentionally, repeating this intersection between an older theological anti-Catholicism and the contemporary progressive hostility toward the Church's hierarchical structure and conservative stance on LGBTQ rights and abortion.

What was perhaps the most revealing aspect of the "Constable affair" was columnist Janice Kennedy's defence of the cartoon in the *Ottawa Citizen*. Kennedy ardently defended satire as a "linchpin of civilization," comparing Constable to Jonathan Swift and Mordecai Richler. She did not understand how this cartoon could be viewed as offensive: Nazi had become "culturally synonymous with tyranny," and since Ratzinger (and John Paul II before him) had "authoritarian impulses," this comparison was apt. "[S]o if the shoe fits ..." was Kennedy's conclusion, believing that those who were assailing the paper, Constable, and Rebick reeked of "Chairman Mao or Big Brother."[108] Yet again, infamous totalitarian dictators were invoked in the discourse surrounding a controversy over the Church; yet again it was taken for granted that the Church deserved these attacks, with rejection of these attacks construed as coming from blind followers. Certainly, Richard Bethell's letter to the editor calling for Constable and Rebick to be prosecuted for hate crimes and comparing them to the KKK was hyperbolic.[109] Dismissing offence being taken at such a cartoon by Catholics (or non-Catholics), however, is representative of a larger historical and intellectual understanding of

Catholicism in Canada and how it does not fit in a modern, secular, democratic society.

Another example of this strain of anti-Catholicism occurred when Catholic bishops in Canada publicly opposed Governor General Adrienne Clarkson sending congratulations to two recently married same-sex couples in Toronto who invited her to their weddings. While this is a controversial issue and the position of the official Catholic Church concerning LGBTQ issues is certainly open to criticism, the reaction to these bishops' public stand, by letter writers to the *Globe and Mail* at least, often degenerated into anti-Catholic stereotypes. Brendan Foley of St. John's asked "Is Canada a theocracy or a pluralist democracy?" Foley added the rhetorical question "Do we have citizen bishops or ayatollahs in cerise?" referring to the authoritarian regime of Iran, a comparison the CPL would certainly endorse and yet again linking contemporary Islamophobia with anti-Catholicism. He ended by telling the bishops that this was what liberty looked like in a "secular state, without prejudice." Lindsay Tabah and Mike Wladyka appealed to an even more explicitly anti-Catholic narrative, looking to the dark Catholic past as an explanation for the Church's present actions. According to Tabah, Catholicism "embodie[d] a history of intolerance, violence and fear," while Wladyka of Port Hope, Ontario, concluded that "Bishops have been blasting perceived heresies since the Inquisition. The Earth is no less round and the sun no less central to it." Wladyka sent his love and support to the recently married couples, reassuring them that these bishops represented only a "meagre world view" and knew nothing of true love.[110]

John Saddy perhaps best summarized this strain of anti-Catholicism in his short letter when he appealed to the centuries-old stereotype of Catholic priests and officials as sexual perverts.[111] Clearly, according to Saddy, anyone comfortable with their own sexuality would have no problem with same-sex marriage, something impossible for a celibate clergy engaged in systematic hypocrisy: "when the world's largest employer of homosexuals and lesbians, the Roman Catholic Church, condemns gay weddings, it is the epitome of hypocrisy."[112] This writer confusingly seems to be equating joining the priesthood or becoming a nun with unprofessed homosexuality, a sweeping generalization, which in itself castigates homosexuality as an abnormal development while simultaneously defending the rights of same-sex marriage. Celibacy, or homosexuality for that matter, simply did not fit into this correspondent's vision of the modern world, and anyone who "chose it" was clearly perplexed about his or her own "natural" sexuality. Jenkins notes that the trope of the priesthood as refuge for the homosexual, interpreting this as evidence that the Catholic Church promoted depraved sexuality, was a prominent theme in sensationalistic nineteenth-century anti-Catholic literature. When adapted to contemporary society, this stereotype defends sexual pluralism while rebuking the hierarchy for hindering the "psycho-sexual development" of its clergy; the Church thus acted as a form of "institutionalized closet."[113]

The trope of the priest as irredeemable sexual pervert also appears in the rhetoric surrounding recent revelations about the Church obfuscating investigations into groups of priests who had been committing sexual assaults and acts of pedophilia for decades.[114] Judy Rebick's rabble.ca has provided a forum for both intelligent criticisms of the Church's actions and for anti-Catholic diatribes and jokes. An example of intelligent criticism is Sharon Fraser's blog entry "The Priests and the Patriarchy." "To suggest that priestly celibacy is the problem," Fraser writes, "implies that child sexual abuse doesn't exist in all other segments of society." For Fraser, the child sex-abuse scandals in the Catholic Church, while of course horrifying and resulting partially from priests "living at the heart of patriarchy," were the result of power and entitlement, not Catholicism. Pedophilia was not about sexual distortion or celibacy, it was about power and a rejection of the humanity of the victims.[115] A striking example of an anti-Catholic diatribe appeared in a post by veteran progressive journalist Murray Dobbin on 31 March 2010, entitled "The Catholic Church: Pedophiles and Sadists."[116] Dobbin was responding to recent revelations that the Vatican, including, apparently, then-Cardinal Joseph Ratzinger (later Benedict XVI), knew about a priest assaulting young deaf boys in a school in Wisconsin and did nothing to stop him.[117] This is a horrifying case that should elicit a strong criticism of the Church's actions, as should any blocking of the proper prosecution of pedophiles by Church officials. Dobbin's post embodies both the passions this issue should evoke and Jenkins's "new anti-Catholicism," in which very real occurrences of sexual abuse are used as evidence to reaffirm pre-existing hostility toward the Church for a host of reasons (e.g., its undemocratic structure, its hostility towards LGBTQ rights, its largely pro-life stance).[118] Dobbin asked what it would take for Catholics to turn their backs on the Church, which, as far as he could tell, was "little more than an organized pedophile ring," serving as a respectable front for the most depraved people to engage in their most disgusting impulses. The entire Church, from the Vatican to the smallest parish, should be shuttered, sold, and the money sent to pay for condom distribution in Africa to "solve" the AIDS crisis, a crisis which the Church had exacerbated. The Church was simply "too profoundly sick to be capable of redeeming itself." If individual Catholics did not leave the Church now, they were complicit in the crimes of their Church. Dobbin went beyond even these monolithic condemnations, stating that the physical and sexual torment the Church inflicted on people was almost equalled by the mental anguish it caused by telling children they could be damned to hell if they sinned. Dobbin's equation here of Catholicism with pedophilia (at least in its consequences) goes far beyond legitimate criticism of the Church. It represents the continuation into the twenty-first century of many of the anti-Catholic tropes detailed in this study, especially the belief that Catholicism was a distorting force in modern society. His conclusion goes even further, however: "Pedophiles and sadists. If there was a vengeful God all of these monsters would have been struck dead by lightning long ago, the Pope among them."[119] Clearly, anti-Catholic narratives remain, at least in some circles.

In January 2016, the newly elected NDP government of Alberta released guidelines for public and separate schools in the province protecting the rights of LGBTQ students, including allowing the formation of gay-straight alliances. Bishop Fred Henry, the outspoken and intensely conservative bishop of Calgary, released a controversial statement accusing these new guidelines of promoting the "madness of relativism" and as "breath[ing] pure secularism," denying what for Henry was the foundational Catholic belief that human sexuality was a rigidly defined expression of divine creation. Even more inflammatory were Henry's charges that the legislation was a "forceful imposition of a particular narrow-minded anti-Catholic ideology."[120] Henry's remarks were met with some support, but mostly elicited widespread condemnation, both from within and outside of the Catholic community. One of the common refrains was that Henry and his confreres had "slithered in from a bygone era," that they, and the province with its separate schools, were clinging to an archaic system and understanding of pluralism and tolerance and were thus either to be dismissed or were worthy of pity.[121]

Undoubtedly, Henry's language is intemperate. It is no secret that the Catholic Church's treatment and understanding of LGBTQ rights has proven a troubling limitation for an institution and faith claiming to be based on universal love and fellowship. Nevertheless, what is revealing for this study is the reliance on old anti-Catholic stereotypes in the opinions of those hostile to Henry. One letter-writer to the *Edmonton Journal* saw Henry's labelling of the NDP as totalitarian "the pot calling the kettle black." The writer continued in his equation of Catholicism with totalitarianism: "Ever since the Emperor Constantine made Christianity the state religion of the Roman Empire, the Roman Catholic Church has been totalitarian." Rork Hilford of Calgary brought Canadian history into his expression of displeasure with Henry, believing schools were for educating students, not "forcing religious dogma down their throats." Hilford added that it was foolish to have religion and education linked in Alberta, calling for "another Manitoba Schools Question referendum," a strange proclamation, as there had never been a referendum on the Manitoba Schools Question in the first place.[122]

Former PC minister of education from 1976 to 1986, Dave King, provided perhaps the most comprehensive and revealing dismissal of Henry and his camp in his letter to the editor of the *Edmonton Journal*. King believed that Henry's comments demonstrated what King has suspected all along: the existence of these schools – of any publicly-funded religious schools – violates the principles of a civil democracy. It promotes not only favouritism for one faith tradition, but it tacitly offers support for the Henry model of inclusion, based on charity and noblesse oblige, not on the democratic principles of equality. King explained at the core of this undemocratic model is the fact that, if pushed enough, Henry and other Catholics would have to admit that decisions regarding these issues could only be decided by the pope, not the clergy or the laity, as the pope is where all authority lies in Catholicism. King closes the article by asking his audience if they are satisfied with a model of decision-making and inclusion that was so clearly "hierarchical."[123] Apparent here, yet again, is the subtle insinuation that Catholics cannot act rationally in a modern, pluralistic society, but instead rely on the dictates of their clergy and, in the end, the pontiff himself.

Henry's invocation of anti-Catholicism is complex, as providing for the protection of students, regardless of sexual orientation or identity, does not fit into the definition of anti-Catholicism argued throughout this study. The conflict here is based on a fundamental disagreement as to the nature of sexuality between one segment of the Church and a government providing for its citizens. As stated several times, criticism of the Church or Catholicism is not anti-Catholic, nor is embracing ideological and/or moral principles counter to Catholic doctrine, or to an interpretation of Catholic doctrine. What is important to this study is that those commenting on this controversy replicated the meanings, tropes, and historical assumptions comprising the discourse of anti-Catholicism in expressing their distaste for Henry's ideas. It shows that anti-Catholicism did not disappear in post-1960s Canada, replaced with a purely secular and tolerant Canadian identity, as Patrick Allitt has cautiously noted occurred in post-1960 America amid the controversies surrounding the election of John F. Kennedy and the integration of "white ethnics" into wider American culture. Allitt follows this claim with the caveat that these prejudices undoubtedly still exist among Americans, but that their decline in the public sphere has undermined its cultural and intellectual currency.[124] In Canada, the "vulgar" language of the CPL and fundamentalist Protestants has become marginalized. Yet public utterances steeped in the meanings produced by anti-Catholicism remain, particularly among those who consider that a Catholic Church contributes nothing to the nation – perhaps the world – other than conservative reaction.

CONCLUSION

Not Quite Us?

Anti-Catholicism in twentieth-century Canada provides an analytical framework through which to analyze the complex and constantly shifting nature of English-Canadian nationalism and conceptions of identity. A wide swath of Canadian intellectuals, politicians, organizations, Protestant leaders, and private Canadians constructed their vision of an ideal Canada through the first several decades of the twentieth century in opposition to its perceptions of Catholicism. Examining expressions of Canadian identity through the lens of anti-Catholicism also allows us to question the narrative that Canadian nationalism sharply transformed from a conservative, ethnic nationalism to a progressive, "universal" civic nationalism. Instead, I have posited that this dichotomization is itself the result of a normative framework created by academics and civic nationalists. Civic nationalism in Canada was exclusionary and contained many of the elements of an older ethnic nationalism, demonstrated by the continuing perception of Catholicism as an alien/rival religious/social system that did not "fit" into the ideal liberal Canada. Values believed to be "universal," such as liberty, freedom, and parliamentary democracy, were distinctively Protestant values, with observable British roots, for which Catholics were unsuitable. Thus, the basis of civic nationalism was a contingent universalism still anchored in the earlier language of an Anglo-Protestant Canada.

While this is the core pattern revealed by studying Canadian anti-Catholicism in this period, anti-Catholicism itself shifted and was never one-dimensional. There have always been those anti-Catholics who focus on theology, others on the alleged inherent disloyalty and/or authoritarianism of Catholics, and others who have been

Conclusion

concerned with the sexual and moral distortedness of the Church and its followers. What connects these discursive threads is a caricatured vision of the Church and Catholicism as a monolithic institution and system harmful to its adherents and to society in general, due to its foolish, even totalitarian, teachings, which have prevented individual self-realization. Some interpreted it not as a religious system or institution at all, but instead as a power-hungry political organization determined to constantly expand its already-global influence.

This "way of thinking" remains in Canadian society, manifesting itself not only in continued anti-Catholicism, but in Islamophobia and anti-Semitism. Anti-Catholicism, Islamophobia, and anti-Semitism should not be equated, however. Each tradition contains its own tropes and narrative(s) and has different, often tragic, real-world consequences. They have a "family resemblance," in which not all contain the same components at any one time, but a recognizable pattern emerges for analysis and comparison.[1] This pattern is often dependent on the creation of a "unifying Other," reflecting the unwanted elements of the Self, although this is always historically contingent. Islamophobia and anti-Catholicism, especially, are both shaped by the conflation of Western values with secularization, individualism, and universality. Islam and Catholicism are anachronisms *and* rivals in unsure modern times in these frameworks, whether working through secret political channels, overwhelming countries with immigration and/or a high birth rate, or perpetuating harmful social, political, and cultural values. These religions (perhaps not even religions, according to some), or at least the interpretations of them by commentators, challenge Western assumptions of the certainty and rationality of liberal democracy. Anti-Catholicism in this study reveals the complex processes that underlie visions of the modern nation, as well as those that underlie visions of an ideal citizenry.

The decoupling of anti-Catholicism in Canada from any specific immigrant or ethno-linguistic group represented the gradual "universalizing" of anti-Catholicism during the Cold War. Although residual anger at Catholic Quebec for its attitude toward the war remained in some circles, the discourse was gradually emptied of overt ethnic rhetoric as Canada and Western civilization faced a more daunting nemesis. Anti-Catholicism focused on the conflict of values between the liberal-democratic world and a Catholicism now compared to the new totalitarian threat, the Soviet Union. Protestants saw both Catholicism and communism as rival forms of (counter-)modernity, with Catholicism presenting a systematic alternative to the liberal-democratic ideal of the world. Catholicism was not simply an ossified medievalism any longer, but necessitated monitoring as an internationally powerful, potentially destabilizing, force in a tense world. In the face of an increasingly dangerous world, organized mainstream Protestantism expressed a desire for ecumenism to meet the totalitarian materialist threat. Through an analysis of the material, however, it is also clear that in Canada this threat was not perceived to be solely the Soviet Union but also a hierarchical Catholic Church.

Postwar anti-Catholicism provides the historian with the opportunity to revise earlier research into national identity in this period. Anti-Catholicism, as expressed in respectable, mainstream venues, became "universalized," but not completely severed from the conservative, ethnic nationalism of a previous era. Instead, these forms of nationalism blended into each other, and civic nationalism, while ostensibly dedicated to tolerance and liberty, repeated much of the discourse of an earlier nationalism obsessed with the British connection. It was this Britishness that was itself universalized in the minds of Canadian nationalists, as these universal values were distinctly within the British tradition, including an implicit devotion to a Protestant conception of world history and socio-cultural relations.

As the eminent British Marxist Raphael Samuel once stated, exhortations of pluralism have never prevented "British characteristics" from being exclusionary.[2] Many Canadians still perceived Catholicism as an alien faith that did not respect the normative civic values of Canada, such as democracy, freedom, and tolerance. It perpetuated sectarianism, parochialism, and, in the case of French Canada, aggressive nationalism. To oppose Catholicism into the 1960s and 1970s, and even the 1980s and 1990s, was therefore to oppose intolerance and narrow-mindedness. While the older, "vulgar" anti-Catholicism may have declined in respectability in the mainstream, anti-Catholicism did not exist only on the margins to be laughed at and dismissed. Anti-Catholicism did not disappear from Canadian discourse. It has constantly shifted in composition, reflecting the symbiotic relationship anti-Catholicism has shared with a central question in Canadian history: who is an ideal Canadian and how can this ideal be cultivated and protected? For many Canadians over the years, the answer to this question did not include Roman Catholics. For many Canadians now, it still does not include "the Other."

Notes

INTRODUCTION

1 These pictures are in the A.R. Kaufman fonds (hereafter ARK), Waterloo University Archives (hereafter WUA), box 1, file 23.
2 Notable exceptions are Christie, "Look Out for Leviathan," 63–94; Kenny, "A Prejudice that Rarely Utters Its Name," 639–72; Pitsula's *Keeping Canada British*. These build on the classic work of Miller, such as "Anti-Catholic Thought in Victorian Canada," 474–94. As recently as 2008, Bramadat and Seljak have noted the paucity of studies on anti-Catholicism. Bramadat and Seljak, "Charting the New Terrain," 39, n11.
3 I am influenced here by Gauvreau, "Beyond the Search for Intellectuals," 53–90.
4 Wahrman, "Change and the Corporeal in Seventeenth- and Eighteenth-Century Gender History," 584–602.
5 See note 2. Also see Miller's *Equal Rights* for the only Canadian study dedicated (mostly) to anti-Catholicism.
6 Jenkins, *The New Anti-Catholicism*, 6–8, 20–4, 32–3.
7 Massa, *Anti-Catholicism in America*, 7–16. As will be discussed, the secularity of Canada has often been equated with the Protestantism of Canada, not the total privatization of faith.
8 Porter, *The Vertical Mosaic*, 74–5, 101–3, 170–2, 289. On the other hand, Porter tends to fall into the prevailing stereotypes of the time, referring to Protestant societies as more materialistic and well-developed, and Catholics as coming from less-industrialized places. Porter seems to suggest that this may be an explanation for Catholic under-representation in positions of power in Canadian society. He is careful to point out, however, that religion is not deterministic of social status and that the place of Catholics

in society was not doctrinally based but the result of socio-historical factors, particularly the difficulty immigrants faced integrating into a predominantly Anglo-Protestant society. Porter, 95–100. McGowan notes that Porter was largely reaffirming statistically for many Anglo-Protestants what they had been told for decades by ministers and intellectual and cultural leaders (he mentions Arthur Lower specifically): that "Catholics in Canada were the nation's hewers of wood and drawers of water." McGowan, "Roman Catholics (Anglophone and Allophone)," 79–80.

9 McAuley and Nesbitt-Larking, *Contemporary Orangeism*, 17–19, 19–22 discuss both the Order's longevity in Ontario, Newfoundland, and New Brunswick, along with its gradual decline post-1960s.

10 Roy has written an excellent article on Catholics in BC. See her "The Maillardville, BC, School Strike," 63–88. Statistics Canada, 2001 Census and 2006 Census of Population. Marks has offered an alternative explanation of the lower (again, relatively) levels of anti-Catholicism in British Columbia in her recent *Infidels and the Damn Churches*. For Marks, the higher level of irreligion, coupled with the intense anti-Asian sentiment within the white population, tended to unify Protestants and Catholics against a "common enemy." Marks, *Infidels and the Damn Churches*, 90–6.

11 Perry Rockwood was a particularly anti-Catholic fundamentalist preacher in Truro, Nova Scotia. See his *Triumph in God*. Dalton Camp has a good profile of the religious divides in New Brunswick and Nova Scotia politics during much of the first three-quarters of the twentieth century. See Camp, *Gentlemen*, 32, 68–70, 149–54. Also see Henderson's biography *Angus L. Macdonald*. New Brunswick and Newfoundland have been referred to as strongholds (along with the "hub" of Ontario) for the Orange Order past its glory years of the early-twentieth century. See Eric Kaufmann, "The Orange Order in Ontario, Newfoundland, Scotland, and Northern Ireland: A Macro-Social Analysis," 42–68, Fitzgerald, "'British Union,' the Orange Order, and Newfoundland's Confederation with Canada, 1948–49," 146–69, and Wilson, "Introduction: 'Who Are These People?'" 9–24, in Wilson, ed., *The Orange Order in Canada*. Finally, Hayday discusses the ardency of the anti-bilingualism movement, which bled into anti-Catholicism, in New Brunswick in his *So They Want Us to Learn French*, 76–8.

12 See Cook's praise of the Trudeauvian neutral nation-state, *The Maple Leaf Forever*, x. Breton shares Cook's perspective, adding that Canada needed a strict civic nationalism, as ethnic nationalism would hinder a diverse nation such as Canada. See Breton, "From Ethnic to Civic Nationalism," 87. Ignatieff is a more-recent proponent of the positivity and necessity of civic nationalism. See Ignatieff, *Blood and Belonging*.

13 Igartua, *The Other Quiet Revolution*, 4, 136, 164, 222–6. Buckner, while agreeing that the ethnic conception had largely disappeared by the late 1960s, believes that these two forms of Canadian nationalism coexisted for some time, and that there was no sudden disappearance of the Canadian allegiance to Britishness. See Buckner, "Canada and the End of Empire," 122–4. Resnick counsels that English Canadians need to stop their "holier than thou" attitude toward Quebec nationalism being ethnic, as there was ethnic content in English-Canadian nationalism for decades, condemning this binary as useless for solving problems in multinational states. Confusingly, Resnick also believes that all nationalism in Canada is essentially now civic nationalism, just in different forms. Resnick, "Civic and Ethnic Nationalism," 282–93.
14 Champion, *The Strange Demise of British Canada*, 7–8, 38–9.
15 Bramadat and Seljak, "Charting the New Terrain," 10–11, 25. Bramadat and Seljak maintain that the three pillars of English-Canadian nationalism until at least the 1960s were Protestantism, British culture, and institutions, and a belief in modern political, economic, and scientific progress.
16 Yack, "The Myth," 194–8.
17 Ibid., 203, 196.
18 Anthony Smith, in his seminal studies of nationalism, has also critiqued the normative binary of civic and ethnic nationalism, influenced as it is by Hans Kohn's Western-Eastern binary of nationalism. According to Smith, European-trained historians became enamoured with Kohn's understanding of Western (civic) nationalism as enlightened and liberal, ignoring how the civic nation has been used to justify exclusion in actual practice. "Civic nationalism's failure to endorse minority group rights may be consonant with liberal individualism and individual human rights," Smith writes, "but only by conveniently overlooking the group rights accorded to the majority (host) nation." Smith, *Cultural Foundations of Nations*, 16–17, and *Nationalism*, 41.
19 Darian-Smith, Grimshaw, and McIntyre, "Introduction," 14; Schwarz, "Shivering in the Noonday Sun," in *Britishness Abroad*, 20–6.
20 Vance, *Maple Leaf Empire*, 221–2.
21 Belich, "Rise of the Angloworld," 41.
22 Jenkins, *New Anti-Catholicism*, 6–8.
23 Ibid., 5–8; McGreevy, "Thinking on One's Own," 98.
24 Esposito and Kalin, "Introduction," in Esposito and Kalin, eds., *Islamophobia*, xii–xiii.
25 Massa, *Anti-Catholicism in America*, 7–16.
26 Semati, "Islamophobia," 265–7.

27 Ibid., 265–7.
28 Chris Allen, *Islamophobia*, 189–90.
29 Said, *Orientalism*, 3; Allen, *Islamophobia*, 195–6.
30 Sayyid, *Fundamental Fear*, 4–5, 13–15.
31 Mendelson, *Exiles from Nowhere*, 1–4.
32 I am borrowing from Craig Calhoun's use of Ludwig Wittgenstein's "patterns as family resemblances" in his analysis of nationalism. Calhoun, *Nationalism*, 5–6.
33 Mendelson notes that this was a major component of anti-Semitism, combining Christian theological supercessionism and triumphalism. Mendelson, *Exiles from Nowhere*, 4.
34 Malcom, "Loyal Orangemen," 219, 242, n37.
35 Gross, *War Against Catholicism*, 22–8.
36 Werner and Harvard, "European Anti-Catholicism," 17–20. Also see Homi K. Bhabha's classic works on the complex reciprocal natures of the "self" and "other": "Of Mimicry and Man," 125–33, and "The Other Question," 66–84.
37 Christie and Gauvreau, "Introduction," 4–9, 24–6. Gauvreau and Christie also speculate that Canada perhaps experienced this public religious decline later than many European nations, especially Britain, due to its pre-existing history of religious pluralism leading to a revitalization of various denominations at different times. Also see Bramadat and Seljak, "Charting the New Terrain," 12–15.
38 Bramadat and Seljak, "Charting the New Terrain," 11–15.
39 Gary R. Miedema, *For Canada's Sake*, xv–xviii, 13, 21–7.
40 Bramadat and Seljak, "Charting the New Terrain," 15.
41 Noll and Nystrom, *Is the Reformation Over?* 11–13, briefly discusses the rapprochement between conservative evangelicals and Catholics in Canada.
42 Tumbleson, *Catholicism*, 13.

CHAPTER ONE

1 Woodsworth, *Strangers within Our Gates*, 293.
2 Kirkconnell to His Parents, December 23, 1917, file 10, vol. 3, Watson Kirkconnell fonds (hereafter WK), Acadia University Archives.
3 Ferguson, *Remaking Liberalism*, xv.
4 Ibid., 28–9.
5 English, *The Decline of Politics*, 5–7, 86–7.
6 Gauvreau and Christie, *Full-orbed Christianity*, xiii–xiv.
7 McGowan, "To Share in the Burdens of Empire," 177–9.

8 McLaughlin draws attention to the continued importance of Irish-Catholic nationalism and Irish-Protestant Orangeism in Canada, particularly how the former served to isolate aspects of the Irish-Canadian population. McLaughlin's conclusion, however, that the importance of Irish nationalism in Canada in this period does not lie in its predominance in the community but in its very existence does not refute McGowan's larger conclusion regarding an Irish-Catholic desire for greater involvement in the mainstream of Canadian society. McLaughlin, *Irish Canadian Conflict*, 17–22.
9 Pincus, *Protestantism and Patriotism*, 6–7, 446–8.
10 Valverde, "When the Mother of the Race Is Free," 5–6.
11 My thanks to Jennifer Henderson's *Settler Feminism*, 165–9, for drawing my attention to this source. For biographical information, see the same work, Chapter 3.
12 Murphy, *Impressions*, 14–17, 31–2, 136–8.
13 Ibid., 78–9, 106–7, 86–7.
14 Murphy, *Seeds of Pine*, 178–80; Murphy, *Open Trails*, 127.
15 Forsey to Mother, August 25, 1928, file 5, vol. 58, Eugene Forsey fonds (hereafter EF), Library and Archives Canada (hereafter LAC).
16 Forsey to Mother, September 13, 1928, file 5, vol. 48, EF. Franchot has noted that Protestant "tourists" often used visits to Catholic Churches or Rome itself to construct one's identity as more progressive, open, and separated from the horrors of a medieval past. Franchot, *Roads to Rome*, Chapters 2 and 9.
17 Canadian philosopher John Watson termed this the moral imperative, an idealized view of human existence that posited a moral order in an industrializing society through concrete, individual Christian choices. Quoted in Milligan, *Eugene A. Forsey*, 36–41.
18 Forsey to Mother, March 18, 1927, file 9, vol. 45, EF.
19 Referring to Catholics as "these people," as a monolithic mass that was completely distinct from the mainstream of society, was a common rhetorical device. It was not novel, as John Holland, the grand secretary of the Loyal Orange Lodge of British America, used it at a mass meeting in 1856: "'Wherever these people predominate,' he told a cheering crowd, 'there the peace and happiness and comfort of the community is destroyed.' 'These people' had no mind of their own he continued; they were mentally enslaved by their priests, and the results were plain to see – they were 'bad farmers,' with a well-deserved reputation for drinking, fighting and rioting." Wilson, "Orange Influences of the Right Kind," 92–3.
20 This book went through four editions between 1907 and 1916, with total sales reaching twenty thousand in Sellar's lifetime, a good number for a

book written by a rural newspaperman. Sellar's son estimated in 1959 that the book had reached a circulation of at least fifty thousand as it continued to be published by Horatio Hocken's Orange-leaning publishing company, Ontario Press. Hill, *Voice of the Vanishing Minority*, 272, 281–2. Hocken was the editor of the *Orange Sentinel*, as well as the one-time mayor of Toronto.

21 Nordstrom, *Danger on the Doorstep*, 54–5.
22 Morgan, ed., *Men and Women of the Time*, 1009.
23 Hill, *Voice of the Vanishing Minority*, 213. This was the opinion expressed by the *Progrès de Valleyfield* newspaper in the 1890s.
24 Sellar, *Tragedy*, 117–18, 153–4, 52, 79.
25 This was a goal of many figures in this period. See Kohn, *This Kindred People*, 20–6.
26 Sellar, *Tragedy*, 91, 330.
27 Ibid., 196, 271–3, 218–21, 312. Hill, *Voice of the Vanishing Minority*, 288–99. Hill places Sellar in the context of current Canadian debates about the alleged power of Quebec in the federal government, using him as a symbol of opposition to the "prostrating" of English Canadians on the "altar" of national unity.
28 Sellar, *Tragedy*, 312, 344–7.
29 See Miller, *Equal Rights*. Sellar, *Tragedy*, 349.
30 For an excellent analysis of the centrality of anti-Catholicism to fundamentalist theology in the early twentieth century, see Marsden, *Fundamentalism and American Culture*, 49–57, 66–7.
31 Kee, *Revivalists*, 53–66.
32 Oswald Smith, *Is the Antichrist at Hand?* 13, 22, 36–7.
33 Hislop, *The Two Babylons*, 1–3.
34 See Beard, *The Pope of Rome Is Antichrist*; Keach, *Antichrist Stormed*; Martin Luther, *A Faithful Admonition*.
35 Oswald Smith, *Is the Antichrist at Hand?* 36–7, 88–9.
36 Kee, *Revivalists*, 58. According to Brian Alexander McKenzie, Bingham's periodical had a circulation between three and eight thousand issues from 1916 to 1935, proving that it was at least a modest part of the intellectual and cultural landscape of English-speaking Canada. See McKenzie, "Fundamentalism," 71–3. By the end of his life in 1942, Bingham had overseen the SIM since 1893 and its growth into the largest Christian mission in Africa and the second-largest Christian mission in the world, second only to the China Inland Mission (McKenzie, 51). In addition, Bingham was a founding member of T.T. Shields's Second World War anti-Catholic organization, the Canadian Protestant League (see *Gospel Witness*,

23 October 1941), he sat on the board of the fundamentalist Toronto Bible College, and was a vigorous supporter of the Inter-Varsity Christian Fellowship (Stackhouse Jr, *Canadian Evangelicalism*, 186). John McNicol, the principal of Toronto Bible College, was also on the editorial board of Bingham's *Evangelical Christian* and was friends with Bingham.

37 "The Drift Rome-Ward," *Evangelical Christian*, July 1923.
38 Oswald Smith, *The Peoples Church*, 87. Smith revealed that Jaffray gave him $20,000 for the founding of the church. Saywell defines Jaffray as inheriting a highly moral newspaper from his father and transforming it into a platform for his own fundamentalism. This caused the newspaper to be faced with financial ruin, and thus it was easily bought by George McCullagh in 1936. Saywell, *"Just Call Me Mitch,"* 280. McKenzie, "Fundamentalism," 59–61.
39 The apoliticism of early fundamentalists (1890s to 1920s) in both Canada and the US has been noted numerous times, particularly after the embarrassment of the Scopes Monkey Trial. Horowitz has provided a provocative challenge to this convention, regarding the retreat of American fundamentalists from the "secular world" after Scopes as "overstated." In Canada, however, there has been less evidence that fundamentalists were significantly politically engaged, but there has been less scholarly attention paid to fundamentalism in general in Canada outside of individuals such as Shields or William Aberhart. See Marsden, *Fundamentalism*, for the conventional American narrative and Horowitz, *America's Right*, 72–8, for the challenge. For fundamentalism in Canada see Stackhouse Jr, *Canadian Evangelicalism*.
40 Pulkingham, "A Common Interest?" 7–8.
41 Woodsworth, *Strangers*, 110, 281. On the frontispiece of this work it states that this was specifically released through the Young People's Forward Movement Department of the Missionary Society and that the book had already sold eight thousand copies.
42 Coleman, *White Civility*, 176.
43 Barber, "Nationalism, Nativism, and the Social Gospel," 189–92.
44 Woodsworth, *Strangers*, 303, 288, 310. Italics in original.
45 Ibid., 293.
46 Scholars have noted that Connor was the most popular Canadian writer at the beginning of the twentieth century, allegedly even read by presidents and prime ministers. See Watt, "Western Myth," 26–7, and J. Lee Thompson and John H. Thompson, "Ralph Connor," 159.
47 Connor, *The Colporteur*, 4–5, 11, 14–21, 31, 25.
48 Ibid., 25.

49 McKillop, "Nationalism, Identity," 5–6.
50 Murphy, *Impressions*, 1–2.
51 Coleman, *White Civility*, 171–3.
52 The most detailed recent study of the controversies surrounding Regulation 17 is Cecillon's *Prayers, Petitions, and Protests*, 1–15, 75–6.
53 Sellar, *Tragedy*, 311.
54 Sissons, *Bi-lingual Schools*, 108.
55 For the former characterization, see Dutil, "Against Isolationism," 125. For the latter see Heick, "The Character and Spirit of an Age," 20. The *Bonne Entente* movement was started by two Toronto Liberals, J.M. Godfrey and Arthur Hawkes, ostensibly to heal the divide between French and English Canada. Brown and Cook believe it was more cynical: to retrieve investment by French businesses angered by Regulation 17 and, for Godfrey anyway, to convince French Canadians that coalition government and conscription were positives. Cook and Brown, *Canada, 1896–1921*, 265–6.
56 In August 1913, the Whitney government, facing massive opposition, gave the minister of education, on the advice of the inspector, the authority to extend French instruction in any schools beyond the first two years and beyond the one-hour limit. Regulation 17 was also adjusted to put the Catholic inspector on an equal level with the Protestant inspector, but the inspection was still designed to emphasize English. Cecillon, *Prayers, Petitions, and Protests*, 90.
57 Sissons was also against the Ottawa Separate School Board, who refused to recognize the validity of the Regulation and instead pulled its students out of their schools. The board had to be replaced with a temporary commission to ensure the proper functioning of schools. Sissons, *Bi-lingual*, 108–13, 184–7, 207–15.
58 Sissons, *Bi-lingual*, 187–90, 112–13.
59 Ferguson, "British-Canadian Intellectuals," 314–15.
60 Sissons, "The Schools of Manitoba: No. 9," *Globe*, 23 November 1912. This was one part of a nine-part series that ran from early October 1912 to this issue. Sissons noted in his memoirs that, when doing research for his book, *Church and State*, he was better received by the departments of education in provinces where "no special privileges were extended to any religious body and where consequently there were no political complications." Sissons, Nil alienum, 252–3.
61 Walker, *Catholic Education: A Documentary Study*, 289–90; "Calls Bilingualism National Outrage," *Globe*, 17 August 1916.
62 "Rowell Scores Nationalists," *Globe*, 7 December 1917.

63 English, *Decline of Politics*, 109–11; Stephen Leacock, "Democracy and Social Progress," 15–20.
64 For classic studies of race and first-wave feminism, see Valverde's "When the Mother of the Race Is Free" and Bacchi's *Liberation Deferred?* Chapter 7. More recently, Fiamengo, while acknowledging the importance of no longer sanctifying early women's-rights activists, has criticized historians of first-wave feminism for oversimplifying the white supremacy of early feminists. See Fiamengo, "Rediscovering Our Foremothers Again," 85–7. Jennifer Henderson is an exception to the ignoring of anti-Catholicism, as she examines Emily Murphy's anti-Catholicism in *Settler Feminism*, 165–9. Henderson also represents a more recent, literary-criticism-based analysis of the racial attitudes of first-wave feminists in Canada.
65 Plumptre, "Some Thoughts on the Suffrage in Canada," 304–5, 312–15. Wells's own anti-Catholicism was most prominently displayed in his book *Crux Ansata: An Indictment of the Roman Catholic Church* (London: Penguin, 1943). Biographical information is from Forestall with Moynagh, eds., *Documenting First Wave Feminisms*, 297.
66 Murphy, *Janey Canuck in the West*, 30–1.
67 Kirkconnell to Mother, 5 December 1917, file 10, vol. 3, WK.
68 S.D. Chown, "An Open Letter on the Duty of the Hour," *Christian Guardian*, 12 December 1917. This quotation is from a letter to K. Kingston, found in Bliss, "Methodist Church," 222.
69 Baillargeon traces the origins of this phrase to Jesuit Louis Lalande in 1918. Baillargeon, *Babies for the Nation*, 46–59, 268n61.
70 Brown's own anti-Catholicism has been well-documented. See Careless's entry for Brown in the *Dictionary of Canadian Biography*, http://www.biographi.ca/en/bio/brown_george_10E.html, accessed 20 June 2014.
71 Sellar, *George Brown*, 27, 2, 25–6, 32, 18–19.
72 Memorandum from Robert Borden to C.J. Doherty, J.D. Reid, and G.E. Foster, 13 November 1917, Robert Borden fonds (hereafter RB), vol. 16, LAC. This memo is quoted by English, *Decline of Politics*, 191–2, to demonstrate Borden's frustration and his resort to anti-French discourse. Borden to Denison, 21 Dec. 1917, vol. 16, RB.
73 Borden to Morrison, 25 October 1917, vol. 140, RB. In the most comprehensive study of 1917, Dutil and MacKenzie have pointed out that, while the Quebec Church was opposed to conscription – although not opposed to the war effort in general – the Catholic Church in much of the rest of Canada was very supportive of the war effort and even encouraged enlistment to an extent. Dutil and MacKenzie, *Embattled Nation*, 154–5.

74 For example, citizens of the area claimed they saw cannon being secretly brought into the novitiate, while others were sure that secret tunnels were being constructed underneath it to engage in treachery. Leo Johnson, *Guelph*, 314. Immediately after the Easter Riots in Quebec City, there was also concern that French Catholics were hoarding ammunition and weapons in local Catholic churches. Auger, "On the Brink of Civil War," 523.

75 "Many Young Men in Quebec Are Taking to the Woods," *The Sentinel*, 30 May 1918. The quoted author, Gaston Maillet of the French weekly *L'Autorité*, advocated the government forcing these men to perform their duty. Admittedly, as Daniel Byers has noted in his excellent research into military recruitment in the First World War, 68 per cent of the defaulters under the MSA by the end of the war were French Canadian. What is revealing is not the frank discussion of *why* French Canadians would be opposed to conscription, but the conspiratorial and anti-Catholic theories surrounding this fact. Byers, *Zombie Army*, 196.

76 Hogan, "The Guelph Novitiate," 57; Johnson, *Guelph*, 314.

77 Hogan, "The Guelph Novitiate," 58–9.

78 Middleton and Chisholm, *Report*, 61.

79 Hogan, "The Guelph Novitiate," 65–7. There is confusion about this point, as Rutherdale notes that the original memo was lost, causing great consternation at the later inquiry as to whether the exact wording was "cleaned out" or "cleaned up." I am using the phrase that both Rutherdale and Hogan use more often. Rutherdale, *Hometown Horizons*, 182. In the official inquiry, the commissioners state that the original expression was "cleaned up," but that a transcription error caused it to be forwarded as "cleaned out." Middleton and Chisholm, *Report*, 61.

80 Hogan, "The Guelph Novitiate," 66. The commission concluded that the press ban was designed to avoid "arous[ing] in other parts of the Dominion the feeling that members of the Catholic Church were not being treated fairly under the law." Middleton and Chisholm, *Report*, 67.

81 The most serious violent outburst regarding conscription took place over the Easter weekend, 1918, in Quebec City, which saw riots by French Canadians opposed to the implementation of compulsory service. Four to five civilians were killed by troops. Auger notes that it is not clear how many civilians died, as four were confirmed, but *Le Devoir* reported at the time that one more civilian had died from his injuries in hospital. See Auger, "On the Brink of Civil War," 519–20.

82 Dutil and Mackenzie, *Embattled Nation*, Chapter 9, is a comprehensive breakdown of the results of the election, which saw Union triumph in all provinces outside of Quebec and win 57.1 per cent of the popular vote.

83 "Guelph Excited by Gossip about Jesuit College," *Toronto Star*, 19 June 1918.
84 "Novitiate Affair Is Discussed in Some Protestant Pulpits," *Guelph Evening Mercury*, 24 June 1918. Rev. H.G. Christie of Guelph accused Justice Minister Doherty of deviously crafting the MSA to protect Catholic students from conscription. See Hopkins, *Canadian Annual Review, 1918*, 458.
85 The Catholic Unity League, *Double Collapse*, 9.
86 "Novitiate Affair Is Discussed in Some Protestant Pulpits," *Guelph Evening Mercury*, 24 June 1918.
87 *Double Collapse*, 23; Middleton and Chisholm, *Report*, 69. In the House of Commons, MP Sam Hughes, no friend of the Roman Catholic community, mentioned Palmer was central to the government decision to formally investigate the events of the Guelph Raid. See House of Commons Debates, Sam Hughes, 7 April 1919, 1219–1221. See Haycock, *Sam Hughes*, 26–55, 114–15.
88 "Ottawa's Move Is Now Awaited by Guelph Folk," *Toronto Star*, 22 June 1918.
89 For both texts and a good analysis, see Schultz, ed., *A Veil of Fear*. According to Schultz, vii, *Maria Monk* sold three hundred thousand copies at home and abroad by 1860, becoming one of the best-selling books in the North Atlantic Triangle.
90 George Nunan, "The Guelph Raid: Visit of the Military Police to the Novitiate, June 7, 1918," 19 August 1963 copied by Horatio P. Phelan; Doherty provided two recollections of the raid, one "The Guelph Raid," in 1961 and another on 21 August 1963, also copied by Horatio P. Phelan, Box D-509, The Archive of the Jesuits in Canada (hereafter AJC).
91 Bourque to Mewburn, 8 June 1918, Box D-509, AJC.
92 "Novitiate Affair Is Discussed in Some Protestant Pulpits," *Guelph Evening Mercury*, 24 June 1918.
93 "Guelph Ministers Demand Fair Play under M.S. Act," *Globe and Mail*, 24 June 1918.
94 Motion moved by R.C. Jackson and R.J. Edgar, 15 July 1918, Correspondence, Royal Black Preceptory fonds (hereafter RBP), Glenbow Museum Archives (hereafter GMA); "Guelph Ministers Say Real Quarrel Is with Law Makers," *Ottawa Citizen*, 24 June 1918.
95 Dutil and MacKenzie, *Embattled Nation*, 156.
96 Woodsworth, *My Neighbour*, Introduction by Richard Allen, x.
97 Cook and Brown, *Canada, 1896–1921*, 2–3. At the Pre-Assembly Congress of the Presbyterian Church in 1913, Rev. J.G. Shearer expressed

his concern with the nature and ethnic composition of the cities. He was afraid that, if the churches failed to minister to the shifting population and protect Canadian institutions, the cities would begin to crumble and thus inevitably the nation itself. Rev. J.G. Shearer, "Redemption," 171–3.

98 Woodsworth, *My Neighbour*, 101–4.
99 Ibid., 104.
100 McGowan, "Portion for the Vanquished," 219; Fay believes that huge amounts of immigration "challenged the devotional and jurisdictional edifice" of the Church in Canada. See Fay, *History of Canadian Catholics*, 151, 159–60, 164–9, 177.
101 Fay, *History of Canadian Catholics*, 160.
102 McNaught, *Prophet in Politics*, 91–4.
103 Woodsworth, *My Neighbour*, 104.
104 Jennifer Henderson, *Settler Feminism*, 170–1. See *Janey Canuck in the West*, *Open Trails*, and *Seeds of Pine*.
105 Murphy, *Open Trails*, 72–3; Murphy, *Seeds of Pine*, 26.
106 Murphy, *Seeds of Pine*, 212–21.
107 Ibid., 12–13, 212–21.
108 Cook and Brown, *Canada, 1896–1921*, 11, 71–4, 83, 303; Barber, "Nationalism, Nativism," 215–17; Gauvreau and Christie, *Full-orbed Christianity*, 166–72. For a good analysis of the visions of "the West" in Canada, mostly formulated by Easterners, see Owram, *Promise of Eden*, 32–3, 48–9, 76–8.
109 Gordon, "The Canadian Situation," 87–9.
110 Amaron, *Future of Canada*, 2.
111 Ward and Smith, *Jimmy Gardiner*, 19.
112 See Kyba, "J.T.M. Anderson," 114–17; George Hoffman, "Saskatchewan Catholics," 65–9; Robin, *Shades of Right*, especially Chapters 2–3; the most recent account is Pitsula, *Keeping Canada British*, especially Chapters 7–8.
113 Kyba, "Anderson," 110.
114 Anderson, *Education of the New Canadian*, 31–2, 39, 83, 196–8.
115 Ibid., 97, 60–1, 25.
116 Barber, "Nation-Building in Saskatchewan," 218–22. For his memoirs, see England, *Living, Learning, Remembering*.
117 Crowley, *Marriage of Minds*, 260.
118 England, *Central European*, vii–viii, xiv; for a scholarly – if brief – analysis, see Wurtele, "Assimilation," 122–33.
119 England, *Central European*, 220.
120 Ibid., 91, 167, 192–3.

121 Ibid., 225. Italics appear in the original.
122 Ibid., 147.
123 According to Tyner and Inwood, "Geography of Race," 801–6, and Roediger, *How Race Survived*, 153–68, this was the most common division of the white race at the time. England, *Central European*, 41–3.
124 Gauvreau, "Protestantism Transformed," 79–83.
125 England, *Central European*, 46, 100–1, 211.
126 Kyba, "Ballots and Burning Crosses," 107–8, 116. For a succinct study of Lloyd's career, see Kitzan, "Preaching Purity," 291–311.
127 Kitzan, "Preaching Purity," 297–9.
128 Mancuso, "For Purity or Prosperity," 1–23.
129 Gray, *The Roar of the Twenties*, 247; William H. Katerberg, "Protecting Christian Liberty," 9–10; Palmer, *Patterns of Prejudice*, 98–106.
130 Cook and Brown, *Canada, 1896–1921*, 58–60. Rev. Cecil Swanson remembered Lloyd as being held in high esteem among the Anglican community, even if not everyone shared his nativist sentiments. See Palmer, *Patterns of Prejudice*, 198, n18. For a favourable evaluation of Lloyd's life and accomplishments, see B.A. McKelvie, "The Fighting Bishop," *Maclean's*, 1 September 1936.
131 Lloyd, *Trail of 1903*, frontispiece, 29.
132 Ibid., 91. Barber notes that the Fellowship was designed to spread the empire and the Church of England to the polyglot masses of Western Canada. Barber, "The Fellowship," 154–66. Vance, in *Maple Leaf Empire*, 129, mentions this organization as emerging from the legislation after, not during, the Great War, which was designed to encourage British missionaries to come to Western Canada.
133 Lloyd, "Building of the Nation," 4. Lloyd provided a series of articles for the *Banff Crag and Canyon* from August to November 1928 similarly entitled "Nation-Building," railing against the evils of Liberal immigration policy.
134 Lloyd, "Building of the Nation," 5–6, 12. Lloyd explicitly used the term "Mongrel Canada" when he released an open letter to the newspapers condemning Canada's immigration policy in contrast to Australia's "white-only" policy. See George Exton Lloyd, "British Australia; Mongrel Canada," *Globe*, 28 April 1928.
135 All letters from the NAC are anonymous unless otherwise noted. Letter to Robert Forke from Master of Council S217, 28 November 1928, also contains the "Al Smith" statement. For letters claiming that a plethora of Catholic priests were employed by the government, see letter to Robert Forke from the Master of Council 101, 5 May 1928; to Deputy Minister

from Master of Council S217, February 1928; to Mackenzie King from Secretary of Council, 8 May 1928; letter to Mackenzie King from the National Association of Canada, undated. Immigration Branch fonds (hereafter IB), volume 335, file 348818, LAC.

136 Letter to A.P. Bigelow from Robert Forke, 23 April 1929; to Master Council, S217 from Acting Deputy Minister, 22 February 1929; to Kyle McMaster from [unclear], 1 February 1930, IB.

137 Letter to Master of the National Association of Canada from Robert Forke, 9 May 1928, IB.

138 Kitzan, "Preaching Purity," 306.

139 Katerberg, "Protecting Christian Liberty," 6.

140 Pitsula, *Keeping Canada British*, 162–73.

141 Kyba, "Anderson," 125.

142 Ibid., 116–19, 125, 131–5. Kyba claims that Anderson represented those who saw in schools only a neutral institution. The Tories under Anderson won no seats in the 1934 election, and the party would not form a government in Saskatchewan again until 1982.

143 Batzold, "Some Facts," 11–12, 7.

144 "Ku Klux Klan Accused of Dynamite Outrage in the Town of Barrie," *Globe*, 22 June 1926; Harry Hertz, "KKK Busy Again in Alberta: Activities Elsewhere Sporadic," *Edmonton Journal*, n.d. (1929?). Found in the file Ku Klux Klan in Canada, GMA. This event is briefly described among other instances of Klan violence in Robin, *Shades of Right*, 15. Sher details how, in 1922, fires destroyed Catholic institutions, including a rest home in Oka, which were widely suspected to be the fault of the Klan. That same year, St Boniface College, near Winnipeg, was destroyed by a fire that killed ten Catholics; again it was widely believed to be caused by the Klan. Sher, *White Hoods*, 26. Pitsula, *Keeping Canada British*, 1, 17–19.

145 "Two More Klansmen Arrested at Barrie Following Outrage," *Globe*, 23 June 1926.

146 "Outrage at Barrie Repudiated by Klan to Hon. W.F. Nickle," *Globe*, 25 June 1926. This article mistakenly refers to Lord as "A.H. Lord"; there is no evidence for an A.H. Lord in the New Brunswick legislature. Interestingly, Jimmy Gardiner was warned by a friend before the 1929 election about a Klansman who was travelling west as a Bible-school organizer. He was a New Brunswick Tory MLA named J.S. Lord, or "Dirty Jim" Lord of Saint Stephen. The Klan was clearly not limited only to the Prairies or Ontario. See Ward and Smith, *Jimmy Gardiner*, 92; for the nickname "Dirty Jim" Lord see Robin, *Shades of Right*, 11–12. Thank you to the Provincial Archives of New Brunswick for the information about Lord.

147 W.E. Sieber, Protestant Home News Letter, 1935, box 1, Springbank Loyal Orange Lodge fonds, GMA.
148 This view is best represented by Bartley, "A Public Nuisance." While Bartley focuses solely on Ontario and claims that there was no political room for the Klan there, as demonstrated earlier, even in that province the Klan was not just a minor inconvenience but perpetuated and exacerbated anti-Catholicism. Pitsula, *Keeping Canada British*, 1, 5–8, 14–19.
149 Gibbon, *Canadian Mosaic*, ix. Gibbon mentions an American author, Victoria Hayward, as the first to use the term mosaic to describe the Canadian people in *Romantic Canada* (Toronto: Macmillan and Company, 1922). Biographical information is from Forestall with Moynagh, eds., *Documenting First Wave Feminisms*, 93.
150 Foster, *Our Canadian Mosaic*, 135.
151 Ibid., 5, 9–11, 21–2, 49–50.
152 Ibid., 63, 80–1, 99.
153 Ibid., 43, 88, 98, 129.
154 Ibid., 29.
155 Ibid., 126–33, 80–1, 147–50.
156 Connor, *The Foreigner*, 14, 105, 157–8.
157 Woodsworth, *My Neighbour*, 201.
158 Connor, *The Foreigner*, 157–8.
159 Ibid., 97.
160 Ibid., 254, 266–7, 339.

CHAPTER TWO

1 Scott, *Canada Today*, 17.
2 "Roman Catholic Pressure on Publishers Is Alleged," *Toronto Star*, 7 June 1938.
3 McLaren and McLaren, *Bedroom and the State*, 93–6.
4 Oswald Smith, *Is the Antichrist at Hand?* 13, 22, 60–5, describes Mussolini as a candidate for being Antichrist. In a letter from his trip to Italy in 1928, Forsey expressed his anger at the dictatorial moral customs of the local Catholic population and the ubiquitous, lazy "Fascist militiaman" on each streetcar. Forsey to Mother, 13 September 1928, file 5, vol. 48, EF. Thompson and Seager mention that Camillien Houde's support of Mussolini made him very popular in 1920s Montreal. See *Canada, 1922–1939*, 247.
5 Gauvreau, *Catholic Origins*, 9–12, 23.
6 Baum, *Catholics and Canadian Socialists*, 72–9.

7   Fay, *History of Canadian Catholics*, 202–3, 207–8, 238–9.
8   Gauvreau, *Catholic Origins*, 18. Gregory Baum mentions that most convinced corporatists in Canada were opposed to submitting the control of any economic council to the state, a situation they derided as "political corporatism" and as the foundation for fascism. Baum, *Catholics and Canadian Socialism*, 180.
9   Bliss and Grayson, ed., *Wretched of Canada*, xiv; Manley, "Audacity," 9–41.
10 For an excellent recent thesis that revises the standard interpretation of pre–Quiet Revolution Quebec as a clerically stultified, proto-fascist society, see Dumas, "L'Église." For Dumas's discussion of the 1930s, see Chapters 2 to 4.
11 See Horn, *The Great Depression*, 16.
12 See McLaren and McLaren, *Bedroom and the State*; and Angus McLaren, *Our Own Master Race*.
13 Horn, *The Great Depression*, 16; Thompson, *Ethnic Minorities*, 11.
14 Silcox was exposed to progressive Christian social thought when he was educated at Brown University, a centre for Christian sociology in the early-twentieth century, and became convinced that the wedding of Christianity and the modern social sciences was central to the future of the faith. As Christie and Gauvreau point out, however, he began to question this simple, pragmatic social Christianity for not emphasizing the need for spiritual solutions and inner piety to social and economic problems. Gauvreau and Christie, *Full-orbed Christianity*, 103, 161–2.
15 Wolffe, *Protestant Crusade*, 131–41.
16 Campbell, *Respectable Citizens*, 11–14, 177–8.
17 McAree, "Church Has Right to Protect Its Members," *Globe and Mail*, 21 June 1938.
18 McAree, "Church Claps Gun to Publisher's Head," *Globe and Mail*, 7 June 1938.
19 Eayrs, "Prohibited Reading," *Globe and Mail*, 9 June 1938.
20 McAree, "Church Has Right to Protect Its Members," *Globe and Mail*, 21 June 1938.
21 "Vote Unanimous Protest Against Separate Schools: Protestants Rise Together Against Catholic Demands," *Toronto Telegram*, 4 March 1936. McGowan, "Air Wars," 11–12.
22 "Zeidman 'Fired' by Catholics, Says L.O.L. Head," *Globe*, 19 March 1936.
23 "Birth Control Broadcast Ban Opens Dispute," *Globe and Mail*, 4 January 1937. The CBC was both broadcaster and regulator of the airwaves in Canada until 1958, when private broadcasters gained a regulatory board

independent of the CBC after a long battle. In 1938 a CBC body was formed, the National Religious Advisory Council, which was dedicated solely to regulating religious broadcasting. Kuffert, *A Great Duty*, 120, 145, 198.

24 "Birth Control Broadcast Ban Opens Dispute," *Globe and Mail*, 4 January 1937; Kaufman, *Birth Control Trial*, 7.
25 "Rome's Hand Is Seen in Ban of Broadcast" *Globe and Mail*, 14 January 1937. McGowan notes that the CBC was inundated with protests from Orangemen and other supporters of Zeidman. McGowan, "Air Wars," 14.
26 "Birth Control Broadcast Ban."
27 See Silcox and Fisher, *Catholics, Jews, and Protestants*, where the stated goal was to overcome social forces of isolation, indifference, and difficulties between the groups to foster understanding.
28 "Ask Backing of Air Talks," *Globe and Mail*, 17 January 1938; "Pastor of Evangel Temple Will Discuss Protestant Broadcast Problem," *Globe and Mail*, 22 January 1938. McGowan notes that Zeidman's claim to not have equal airtime to the Catholic Church was disingenuous; he was simply attacking his Catholic nemesis, Father Charles Lanphier, who was broadcast on a CBC-owned station. Many Protestants, just not Zeidman, had equal or more airtime than Lanphier on this station. McGowan, "Air Wars," 12–13.
29 Silcox to Major Gladstone Murray, 16 November 1937, file 4, box 11, C.E. Silcox fonds (hereafter CES), United Church of Canada Archives (hereafter UCA). All emphasis in this letter is from the original.
30 Ibid.
31 McGowan, "Air Wars," 17–18.
32 "Church Fire Follows Threat," *Globe and Mail*, 28 March 1938.
33 Mills, "When Democratic Socialists Discovered Democracy," 3.
34 Djwa, "Introduction," in Djwa and MacDonald, *On F.R. Scott*, ix–xxii.
35 S. [F.R. Scott, pseud.], "Embryo Fascism in Quebec," *Foreign Affairs* 16 (April 1938): 454–8. Emphasis in original.
36 Robin, *Shades of Right*, 102, 106–9, 183, 219. Dumas, "L'Église," 200–2, 249–50.
37 Mills, "When Democratic Socialists Discovered Democracy," 10–12.
38 Djwa, *Politics of the Imagination*, 168–9.
39 S., "Embryo Fascism," 461–4.
40 Scott, "French Canadian Nationalism," in Horn, *A New Endeavour*, 32–4.
41 Scott, "The Cardinal Speaks," *Canadian Forum* (hereafter CF) 18 (Jan. 1939); and Scott, "Canada's Future in the British Commonwealth," *Foreign Affairs* 15 (1937): 432.

42 Scott, "Canada's Future," 437, n10. Emphasis mine.
43 Cawley, "Canadian Catholic," 25.
44 Djwa, *Politics of Imagination*, 172.
45 "100,000 Catholics Pledge Anti-Communism Fight," *Montreal Star*, 26 October 1936; for a characterization of Gauthier, see Fay, *History of Canadian Catholics*, 210–11; and Ballantyne, "The Catholic Church," 34.
46 Scott, *Canada Today*, 110, 17.
47 Rosaire Cauchon, "Is Quebec Going Fascist? A Reply from Quebec," *Maclean's*, 15 September 1937; Roberts in "Padlocks and Democrats," *Saturday Night*, 4 February 1939.
48 "Spanish Mission Fails to Get Local Hearing," *Montreal Star*, 24 October 1936.
49 Milligan, *Eugene A. Forsey*, 136.
50 Forsey to Hon. C.H. Cahan, 3 November 1936; to Hon. Thomas Coonan, 2 November 1936; Letter to the Editor to the *Montreal Witness*, 1 November 1936; Personal General Correspondence, 1921–1951, Part 1, vol. 5, EF.
51 Milligan, *Eugene A. Forsey*, 137.
52 Forsey, "Clerical Fascism," CF 17 (June 1937): 90–2.
53 Villeneuve is also the central figure in Scott's article "The Cardinal Speaks," 294–5.
54 In an early article for Groulx's *l'Action française*, Villeneuve proclaimed his total support for this very plan, stating that a French Catholic state in North America would "become ... a modern-day Israel in the midst of an emerging Babylon ... an apostolic nation, a nation of light." Villeneuve, "And Our Dispersed Brethren ...?" in *French Canadian Nationalism*, 202.
55 Delisle, *Myths, Memory, and Lies*, 61. For a sympathetic portrayal of not only Villeneuve but also Maurice Duplessis, see Conrad Black, *Duplessis*, and 106–7 for his attitudinal shift. For Villeneuve's enthusiastic support of the war effort and hesitancy with regard to supporting Marshal Pétain in Vichy France, see Fay, *A History of Canadian Catholics*, 237, 243; and Couture, "Vichy-Free French," 204–5.
56 Dumas, "L'Église," 50–7, 107–16, 121–46, 170–97.
57 Forsey, "Quebec on the Road to Fascism," CF 17 (December 1937): 300; Dumas, "L'Église," 6, 56–7.
58 See Levy, *Baptists of the Maritime Provinces*, 162, 172; Therrien, ed., *Baptist Work*.
59 Forsey, "Under the Padlock," CF 18 (May 1938): 41–4.

60 Forsey, "Quebec Fascists Show their Hand," CF 16 (December 1936): 8–9.
61 Walker, *Catholic Education and Politics*, vol. 3, 1; Saywell, *"Just Call Me Mitch,"* 123–7, 209–10.
62 Saywell, *"Just Call Me Mitch,"* 258–60.
63 Meehan, "East Hastings," 119.
64 "Vote Unanimous Protest Against Separate Schools: Protestants Rise Together Against Catholic Demands," *Toronto Telegram*, 4 March 1936.
65 Meehan, "East Hastings," 114–15. For a recent summary of the by-election, see Adams, "Fighting Fire with Fire," 69–78.
66 Frank O'Connor was the subject of criticism for his perceived influence over Hepburn, much of it revolving around their personal friendship and the "suspicious" fact that O'Connor was a Catholic. See Tory campaign poster "Has O'Connor Government Given East Hastings a Square Deal?" and a speech by Drew in Shannonville, "Drew Bids 'True Liberals' to Oust Hepburn Ministry," *Toronto Star*, 8 December 1936. Contained in file 623, East Hastings (2), 1936, vol. 69, George Drew fonds (hereafter GD), LAC.
67 "Protestant Politicians Intrusion in Religion," *Toronto Star*, 3 December 1936.
68 "Conservative Opportunity," file 623, East Hastings (2), 1936, vol. 69, GD.
69 "Attacks on the Paper," *Globe and Mail*, 1 December 1936.
70 One example of Drew having to defend himself occurred in 1939 when he wanted to pass an amendment promoting national unity between the then-warring federal government under King and Hepburn's provincial Liberals. The Liberals proceeded to raise the issue of Drew's speech in Plainfield as evidence that he knew nothing of national unity, which prompted Drew to give an immediate broadcast to deny the charges once again. See "This Week at Queen's Park," an address by Col. Geo. A. Drew, CFRB, 20 March 1939, file 517a, vol. 57, GD.
71 Saywell, *"Just Call Me Mitch,"* 272. The statement was originally reported in the *Toronto Star*, 28 November 1936, and there is a clipping of it in file 517a, vol. 57, GD.
72 Faulkner, "A Ringside Seat at the Battle of Hastings," *Kingston Whig-Standard*, 7 December 1936. Contained in file 623, vol. 69, GD.
73 "Drew Gives Direct Denial to Hepburn's Statements," *Toronto Star*, 1 December 1936. Contained in file 623, vol. 69, GD.
74 "Education" file 623, vol. 69, GD; Fisher, "Hands Off Hastings, Drew Warns Church: Separate Schools' End Predicted If Religion Meddles in Government," *Toronto Telegram*, 26 Nov. 1936, file 623, vol. 69, GD.

75 Copy of an article detailing Drew's speech from Bancroft, 25 November 1936, file 623, vol. 69, GD. Saywell, *"Just Call Me Mitch,"* 297.
76 Copy of an article detailing Drew's speech from Bancroft, 25 November 1936, file 623, vol. 69, GD.
77 Fisher, "Hands Off Hastings." Drew also compared Hepburn to Mussolini and his Fascist government in Fisher, "British Institutions Lost in School Issue Drew tells Hastings: Church and State Must Be Separated – Declares Concession Will Not Be Final," speech in Deseronto, in file 623, vol. 69, GD.
78 Fisher, "Hands Off Hastings."
79 The Tories won with a majority of 1,136 votes, coming close to trebling their results from 1934. Meehan, "East Hastings," 123.
80 "Beloved and Hated: Fiery T.T. Shields Dies in His 82nd Year," *Globe and Mail*, 5 April 1955; Anglin, "The Battling Baptist," *Maclean's*, 15 June 1949.
81 "May Move Pope to Casa Loma," *Toronto Star*, 30 November 1936, file 623, vol. 69, GD.
82 Saywell, *"Just Call Me Mitch,"* 356–7.
83 "Queen's Park Hooliganism Election Issue, Says Drew," *Toronto Telegram*, 13 November 1936.
84 "Rock-a-bye Five Babies!" *Globe*, 30 May 1934.
85 Mallon, "Nation's Hope Put in Readjustment," *New York Times*, 29 August 1935; "The Intergroup Situation in Canada: A Protestant Viewpoint," file 13, box 5, CES.
86 Silcox, "The Intergroup Situation in Canada," 3–4, 8.
87 Horn, introduction to *The Dirty Thirties*, 14–15.
88 This was the title of a retrospective by Bill Stephenson, "The Great Birth Control Trial," *Maclean's*, 23 November 1957.
89 Dodd, "Canadian Birth Control Movement," 412–18.
90 Kaufman, "Sterilization Notes, Pamphlet No. 7," 5, 14, 16–17, 3.
91 Scrapbook, USA, sterilization and Catholics, 1935-1937, file 27, box 2, ARK. This statement is scrawled in a note attached to an article discussing a debate between Silcox and a Catholic priest concerning contraception.
92 Kaufman, "Sterilization Notes, Pamphlet No. 2," 15.
93 Dodd, "Canadian Birth Control Movement," 414–18; the title of another retrospective is revealing: Hollobon, "Did Dirty Work for Men at Trial, Pioneer of Birth Control says," *Globe and Mail*, 30 November 1978.
94 Dodd, "Canadian Birth Control Movement," 412; Revie, "More than Just Boots!" 125; McLaren, *Our Own Master Race*, 84.
95 Revie, "More than Just Boots!" 130; McLaren, *Our Own Master Race*, 85.

96 Dodd, "Canadian Birth Control Movement," 416.
97 Kaufman, *Birth Control Trial*, 12; McLaren, *Our Own Master Race*, 149–50.
98 Dodd, "Canadian Birth Control Movement," 421; Stortz and Eaton, "Pro Bono Publico," 51, 57.
99 "Birth-Control Charge Said Unique in Anglo-Saxon Law," *Toronto Star*, 23 October 1936.
100 Mary Hawkins testimony, file 27, Dorothea Palmer fonds (hereafter DP), WUA. I would like to credit McLaren and McLaren, *Bedroom and the State*, 101–3, for drawing my attention to Hawkins's and Brandt's arguments. Davis, *Moral and Pastoral Theology*, 168.
101 "Truth (A Child of Mary)," *Toronto Star*, 14 November 1936, Series I, Newspaper Clippings, 1936; Brandt to Hawkins, 15 November 1936, Series E, Correspondence, Planned Parenthood Society of Hamilton papers (hereafter PPSH), Local History and Archives Hamilton. Brandt testimony, file 27, DP.
102 "Launches Attack on Birth Control," *Hamilton Spectator*, 11 October 1933; there was also a series of letters to the editor that pitted McNally against several correspondents in his anti-contraception arguments: see McNally, "Birth Control," 24 January 1934; Donald McLaren, "Replies to Bishop," 25 January (in which McLaren accused McNally of having "one foot in the College of Cardinals and the other in the Middle Ages"); Citizen, "Birth Control," 26 January 1934; Peter Dunn, "Birth Control," 27 January 1934; McNally, "Bishop Replies to Mr. Dunn," 29 January 1934; McLaren, "Replies to Bishop," 30 January 1934 (accusing McNally of acting like a "fourteenth-century Pope"); Dunn, "Rev. Mr. Dunn Explains," 1 February 1934. Also see "For the Public Good: A History of the Birth Control Clinic and the Planned Parenthood Society of Hamilton, Ontario, Canada," Series E, Correspondence, PPSH.
103 Dodd, "Canadian Birth Control Movement," 421.
104 Brandt to Hawkins, 13 February 1937, 12 September 1934, 17 February 1937 Series E, Correspondence, PPSH.
105 "An Outline of the Work and Aims of the Birth Control Society of Hamilton, Indicating the Social, Economic, Political and Religious Aspects of the Subject," 15, Series F, History, PPSH.
106 "Return Mrs. Hawkins as Head of Society," *Hamilton Spectator*, 15 January 1936, Series I, Newspaper Clippings, 1936, PPSH. In an earlier meeting of the BCSH, Hawkins also suggested a eugenical argument of a population hurting the quality of the nation, painting a picture of

couples suffering the "black dread" of "one feeble-minded child, one normal child and then Mongolian idiot twins." "Birth Control Society Holds Annual Meeting," *Hamilton Spectator*, 24 January 1934.

107 "Transcript of Mr. Silcox's Testimony during the Eastview Trial, 1937," 2, 7, 20–1, file 45, box 8, CES.
108 Kaufman, *Birth Control Trial*, 9.
109 "Would Eliminate Racial Tension by Birth Control," *Toronto Star*, 29 October 1936.
110 Scott to Silcox, 23 April 1937, Civil Liberties, 1936–1937, vol. 9, F.R. Scott fonds (hereafter FRS), LAC.
111 Silcox to Scott, 27 April 1937, Civil Liberties, 1936–1937, vol. 9, FRS.
112 Silcox to Scott, 24 April 1937, Civil Liberties, 1936–1937, vol. 9, FRS.
113 Scott to Silcox, 23 April 1937, Civil Liberties, 1936–1937, vol. 9, FRS.
114 Scott to Roger Ouimet, 26 April 1937, Civil Liberties, 1936–1937, vol. 9, FRS.
115 Kaufman to F.W. Wegenast, 20 February 1937, file 33, Box 5, DP.
116 Stortz and Eaton, "Pro Bono Publico," 53, 58–9. Wegenast had this *Telegram* article in his files. File 38, box 5, DP.
117 Wegenast, "Sidelights on the Eastview Trial," file 44, Box 6, file 44, DP.
118 For a recent examination of eugenics in Canada, the role that the science was believed to play in protecting the sanctity of the population and the complexity of everyday Catholics confronting birth control, see Dyck, *Facing Eugenics*.
119 See Pozzi, "The Problem of Birth Control," 209–29.
120 See her numerous letters to the editor of the *Winnipeg Free Press* in the 1930s. For example: "Warning that Price of Cream May Go Sky High," 19 May 1932; "Economic Conditions and Birth Control," 23 April 1932; "A Quintuplet Standard for All Our Children," 18 January 1936; "Babies that Know No Cradle but a Coffin," 16 January 1937.
121 Rogers quotes McCabe from the *American Freeman*. Rogers to Wegenast, 26 April 1937, file 50, box 6, DP. Gauvin's lectures rely on McCabe as a "historian" (which he was not). In his "The Knights of Columbus and Birth Control," delivered in Winnipeg, 24 January 1937, he concluded, "The history of that institution [the Church] is such a nightmare of persecution and horror, of intellectual repression and slavery, that men and women who know its story are everywhere decidedly afraid of it. (Applause)," and that the battle over birth control "brings to the consciousness of non-Catholics a realization of the fact that Rome is still the enemy of human freedom and of commonsense. (Applause)." Gauvin,

"The Knights of Columbus and Birth Control," 24 January 1937; "How the Church Ruined Spain," 7 February 1937.
122 Rogers to Wegenast, 9 February 1937, 26 April 1937, file 50, box 6, DP.
123 Orkin, *The Great Stork Derby*.
124 Examples include: Cavanaugh, "Irene Marryat Parlby"; Pickles, *Imperial Feminism and National Identity*; Dean, *A Different Point of View*; and Devereux, *Growing a Race*.
125 Janey Canuck, "Birth Control: Its Meaning," *Vancouver Sun*, 27 August 1932; "Sterilization of the Insane," *Vancouver Sun*, 3 September 1932; "Should the Unfit Wed?" *Vancouver Sun*, 10 and 17 September 1932; "Over-Population and Birth Control," *Vancouver Sun*, 1 October 1932.
126 McLaren, *Our Own Master Race*, 124–5. See Hurd, "The Immigration Problem," address delivered before the Canadian Club, Toronto, 8 March 1937, folder 5, William Burton Hurd fonds, McMaster University Archives. For Forsey's embrace of this concept see his pamphlet "Does Canada Need Immigrants?" (LSR National Executive: 1937[?]), originally published as "Immigration Ballyhoo," CF 17 (February 1937).
127 Wegenast, the lawyer defending Palmer in her trial, had this lecture in a file labelled Population Problems. File 47, box 6, DP.
128 Hurd, "The Immigration Problem," 6–14.
129 Hurd, "The Decline in the Canadian Birth-Rate," *The Canadian Journal of Economics and Political Science* 3, no. 1 (Feb. 1937), 56–7.
130 Hurd, "Decline of the Anglo-Saxon Canadian," *Maclean's*, 1 September 1937, 13, 45.
131 Ibid.
132 Ibid.
133 See *Tribute to a Nation Builder: An Appreciation of Dr. John Murray Gibbon* (Toronto: Composers Authors and Publishers Association of Canada, Limited, 1946). McKay has referred to him as a "cultural entrepreneur" and a principal figure in the formation of an interwar sense of nationalism in Canada. McKay, *Quest of the Folk*, 57–8.
134 Gibbon, *Canadian Mosaic*, 2, 413–15.
135 Thompson, "Third British Empire," 101–2; McKay, *Quest of the Folk*, 57.
136 Gibbon, *Canadian Mosaic*, 116, 385.
137 Ibid., 276–8.
138 Ibid., 253–4, 308, 323, 327, 413.
139 Ibid., 308.
140 Crowley, *Marriage of Minds*, 260.
141 Kirkconnell, *European Heritage*, 19–21, 82–3, 95, 140–1.

142 Katerberg, *Modernity and the Dilemma*, 218, 48–58.
143 Gibbon, *Canadian Mosaic*, 24.
144 Ibid., 47.
145 Dumas notes that this has become a common refrain in Quebec history as well, a component of the Manichaen narrative of Godbout and Lesage as brave Liberals breaking through the *Grande noirceur*. Interestingly, Dumas also recalls that Villeneuve told Joseph Atkinson of the *Toronto Star* that he hoped Godbout won the 1939 provincial election and publicly told American newspapers a month later that Quebec had voted for Godbout because of their desire for national unity and the war effort! Dumas, "L'Église," 2–3, 209.
146 Kirkconnell, *Canada, Europe*, 111–13, 171, 203.

CHAPTER THREE

1 Gregory Vlastos to Lower, 22 November 1945, AL.
2 Forsey to Mother, 26 May 1942, file 22, vol. 45, EF. Boston Irish Catholics were perceived by some to share the isolationist view of perhaps their most prominent political spokesman, Joseph Patrick Kennedy. For Kennedy's opposition to American intervention in the war as ambassador to Britain, see Michael R. Beschloss, *Kennedy and Roosevelt*, 174, 222–6.
3 Colley, *Britons, 1707–1837*, 29–31.
4 Vance, *Maple Leaf Empire*, 2–4, 221–2; Belich, "Rise of the Angloworld," 41–9.
5 "The Fourth Axis Power," *Gospel Witness*, 29 January 1942; "Shall Papal Quebec's 'No' be Allowed to Limit Canada's War Effort?" *Gospel Witness*, 7 May 1942. All references to this periodical are attributed to Shields, unless otherwise noted.
6 Anthony Burke Smith, *The Look of Catholics*, 2, 8–12, 102–3; Marty, *Modern American Religion*, 3–4, 35–6, 108–10, 130–1. Marty and McGreevy, in *Catholicism and American Freedom*, have begun to question this idea that anti-Catholicism was completely ignored in America during the Second World War, but it appears that unity was emphasized in the face of the Axis threat within much of the Protestant community.
7 This was the opinion of federal Tory leader John Bracken and Ontario Tory Premier George Drew. See Blake, "Parliamentary Success and Political Failure," 177, 183.
8 Christie, "Look Out for Leviathan," 70–1.
9 Adams, "Fighting Fire with Fire," 69–70; C. Allyn Russell, "Thomas Todhunter Shields," 265–6.

10 In an editorially flavoured obituary of Shields, the *Globe and Mail* claimed that Shields generated more religious controversy than any other single figure in Canadian history. "Beloved and Hated: Fiery T.T. Shields Dies in his 82nd Year," *Globe and Mail*, 5 April 1955. Adams, "Fighting Fire"; Russell, "Thomas Todhunter Shields"; Wicks, "T.T. Shields"; Tarr, *Shields of Canada*, which is a hagiography of Shields; Stackhouse Jr, *Canadian Evangelicalism*, Chapter 1, "T.T. Shields: The Fundamentalist Extreme."

11 "A Challenging Answer to Premier King and Other Parliamentary Critics," *Gospel Witness*, 4 March 1943; "Quebec's Official Governmental and Ecclesiastical Attitude Toward War," *Gospel Witness*, 30 January 1941.

12 Reilly, "Baptists," 182. In a letter to H.H. Bingham, representative for the chaplaincy service in the Department of Defence, E.H.S. Ivison claimed that the major problem was that there were a series of bureaucratic mishaps. The responsibility apparently eventually rested with a young assistant, "Connolley," who was a Catholic and who organized the service through Bishop Nelligan and ignored the Protestant component. E.H.S. Ivison to H.H. Bingham, 14 September 1941, file 29d, box 4, Inter-Church Committee on Protestant–Roman Catholic Relations (hereafter ICC), UCA.

13 These angry Protestants included *United Church Observer* (UCO) editor A.J. Wilson and general secretary of the Canadian Baptist Foreign Missions Board, Rev. Dr J.B. McLaurin. "Pontifical Mass on Parliament Hill," GW, 18 September 1941. The initial executive of the CPL was Shields, president; Leslie Saunders, secretary-treasurer; and vice-presidents, Rev. J.H. Barnes (Rector, St Peter's Anglican Church) and T. Christie Innes (Knox Presbyterian Church). See "The Canadian Protestant League," *Gospel Witness*, 23 October 1941.

14 Stackhouse Jr notes that most members did not renew their membership after one year, and it remained a small-but-loud organization for the remainder of the 1940s, until Shields himself was ousted as the president and as the head of the Union of Regular Baptists in a divisive denominational battle. Reilly has mentioned that Shields became quite frustrated with the lack of practical success of the CPL, and he and close colleague H.C. Slade quickly realized that the league was essentially a rump of Union members and revolved almost entirely around the personality of Shields. See Stackhouse Jr, *Canadian Evangelicalism*, 32–3, 215, nn39–40; Reilly, "Baptists," 186–7.

15 Wicks, "T.T. Shields," Appendix C, "Constitution of the Canadian Protestant League," approved on 12 October 1941; "The Canadian Protestant League," *Gospel Witness*, 23 October 1941.

16 "The Canadian Protestant League," *Gospel Witness*, 23 October 1941.

17 House of Commons Debates, 4 March 1941, 1208–10; 4 June 1941, 3467. According to Wicks, Shields extended the name of his periodical from the *Gospel Witness* to the *Gospel Witness and Protestant Advocate* in October 1942. Wicks, "T.T. Shields," 54.
18 House of Commons, 22 July 1942, 4514.
19 House of Commons, 23 February 1943, 653–6.
20 House of Commons, 23 February 1943, 663–4. For a discussion of these parliamentary debates see Adams, "Fighting Fire," 92–5.
21 The yeas were Roy; Independent Frederic Dorion of Charlevoix-Saguenay, who had seconded Roy's amendment; J. Emmanuel d'Anjou, Bloc (Rimouski); Pierre Gauthier, Bloc (Portneuf); Lacombe; Edouard Lacroix, Liberal (Beauce); Wilfrid Lacroix; Jean-Francois Pouliot, Liberal (Temiscouata). House of Commons, 23 February 1943, 668.
22 House of Commons, 20 May 1943, 2839, 2862–63.
23 "A Challenging Answer to Premier King and Other Parliamentary Critics," *Gospel Witness and Protestant Advocate*, 4 March 1943.
24 "Religion in Parliament," *Globe and Mail*, 25 February 1943.
25 "*The Gospel Witness* and Its Parliamentary Critics," *Gospel Witness and Protestant Advocate*, 25 February 1943.
26 This is the name commonly attributed to the radical separatists in Quebec in the interwar period, although Groulx's separatism has been the subject of rethinking. Michel Bock, translated by Ferdinanda Van Gennip, *Nation Beyond Borders*, 17–27; Mann, *Dream of Nation*, 227–32.
27 McAree, "Disloyal Order Active in Quebec," *Globe and Mail*, 17 March 1943.
28 McAree, "Dr. Shields Offers Reasoned Defense," *Globe and Mail*, 30 March 1943.
29 Ibid.
30 House of Commons, 5 June 1943, 4337–40.
31 "About the *Observer*," http://www.ucobserver.org/about/ (accessed 6 September 2011).
32 Byers has provided a detailed analysis of the Zombies, as well as French-Canadian participation in the armed forces in general in the Second World War. National Defence HQ reported in March 1944 that French Canadians composed 19.1 per cent of the armed forces, including conscripts. Byers also calculates that roughly 95,000 French Canadians volunteered and about 132,000 French Canadians were involved in the armed forces overall. Byers believes this absolute amount of participation, when contextualized with the amount of isolation felt by French Canadians, belies the stereotype that French Canadians were drastically underrepresented in

volunteer service or in service in general, and helped facilitate, modestly, some of the bilingual gains of the postwar years. Byers, *Zombie Army*, 7–8.
33 "National Unity," UCO, 15 July 1943.
34 The use of the phrase "appeasement" when referring to French Canada and the Catholic Church in Canada was common in the Second World War. For example, it appeared in various letters to Drew. See letters from Tom C. Mewburn to Drew, 14 September 1944, file 473, vol. 54; Thomas Mungovan to Drew, 10 August 1944; George H. Ross to Drew, 11 August 1944, file 473a, vol. 54, GD. Caputi examines how influential the "guilty men" thesis was during the war. This was postulated by a left-leaning group dubbed CATO in 1940, which claimed that Chamberlain and his associates were weak fools who submitted to the demands of a stronger, aggressive foe, forever causing "appeasement" to become a pejorative term. Caputi, *Neville Chamberlain*, 16–18.
35 "National Unity," UCO, 15 July 1943; Whidden, "The Protestant Strategy in Protestant-Catholic Canada," June 1943, 1–2, file 137, vol. 14, ICC. Whidden also became an influential member of the ICC.
36 Wicks, "T.T. Shields," 97, quoted in *Gospel Witness and Protestant Advocate*, 21 January 1943.
37 Airhart's study *Church with the Soul* contains an excellent, if brief, analysis of the continuing concern with Catholicism in the United Church during wartime. According to Airhart, much of this reflected the anxieties caused by not only a nation at war, but by the increasing speed at which Protestantism and Britishness lost currency as signifiers of unity. Airhart, *Church with the Soul*, 126–56.
38 Silcox, "Religious Peace in Canada?" *Food for Thought*, October 1941, 16.
39 The plebiscite resulted in a 62.31 per cent affirmative against a 36.59 per cent negative, but within Quebec, from a 75.71 per cent turnout, the result was 27.09 per cent affirmative against 71.57 per cent negative. In Granatstein and Neary, eds., *The Good Fight*, 227.
40 The most detailed study of the NRMA troops and the government's policies is Byers's excellent *Zombie Army*. Yet even Byers is unsure of how the term "zombie" became attached to these troops. It is clearly pejorative, however, and refers to the monsters from 1930s horror movies who blindly followed their masters. Byers, *Zombie Army*, 6, 105–9.
41 House of Commons, 16 June 1942, 3389–96.
42 Silcox, "The Higher Rationale of Conscription," *Saturday Night*, 27 September 1941.
43 Silcox, "We Must Have Faith in French Canada," *Saturday Night*, 21 March 1942.

44 Silcox, "Open Letter to Louis St Laurent," *News*, 27 June and 4 July 1942.
45 Forsey to Meighen, 30 June 1942; Meighen to Forsey, 3 July 1942, vol. 222, Arthur Meighen fonds (hereafter AM), LAC through QUA.
46 Silcox, "We Must Have Faith in French Canada."
47 Silcox to Drew, 10 August 1944, file 473a, vol. 54, GD.
48 Silcox, *Must Canada Split?* iii–v, 9–13, 14–15.
49 See Silcox's "Problem Side of Family Allowances," *Saturday Night*, 23 October 1943, and "Look Out! Leviathan's on the Horizon Again," *Saturday Night*, 30 September 1944.
50 Christie, "Sacred Sex," 352.
51 Hayek, *Road to Serfdom*, 2–4, 8–9.
52 Silcox to Gladstone Murray, 25 January 1945; Murray to Silcox, 25 January 1945, file 5, box 11, CES.
53 "Ninth Draft of the Report of the Commission on the Church, Nation, and World Order," 1944, file 46, box 46, 31–2. Arthur Lower fonds (hereafter AL), QUA.
54 Ibid., 31–3.
55 Lower, "Comments and Suggestions on the Ninth Draft of the Commission on the Church, Nation, and World Order," April 1944, 5–6, file 44, box 46, AL.
56 Gordon Sisco to Lower, 4 May 1944, file 46, box 46, AL.
57 Commission, *Church, Nation*, 36.
58 Silcox advised the CCNWO in its preparation of the material, and it had among its executive R.B.Y. Scott, to be discussed later, and J.R. Mutchmor, who was an eventual member of the ICC. Airhart, *Church with the Soul*, 132–3.
59 Lower to M. Seraphin Marion, 22 January 1944, file 35, vol. 7, AL.
60 Lower, "Two Ways of Life," 5, 9–10. Lower eventually grudgingly accepted conscription after attacking ardent conscriptionists for dividing the nation. In a letter to C.G. Power, Lower explained that King and the Liberals had done everything they could to compromise. Those remaining opponents of conscription in French Canada had to join with the Liberals or risk allowing the Orange Order and the Tories to implement their harmful vision. Lower to Power, 25 November 1944, file 23, vol. 1, AL.
61 Both Heick and Berger see this speech as representing an essential aspect of Lower's developing thought. Heick, "The Character and Spirit of an Age," 124–8.
62 Lower, "Two Ways of Life," 10–13.
63 Ibid., 17–18.

64 Ibid., 7–9.
65 His position on immigration covered much of his career and was represented in many different mediums: see Lower, "The Case Against Immigration," *Queen's Quarterly*, 37 (1930): 557–74; Lower, *My First Seventy-Five Years*, 164–5. Berger has noted Lower's desire to belong to a homogeneous national community and to show how history could be used to promote this vision. Berger, *Writing of Canadian History*, 112–13.
66 Lower, "Two Ways of Life," 9–10.
67 Vlastos to Lower, 22 November 1945; Lower to Vlastos, 28 January 1946, file 25, vol. 1, AL.
68 Lower to Sisco, 25 March 1943; Sisco to Lower, 16 February 1943, file 44, box 46, AL.
69 C. de Mestral, "Look Towards a Reformation," UCO, 15 October 1943.
70 Scott and de Mestral, "English-French Relations," 2–3, file 12, vol. 1, Commission on the Church, Nation, and World Order, UCA. Caccia notes that Hurd's study of the 1941 census, *Ethnic Origin and Nativity of the Canadian People, 1941*, remained an internal government document, due to the changing conceptions of race during the war. It needed to be revised when it was finally released in the 1960s. Caccia, *Managing the Canadian Mosaic*, 55.
71 R.B.Y. Scott and de Mestral, "English-French Relations," 5.
72 Ibid., 6–10.
73 Reilly, "Baptists," 183.
74 Kirkconnell, "The Twilight of Canadian Protestantism," *Canadian Baptist*, 1 December 1942.
75 Perkin, "There Were Giants in the Earth in Those Days," 95–101; Caccia, *Managing the Canadian Mosaic*, 55, 93, 110–13, 175.
76 While not completely ignoring the liberal assimilationist tendencies of Kirkconnell and Gibbon, Palmer exaggerates when he states that "Gibbon and Kirkconnell were voices crying in the wilderness – a wilderness of discrimination and racism." Palmer, "Reluctant Hosts," 136. Smale has recently agreed with George G.F. Stanley's maxim that Kirkconnell was a "prophet of Canadian multiculturalism." Smale, "For Whose Kingdom?" 385.
77 Kirkconnell, "The Twilight of Canadian Protestantism," *Canadian Baptist*, 1 December 1942.
78 Ibid.
79 Ibid.
80 Owram, *The Government Generation*, 254–67; Kuffert, *A Great Duty*, 29–33; Cook, "Canadian Freedom," 40.
81 Cook, "Canadian Freedom," 40.

82 Granatstein, *Canada's War*, 102, n. Kaplan lists this as a major reason behind the banning and interning of Witnesses. See Kaplan, *State and Salvation*, xi, 67. See Penton, *Jehovah's Witnesses in Canada*, 144, for the "Christian" letter.
83 House of Commons, 21 July 1943, 5206–11.
84 There was suspicion around the historic pacifist groups, especially the Doukhobors, due to the past violent activities of the Sons of Freedom wing of the group. Palmer, "Ethnic Relations," 19.
85 House of Commons, 21 July 1943, 5215.
86 Janeway, "Roosevelt vs Hitler: the U.S. Wages World Diplomatic War," *Life*, 5 May 1941.
87 House of Commons, 8 May 1941, 2652. It was also opposed by Willson Woodside, "The Forty-Ninth and Fiftieth States," *Saturday Night*, 10 May 1941.
88 Armstrong, *French Canadian Opinion*, 2–4, 34.
89 Couture, "Vichy-Free French," 202–4. Fay agrees in *History of Canadian Catholics*, 221, 236.
90 Courteaux, *Canada between Vichy and Free France*, vii–xi, 30–45, 88–97; Meren, *With Friends Like These*, 13–14. I realize that it was unlikely that various Tories outside of government circles could have known about these largely secret deals. Nevertheless, the irony of the arch-Tories attacking the Liberals for kowtowing to French-Canadian traitors while fulfilling promises to their allies in Britain and the United States should not be lost. It encapsulates the fever pitch of anti–French Canadianism that spread across English Canada during the two conscription crises of the Second World War.
91 Couture, "Vichy-Free French," 203.
92 Roy, "The Province of Quebec and Marshal Pétain," *Saturday Night*, 14 September 1940, reprinted from an editorial in *L'Action Catholique*.
93 Fay, *History of Canadian Catholics*, 237–8; Couture, "Vichy-Free French," 208; for a primary source account of the debate over Frigon, see Gibson and Robertson, eds., *Ottawa at War*, 304–6.
94 Shields, "The Fourth Axis Power," *Gospel Witness*, 29 January 1942.
95 McAree, "Disloyal Order Active in Quebec," *Globe and Mail*, 17 March 1943.
96 Calculations made by author using the publisher's search option in the *Globe and Mail*.
97 "Grave Decisions Face Ottawa," *Globe and Mail*, 19 May 1941.
98 "Send Him Packing," *Globe and Mail*, 17 September 1942. Dumas outlines in great detail how Villeneuve's enthusiastic pro-war stance divided the

province, gaining support from some French-Canadian Catholics in his calls for buying victory bonds and enlistment, and being viewed as an "imperialist" by *nationalistes*. The ubiquitous Abbé Groulx even asked Villeneuve to tone down his pro-war activities or risk making the *nationaliste* publicly anti-clerical. Dumas, "L'Église," 242–57.

99 "Why Still Boycott Russia," *Globe and Mail*, 9 September 1941; "Evading the Issue," *Globe and Mail*, 16 October 1942.
100 "De Gaulle Stirs French Canada," *Globe and Mail*, 9 April 1941.
101 Scott, *Canada and the United States*, 28–30.
102 Forsey to Mother, 13 October 1940, file 20, vol. 45, EF.
103 Forsey to Mother, 26 May 1942, vol. 45, file 22, EF.
104 Howes, *Inside Quebec*, 18–19; Horn, *League for Social Reconstruction*, 57.
105 Howes, *Inside Quebec*, 14–18.
106 Ibid., 20–5.
107 Letter to the Editor, CF 22 (August 1942), attached to a letter from Forsey to Meighen, 15 July 1942, vol. 222, AM. Scott was furious with Forsey, believing that he had undermined the cause of the CCF in Quebec and attacked him personally. Forsey simply responded that he could not allow Scott to spread falsehoods, no matter the reason. Scott to Forsey, 11 August 1942 and 25 August 1942; Forsey to Scott, 21 August 1942, file French Canada, vol. 10, EF.
108 In late 1944, at the height of the second conscription crisis, of the 60,000 Zombies, 39 per cent were from Quebec, 27 per cent were Ontarians, and 37 per cent were from the rest of Canada. French Canadians made up 29 per cent of the population as of 1941 (although it is not clear exactly what number of these Quebeckers were Francophones). Byers, "Canada's Zombies," 159–65. *Historical Statistics of Canada*, Series A1 and A185–237. For example, some French soldiers were told that they needed to "Speak white," which meant English, while in the armed forces. Morton and Granatstein, *Victory, 1945*, 219.
109 Forsey to Meighen, 15 July 1942; Forsey to Meighen, 15 March 1942; Forsey to Meighen, 16 May 1944, respectively, vol. 222, AM.
110 Soucisse, "Two Letters on the Present Feud Between Quebec and the Rest," *Saturday Night*, 12 August 1944.
111 Forsey to B.K. Sandwell, 28 September 1944, vol. 222, AM.
112 See Scott's efforts: Scott to David [Lewis, it appears], 24 June 1942, file 3, vol. 12, FRS; "What did 'No' Mean," CF 22 (June 1942) and "Gare Aux Mots!" originally in *Culture* 6, no. 3 (Sept. 1945); Horn, *A New Endeavour*. For a first-hand recollection of these efforts see Ballantyne, "The Catholic Church and the CCF."

113 For a more conservative evaluation of Bouchard, see Black, *Duplessis*, 275. Demers, however, has noted that Bouchard became involved in the *Union des Latins d'Amérique*, rejecting chauvinistic "Latinism" but embracing the transnational character of the organization and an open "Latinity," dedicated as it was to making connections between Quebec and Latin America. Demers, *Connected Struggles*, 108.
114 Senate, 21 June 1944, 210–17.
115 T.-D. Bouchard, "The Struggle for Quebec," *Maclean's*, 1 October 1944.
116 Many French Canadians, for their part, rejected Bouchard's claims, or at least believed he exaggerated them. St Laurent minimized them, while Frédéric Dorion labelled Bouchard a Quebec Quisling and a Freemason. "Godbout's Ottawa Visit Is Sequel to Secret Society Plot Allegations: St Laurent Asserts Alleged Secret Group Not So Influential," Kenneth Cragg, *Globe and Mail*, 23 June 1944.
117 McAree, "Hierarchy Dictation Defied by Laurier," *Globe and Mail*, 11 July 1944.
118 "Order of Cartier Will Bear Watching," *Orangeville Banner*, from the *Globe and Mail*, 20 July 1944.
119 Corolyn Cox, "Outspoken French Senator Takes All Canada for His Homeland," *Saturday Night*, 12 August 1944; "Advises Canadian Women Hold International Ties," *Globe and Mail*, 22 January 1943.
120 Dumas, "L'Église," 241–2, 258–68.
121 Owram, *Government Generation*, 314–5; Christie, *Engendering the State*, 265, 285–6, 295–300; Blake, *From Rights to Needs*, Chapters 1–4. For the scholarly literature acknowledging the racial and religious aspect of opposition to family allowances, see Owram, *Government Generation*, 313; Christie, *Engendering the State*, 13.
122 House of Commons, 25 July 1944, 5363; for Bracken's opinion see Kendle, *John Bracken*, 212; Grant Dexter, *Family Allowances*, 3; "A Strange Performance," *Globe and Mail*, 31 July 1944.
123 Bruce to Drew, 22 July 1944, vol. 20, file 176, GD.
124 Bruce supported the sterilization of the feeble-minded as early as 1936, while still lieutenant-governor, praising the efforts of Nazi Germany in this regard in a dinner speech to the Toronto Council on Social Welfare, 24 April 1936. The speech was published in Silcox's *Social Welfare*, September 1936, as "Sterilization and Imbecility."
125 House of Commons, 25 July 1944, 5365. Kenneth Cragg, "House Votes, 139 to 0, for Second Reading of Baby Bonus Bill," *Globe and Mail*, 29 July 1944. Bruce was convinced that his suspension was at least

partially due to a grudge King held against him for asking that he resign as prime minister in the House on 23 May 1940. Bruce, *Varied Operations*, 2.

126 "A Man of Rare Courage," in "When Politicians Were He-Men," *Globe and Mail*, 3 August 1944, McCullagh labelled those that did not speak out as "panty-waists"; Judith Robinson, from *News*, "The Measure of a Parliament," *Globe and Mail*, 5 August 1944.

127 Bailey to Bruce, 8 August 1944; Guillet to Bruce, 3 August 1944, file 176, vol. 20, GD.

128 Bruce, *Varied Operations*, 282–6, 301–7, 325–30.

129 Blake, "Parliamentary Success," 173–4.

130 Bracken publicly stated that the bill was a bribe in a speech in Ottawa, but he was not sitting in the House, so he did not vote on the issue. "Allowance Step Political Bribe Bracken Says," *Globe and Mail*, 26 June 1944.

131 Premier George A. Drew, Progressive Conservative Rally at Richmond Hill, 2 August 1944, 1, 5, file 182, vol. 305, GD. Drew and Bruce were in correspondence with each other concerning many issues on which they shared opinions, such as conscription and family allowances. See file 176, vol. 20, GD.

132 Drew to Hugh Farthing, 12 March 1945, file 474, vol. 54, GD.

133 George Drew, "Where Ontario Stands," transcription of broadcast 9 August 1944, 3–5, Family Allowances, 1944–45, 1952–53, vol. 437, GD. Bryden views this speech as reflecting both Drew's impetuousness and frustration with the early collapse of his dream of an autonomous province with federal recognition. Family allowances were the "last straw." Bryden, *"A Justifiable Obsession,"* 18–21.

134 Drew, "Where Ontario Stands," transcription of broadcast, 9 August 1944, 5, Family Allowances, 1944–45, 1952–53, vol. 437, GD.

135 Harry M. Robbins to Drew, 7 May 1952, Correspondence, Progressive Conservative Associations, 1952, vol. 445, GD. Robbins was the PR Officer for the PC Party in Ontario warning Drew that his old statements were going to be used against him in the federal election. In a compilation of editorial opinion from Quebec, the anonymous author concluded that the Liberals would undoubtedly use Drew's statements against him. "This Week in Quebec," Press Information Bureau, 16 October 1944, file 1189, vol. 18, GD.

136 Drew, "Where Ontario Stands," transcription of broadcast, 9 August 1944, 7, Family Allowances, 1944–45, 1952–53, vol. 437, GD. Bryden is

convinced that the unanimous support for family allowances in the House and its widespread popularity in Canada eventually isolated Drew and his compatriots, although he was still a sitting premier and future leader of a major federal party. Bryden, *"A Justifiable Obsession,"* 18–21.
137 "Standing up for Fair Play" to Drew, file 473, vol. 54, GD.
138 Kaufman to Drew, 10 August 1944, file 473a, vol. 54, GD.
139 Colin S. Macdonald to Drew, 14 August 1944, file 473a, vol. 54, GD. This concomitant anti-French/anti-Catholic perspective was also present in letters from A.D. Peters, who claimed King had sold Canada to the pope and "his minions," and from W.W. Marshall, who blamed Cardinal Villeneuve and the Vatican for the introduction of this evil legislation. Letter from Peters, 12 August 1944, from Marshall, 10 August 1944, same file, GD.
140 G. Scott to Drew, 10 August 1944, file 473a, vol. 54, GD.
141 A.E. Willard to Drew, 12 August 1944, file 473a, vol. 54, GD.
142 Thomas Pryde to Drew, 9 August 1944, file 473a, vol. 54, GD. In the same file are letters of endorsement from the Algoma PC Association, 16 August 1944, and the Beaches-Danforth PC Association, 14 August 1944.
143 List of correspondents, file 473, vol. 54, GD.
144 Jack Walker to Drew, 11 August 1944, file 573a, vol. 54, GD.
145 "Drew on Family Allowances," *Ottawa Journal*, 11 August 1944. "Canada Is Growing," file 473, vol. 54, GD.
146 "Orangeman Says Tenth of Baby Bonus to Go in R.C. Church Coffers," *Globe and Mail*, 7 August 1944.
147 Ibid.
148 Kenneth Cragg, "Supports Baby Bonus Properly Administered, Drew Replies to Critics," *Globe and Mail*, 30 September 1944. Drew was at the Eastern Ontario PC Association.
149 Drew to Hugh Farthing, 21 August 1944, file 474, vol. 54, GD. Farthing was the brother of Tory intellectual and monarchist John Farthing, who will be discussed in the next chapter. He was a lawyer in Calgary.
150 Granatstein, *Politics of Survival*, 15–18.
151 Silcox, *Revenge*, iii–iv.
152 Silcox, "Problem Side of Family Allowances," *Saturday Night*, 23 October 1943.
153 Silcox, *Revenge*, 22–3.
154 Ibid., 16–17.
155 Ibid., 11, 23.
156 Rooke and Schnell, *No Bleeding Heart*, 123.

157 See Whitton's series of articles in *Saturday Night*, 24 February to 31 March 1945, and her letters to the *Ottawa Citizen*, 3 to 5 July 1944. Also, Whitton, *The Dawn of an Ampler Life*. Rooke and Schnell, *No Bleeding Heart*, 82, 111–16.
158 Whitton, *Baby Bonuses*, 44.
159 Ibid., 18–23, 40–1.
160 Ibid., 35–8.
161 Ibid., 37.
162 Ibid., 37–8.
163 Ibid.
164 Gould, *Family Allowances in Canada*, 9–11, 24–30.
165 Stepler, *Family Allowances for Canada*, 28.
166 Rooke and Schnell, *No Bleeding Heart*, 124.
167 Drew to Leonard Brockington, 19 February 1942, file 172, vol. 19, GD.
168 Drew to William O. Langdon, file 789, vol. 85, GD.
169 Langdon to Drew, 23 February 1942, file 789, vol. 85, GD. Byers notes that most deserters and defaulters *were* French Canadian; of the over six thousand still at large in 1946, 73.3 per cent were from Quebec. He provides a more nuanced analysis than many obstinate Anglo-Protestants of the time, who believed French Canadians were cowardly and disloyal. For Byers, this reflected the increased isolation of French-Canadian Zombies across Canada and the increasing tensions between French and English Canadians over conscription. The latter influenced the Godbout government to refuse to help the federal government in its tracking of deserters, angering many Anglo-Protestants. Byers, *Zombie Army*, 192–6.
170 Ralph Allen, *Ordeal by Fire*, 418, 443–9; Black, *Duplessis*, 243; Dumas, "L'Église," 244–5, 252–3. For such statements, see "Minister in Quebec Supports Separatist Chaloult's Motion," *Globe and Mail*, 3 February 1944; "'English Soldier Worst in the World,' Says French-Canadian Politician," *Globe and Mail*, 13 July 1944, originally from the *Montreal Daily Star*; Maxime Raymond, House of Commons, 7 May 1941, 2637–42.
171 Byers, *Zombie Army*, 204–7, 233–4; Granatstein and Hitsman, *Broken Promises*, 207–38.
172 Stacey, "Through the Second World War," 294–5; Drew certainly believed that the results of the by-election were fundamental to the future of Canada. Drew to Hugh Farthing, 12 March 1945, file 474, vol. 54, GD; "Pens Fear Political Applecart Is Doomed by By-Election," *Globe and Mail*, 26 January 1945, describing an article in a recent issue of the

New York Herald-Tribune; "Canada at War: Vital By-Election," *Time*, 15 January 1945; Wilfrid Eggleston, "Apparently Mr King Misjudged the Resentment of the People," *Saturday Night*, 17 February 1945; "Canada at War: Tory Triumph," *Time*, 12 February 1945.

173 "King Asks Grey North to Bury Partisan Views," *Globe and Mail*, 13 January 1945; John E. Dolphini [?], president of the North Grey Liberal Association, "An Open Letter to the Electors of North Grey," *Owen Sound Daily Sun-Times*, 10 January 1945; "King Assures that Federal Election Near," *Owen Sound Daily Sun-Times*, 13 January 1945.

174 "Who Fights in Grey North?" *Owen Sound Daily Sun-Times*, 15 January 1945, originally from *Saturday Night*; "Canada at War: Vital By-Election," *Time*, 15 January 1945; perhaps the clearest statement of this came from the Tory *Globe and Mail*: "Citizens of Grey North today go to the polls in a by-election whose sole issue is human lives." Quotation from "Officers Prove McNaughton's Guilt," *Globe and Mail*, 5 February 1945.

175 "Is McNaughton Conducting Feud, Is Case's Query," *Owen Sound Daily Sun-Times*, 18 January 1945. The *Globe and Mail* painted King's attempt to get McNaughton seated as another example of his fascist inclinations. See "In Case You're Interested: It Can Happen Here," *Globe and Mail*, 25 January 1945.

176 "Case Objects to 'Outsiders' in Grey North," *Globe and Mail*, 9 January 1945; "Diefenbaker at Meaford Demands Equality of Service and Sacrifice," *Owen Sound Daily Sun-Times*, 23 January 1945.

177 "Bracken at Meaford on Thursday Eve," *Owen Sound Daily Sun-Times*, 2 February 1945; Granatstein, *Politics of Survival*, 184. This is not to say there were no conflicts between Zombies and the army. See Byers, *Zombie Army*, 199–200, 233–5.

178 Granatstein, *Canada's War*, 393.

179 Kendle, *John Bracken*, 218.

180 "Says McNaughton Vote Is One for Enslavement to Roman Catholic Rule," *Owen Sound Daily Sun-Times*, 5 January 1945.

181 Granatstein, *Canada's War*, 390.

182 "Shields Is Scored by Altar Society St. Mary's Church," *Owen Sound Daily Sun-Times*, 12 January 1945; I. Norman Smith, "Ottawa Journalist Gives Picture of Owen Sound," *Owen Sound Daily Sun-Times*, 27 January 1945, originally from the *Ottawa Journal*; "Internment of T.T. Shields Asked by Quebec City Council," *Globe and Mail*, 13 January 1945.

183 Mackenzie King Diary, 23 December 1944; 5 February 1945.

184 Granatstein and Hitsman, *Broken Promises*, 236–7; Bothwell, Drummond, and English, *Canada*, 334; Kendle, *John Bracken*, 219–20; Morton and Granatstein, *Victory, 1945*, 63. Case won with the following results: Case, 7,333, McNaughton, 6,097, and the CCF candidate Col. A.E. Godfrey, 3,118. Swettenham, *McNaughton*, Vol. 3, 77.
185 Eggleston, "Apparently Mr King Misjudged the Resentment of the People," *Saturday Night*, 17 February 1945.
186 John Marshall, "North Grey Typical Riding?" *Owen Sound Daily Sun-Times*, 1 February 1945. He was the Ottawa correspondent for the *Windsor Star*.
187 "'Victory for the Boys' – Case, 'Lost First Skirmish' – Andy," *Ottawa Journal*, 6 February 1945. McNaughton also referred to Tory bribery, distribution of liquor, and reactionary ideology as important causes of his defeat. King diary, 7 February 1945.
188 King diary, 16 February 1945.
189 Bothwell, Drummond, and English, *Canada*, 335; Granatstein, *Politics of Survival*, 196; Blake, *From Rights to Needs*, 159.
190 Bruce to Forsey, 2 August 1945, Bruce, Honourable Herbert, 1943–1962, Vol. 3, EF.

CHAPTER FOUR

1 Lower, *This Most Famous Stream*, 35–7.
2 Lower to Pickersgill, 14 June 1956, file 41, box 7, AL. According to Rudin, Guy Frégault represented the "Montreal school" of Quebec history, characterized as believing that Quebeckers never truly recovered from the Conquest, viewing Anglo domination as the major characteristic defining the marginalized socio-economic status of French Canadians in Canada. Rudin, *Making History*, 93–128.
3 Lower to Pickersgill, 14 June 1956. Lower agreed with the recent editorial by *Maclean's*, which opposed the banning of Robeson on the principle that this violated the very liberties that a democracy was supposed to represent in the face of Soviet Communism. "Barring Robeson Helps the Reds," *Maclean's*, 26 May 1956.
4 Lower to George Grube, 17 May 1939, file 13, box 1, AL. Lower advised the professor to write a book on the reactionary elements in Ontario, such as the Orange Order, drawing particular attention to the circle around George McCullagh, the fiercely pro-British editor of the *Globe and Mail*, and Drew. Lower even went so far as to label Drew another

Hitler, but without the ability. Lower to Charlie [?], 14 April 1940, file 14, vol. 1, AL.

5 Christie has provided two invaluable studies that include a brief discussion of anti-Catholicism in this era: "Look Out for Leviathan" and "Sacred Sex." There is also an article specifically addressing Baptists and the ICC and the CPL, by Reilly, "Baptists and Organized Opposition." However, this article focuses only on Baptists, and provides an extremely uncritical account of anti-Catholicism in postwar Canada.
6 Christie and Gauvreau, "Introduction," 6–9.
7 The most blatant example of this idea of Protestantism and Catholicism as competing systems in this period comes from Harold Fey, who contributed a series of articles for *Christian Century* in 1944, the first one revealingly entitled "Can Catholicism Win America?" 29 November 1944.
8 Herberg, *Protestant-Catholic-Jew*, 260.
9 Silcox, "Why Are We Protestants?" 2–7, file 72, box 6, CES.
10 Silcox, "Paganism and Papalism," UCO, 1 May and 15 May 1946.
11 Silcox, "Protestantism and Catholicism: Their Similarities and Differences, Introductory Lecture," 6 Feb. 1955, file 83, box 6, CES, 11–12, 20. Italics in the original.
12 Innis, "The Church in Canada," *The Time of Healing*, 22nd Annual Report of the Board of Evangelism and Social Service, United Church of Canada, 1947, 53–4, file 16, box 26, Harold Innis fonds (hereafter HI), University of Toronto Archives.
13 Silcox to Innis, 20 July 1947, file 3, box 8, HI.
14 Lower to the Editor, *The Native Son*, 18 March 1944, file 22, box 1, AL.
15 It seems that Lower's initial title for this book was explicitly religious: *Foundations of Our Faith*. See "Occasional Diary," vol. 51, AL.
16 Lower, *This Most Famous Stream*, x, vii–viii, ix.
17 Ibid., viii, 5–6, 30.
18 Ibid., 34.
19 Ibid., 34–7.
20 Ibid., 39–40, 131–2, 192.
21 This thesis is named after the great German sociologist Max Weber and the influential British socialist historian R.H. Tawney. For an analysis of Weber's thesis in relation to Catholicism, see McGreevy, *Catholicism and American Freedom*, 176–8; Jenkins, *New Anti-Catholicism*, 32–4.
22 Lower, *Colony to Nation*, 67. *Colony to Nation* went through five editions, including five printings in three editions within the first ten years of publication. Publisher Longmans Canada had trouble fulfilling all the requests from non-academic Canadians for the text. In addition to the Governor

General's Award, it won the Imperial Order of the Daughters of the Empire award and the Royal Society of Canada's Tyrell Medal. See Edwardson, "Narrating a Canadian Identity," 60.
23 Wright, *Professionalization of History*, 151–3; Edwardson, "Narrating a Canadian Identity," 60–1.
24 Lower, *Colony to Nation*, 66–9, 68n11, 181.
25 Ibid., 66–9, 25–7.
26 Lower's clipping of Lunn's article has "cheap journalism" scrawled across it. Lunn, "The Angry Professor Who Pulls Canada Apart," *Star Weekly Magazine*, 27 June 1959, clipping, file 5, box 62, AL
27 Lower, *This Most Famous Stream*, 58; this sentiment is also present in *Canadians in the Making*, 274.
28 Mendelson, *Exiles from Nowhere*, 2–3.
29 Lower to Nelson, 15 February 1956, file 5, box 3, AL.
30 Lower to Sister Mary Jean, May 1956, file 5, box 3, AL.
31 I have chosen to use the United Church as an example because it was the largest Protestant denomination in the country. See *Historical Statistics in Canada*, series A164-184. I was also influenced by Airhart's discussion of the United Church and Vatican II in *Church with the Soul*. For a profile of other reactions to Vatican II, see Attridge, Clifford, and Routhier, eds., *Vatican II*.
32 Forrest, "The Men Who Ponder the Church's Faith," UCO, 1 Oct. 1961. "Let's Wait and See – And Pray," UCO, 1 October 1962.
33 For negative reactions see "R.C.s Pleased – I'm Displeased," letters from W.R. Will, John Bailey, John M. Weir, UCO, 15 November 1962; "Roman Catholics," letters from Allan Diamond, Miss B. McCracken, UCO, 1 December 1962. For positive reactions, see "United Church and R.C.s," letters from Rev. Barry D. Moore, Mrs W.E. Morton, Rev. Morley P. Bentley, UCO, 1 January 1963. For a discussion of this decision and the United Church's reaction to Vatican II, see Airhart, *Church with the Soul*, 197–8,
34 "Editor's Observations," UCO, 1 December 1962.
35 "An Infallible Pope!" UCO, 15 June 1962.
36 Forrest, "A Protestant at Vatican II," UCO, 15 November 1962.
37 Airhart, *Church with the Soul*, 244–8, 271–2.
38 McLeod, *"Thus in the Stilly Night,"* Appendix D: "The Address of the Moderator the Right Rev. Hugh A. McLeod to the Twentieth General Council of the United Church," 12 September 1962, 283–9. Airhart, *Church with the Soul*, 185–6, 196–8, 202–4.
39 McLeod, "The Address of the Moderator," 283–9.

40 Hugh McLeod to My Dear Friends, 1 October 1962, Office of the Moderator fonds (hereafter OM), file 2, box 12, UCA.
41 "The News in Brief," *Globe and Mail*, 14 September 1962; "Moderator's Charge Rouses All Faiths," *Globe and Mail*, 14 September 1962.
42 "Up Front," *UCO*, 1 October 1962; "Up Front" and "Is Canada to Become Roman Catholic?" *UCO*, 1 September 1962.
43 "Immigration and R.C.s," 15 October 1962, *UCO*.
44 "Catholics: Immigration and Education," *UCO*, 15 October 1962.
45 Bryden, *"Justifiable Obsession,"* 54–7.
46 *Toronto Daily Star*, 25 June 1949. They also ran headlines before the election that read "Shall Duplessis Rule Canada?" and, over a picture of Houde and Duplessis, "Shall These Two Men Become Canada's Real Rulers?" *Toronto Daily Star*, 22 June 1949 and 25 June 1949, respectively. "History of Federal Ridings since 1867: Papineau, Quebec (1949–1988)," Parliament of Canada, http://www.parl.gc.ca/About/Parliament/FederalRidingsHistory/hfer.asp?Include=Y&Language=E&rid=532&Search=Det. (accessed 24 October 2012). Houde won 12,611 votes in the riding of Papineau, while PC Wilfred Kendall won only 587.
47 D'Arcy Birmingham to Drew, 11 August 1953; response from Drew, 14 August 1953, Election 1953, Correspondence, A-B, vol. 436, GD.
48 Casey, *The Making of a Catholic President*, 189.
49 Mrs G.H. Dresser to Drew, 15 August 1953. Drew responded 25 August 1953, Elections 1953, Correspondence, C-D, vol. 436, GD.
50 W.B. Rollason to Drew, 11 August 1953, Drew responded 29 August 1953, Elections 1953, Correspondence, Miscellaneous, vol. 436, GD.
51 L.W. Murphy to Drew, 4 March 1955, Drew responded 9 March 1955, file 449, vol. 210, GD.
52 Drew to Brigadier John H. Price, 12 August 1953, Elections 1953, Correspondence, Miscellaneous, vol. 436, GD.
53 Drew to Leon Balcer, 11 August 1953, Elections 1953, Correspondence 1953, A-B, vol. 436, GD.
54 Drew to Hugh Farthing, 12 March 1945, file 474, vol. 54, GD.
55 Drew to Farthing, 12 March 1945; Gotlieb, "George Drew and the Dominion-Provincial Conference on Reconstruction of 1945–46," *CHR* 66 (1985): 30. I would like to thank Gotlieb for drawing my attention to the last two quotations.
56 Drew to Hugh Farthing, 27 June 1945, file 474, vol. 54, GD.
57 Drew to James Jackson, General Secretary of the Grand Orange Lodge of Ontario West, 29 May 1956. Jackson had sent a particularly intense rebuke of Balcer on 25 May 1956, stating "We desire to emphasize that

any encroachments of Romanism or any surrender of British traditions is, and will be resisted by every means within our power as members of this patriotic association," file 20, vol. 228, GD.
58 Farthing, *Freedom*, preface by Robinson, v–vi, "Introduction," Fulton, xvi. Christian and Campbell, *Political Parties*, 110–13.
59 Farthing, *Freedom*, 49.
60 Ibid., 4–9, 75.
61 Ibid., 13–18, 21, 89.
62 Ibid., xiii–xiv.
63 Ibid., 86.
64 Massolin, *Canadian Intellectuals*, 251–3. This was one of the many concerns percolating in Canadian conservatism/Conservatism during the High Liberal years of the 1940s and 1950s.
65 Farthing to Forsey, 25 January 1952, Farthing, John, Part 3, 1943, 1952–1954, vol. 3, EF.
66 Ibid.
67 Ibid.
68 Farthing, *Freedom*, 172–5.
69 Forsey to H.C. Farthing, 23 April 1957, Personal General Correspondence, Part 2, 1957, vol. 5, EF.
70 Creighton, "Eugene Alfred Forsey," in Forsey, *Freedom and Order*, 9–10. Correspondence w. Eugene Forsey, 1944–1964, vol. 26, Donald Creighton fonds, LAC.
71 Forsey to Meighen, 18 February 1952, vol. 223, AM.
72 Farthing to Forsey, 9 February 1952, vol. 220A, AM.
73 Judith Robinson to Forsey, 1952, Robinson, Judith, 1945, 1952, vol. 5, EF.
74 Saunders was a Salvationist and mayor of Toronto from 1954 to 1955, through appointment, after the sitting mayor resigned to become head of the Toronto Transit Commission. Saunders, *An Orangeman in Public Life*, 116–17.
75 Kirkconnell, "Authentic Research Means That All Relevant Facts Are Studied," *Saturday Night*, 8 February 1947. Saunders, "Communism in R.C. Countries," *Protestant Action*, July-August 1954.
76 Mrs Blake, "No Vatican Envoy," *Protestant Action*, April 1954.
77 Lay Preacher, "McCarthyism," *Protestant Action*, April 1954.
78 "Persecution," *Prairie Overcomer*, June–July 1950.
79 For the long, complex story of the treatment of Jehovah's Witnesses in Quebec, particularly during the Duplessis years, see Kaplan, *State and Salvation*.
80 "Brethren Deny Link to Witnesses," *Globe and Mail*, 22 April 1950; "'Mob Rule' in Quebec," *Ensign*, 29 April 1950, in file 337, John H. Blackmore

fonds (hereafter JHB), GMA. The *Ensign*, a Catholic journal, noted that the Witnesses called themselves "Les Evangelistes de Jehovah" in French, and that the Brethren had become known as "Les Evangelistes" in Quebec, perhaps contributing to the confusion.

81 "Persecution," *Prairie Overcomer*, June-July 1950.
82 See Stingel, *Social Discredit*, 140–1 and Appendix A, 194–5, for a short biography of Blackmore. In 1953, Blackmore added to his reputation when he openly praised Joe McCarthy and his tactics as defending Western liberties. See Harvey Hickey, "Franking Scope Questioned: Charge Anti-Semitic Data Mailed by MP's Secretary," *Globe and Mail*, 20 November 1953.
83 House of Commons, 24 April 1950, 1827–1829.
84 Blackmore to Purcell, 16 May 1950, file 337; Blackmore to Mrs C.M. Vander Lee, 27 May 1950, file 337, JHB.
85 Blackmore to M.O. Rollefson, 2 May 1950, file 337, JHB.
86 Blackmore to CPL, 16 May 1950; Blackmore to Edward Morris, 1 and 5 June 1950, file 337, JHB.
87 Edward Morris to Blackmore, 1 June 1950, file 337, JHB.
88 Blackmore to Manning, 29 May 1950; Manning to Blackmore, 3 June 1950, file 337, JHB.
89 James Watt, "History of the Inter-Church Committee on Protestant–Roman Catholic Relations, 1944 to 1973," Inter-Church Committee Collection, finding aid 73, 1, UCA. The objectives of the ICC are stated clearly in the *Brief of the Inter-Church Committee*.
90 Moir has referred to the United Church as its "step-parent." Moir, "Toronto's Protestants," 323.
91 Watt, "History of the Inter-Church Committee," Appendix.
92 Walker, *Catholic Education and Politics*, vol. 3, 23.
93 Inter-Church Committee on Protestant–Roman Catholic Relations, *Protestant- Roman Catholic Relations*, 5.
94 Saywell, *"Just Call Me Mitch,"* 258–63, 299–300; Walker, *Catholic Education in Ontario: A Documentary Study*, 1.
95 Inter-Church Committee (ICC), *Brief Submitted*, 26–7, 33–4.
96 ICC, *French Language*, 10.
97 Walker, *Catholic Education in Ontario*, vol. 3, 67, 79–80.
98 ICC, *French Language*, 10.
99 ICC, *Hope Report*, 6–7.
100 Kirkconnell, "Canadian Baptists and the World Council of Churches," *Maritime Baptist*, 18 February 1948.

101 Kirkconnell, "Tide of Anti-Catholic Propaganda Rising," *Saturday Night*, 4 January 1947, 6.
102 Kirkconnell, "Authentic Research Means That All Relevant Facts Are Studied," *Saturday Night*, 8 February 1947, 4; for the original request from the ICC, see George A. Cornish to Kirkconnell, 9 December 1946, file 2, vol. 52, WK. Kirkconnell also turned down membership offered by Rev. H.H. Bingham. Kirkconnell to Bingham, 18 January 1946, file 29d, vol. 4, ICC. Kirkconnell to Bingham, 11 December 1946, file 2, vol. 52, WK.
103 Kirkconnell to Bingham, 10 November 1945, file 29d, vol. 4, ICC.
104 Kirkconnell, "Tide of Anti-Catholic Propaganda Rising," *Saturday Night*, 4 January 1947, 6.
105 Kirkconnell to Farmer, 22 March 1947, file 25, box 53, WK.
106 Letter to Mr Brant, 23 November 1954, file 60, box 36, WK.
107 Wade was an American-born professor of French-Canadian history, who came from a religiously mixed family but was raised Catholic. He is best-known for his epic study *The French Canadians, 1760–1945*. Griffiths, "Hugh Mason Wade," in *Mason Wade, Acadia and Quebec: The Perception of an Outsider*, 2–3.
108 Kirkconnell, "Religion and Philosophy: An English-Canadian Point of View," 42–7, 54–5. See McEvoy, "Establishment of Diplomatic Relations," 66–84 and "Religion and Politics," 121–44, for discussions of Protestant hostility toward state relations with the Vatican.
109 Kirkconnell, "Religion and Philosophy," 54–5.
110 John A. Stevenson, "Where Will Pius XII Go If Reds Win Italy?" *Saturday Night*, 22 November 1947; Kirkconnell, "Religion and Philosophy," 54–5.
111 Bossy, *A Call*, 24–5, 34–6.
112 Walter J. Bossy to Louis St Laurent, Stuart Sinclair, Walter Harris, and Howard Prentice, 27 March 1953, file 126, box 13, ICC.
113 Minutes, Meeting of the ICC, Toronto, 15 December 1955, file 126, box 13, ICC.
114 Rev. Ralph Latimer, "Confidential," 1–3, file 126, box 13, ICC.
115 Latimer, "Confidential," 3–4, file 126, box 13, ICC.
116 For a good social history of the reaction to, and treatment of, European immigrants and DPs in this period, see Iacovetta, *Gatekeepers*.
117 W.W. Judd to George Cornish, 30 January 1956, file 126, box 13, ICC
118 W.W. Judd to the ICC, 9 January 1956, file 126, box 13, ICC.
119 Rev. James Craig to Rev. George Pidgeon, 9 March 1956, file 126, box 13, ICC.

120 Ralph Latimer to George Cornish, 23 January 1956, file 126, box 13, ICC.
121 Entry for the Ernest E. Long fonds, UCA, "Administrative History."
122 W.G. Berry to V.T. Mooney, 14 May 1969, file 29, vol. 3, ICC.
123 Elizabeth Diamond, Alix McEwen, and Patricia Birkett, revised by Cheryl DiMaria and Robert Fisher, "Administrative History," Canadian Council of Churches (hereafter CCC) Finding Aid, LAC, no. 766. Also see, the "The Canadian Council of Churches, Constitution," file 7, vol. 101, CCC.
124 Mooney to Rev. R.M. Bennett, 18 November 1967, file 29b, vol. 3, ICC.
125 Rev. Wilfred Butcher to V.T. Mooney, 6 March 1967; Mooney to Butcher, 6 April 1967, file 29b, vol. 3, ICC.
126 W.G. Berry, "What We Have Done," 3 January 1966, file 20, vol. 37, CCC.
127 R.M. Bennett to Rev. Dr R.W. Henderson, 27 November 1967, file 16, vol. 121, CCC. Henderson was the chairman of the Developments and Priorities Committee of the CCC.
128 Mooney to Rev. R.M. Bennett, 19 December 1967, file 29b, vol. 3, ICC.
129 For example, "Catholicism Considered in Relation to Protestantism," file 60, vol. 101, CCC, or Robert Rouquette, "The Holy Office and the Oecumenical [sic] Movement," file 48, vol. 101, CCC.
130 See vol. 121, file 16 and vol. 43 file 8, CCC.
131 "Dogma of the Assumption," "Archbishop of York on the Proposed Dogma of the Assumption," file 34, vol. 101, CCC.
132 H.E. Wintemute to W.J. Gallagher, 25 September 1951, file 34, vol. 101, CCC.
133 Anonymous, "Implications of Diplomatic Representation at the Vatican," n.d., 2–3, file 81, vol. 102, CCC.
134 Rev. Ernest E. Long and Ivor D. Williams, "Civil and Religious Liberty," 5, 10–11, file 28, vol. 101, CCC.
135 Long and Williams, "Civil and Religious Liberty," 14.
136 Forsey opposed this doctrine so fiercely that he left the newly formed New Democratic Party when it endorsed it at its founding convention. Forsey, *A Life on the Fringe*, 205–6.
137 Forsey, "Canada – Two Nations or One?" in Forsey, *Freedom and Order*, 258–9.
138 Fraser, *René Lévesque*, 35.
139 "Opposed to Teaching Public School French, Clergyman in Dutch," *Globe and Mail*, 20 December 1962; "Minister Says Quebec Is 300 Years Behind," *Ottawa Citizen*, 15 December 1962.
140 "Opposed to Teaching Public School French," *Globe and Mail*; "Minister 'Snowed Under': French Stand Creates 'Mail Storm,'" *Hamilton Spectator*, 14 June 1963.

141 "'Emotional Urge': French in Schools Not a Need: Trustee," *Globe and Mail*, 30 January 1964.
142 MacLennan, "Quebec No Clerical-Fascist State, Culture Exploding!" *Toronto Star*, 18 December 1962. Emphasis added by author.
143 Dumas, "L'Église," 3–4, 321–6.
144 MacLennan to Lower, 2 March 1964, file 32, box 7, AL.
145 Lower to MacLennan, 5 December 1970, file 32, box 7, AL; Taine, *History*, 104–6, 109–15, 137–8, 167–9; Jones, "Hippolyte Adolphe Taine."
146 MacLennan to Lower, 17 January 1971, file 32, box 7, AL.
147 Lower, "Possible Outline for a Draft of a Brief on Biculturalism," 5 February 1964, file 7, box 61, AL.

CHAPTER FIVE

1 Richard J. Doyle, "Davis's motive on schools remains a mystery," n.d., n.t., L.S. Garnsworthy papers (hereafter LG), Separate School Funding: clippings, Anglican Diocese of Toronto Archives.
2 Lower, *A Pattern for History*, 15–27, 323, 347.
3 Bramadat and Seljak, "Charting the New Terrain," 11–15.
4 Miedema, *For Canada's Sake*, xv–xviii, 13, 21–7.
5 Noll has explained this transformation in Canadian society as resulting from 1) large structural factors in Canadian history, particularly the inability of Canadian institutions to adapt to a rapidly changing society due to their more hierarchical nature; 2) contingency, especially the slow, contentious embracing of social Christianity by the mainline Protestants and Catholics. This embrace was too late for Noll, as society had already moved on, with the state and the new ideology of multiculturalism facilitating Canadian cohesion, not religion. Noll, *What Happened*, 54–6.
6 Noll and Nystrom, *Is the Reformation Over?* 11–13. For a good discussion of the coalition of Catholics and evangelicals in the American religious right in the 1970s, see Allitt, "Transformation," 144–56.
7 McGowan, "Roman Catholics (Anglophone and Allophone)," 89–90.
8 Jenkins, *New Anti-Catholicism*, 32.
9 Boyd, with Kenneth McDonald, *The National Dilemma*, v; Boyd, *Rebel Engineer*, 187–9; "Biography/History," Winnett Boyd fonds, Trent University Archives, http://www.trentu.ca/admin/library/archives/99-008.htm (accessed 11 September 2012); Hayday, *So They Want Us to Learn French*, 86.
10 Boyd, "Foreword," in Allison, *French Power*, ix.

11 English refers to Andrew's book as the most extreme example of English-Canadian displeasure with bilingualism in the 1960s and 1970s. English notes it went through ten printings between 1977 and 1978. English, *Just Watch Me*, 346. Boyd claimed by 1978 it had sold 120,000 copies. Boyd, "Foreword," in Allison, *French Power*, vii.
12 Andrew, *Bilingual Today, French Tomorrow*, i–iv, 1–5, 13–17, 27–30.
13 Ibid., 57–9. For an excellent analysis of organized anti-bilingualism and the concern among many Anglophones that it would cause a loss in jobs, see Hayday, *So They Want Us to Learn French*, 17–19, 30–2.
14 Andrew, *Enough!* vi–vii, 17, 55–7; Hayday, *So They Want Us to Learn French*, 111–13.
15 Russell, *Canadian Crucible*, 243–4; Allison, *French Power*, 56–7.
16 Allison, *French Power*, 61–70, 76.
17 Ibid., 75–6.
18 Boyd, *Rebel Engineer*, 179–81, 187–9.
19 Norman Webster, "Tough Book to Stomach," *Globe and Mail*, 6 September 1977.
20 Hayday, *So They Want Us to Learn French*, 17–19, 84–6.
21 Francis, *Fighting for Canada*, 8–11.
22 Gratton, *French Canadians*, Chapter 2, "La Patente." For Gratton's sexual impropriety, see "MP Seeks Probe of PMO Official after Allegations of Sexual Misconduct," *Globe and Mail*, 8 November 1986.
23 *L'Autorité* was quoted approvingly in Judith Robinson's conservative Toronto paper *News* in 1944 when it claimed that the Order was the secret society underlying the isolationism and nationalism in Quebec: "For several years we have had in Quebec, a Ku Klux Klan in many ways reminiscent of the American Ku Klux Klan ... Our Klansmen of Quebec have quite simply replaced Catholics by Protestants, and instead of Negroes have the English." Press Information Bureau, "Quebec's Ku Klux Klan Parent of Bloc Populaire," *News*, 29 April 1944.
24 Champion, *Strange Demise*, 163–9.
25 Francis, *Fighting for Canada*, 168–84.
26 Ray Conlogue, "Friends of Sovereignty," *Globe and Mail*, 6 November 1996.
27 Francis, "Diane Francis Replies," *Globe and Mail*, 4 December 1996; Aubin's article appeared as "For the Record, Ms Francis...," *Globe and Mail*, 16 November 1996.
28 Hayday, *So They Want Us to Learn French*, 8.
29 Lower, *Pattern of History*, 153–5, 159–70, 281.

30 Letter from Bill Davis to V.T. Mooney, 8 October 1968, vol. 3, file 29a, ICC.
31 Letter from Davis to Mooney, 29 January 1971, vol. 3, file 29, ICC: "Since I assumed my present portfolio [minister of education] I have made every effort to build the Ontario educational system into one of the finest in the world, and I cannot agree to any proposal which would in any way weaken it or which would not be in the best interests of all the people in this province."
32 "Statement to the Prime Minister of Ontario by the Inter-Church Committee on Protestant–Roman Catholic Relations," 30 May 1968, presented to Robarts and Davis; for an example of a meeting between the ICC and Robarts and Davis, see Mooney to Albaugh, 9 May 1968, vol. 3, file 29a, ICC.
33 "A New Separatism in Ontario?" vol. 3, file 29, ICC.
34 Mooney to Davis, 4 November 1971; Davis to Mooney, 22 November 1971, file 29, vol. 3, ICC.
35 Airhart sees the disbanding of the ICC as representative of the increasing acceptance of Catholicism in Canadian society by the majority of those in the United Church. Airhart, *Church with the Soul*, 244–5.
36 Mooney to Berry, 4 March 1971, file 29, vol. 3, ICC.
37 James Craig to Ralph Latimer, 3 March 1971, file 29, vol. 3, ICC. Italics in original.
38 V.T. Mooney to Rev. A. Leonard Griffith, 30 April 1968, file 29c, vol. 3, ICC; Mooney to Rev. Donald Bruce Macdonald, 21 January 1972, file 29, vol. 3. This sentiment is present again in a letter from Mooney to Rev. Arthur W. Currie, 27 November 1970, file 29, vol. 3.
39 MacDonald, *Happy Warrior*, 261. Manthorpe, in his study of the Tory dynasty, referred to an anonymous Toronto newspaper executive, who claimed as soon as Davis opposed the extension of Catholic schools that he would win the 1971 election, because it would galvanize the traditional anti-Catholic, pro-Orange feeling in Ontario. Jonathan Manthorpe, *The Power and the Tories*, 155–6.
40 MacDonald, *Happy Warrior*, 261–2. John Cruickshank and Robert Matas, "Miller Accuses Archbishop of Reopening Religious Wounds," *Globe and Mail*, 26 April 1985; Robert Matas, "United Schools Unattainable, Davis Decided," *Globe and Mail*, 25 March 1985. Goodman, *Life of the Party*, 269; Dana Flavelle, "Catholic Teachers Protect System," *Toronto Star*, 24 September 1985.
41 Cheryl Agoston, "Cardinal Denies He Made Deal with Davis," *Catholic Register*, 27 April 1985; "Anglican Archbishop Critical: Top Clerics Split

over RC Financing"; Robert Matas, "United Schools Unattainable, Davis Decided," *Globe and Mail*, 25 March 1985; Hoy, *Bill Davis*, 262–9; Dixon, "William Davis," 21–7.

42 Dixon, "William Davis," 21–7; Speirs, *Out of the Blue*, 21–5; Hoy mentions the lawsuit, but privileges the alleged arrangement with Carter, as well as Carter's threats. Hoy, *Bill Davis*, 265.

43 Orland French, "Was Davis Marooned in Corner?" *Globe and Mail*, 15 April 1985; J. Wood, "Re: Ontario's Non-Issue," *Globe and Mail*, 24 April 1985.

44 Allan Fotheringham, "King Billy and His Orangemen," *Maclean's*, 6 February 1981.

45 Letter from Garnsworthy to Davis, 14 June 1984, file 12, 2009-260-002, Ecclesiastical Province of Ontario fonds, Algoma University.

46 Garnsworthy, "The Archbishop Urges Dialogue on Funding," *The Anglican*, September 1984, LG; Robert Matas, "Not alone on school financing issue, renegade Tory says," *Globe and Mail*, 4 July 1985.

47 Stanley Oziewicz, "Primate Dislikes Hitler-Davis Equation," *Globe and Mail*, 27 April 1985.

48 Richard J. Doyle, "Davis's Motive on Schools Remains a Mystery," n.d., n.t., LG; Robert Matas, "Primate Attempts to Ease Rift over Schools," *Globe and Mail*, 12 July 1984.

49 John Allemang, "Outspoken Anglican Plans to Just Fade Away," *Globe and Mail*, 22 November 1988.

50 Robert Matas, "Primate Attempts to Ease Rift over Schools," *Globe and Mail*, 12 July 1984. Orland French, "Nice Nelly Approach Just Not On," *Globe and Mail*, 29 August 1985. For a study of the Keegstra case, see Bercuson and Wertheimer, *A Trust Betrayed: The Keegstra Affair*.

51 Theresa Tedesco, "Archbishop Get Cheers with Call for Inquiry," *Globe and Mail*, 4 November 1985.

52 Whitaker, "Rash Act to Aid Catholic Schools?" *Globe and Mail*, 11 April 1985; Frank Jones, "Cardinal Off Base with Bigotry Remark," *Toronto Star*, 19 September 1985.

53 Ron Seberras, "Dual System Is History," *Toronto Star*, 16 October 1984.

54 MacDonald, *Happy Warrior*, 261–2.

55 Orland French, "Nasty Potential in Funding," *Globe and Mail*, 9 May 1985.

56 John Allemang and Donn Downey, "Ex-archbishop's Views on RC School Funding Helped Topple Tories," *Globe and Mail*, 27 January 1990.

57 Speirs, *Out of the Blue*, 118–19.

58 Wolffe, "Anti-Catholicism and the Evangelical Identity," 193.

59 Speirs, *Out of the Blue*, 181.
60 Michael McAteer, "Anti-Catholic Comics for Sale Despite Threats of Legal Action," *Toronto Star*, 12 November 1983; Trish Crawford, "MPP Tables Anti-Catholic Comic," *Toronto Star*, 26 October 1983; Tom Harpur, "Hellfire and Damnation Comic Books Attack Bible Scholars, Catholics, Jews," *Toronto Star*, 28 March 1981; Suzanne Goldenberg, "Rise in Anti-Catholic Tracts Attributed to Pope's Visit," *Globe and Mail*, 19 July 1984; Victory Paddy, "Evangelical Comics Prove Unfunny," *Maclean's*, 3 August 1981.
61 See the Chick Publications website, http://www.chick.com/. For academic studies of Chick's publications and his anti-Catholicism, see Borer and Murphee, "Framing Catholicism," 95–112; Massa, *Anti-Catholicism in America*, Chapter 7.
62 Tom Harpur, "Hellfire and Damnation Comic Books Attack Bible Scholars, Catholics, Jews," *Toronto Star*, 28 March 1981; George Johnson, *Architects of Fear*, 86–90.
63 Michael McAteer, "Anti-Catholic Comics for Sale Despite Threats of Legal Action," *Toronto Star*, 12 November 1983.
64 Andrew Nikiforuk, "2,000 Hear Hero of Religious Comics," *Globe and Mail*, 19 April 1982; Dominion *Law Report*, 1982, 413–16.
65 "U.S. Men Arrested with Hate Literature," *Globe and Mail*, 17 September 1984; Michael Tenszen, "Plan for Papal Visit Brings Hate Tracts," *Globe and Mail*, 20 April 1984.
66 "Books by Avro Manhattan," *Globe and Mail*, 21 April 1984; Nigel Russell, F.E. Krueger, "Hatred Dressed Up," *Globe and Mail*, 27 April 1984; Robert Matas, "Bishop Says Pope's Trip Could Incite Bigots," *Globe and Mail*, 13 February 1984.
67 Trish Crawford, "Crackdown Threatened on Anti-papal Literature," *Toronto Star*, 14 February 1984; "4 People Charged with Distributing Anti-RC Literature," *Globe and Mail*, 14 September 1984.
68 "Church Members Willing to Go to Jail to Defend Right to Protest the Pope," *Toronto Star*, 29 February 1984.
69 Walter Stefaniuk, "Pope Throws Off Carefully Timed Schedules to Mix with Crowds," *Toronto Star*, 14 September 1984.
70 William H. Jones, "Pope Pomp and Junk," *Canadian Baptist*, March 1984.
71 Ibid.
72 Brian Stiller, "Here Comes the Pope," *Faith Alive*, 1984.
73 Don Anderson, Memo to CCC Officers and Staff, General Secretaries of CCC member churches, 12 July 1983; CCC Papal Visit Advisory

Committee, Aide Memoire, 20 December 1983; Clarke MacDonald, Statement re Pope John Paul II – visit to Canada – September 1984, December 19, 1983, file Papal Visit, box 5, Clarke MacDonald, OM.

74 "About Us: Our Trust from the Past," Canadian Protestant League, 2011, http://www.canadianprotestant.org/?page_id=7 (accessed 11 September 2012).

75 "Store," Canadian Protestant League, http://www.canadianprotestant.org/?page_id=160&cpage=1 (accessed 11 September 2012). *The Protestant Challenge*, Canadian Protestant League, http://www.canadianprotestant.org/?page_id=59 (accessed 11 September 2012). In the Spring/Summer, 2008 issue, dedicated to denouncing the separate-school system in Ontario, the periodical reprinted a vicious sermon by Shields from 1951 entitled "The Separate School Question: Its Principle and History."

76 In this same issue of *The Protestant Challenge* there is an article about state sanctioning of "honour killing," while listed in the bookstore are books with titles such as *The Islamic Invasion*, by Robert Morey and *Who Is This Allah?* by G.J.O. Moshay. See "Store," Canadian Protestant League, http://www.canadianprotestant.org/?page_id=160.

77 "Our Beliefs," Toronto Free Presbyterian Church, http://torontofpc.ca/our-beliefs/ (accessed 3 February 2016).

78 Minutes of Cavan Township Council Meetings, 4 October 1977, 1976–77; "Only Bigots Need Apply," *Globe and Mail*, 6 October 1977.

79 See Greer, "The Cavan Blazers," 34–8; and Eric P. Kaufmann, *The Orange Order*, 13, for examples of this characterization.

80 Rudy Platiel, "The Cavan Blazers Are a Bitter Memory of Religious Bigotry," *Globe and Mail*, 7 October 1977. Greer has referred to the Cavan Blazers as the militant arm of the Orange Order in the Peterborough area. Some of their activities included burning down a series of cottages a Catholic resident of the area had built for his Catholic brethren, so that they would not settle in the township, and setting Catholic Patrick Maguire's house on fire when he invited a priest over to say mass. This incident inspired one of their slogans, "To hell with the Pope and Paddy Maguire." Greer, "The Cavan Blazers," 34–8. The Blazers were invoked numerous times in the reaction to this incident. See "Church Leaders Condemn Cavan's Monastery Action," *Peterborough Examiner*, 6 October 1977; Gene Allen, "Anglican Service Was Quiet, No Sermons Decrying Bigotry," *Peterborough Examiner*, 11 October 1977; Paul J. Brennan, "Councillors Are Living in Cavan Past, Reader Says," *Peterborough Examiner*, 15 October 1977.

81 "Church Leaders Condemn Cavan's Monastery Action," *Peterborough Examiner*, 6 October 1977.
82 Carola Vyhnak, "McMurty Backs Monks in Battle for a Monastery," *Toronto Star*, 6 October 1977.
83 Quoted in McMurtry, *Memoirs*, 235–6.
84 "Three Sins," 7 October 1977, *Toronto Sun*. McMurtry, *Memoirs*, 235–6. Thanks to Roy McMurtry for drawing my attention to this cartoon.
85 There in fact was a building/zoning freeze in the area implemented by the Ontario government to prevent "checkerboard" land development. See "The Cavan Blazers Are a Bitter Memory of Religious Bigotry," *Globe and Mail*, 7 October 1977"; "Rights Commission Question Cavan Council about Its Bar Against Quebeckers' Monastery," *Globe and Mail*, 15 October 1977. Disappointingly, when I filed a request to see the complaint file in the Ontario Human Rights Commission fonds for the Cavan incident, it was the only case file that was missing. See Provincial Archives of Ontario, Human Rights Commission complaint case files, index, Case no.-5215, Type: A, Respondent: Township of Cavan, Location, Cavan, Complainant, Canadian Civil Liberties Association, Comp. Category, Catholic, Date, 10/7/77, Disp. Date, 11/9/77, Prov. No. 2, Disposition, Settled, N.M.
86 "Cavan Township Says It Regrets Stand on Monks," *Globe and Mail*, 10 November 1977; "Cavan Ordered to Include Clause: No Discrimination," *Millbrook Reporter*, 16 November 1977.
87 Division vote slip, n.d., Minutes of Cavan Township Council Meetings, 1976–1977; "Church Leaders Condemn Cavan's Monastery Action," *Peterborough Examiner*, 6 October 1977; "Monks Give Up on Cavan," *Peterborough Examiner*, 7 October 1977.
88 Massa, *Anti-Catholicism in America*, 14–16.
89 Cuneo, *Catholics Against the Church*, 57–65.
90 Ibid., ix–xiii.
91 Stanley Oziewicz, "Rabbi Supports Cardinal on Demonstration Plans," *Globe and Mail*, 13 February 1985.
92 Cuneo, *Catholics Against the Church*, 57–65.
93 Dr Cassidy is currently president of the intensely traditionalist Catholic Our Lady Seat of Wisdom Academy in Barry's Bay, Ontario. Our Lady Seat of Wisdom College website, https://www.seatofwisdom.ca/academics/faculty/kcassidy/ (accessed 29 August 2016).
94 Michael McAteer, "Canadian Catholics Start League to Battle Attacks Against Them," *Toronto Star*, 6 April 1985. The CCRL still exists. Its stated purpose is to "comba[t] anti-Catholic defamation, working with the media

to secure a fair hearing for Catholic positions on issues of public debate, and lobbying government and intervening in court challenges in support of law and policy compatible with a Catholic understanding of human nature and the common good." The CCRL's website boasts that the CCRL has been involved in over forty court interventions, over seven hundred anti-defamation actions, and over six thousand media appearances. "About the Catholic Civil Rights League," https://ccrl.ca/about/ (accessed 25 August 2016).

95 "Religion and Argument," *Globe and Mail*, 13 March 1985; Hugh Reynolds (no title), *Globe and Mail*, 26 March 1985; Stanley Oziewicz, "New RC Group to Fight Anti-Catholicism," *Globe and Mail*, 12 March 1985. See Rebick's account of the modern feminist movement in Canada, *Ten Thousand Roses: The Making of a Feminist Revolution*, 47–52, 160–2, 188, 248, for details on the Catholic Church and the women's-rights movement, particularly the pro-choice movement, where Rebick and other women on the ground recall the Church and Catholics both supporting women's rights and opposing access to abortion. For her activism regarding access to abortion and the OCAC, see Weir, "Social Movement Activism in the Formation of Ontario New Democratic Party Policy on Abortion, 1982–1984," *Labour/Le Travail* 35 (1995): 174–85.

96 H.R. Hallman, "Catholic Rights," *Globe and Mail*, 29 March 1985.

97 Barry Jessup, "Old and New Sins," *Globe and Mail*, 25 May 1985; Wendell W. Waters, "Standards Challenged," *Globe and Mail*, 6 June 1985; Orland French, "Rights at Mercy of Dogma," *Globe and Mail*, 30 July 1985.

98 Ian Dowbiggin, "Why Is Anti-Catholicism Tolerated?" *Globe and Mail*, 24 April 1995; John Stackhouse, "Birth Control Divides UN Talks," *Globe and Mail*, 5 September 1994.

99 Robert Eady, A.D. Brewer, "Anti-Catholicism," *Globe and Mail*, 3 May 1995.

100 Bradley Pascoe, A.M. Catterall, Marc A. Schindler, "Seeing a Problem Where None Exists," Re: Why Is Anti-Catholicism Tolerated – Facts and Arguments, *Globe and Mail*, 26 April 1995; Frances Walsh, "Unholy Ghosts," *Globe and Mail*, 2 May 1995.

101 See Jenkins for the American reaction to very real corruption in Vatican finances in the 1970s and 1980s, as well as the connections between the Institute for Religious Works, the mafia, and the shocking death of Roberto Calvi, a Vatican banker, in 1982. Jenkins also notes that sex-abuse cases in the Church were coming to the public's attention

in America in the early nineties. Jenkins, *New Anti-Catholicism*, 54–5, 133–5.

102 Michael Posner, "Son of Morningside," *Globe and Mail*, 10 May 1997. Thanks to Kenny's "A Prejudice that Rarely Utters Its Name" for drawing my attention to this and the example of the governor-general's reaction to gay marriage. "Enright and the Church," *Globe and Mail*, 15 May 1997.

103 "Unwanted 'Satire' from Judy Rebick," *Catholic Insight*, July-August 2005, contains a blistering indictment of Rebick, referring to her as a "Jewish anti-life, anti-family agitator" (what being Jewish has to do with the controversy is unclear). See Sharon Fraser, "The Editor Strikes Back," rabble.ca, 3 June 2005, http://rabble.ca/news/ithe-editor-strikes-backi (accessed 7 August 2017), for rabble's response and a good summary of the cartoon and reactions. Joanne Laucius, "Nazi-Saluting Pope Infuriates Catholics," *Ottawa Citizen*, 27 May 2005.

104 For example, Jeff deMontigny, "Compromise Values," Bert De Vries, "Spewing Intolerance," *Ottawa Citizen*, 30 May 2005; Catherine Collins, "Real Humour Targets Ourselves, Not Others," *Ottawa Citizen*, 7 June 2005.

105 Karen Rawlines, "Here's the Skinny on Judy Rebick," *Saint John Telegraph Journal*, 2 June 2005.

106 Laucius, "Nazi-Saluting Pope Infuriates Catholics," *Ottawa Citizen*, 27 May 2005.

107 Jenkins, *New Anti-Catholicism*, 162–3.

108 Janice Kennedy, "The Death of Satire: What a Poor and Barren Place the World Will Be," *Ottawa Citizen*, 5 June 2005.

109 Richard Bethell, "Cartoon Attacks the Heart of Catholicism," *Ottawa Citizen*, 30 May 2005.

110 All letters are from "Love and Marriage" section of letters, *Globe and Mail*, 18 January 2001.

111 Verhoeven refers to the criticism of celibacy in increasingly scientific terms in the nineteenth century as a major component of anti-Catholic literature and ideology. Verhoeven, *Transatlantic Anti-Catholicism*, vii, 2–3, also the chapters "Natural or Unnatural? Doctors and the Vow of Celibacy" and "Neither Male nor Female – The Jesuit as Androgyne."

112 John Saddy, "Love and Marriage," *Globe and Mail*, 18 January 2001.

113 Jenkins, *New Anti-Catholicism*, 44, 109–10.

114 A detailed analysis of the media coverage of the current sexual-assault crisis in the Catholic Church is beyond the scope of this study. For a discussion of this see Kenny, "A Prejudice that Rarely Utters Its Name,"

639–40; Jenkins, "'The Perp Walk of Sacramental Perverts': The Pedophile Priest Crisis," *The New Anti-Catholicism*.

115 Fraser, "The Priests and the Patriarchy," rabble.ca, 16 October 2009, http://rabble.ca/blogs/bloggers/sharon-fraser/2009/10/priests-and-patriarchy (accessed 24 August 2017).

116 "About," Murray Dobbin's Blog, https://murraydobbin.ca/about/ (accessed 12 October 2017). Dobbin is a very active columnist for rabble.ca as of the writing of this book. See Murray Dobbin's contributor page, http://rabble.ca/category/bios/rabble-staff/contributor/murray-dobbin (accessed 12 October 2017).

117 Laurie Goodstein and David Callender, "For Years, Deaf Boys Tried to Tell of Priest's Abuse," *New York Times*, 26 March 2010.

118 Jenkins, *New Anti-Catholicism*, 2, 110, 135–43.

119 Dobbin, "The Catholic Church: Pedophiles and Sadists," rabble.ca, 31 March 2010, http://rabble.ca/blogs/bloggers/alex/2010/03/catholic-church-pedophiles-and-sadists (accessed 24 August 2017).

120 Bishop Henry's letter, *Calgary Herald*, 14 January 2016, http://calgaryherald.com/storyline/read-bishop-fred-henrys-full-letter-on-the-new-gay-straight-guidelines-for-alberta-schools (accessed 11 August 2016).

121 Max Maudie, "Mercy and Compassion for Catholic Zealots, as Well as LGBTQ Students," *Edmonton Sun*, 22 January 2016; Kristopher Wells, "Progressive Albertans Are Challenging Province's Bible Belt Stereotypes," *Globe and Mail*, 22 January 2016; Jeremy Klaszus, "Calgary Bishop Fred Henry: A Living Case Against Catholic School Funding in Alberta," *Calgary Metro*, 31 January 2016, http://www.metronews.ca/views/calgary/urban-compass/2016/01/31/bishop-fred-henry-case-against-catholic-school-funding.html (accessed 3 August 2016).

122 J.E. Logan, "A Case of It Takes One to Know One," *Edmonton Journal*, 16 January 2016; Gordon Hunter, "Risible," *Calgary Herald*, 18 January 2016; Rork Hilford, "Kids First," *Calgary Herald*, 18 January 2016.

123 Dave King, "Bishop's Views Put Catholic Schools at Odds with Democracy," *Edmonton Journal*, 3 February 2016.

124 Allitt, "Transformation," 154.

CONCLUSION

1 Calhoun, *Nationalism*, 5–6.
2 Samuel, "The 'Little Platoons,'" xxii.

Bibliography

ARCHIVAL SOURCES

The Archive of the Jesuits in Canada (AJC)
John H. Blackmore fonds, Glenbow Museum Archives (JHB)
Robert Borden fonds, Library and Archives Canada (through Queen's University Archives) (RB)
Canadian Council of Churches fonds, Library and Archives Canada (CCC)
Cavan Township Council Meetings, Minutes, 1977–1978
Commission on the Church, Nation, and World Order, United Church of Canada Archives
Donald Creighton fonds, Library and Archives Canada
George Drew fonds, Library and Archives Canada (GD)
Ecclesiastical Province of Ontario fonds (Anglican Church), Algoma University Archives
Eugene Forsey fonds, Library and Archives Canada (EF)
L.S. Garnsworthy papers, Anglican Diocese of Toronto Archives (LG)
House of Commons Debates
Human Rights Commission Complaint Case Files, Provincial Archives of Ontario
William Burton Hurd fonds, McMaster University Archives
Immigration Branch fonds, Library and Archives Canada (IB)
Harold Innis fonds, University of Toronto Archives (HI)
Inter-Church Committee on Protestant–Roman Catholic Relations fonds, United Church of Canada Archives (ICC)
A.R. Kaufman fonds, University of Waterloo Archives (ARK)
Watson Kirkconnell fonds, Acadia University Archives (WK)
Ku Klux Klan file, Glenbow Museum Archives

Arthur Lower fonds, Queen's University Archives (AL)
Arthur Meighen fonds, Library and Archives Canada (through Queen's University Archives) (AM)
Office of the Moderator fonds, United Church of Canada Archives (OM)
Dorothea Palmer fonds, University of Waterloo Archives (DP)
Planned Parenthood Society of Hamilton Papers, Local History and Archives Hamilton (PPSH)
Royal Black Preceptory fonds, Glenbow Museum Archives
F.R. Scott fonds, Library and Archives Canada (FRS)
C.E. Silcox fonds, United Church of Canada Archives (CES)
Springbank Loyal Orange Lodge fonds, Glenbow Museum Archives

NEWSPAPERS / PERIODICALS

Globe and Mail
Gospel Witness and Protestant Advocate
Maclean's
Ottawa Citizen
Owen Sound Daily Sun-Times
Peterborough Examiner
Protestant Action
Saturday Night
Toronto News
Toronto Star
Toronto Telegram
United Church Observer

BOOKS AND ARTICLES

Adams, Doug. "Fighting Fire with Fire: T.T. Shields and His Confrontations with Premier Mitchell Hepburn and Prime Minister Mackenzie King, 1934–1948." In *Baptists and Public Life in Canada*, edited by Gordon Heath and Paul Wilson, 52–104. Hamilton: McMaster Divinity College Press, 2012.

Airhart, Phyllis. *A Church with the Soul of a Nation: Making and Remaking the United Church of Canada*. Montreal and Kingston: McGill-Queen's University Press, 2014.

Allen, Chris. *Islamophobia*. England: Ashgate, 2010.

Allen, Ralph. *Ordeal by Fire: Canada, 1910–1945*. Toronto: Doubleday Canada, 1961.

Allison, Sam. *French Power: The Francization of Canada*. Richmond Hill: BMG Publishing, 1978.
Allitt, Patrick. "The Transformation of Catholic-Evangelical Relations in the United States: 1950–2000." In *The Sixties and Beyond: Dechristianization in North America and Western Europe, 1945–2000*, edited by Nancy Christie and Michael Gauvreau, 144–56. Toronto: University of Toronto Press, 2013.
Amaron, Calvin E. *The Future of Canada: The Extraordinary Privileges of the Roman Catholic Church in Quebec*. Ville de St Paul: N. Gelinas, 1912[?].
Anderson, J.T.M. *The Education of the New Canadian: A Treatise on Canada's Greatest Educational Problem*. Toronto: J.M. Dent and Sons, 1918.
Andrew, Jock V. *Bilingual Today, French Tomorrow: Trudeau's Master Plan and How It Can Be Stopped*. Richmond Hill: BMG Publishing, 1977.
– *Enough! (Enough French, Enough Quebec)*. Kitchener: Andrew Books, 1988.
Armstrong, Elizabeth H. *French Canadian Opinion on the War: January 1940–June 1941*. Toronto and Halifax: The Ryerson Press, 1942.
Attridge, Michael, Catherine E. Clifford, and Gilles Routhier, eds. *Vatican II: Experiences canadiennes/Canadian Experiences*. Ottawa: University of Ottawa Press, 2011.
Auger, Martin F. "On the Brink of Civil War: The Canadian Government and the Suppression of the 1918 Easter Riots." *Canadian Historical Review* 89 (2008): 503–40.
Bacchi, Carol. *Liberation Deferred? The Ideas of the English-Canadian Suffragists, 1877–1918*. Toronto: University of Toronto Press, 1983.
Baillargeon, Denyse. *Babies for the Nation: The Medicalization of Motherhood in Quebec, 1910-1970*. Translated by W. Donald Wilson. Waterloo, ON: Wilfrid Laurier University Press, 2009.
Ballantyne, G.M. "The Catholic Church and the CCF." The Canadian Catholic Historical Association, *Report* (1963): 33–45.
Barber, Marilyn, "The Fellowship of Maple Leaf Teachers." In *The Anglican Church and the World of Western Canada, 1820–1970*, edited by Barry Ferguson, 154–66. Regina: University of Regina, 1991.
– "Nation-Building in Saskatchewan: Teachers from the British Isles in Saskatchewan Rural Schools in the 1920s." In *Canada and the British World: Culture, Migration, and Identity*, edited by Phillip Buckner and R. Douglas Francis, 215–33. Vancouver: University of British Columbia Press, 2006.

- "Nationalism, Nativism, and the Social Gospel: The Protestant Churches' Response to Foreign Immigration in Western Canada, 1897–1914." In *The Social Gospel in Canada*, edited by Richard Allen, 186–226. Ottawa: National Museum of Canada, 1975.
Bartley, Allan. "A Public Nuisance: The Ku Klux Klan in Ontario, 1923–27." *Journal of Canadian Studies* 30 (1995): 156–74.
Basavarajappa, K.G., and Bali Ram. "Section A: Population and Migration." *Historical Statistics in Canada, Second Edition*. Ottawa: Social Science Federation of Canada, Statistics Canada, 1983.
Batzold, Chas. E. "Some Facts about the Canadian Knights and Ladies of the Ku Klux Klan." Vancouver: Executive Chambers of the Imperial Palace of the Invisible Empire, 1926.
Baum, Gregory. *Catholics and Canadian Socialism: Political Thought in the Thirties and Forties*. Toronto: James Lorimer, 1980.
Beard, Thomas, *Pope of Rome Is Antichrist*. London: 1625.
Belich, James. "The Rise of the Angloworld: Settlement in North America and Australasia, 1784–1918." In *Rediscovering the British World*, edited by Phillip Buckner and R. Douglas Francis, 39–57. Calgary: University of Calgary Press, 2005.
Bercuson, David and Douglas Wertheimer. *A Trust Betrayed: The Keegstra Affair*. Toronto: Doubleday, 1985.
Berger, Carl. *The Sense of Power: Studies in the Ideas of Canadian Imperialism, 1867–1914*. Toronto: University of Toronto Press, 1970.
- *The Writing of Canadian History: Aspects of English-Canadian Historical Writing since 1900*. Toronto: University of Toronto Press, 1986.
Beschloss, Michael R. *Kennedy and Roosevelt: The Uneasy Alliance*. New York: W.W. Norton, 1980.
Bhabha, Homi K. "Of Mimicry and Man: The Ambivalence of Colonial Discourse." *October* 28 (1984): 125–33.
- "The Other Question: Stereotype, Discrimination and the Discourse of Colonialism." In *The Location of Culture*, Bhabha, 66–84. London: Routledge, 1994.
Black, Conrad. *Duplessis*. Toronto: McClelland and Stewart, 1977.
Blake, Raymond B. *From Rights to Needs: A History of Family Allowances in Canada, 1929–92*. Vancouver: University of British Columbia, 2009.
- "Parliamentary Success and Political Failure: Family Allowances and the Progressive Conservative Party." In *Engaging the Enemy: Canada in the 1940s*, edited by Andrew Hiscock and Muriel Chamberlain, 173–90. Wales: University of Wales Canadian Studies Group, 2006.
Bliss, Michael. "The Methodist Church and World War I." *Canadian Historical Review* 49 (1968): 213–33.

Bliss, Michael, and L.M. Grayson, eds. *Wretched of Canada: Letters to R.B. Bennett, 1930–1935*. Toronto: University of Toronto Press, 1971.

Bock, Michel. *A Nation Beyond Borders: Lionel Groulx on French-Canadian Minorities*. Trans. by Ferdinanda Van Gennip. Ottawa: University of Ottawa Press, 2014.

Borer, Michael Ian, and Adam Murphee. "Framing Catholicism: Jack Chick's Anti-Catholic Cartoons and the Flexible Boundaries of the Culture Wars." *Religion and American Culture* 18 (2008): 95–112.

Bossy, Walter J. *A Call to Socially Minded Christian Canadians*. Montreal: The Classocracy League of Canada, 1934.

Bothwell, Robert, Ian Drummond, and John English. *Canada, 1900–1945*. Toronto: University of Toronto Press, 1987.

Boyd, Winnett. *Rebel Engineer: The Life and Work of Winnett Boyd*. Bobcaygeon: Transcontinental Printing, 1998.

Boyd, Winnett, with Kenneth McDonald. *The National Dilemma and the Way Out*. Richmond Hill: BMG Publishing Limited, 1975.

Bramadat, Paul, and David Seljak. "Charting the New Terrain: Christianity and Ethnicity in Canada." In *Christianity and Ethnicity in Canada*, edited by Paul Bramadat and David Seljak, 3–48. Toronto: University of Toronto: 2008.

Breton, Raymond. "From Ethnic to Civic Nationalism: English Canada and Quebec." *Ethnic and Racial Studies* 11 (1988): 85–102.

Bruce, Herbert. "Sterilization and Imbecility." *Social Welfare* (September 1936): 95–7.

– *Varied Operations*. Toronto: Longman, Green, 1958.

Bryden, P.E. *"A Justifiable Obsession": Conservative Ontario's Relations with Ottawa, 1943–1985*. Toronto: University of Toronto Press, 2013.

Buckner, P.A. "Canada and the End of Empire, 1939–1982." In *Canada and the British Empire*, edited by P.A. Buckner, 107–26. New York: Oxford University Press, 2008.

Byers, Daniel. "Canada's Zombies: A Portrait of Canadian Conscripts and their Experience During the Second World War." In *Forging a Nation: Perspectives on the Canadian Military Experience*, edited by Bernd Horn, 155–76. St Catharines: Vanwell Publishing, 2002.

– *Zombie Army: The Canadian Army and Conscription in the Second World War*. Vancouver: UBC Press, 2016.

Caccia, Ivana. *Managing the Canadian Mosaic in Wartime: Shaping Citizenship Policy, 1939–1945*. Montreal and Kingston: McGill-Queen's University Press, 2010.

Calhoun, Craig. *Nationalism*. Minneapolis: University of Minnesota Press, 1997.

Camp, Dalton. *Gentlemen, Players, and Politicians*. Toronto: McClelland and Stewart, 1970.

Campbell, Lara. *Respectable Citizens: Gender, Family, and Unemployment in Ontario's Great Depression*. Toronto: University of Toronto Press, 2009.

Caputi, Robert J. *Neville Chamberlain and Appeasement*. Selinsgrove: Susquehanna University Press, 2000.

Casey, Shaun. *The Making of a Catholic President: Kennedy vs Nixon, 1960*. Oxford: Oxford University, 2009.

Catholic Unity League. *A Double Collapse of Bigotry: The Case of Bishop Budka, the Raid on the Guelph Novitiate*. London: St Peter's Seminary, 1919.

Cavanaugh, Catherine. "Irene Marryat Parlby: An 'Imperial Daughter' in the Canadian West, 1896–1934." In *Telling Tales: Essays in Western Women's History*, edited by Catherine Cavanaugh and Randi Warne, 100–22. Vancouver: UBC Press, 2000.

Cawley, Art. "The Canadian Catholic English-language Press and the Spanish Civil War." Canadian Catholic Historical Association *Study Sessions* 49 (1982): 25–51.

Cecillon, Paul. *Prayers, Petitions, and Protests: The Catholic Church and the Ontario Schools Crisis in the Windsor Border Region, 1910–1928*. Montreal and Kingston: McGill-Queen's University Press, 2013.

Champion, C.P. *The Strange Demise of British Canada: The Liberals and Canadian Nationalism, 1964–1968*. Montreal and Kingston: McGill-Queen's University Press, 2010.

Christian, William, and Colin Campbell. *Political Parties and Ideologies in Canada: Liberals, Conservatives, Socialists, Nationalists*. Toronto: McGraw-Hill Ryerson, 1983.

Christie, Nancy. *Engendering the State: Family, Work, and Welfare in Canada*. Toronto: University of Toronto Press, 2000.

– "'Look Out for Leviathan': The Search for a Conservative Modernist Consensus." In *Cultures of Citizenship in Post-War Canada, 1940–1955*, edited by Nancy Christie and Michael Gauvreau, 63–94. Montreal: McGill-Queen's University Press, 2003.

– "Sacred Sex: The United Church and the Privatization of the Family in Post-War Canada." In *Households of Faith: Family, Gender, and Community in Canada, 1760–1969*, edited by Nancy Christie, 348–76. Montreal: McGill-Queen's University Press, 2002.

Christie, Nancy, and Michael Gauvreau. "Introduction: 'Even the Hippies Were Only Very Slowly Going Secular': Dechristianization and the

Culture of Individualism in North America and Western Europe." In *The Sixties and Beyond: Dechristianization in North America and Western Europe, 1945–2000*, edited by Christie and Gauvreau, 3–38. Toronto: University of Toronto Press, 2013.

Coleman, Daniel. *White Civility: The Literary Project of English Canada*. Toronto: University of Toronto Press, 2006.

Colley, Linda. *Britons: Forging the Nation, 1707–1837*. London: Pimilco, 1994.

Commission on Church, Nation, and World Order. *Church, Nation and World Order: A Report*. Toronto: Board of Evangelism and Social Service, 1944.

Connor, Ralph. *The Colporteur*. Toronto: Women's Missionary Society, Methodist Church Canada, nd.

– *The Foreigner: A Tale of Saskatchewan*. Toronto: The Westminster Company, 1909.

Cook, Ramsay. "Canadian Freedom in Wartime, 1939–1945." In *His Own Man: Essays in Honour of Arthur Reginald Marsden Lower*, edited by W.H. Heick and Roger Graham, 37–53. Montreal and London: McGill-Queen's University Press, 1974.

– *The Maple Leaf Forever: Essays on Nationalism and Politics in Canada*. Toronto: Macmillan of Canada, 1977.

Cook, Ramsay, and Robert Craig Brown. *Canada, 1896–1921: A Nation Transformed*. Toronto: McClelland and Stewart, 1974.

Courteaux, Olivier. *Canada between Vichy and Free France, 1940–1945*. Toronto: University of Toronto Press, 2013.

Couture, Paul M. "The Vichy-Free French Propaganda War in Quebec, 1940–1942." Canadian Historical Association *Historical Papers* 13 (1978): 200–16.

Crowley, Terry. *Marriage of Minds: Isabel and Oscar Skelton, Reinventing Canada*. Toronto: University of Toronto Press, 2003.

Cuneo, Michael. *Catholics Against the Church: Anti-Abortion Protest in Toronto, 1969–1985*. Toronto: University of Toronto Press, 1989.

Darian-Smith, Kate, Patricia Grimshaw, and Stuart McIntyre. "Introduction: Britishness Abroad." In *Britishness Abroad: Transnational Movements and Imperial Cultures*, edited by Darian-Smith, Grimshaw, and McIntyre, 1–15. Victoria: Melbourne University Press, 2007.

Davis, Henry. *Moral and Pastoral Theology. Vol. 2: Commandments of God, Precepts of the Church*. London: Sheed and Ward, 1938.

Dean, Misao. *A Different Point of View: Sara Jeannette Duncan*. Montreal and Kingston: McGill-Queen's University Press, 1991.

Delisle, Esther. *Myths, Memory, and Lies: Quebec's Intelligentsia and the Fascist Temptation, 1939–1960.* Translated by Madelaine Hébert. Montreal: Robert Davies Multimedia, 1998.

Demers, Maurice. *Connected Struggles: Catholics, Nationalists, and Transnational Relations between Mexico and Quebec, 1917–1945.* Montreal and Kingston: McGill-Queen's University Press, 2014.

Devereux, Cecily. *Growing a Race: Nellie L. McClung and the Fiction of Eugenic Feminism.* Montreal and Kingston: McGill-Queen's University Press, 2005.

Dexter, Grant. *Family Allowances.* Winnipeg: Winnipeg Free Press, 1944.

Dixon, Robert. "William Davis and the Road to Completion in Ontario's Catholic High Schools, 1971–1985." Canadian Catholic Historical Association *Historical Studies* 69 (2003): 7–33.

Djwa, Sandra. *The Politics of the Imagination: A Life of F.R. Scott.* Toronto: McClelland and Stewart, 1987.

Djwa, Sandra, and R. St J. MacDonald, eds. *On F.R. Scott: Essays on His Contributions to Law, Literature, and Politics.* Montreal: McGill-Queen's University Press: 1983.

Dodd, Dianne. "The Canadian Birth Control Movement on Trial, 1936–1937." *Histoire sociale-Social History* 16 (1983): 411–28.

Dumas, Alexandre. "L'Église face à Duplessis: le clergé catholique face à la politique Québécoise de 1930 à 1960." PhD thesis, Université McGill, 2016.

Dutil, Patrice. "Against Isolationism: Napoleon Belcourt, French Canada, and 'La grande guerre.'" In *Canada and the First World War: Essays in Honour of Robert Craig Brown,* edited by David MacKenzie, 96–137. Toronto: University of Toronto Press, 2005.

Dutil, Patrice, and David MacKenzie. *Embattled Nation: Canada's Wartime Election of 1917.* Toronto: Dundurn, 2017.

Dyck, Erika. *Facing Eugenics: Reproduction, Sterilization, and the Politics of Choice.* Toronto: University of Toronto Press, 2013.

Edwardson, Ryan. "Narrating a Canadian Identity: Arthur R.M. Lower's *Colony to Nation* and the Nationalization of History." *International Journal of Canadian Studies* 26 (2002): 59–76.

England, Robert. *The Central European Immigrant in Canada.* Toronto: Macmillan Company in Canada, 1929.

– *Living, Learning, Remembering.* Vancouver: Centre for Continuing Education, 1980.

English, John. *The Decline of Politics: The Conservatives and the Party System, 1901–1920.* Toronto: University of Toronto Press, 1977.

- *Just Watch Me: The Life of Pierre Elliott Trudeau, 1968–2000.* Toronto: Alfred A. Knopf Canada, 2009.
Esposito, John L., and Ibrahim Kalin, eds. *Islamophobia: The Challenge of Pluralism in the 21st Century.* Oxford University Press, 2011.
Farthing, John. *Freedom Wears a Crown.* Toronto: Kingswood House, 1957.
Fay, Terence J. *A History of Canadian Catholics: Gallicanism, Romanism, and Canadianism.* Montreal and Kingston: McGill-Queen's University Press, 2002.
Ferguson, Barry. "British-Canadian Intellectuals, Ukrainian Immigrants, and Canadian National Identity." In *Canada's Ukrainians: Negotiating an Identity*, edited by Lubomyr Luciuk and Stella Hryniuk, 304–25. Toronto: University of Toronto Press, 1991.
- *Remaking Liberalism: The Intellectual Legacy of Adam Shortt, O.D. Skelton, W.C. Clark, and W.A. Mackintosh, 1890–1925.* Montreal and Kingston: McGill-Queen's University Press, 1993.
Fiamengo, Janice. "Rediscovering Our Foremothers Again: The Racial Ideas of Canada's Early Feminists, 1885–1945." *Essays on Canadian Writing* 75 (2002): 85–118.
Fitzgerald, John Edward. "'British Union,' the Orange Order, and Newfoundland's Confederation with Canada, 1948–49." In *The Orange Order in Canada*, edited by David A. Wilson, 146–69. Dublin: Four Courts Press, 2007.
Forestall, Nancy M., with Maureen Moynagh, eds. *Documenting First Wave Feminisms.* Vol. 2: *Canada: National and Transnational Contexts.* Toronto: University of Toronto Press, 2014.
Forsey, Eugene. "Clerical Fascism." *Canadian Forum* 17 (June 1937).
- "Does Canada Need Immigrants?" Montreal: League for Social Reconstruction National Executive, 1937[?].
- *Freedom and Order: Collected Essays.* Toronto: McClelland and Stewart Limited, 1974.
- *A Life on the Fringe: The Memoirs of Eugene Forsey.* Toronto: Oxford University Press, 1990.
- "Quebec Fascists Show their Hand." *Canadian Forum* 16 (December 1936).
- "Quebec on the Road to Fascism." *Canadian Forum* 17 (December 1937).
- "Under the Padlock." *Canadian Forum* 18 (May 1938).
Foster, Kate. *Our Canadian Mosaic.* Toronto: Dominion Council, YWCA, 1926.
Franchot, Jenny. *Roads to Rome: The Antebellum Protestant Encounter with Catholicism.* Berkeley: University of California Press, 1994.

Francis, Diane. *Fighting for Canada*. Toronto: Key Porter Books, 1996.
Fraser, Graham. *René Lévesque and the Parti Québécois in Power*. Montreal and Kingston: McGill-Queen's University Press, 2001.
Gauvreau, Michael. "Beyond the Search for Intellectuals: On the Paucity of Paradigms in the Writing of Canadian Intellectual History." In *Thinkers and Dreamers: Historical Essays in Honour of Carl Berger*, edited by Gerald Friesen and Doug Owram, 53–90. Toronto: University of Toronto Press: 2011.
– *The Catholic Origins of Quebec's Quiet Revolution, 1931–1970*. Montreal and Kingston: McGill-Queen's University Press, 2005.
– "Protestantism Transformed: Personal Piety and the Evangelical Social Vision." In *The Canadian Protestant Experience, 1760 to 1990*, edited by George A. Rawlyk, 48–97. Montreal and Kingston: McGill-Queen's University Press, 1990.
Gauvreau, Michael, and Nancy Christie. *A Full-orbed Christianity: The Protestant Churches and Social Welfare in Canada, 1900–1940*. Montreal and Kingston: McGill-Queen's University Press, 1996.
Gibbon, John Murray. *Canadian Mosaic: The Making of a Northern Nation*. Toronto: McClelland and Stewart, 1938.
Gibson, Frederick W., and Barbara Robertson. *Ottawa at War: The Grant Dexter Memoranda, 1939–1945*. Winnipeg: The Manitoba Record Society, 1994.
Goodman, Eddie. *Life of the Party: The Memoirs of Eddie Goodman*. Toronto: Key Porter Books, 1988.
Gordon, Charles W. "The Canadian Situation." In *Pre-Assembly Congress: Addresses, Delivered at the Presbyterian Pre-Assembly Congress, Held in Massey Hall, Toronto, Saturday, May 31st, to Wednesday June 4th, 1913, with Reports of Committees*, 85–94. Toronto: Board of Foreign Missions, Presbyterian Church in Canada, 1913.
Gotlieb, Marc J. "George Drew and the Dominion-Provincial Conference on Reconstruction of 1945–46." *Canadian Historical Review* 66 (1985): 27–47.
Gould, Margaret. *Family Allowances in Canada: Facts versus Fiction*. Toronto: Ryerson Press, 1945.
Granatstein, J.L. *Canada's War: The Politics of the Mackenzie King Government, 1939–1945*. Toronto: University of Toronto Press, 1990.
– *The Politics of Survival: The Conservative Party of Canada, 1939–1945*. Toronto: University of Toronto Press, 1967.
Granatstein, J.L., and J.M. Hitsman. *Broken Promises: A History of Conscription in Canada*. Toronto: Oxford University Press, 1977.

Granatstein, J.L., and Peter Neary, eds. *The Good Fight: Canadians and World War II.* Toronto: Copp Clark, 1995.
Gratton, Michel. *French Canadians: An Outsider's Inside Look at Quebec.* Toronto: Key Porter Books, 1992.
Gray, James H. *The Roar of the Twenties.* Toronto: Macmillan of Canada, 1975.
Greer, Brian. "The Cavan Blazers." In *This Green and Pleasant Land: Chronicles of Cavan Township,* edited by Quentin Brown, 34–8. Millbrook: Millbrook and Cavan Historical Society, 1990.
Griffiths, N.E.S. "Hugh Mason Wade." In *Mason Wade, Acadia, and Quebec: The Perception of an Outsider,* edited by N.E.S. Griffiths and G.A. Rawlyk, 1–11. Ottawa: Carleton University Press, 1991.
Gross, Michael. *The War Against Catholicism: Liberalism and the Anti-Catholic Imagination in Nineteenth-Century Germany.* Ann Arbor: University of Michigan Press, 2004.
Haycock, Ronald G. *Sam Hughes: The Public Career of a Controversial Canadian, 1885–1916.* Waterloo: Wilfrid Laurier University Press/National Museums of Canada, 1986.
Hayday, Matthew. *So They Want Us to Learn French: Promoting and Opposing Bilingualism in English-speaking Canada.* Vancouver: University of British Columbia Press, 2015.
Hayek, Friedrich A. *The Road to Serfdom.* Chicago: University of Chicago Press, 1945.
Heick, W.H. "The Character and Spirit of an Age: A Study of the Thought of Arthur R.M. Lower." In *His Own Man: Essays in Honour of Arthur Reginald Marsden Lower,* edited by W.H. Heick and Roger Graham, 19–35. Montreal and London: McGill-Queen's University Press, 1974.
Henderson, Jennifer. *Settler Feminism and Race Making in Canada.* Toronto: University of Toronto Press, 2003.
Henderson, T. Stephen. *Angus L. Macdonald: A Provincial Liberal.* Toronto: University of Toronto Press, 2007.
Herberg, Will. *Protestant-Catholic-Jew: An Essay in American Religious Sociology.* New York: Doubleday, 1956.
Hill, Robert. *Voice of the Vanishing Minority: Robert Sellar and the Huntingdon "Gleaner."* Montreal and Kingston: McGill-Queen's University Press, 1999.
Hislop, Alexander. *The Two Babylons; or, the Papal Worship Proved to be the Worship of Nimrod and his Wife, with Sixty-One Woodcut Illustrations from Nineveh, Babylon, Egypt, Pompeii, etc.* New York: Loizeaux Brothers, 1959.

Hoffman, George. "Saskatchewan Catholics and the Coming of a New Politics, 1930–1934." In *Religion and Society in the Prairie West*, edited by Richard Allen, 65–88. Regina: Canadian Plains Research Centre, University of Regina, 1974.
Hogan, Brian. "The Guelph Novitiate Raid: Conscription, Censorship, and Bigotry during the Great War." *Canadian Catholic Historical Association Study Sessions* 45 (1978): 57–80.
Hopkins, J. Castell. *The Canadian Annual Review, 1918*. Toronto: The Canadian Review Company, 1918.
Horn, Michiel. *The Great Depression of the 1930s in Canada*. Ottawa: Canadian Historical Association, 1984.
– *The League for Social Reconstruction: Intellectual Origins of the Democratic Left in Canada, 1930–1942*. Toronto: University of Toronto Press, 1980.
– ed. *The Dirty Thirties: Canadians in the Great Depression*. Toronto: Copp Clark, 1972.
– ed. *A New Endeavour: Selected Political Essays, Letters, and Addresses*. Toronto: University of Toronto Press, 1986.
Horowitz, Robert B. *America's Right: Anti-Establishment Conservatism from Goldwater to the Tea Party*. Cambridge, UK: Polity Press, 2013.
Howes, Helen C. *Inside Quebec: The Historical Roots and Current Problems of French Canada's Relation to the War and to Democracy*. Toronto: Fellowship for a Christian Social Order, 1942.
Hoy, Claire. *Bill Davis: A Biography*. Toronto: Methuen, 1985.
Hurd, W. Burton. "The Decline in the Canadian Birth-Rate." *The Canadian Journal of Economics and Political Science* 3 (1937): 40–57.
– *Origin, Birthplace, Nationality, and the Language of the Canadian People*. Ottawa: F.A. Acland, 1929.
Iacovetta, Franca. *Gatekeepers: Reshaping Immigrant Lives in Cold War Canada*. Toronto: Between the Lines, 2006.
Igartua, José. *The Other Quiet Revolution: National Identity in English Canada, 1945–71*. Vancouver: University of British Columbia Press, 2006.
Ignatieff, Michael. *Blood and Belonging*. Toronto: Viking, 1993.
Inter-Church Committee on Protestant–Roman Catholic Relations. *Brief of the Inter-Church Committee on Protestant–Roman Catholic Relations, presented to the Prime Minister and the Members of the Legislative Assembly of Ontario Concerning the Brief presented by the Roman Catholic Bishops of Ontario in October, 1962, and some other Matters*. January 1963.

- *French Language in Elementary Schools of Ontario.* Toronto: Inter-Church Committee on Protestant–Roman Catholic Relations, n.d. [1948?].
- *Is the Hope Report a Dead Issue?* Toronto: Inter-Church Committee on Protestant–Roman Catholic Relations, 1953[?].
- *Protestant–Roman Catholic Relations: Brief Submitted to the Royal Commission on Education*, Brief 113. Toronto: Inter-Church Committee on Protestant–Roman Catholic Relations, 1945.

Jenkins, Philip. *The New Anti-Catholicism: The Last Acceptable Prejudice.* Oxford: Oxford University Press, 2003.

Johnson, George. *Architects of Fear: Conspiracy Theories and Paranoia in American Politics.* Los Angeles: Jeremy P. Tarcher, 1983.

Johnson, Leo. *A History of Guelph.* Guelph: Guelph Historical Society, 1977.

Jones, H.S. "Hippolyte Adolphe Taine." *Oxford Dictionary of National Biography*, http://www.oxforddnb.com.ezproxy.lib.ucalgary.ca/view/article/53266.

Kaplan, William. *State and Salvation: The Jehovah's Witnesses and Their Fight for Civil Rights.* Toronto: University of Toronto Press, 1989.

Katerberg, William. *Modernity and the Dilemma of North American Anglican Identities, 1880–1950.* Montreal: McGill-Queen's University Press, 2001.

- "Protecting Christian Liberty: Mainline Protestantism, Racial Thought, and Political Culture in Canada, 1918–1939." In *Historical Papers, 1995*, edited by Bruce L. Guenther, 5–34. Canadian Society of Church History, 1995.

Kaufman, A.R. *Birth Control Trial.* Kitchener, ON: Parents' Information Bureau Limited, 1937.

- "Sterilization Notes, Pamphlet No. 2." Kitchener: Parents' Information Bureau, 193[?].
- "Sterilization Notes, Pamphlet No. 7." Kitchener: Parents' Information Bureau, 193[?].

Kaufmann, Eric P. *The Orange Order: A Contemporary Northern Irish History.* New York: Oxford University Press, 2007.

- "The Orange Order in Ontario, Newfoundland, Scotland, and Northern Ireland: A Macro-Social Analysis." In *The Orange Order in Canada*, edited by David A. Wilson, 42–68. Dublin: Four Courts Press, 2007.

Keach, Benjamin. *Antichrist Stormed; or, Mystery Babylon the Great Whore, and Great City, Proved to be the Present Church of Rome.* London: 1689.

Kee, Kevin. *Revivalists: Marketing the Gospel in English Canada, 1884–1957*. Montreal: McGill-Queen's University Press, 2006.

Kendle, John. *John Bracken: A Political Biography*. Toronto: University of Toronto Press, 1979.

Kenny, Stephen. "A Prejudice that Rarely Utters Its Name: A Historiographical and Historical Reflection upon North American Anti-Catholicism." *American Review of Canadian Studies* (2002): 639–72.

King, Mackenzie. Diary Online. http://www.collectionscanada.gc.ca/databases/king/index-e.html.

Kirkconnell, Watson. *Canada, Europe, and Hitler*. Toronto: Oxford University Press, 1939.

– *The European Heritage: A Synopsis of European Cultural Achievement*. Toronto: J.M. Dent and Sons, 1930.

– "Religion and Philosophy: An English-Canadian Point of View." In *Canadian Dualism: Studies of French-English Relations*, edited by Mason Wade, 41–55. Toronto: University of Toronto Press, 1960.

Kitzan, Chris. "Preaching Purity in the Promised Land: Bishop Lloyd and the Immigration Debate." In *The Prairie West as Promised Land*, edited by R. Douglas Francis and Chris Kitzan, 291–311. Calgary: University of Calgary Press, 2007.

Kohn, Edward P. *This Kindred People: Canadian-American Relations and the Anglo-Saxon Idea, 1895–1903*. Montreal and Kingston: McGill-Queen's University Press, 2004.

Kuffert, L.B. *A Great Duty: Canadian Responses to Modern Life and Mass Culture, 1939–1967*. Montreal and Kingston: McGill-Queen's University Press, 2003.

Kyba, Patrick. "Ballots and Burning Crosses: The Election of 1929." In *Politics in Saskatchewan*, edited by Norman Ward and Duff Spafford, 105–23. Ontario: Longmans Canada, 1968.

– "J.T.M. Anderson." In *Saskatchewan Premiers of the Twentieth Century*, edited by Gordon L. Barnhart, 109–38. Regina: University of Regina, 2004.

Leacock, Stephen. "Democracy and Social Progress." In *The New Era in Canada: Essays Dealing with the Upbuilding of the Canadian Commonwealth*, edited by J.O. Miller, 11–33. Toronto: J.M. Dent and Sons, 1917.

Levy, George Edward. *The Baptists of the Maritime Provinces*. New Brunswick: Barnes-Hopkins, 1946.

Lloyd, George Exton. "The Building of the Nation: Natural Increase and Immigration." Paper Read in front of the Grand Orange Lodge in Edmonton, 26 July 1928.
– *The Trail of 1903: An Account by the Right Rev. George Exton Lloyd.* Edited by Franklin Lloyd Foster. Lloydminster: Foster Learning Inc., 2002.
Lower, Arthur. *Canadians in the Making: A Social History of Canada.* Toronto: Longmans, Green, 1958.
– *Colony to Nation: A History of Canada.* Toronto: Longmans, Green, 1947.
– *My First Seventy-Five Years.* Toronto: Macmillan of Canada, 1967.
– *A Pattern for History.* Toronto: McClelland and Stewart, 1978.
– *This Most Famous Stream: The Liberal Democratic Way of Life.* Toronto: The Ryerson Press, 1954.
– "Two Ways of Life: The Primary Antithesis of Canadian History." *Report of the Annual Meeting of the Canadian Historical Association* 22 (1943): 5–18.
Luther, Martin. *A Faithful Admonition of a certeyne true pastor and prophete sent unto the Germanes at such a time as certain great princes went about to bring alienes into Germany, [and] to restore the papacy; the kingdom of Antichrist.* Grenewych: Conrad Freeman, 1554.
MacDonald, Donald. *The Happy Warrior: Political Memoirs.* Markham: Fitzhenry and Whiteside, 1988.
Malcom, Allison O'Mahen. "Loyal Orangemen and Republican Nativists: Anti-Catholicism and Historical Memory in Canada and the United States, 1837–1867." In *The Loyal Atlantic: Remaking the British Atlantic in the Revolutionary Era*, edited by Jerry Bannister and Liam Riordan, 211–51. Toronto: University of Toronto Press, 2012.
Mancuso, Rebecca. "For Purity or Prosperity: Competing Nationalist Visions and Canadian Immigration Policy, 1919–1930." *British Journal of Canadian Studies* 23 (2010): 1–23.
Manley, John. "'Audacity, Audacity, Still More Audacity': Tim Buck, the Party, and the People, 1932–1939." *Labour/Le Travail* 49 (2002): 9–41.
Mann, Susan. *The Dream of Nation: A Social and Intellectual History of Quebec.* Montreal and Kingston: McGill-Queen's University Press, 2002.
Manthorpe, Jonathan. *The Power and the Tories: Ontario Politics – 1943 to the Present.* Toronto: Macmillan of Canada, 1974.
Marks, Lynne. *Infidels and the Damn Churches: Irreligion and Religion in Settler British Columbia.* Vancouver: UBC Press, 2017.

Marsden, George. *Fundamentalism and American Culture: The Shaping of Twentieth Century Evangelicalism, 1870–1925.* New York: Oxford University Press, 1980.
Marty, Martin E. *Modern American Religion.* Volume 3: *Under God, Indivisible, 1941–1960.* Chicago and London: University of Chicago Press, 1996.
Massa, Mark. *Anti-Catholicism in America: The Last Acceptable Prejudice.* New York: Crossroad Publishing, 2003.
Massolin, Philip. *Canadian Intellectuals, The Tory Tradition, and the Challenge of Modernity, 1939–1970.* Toronto: University of Toronto Press, 2001.
McAuley, James W., and Paul Nesbitt-Larking. *Contemporary Orangeism in Canada: Identity, Nationalism, and Religion.* London: Palgrave Macmillan, 2018.
McEvoy, Frederick J. "The Establishment of Diplomatic Relations Between Canada and the Vatican, 1969." Canadian Catholic Historical Association *Historical Studies* 68 (2002): 66–84.
– "Religion and Politics in Foreign Policy: Canadian Government Relations with the Vatican." Canadian Catholic Historical Association *Historical Studies* 51 (1984): 121–44.
McGowan, Mark. "Air Wars: Radio Regulation, Sectarianism, and Religious Broadcasting in Canada, 1922–1938." *Historical Papers 2008: Canadian Society of Church History*: 5–25.
– "'A Portion for the Vanquished': Roman Catholics and the Ukrainian Catholic Church." In *Canada's Ukrainians: Negotiating an Identity*, edited by Lubomyr Luciuk and Stella Hryniuk, 218–37. Toronto: University of Toronto Press, 1991.
– "Roman Catholics (Anglophone and Allophone)." In *Christianity and Ethnicity in Canada*, edited by Paul Bramadat and David Seljak, 49-100. Toronto: University of Toronto Press, 2008.
– "'To Share in the Burdens of Empire': Toronto's Catholics and the Great War, 1914–1918." In *Catholics at the "Gathering Place": Historical Essays on the Archdiocese of Toronto, 1841–1991*, edited by Mark McGowan and Brian Clarke, 177–207. Toronto: Canadian Catholic Historical Association, 1993.
McGreevy, John T. *Catholicism and American Freedom.* New York and London: W.W. Norton, 2003.
– "Thinking on One's Own: Catholicism in the American Intellectual Imagination, 1928–1960." *The Journal of American History* 84 (1997): 97–131.

McKay, Ian. *The Quest of the Folk: Antimodernism and Cultural Selection in Twentieth-Century Nova Scotia.* Montreal: McGill-Queen's University Press, 1994.

McKenzie, Brian Alexander. "Fundamentalism, Christian Unity, and Premillennialism in the Thought of Rowland Victor Bingham (1872–1942): A Study of Anti-Modernism in Canada." Doctoral thesis, University of Toronto School of Theology, 1985.

McKillop, A.B. "Nationalism, Identity, and Canadian Intellectual History." In *Contours of Canadian Thought*, edited by A.B. McKillop, 3–17. Toronto: University of Toronto Press, 1987.

McLaren, Angus. *Our Own Master Race: Eugenics in Canada, 1885–1945.* Toronto: McClellend and Stewart, 1990.

McLaren, Angus, and Arlene Tigar McLaren. *The Bedroom and the State: The Changing Practices and Politics of Contraception and Abortion in Canada, 1880–1997.* Toronto: Oxford University Press, 1997.

McLaughlin, Robert. *Irish Canadian Conflict and the Struggle for Irish Independence.* Toronto: University of Toronto Press, 2013.

McLeod, Hugh Alexander, *"Thus in the Stilly Night": Being Recollections of the Very Rev. Hugh Alexander McLeod.* Victoria: 1972.

McMurtry, Roy. *Memoirs and Reflections.* Toronto: University of Toronto/Osgoode Society: 2013.

McNaught, Kenneth. *A Prophet in Politics: A Biography of J.S. Woodsworth.* Toronto: University of Toronto Press, 1960.

Meehan, Peter. "The East Hastings By-Election of 1936 and the Ontario Separate School Tax Question." *Historical Studies* 68 (2002): 105–32.

Mendelson, Alan. *Exiles from Nowhere: The Jews and the Canadian Elite.* Montreal: Robin Brass Studio, 2008.

Meren, David. *With Friends Like These: Entangled Nationalism and the Canada-Quebec-France Triangle, 1944–1970.* Vancouver and Toronto: UBC Press, 2012.

Middleton, W.E., and J.A. Chisholm. "Report of the Commission on Inquiry into the Raid on the Jesuit Novitiate at Guelph." In *Ontario and the First World War, 1914–1918: A Collection of Documents.* Edited by Barbara M. Wilson, 58–69. Toronto: University of Toronto Press, 1977.

Miedema, Gary R. *For Canada's Sake: Public Religion, Centennial Celebrations, and the Remaking of Canada in the 1960s.* Montreal and Kingston: McGill-Queen's University Press, 2005.

Miller, J.R. "Anti-Catholic Thought in Victorian Canada." *Canadian Historical Review* 66 (1985): 474–94.

- *Equal Rights: The Jesuits' Estates Act Controversy*. Montreal: McGill-Queen's University Press, 1979.
Milligan, Frank. *Eugene A. Forsey: An Intellectual Biography*. Calgary: University of Calgary Press, 2004.
Mills, Sean. "When Democratic Socialists Discovered Democracy: The League for Social Reconstruction Confronts the 'Quebec Problem.'" *Canadian Historical Review* 86 (2005): 1–17.
Moir, John. "Toronto's Protestants and Their Perceptions of Their Roman Catholic Neighbours." In *Catholics at the "Gathering Place": Historical Essays on the Archdiocese of Toronto, 1841–1991*, edited by Mark McGowan and Brian Clarke, 313–27. Toronto: Canadian Catholic Historical Association, 1993.
Morgan, Henry James, ed. *Men and Women of the Time: A Hand-Book of Canadian Biography of Living Characters*. Toronto: William Briggs, 1912.
Morton, Desmond, and J.L. Granatstein. *Victory, 1945: Canadians from War to Peace*. Toronto: Harper Collins, 1995.
Murphy, Emily. *The Impressions of Janey Canuck Abroad*. Toronto: n.p., 1902.
- *Janey Canuck in the West*. Toronto: McClelland and Stewart, 1975 [1910].
- *Open Trails*. Toronto: Cassell and Company, Ltd., 1912.
- *Seeds of Pine*. Toronto: Hodder and Stoughton, 1914.
Nordstrom, Justin. *Danger on the Doorstep: Anti-Catholicism and American Print Culture in the Progressive Era*. Notre Dame, IN: University of Notre Dame Press, 2006.
Noll, Mark. *What Happened to Christian Canada?* Vancouver: Regent College Publishing, 2007.
Noll, Mark, and Carolyn Nystrom, *Is the Reformation Over? An Evangelical Assessment of Contemporary Roman Catholicism*. Grand Rapids, MI: Baker Academic, 2005.
Orkin, Mark M. *The Great Stork Derby*. Don Mills, ON: General Publishing, 1981.
Owram, Doug. *The Government Generation: Canadian Intellectuals and the State, 1900–1945*. Toronto: University of Toronto Press, 1986.
- *Promise of Eden: The Canadian Expansionist Movement and the Idea of the West, 1856–1900*. Toronto: University of Toronto Press, 1980.
Palmer, Howard. "Ethnic Relations in Wartime: Nationalism and European Minorities in Alberta during the Second World War." *Canadian Ethnic Studies* 14 (1982): 1–23.

- *Patterns of Prejudice: A History of Nativism in Alberta.* Toronto: McClelland and Stewart, 1982.
- "Reluctant Hosts: Anglo-Canadian Views of Multiculturalism in the Twentieth Century." In *Readings in Canadian History: Post-Confederation,* edited by R. Douglas Francis and Donald B. Smith, 123–39. Toronto: Holt, Rinehart and Winston of Canada, 1982.

Penton, M. James. *Jehovah's Witnesses in Canada: Champions of Freedom of Speech and Worship.* Toronto: Macmillan of Canada, 1976.

Perkin, J.R.C. "'There Were Giants in the Earth in Those Days': An Assessment of Watson Kirkconnell." In *Canadian Baptists and Christian Higher Education,* edited by G.A. Rawlyk, 89–110. Montreal: McGill-Queen's University Press, 1988.

Pickles, Katie. *Female Imperialism and National Identity: The Imperial Order of the Daughters of Empire.* New York: Manchester University Press, 2003.

Pincus, Steven. *Protestantism and Patriotism: Ideologies and the Making of English Foreign Policy, 1650–1668.* Cambridge: Cambridge University Press, 1996.

Pitsula, James. *Keeping Canada British: The Ku Klux Klan in 1920s Saskatchewan.* Vancouver: University of British Columbia Press, 2013.

Plumptre, Adelaide. "Some Thoughts on the Suffrage in Canada." In *The New Era in Canada: Essays Dealing with the Upbuilding of the Canadian Commonwealth,* edited by J.O. Miller, 301–30. Toronto: J.M. Dent and Sons, 1917.

Porter, John. *The Vertical Mosaic: An Analysis of Social Class and Power in Canada.* Toronto: University of Toronto Press, 1965.

Pozzi, Lucia. "The Problem of Birth Control in the United States Under the Papacy of Pius XI." 209–29. In *Pius XI and America,* Proceedings of the Brown University Conference, Providence, 2010, edited by Charles R. Gallagher, David I. Kertzer, Alberto Melloni, 209–29. Berlin: LIT Verlag, 2012.

Pulkingham, Jane. "A Common Interest? Reflections on the Social Legacy of J.S. Woodsworth and the Contemporary Politics of Social Change in Canada." In *Human Welfare, Rights, and Social Activism: Rethinking the Legacy of J.S. Woodsworth,* edited by Jane Pulkingham, 3–41. Toronto: University of Toronto Press, 2010.

Rebick, Judy. *Ten Thousand Roses: The Making of a Feminist Revolution.* Toronto: Penguin Canada, 2005.

Reilly, Brent. "Baptists and Organized Opposition to Roman Catholicism, 1941–1962." In *Costly Vision: The Baptist Pilgrimage in Canada,* edited by Jarold K. Zeman, 181–98. Burlington: Welch Publishing Company, 1988.

Resnick, Philip. "Civic and Ethnic Nationalism: Lessons from the Canadian Case." In *Canadian Political Philosophy*, edited by Ronald Beiner and Wayne Norman, 282–97. Oxford and New York: Oxford University Press, 2001.

Revie, Linda. "More than Just Boots! The Eugenic and Commercial Concerns behind A.R. Kaufman's Birth Controlling Activities." *Canadian Bulletin of Medical History* 23 (2006): 119–43.

Robin, Martin. *Shades of Right: Nativist and Fascist Politics in Canada, 1920–1940*. Toronto: University of Toronto Press, 1992.

Rockwood, Perry. *Triumph in God: The Life Story of Radio Pastor Perry F. Rockwood*. Halifax: Peoples Gospel Hour, n.d.

Roediger, David R. *How Race Survived US History: From Settlement and Slavery to the Obama Phenomenon*. London: Verso, 2008.

Rooke, P.T., and R.L. Schnell. *No Bleeding Heart: Charlotte Whitton, A Feminist on the Right*. Vancouver: University of British Columbia Press, 1987.

Roy, Patricia. "The Maillardville, BC, School Strike: Archbishop W.M. Duke, Catholic Schools, and the British Columbia Election of 1952." *Historical Studies* 80 (2014): 63–88.

Rudin, Ronald. *Making History in Twentieth-Century Quebec: Historians and Their Society*. Toronto: University of Toronto Press, 1997.

Russell, C. Allyn. "Thomas Todhunter Shields, Canadian Fundamentalist." *Ontario History* 70 (1978): 263–80.

Russell, Frances. *The Canadian Crucible: Manitoba's Role in Canada's Great Divide*. Winnipeg: Heartland Associates, Inc., 2003.

Rutherdale, Robert. *Hometown Horizons: Local Responses to Canada's Great War*. Vancouver: University of British Columbia Press, 2004.

Said, Edward. *Orientalism*. New York: Vintage Books, 2003.

Samuel, Raphael. "Introduction: The 'Little Platoons.'" In *Patriotism: The Making and Unmaking of British National Identity. Volume 2: Minorities and Outsiders*, edited by Raphael Samuel, ix–xxxix. London and New York: Routledge, 1989.

Saunders, Leslie. *An Orangeman in Public Life: The Memoirs of Leslie Howard Saunders*. Toronto: Britannia Printers, 1980.

Saywell, John. *"Just Call Me Mitch": The Life of Mitchell F. Hepburn*. Toronto: University of Toronto Press, 1991.

Sayyid, S. *A Fundamental Fear: Eurocentrism and the Emergence of Islamism*. New York: Zed Books, 2003.

Schultz, Nancy Lusignan, ed. *A Veil of Fear: Nineteenth-Century Convent Tales by Rebecca Reed and Maria Monk*. West Lafayette, IN: Purdue University Press, 1999.

Schwarz, Bill. "'Shivering in the Noonday Sun': The British World and the Dynamics of 'Nativisation.'" In *Britishness Abroad: Transnational Movements and Imperial Cultures*, edited by Kate Darian-Smith, Patricia Grimshaw, and Stuart Mcintyre, 19–44. Victoria: Melbourne University Press, 2007.

Scott, F.R. *Canada and the United States*. Boston: World Peace Foundation, 1941.

– "Canada's Future in the British Commonwealth." *Foreign Affairs* 15 (1937).

– *Canada Today: A Study of Her National Interests and National Policy*. London: Oxford University Press, 1938.

– "The Cardinal Speaks." *Canadian Forum* 18 (January 1939).

– [S, pseud.]. "Embryo Fascism in Quebec." *Foreign Affairs* 16 (April 1938): 454–7.

– "French Canadian Nationalism." In *A New Endeavour: Selected Political Essays, Letters, and Addresses*, edited by Michiel Horn, 27–36. Toronto: University of Toronto Press, 1986. Originally published in *Canadian Forum* 15 (1936).

– "What Did 'No' Mean." *Canadian Forum* 22 (June 1942).

Scott, R.B.Y., and Gregory Vlastos. *Towards the Christian Revolution*. Kingston: Ronald P. Frye and Company, 1989 [first edition 1936].

Sellar, Robert. *George Brown: The Globe, Confederation*. Toronto: Britnell's Bookstore, 1917.

– *The Tragedy of Quebec: The Expulsion of Its Protestant Farmers*. Toronto: University of Toronto Press, 1974 [first edition, 1907].

Semati, Mehdi. "Islamophobia, Culture, and Race in the Age of Empire." *Cultural Studies* 24 (2010): 256–75.

Shearer, J.G. "The Redemption of the City." In *Pre-Assembly Congress: Addresses Delivered at the Presbyterian Pre-Assembly Congress, Held in Massey Hall, Toronto, Saturday, May 31st, to Wednesday June 4th, 1913, With Reports of Committees*, 170–4. Toronto: Board of Foreign Missions, Presbyterian Church in Canada, 1913.

Sher, Julian. *White Hoods: Canada's Ku Klux Klan*. Vancouver: New Star Books, 1983.

Silcox, C.E. *Must Canada Split?* Toronto: Ryerson Press, 1944.

– *The Revenge of the Cradles*. Toronto: Ryerson Press, 1945.

Silcox, C.E., and Galen M. Fisher. *Catholics, Jews, and Protestants: A Study of Relationships in the United States and Canada*. New York: Harper and Bros., 1934.

Sissons, C.B. *Bi-Lingual Schools in Canada*. Toronto: J.M. Dent and Sons, 1917.

- Nil alienum: *The Memoirs of C.B. Sissons*. Toronto: University of Toronto Press, 1964.
Smale, Robert. "For Whose Kingdom? Central Canadian Baptists, Watson Kirkconnell, and the Evangelization of Immigrants, 1880–1939." In *Baptists and Public Life in Canada*, edited by Gordon Heath and Paul Wilson, 343–92. Hamilton: McMaster Divinity College Press, 2012.
Smith, Anthony Burke. *The Look of Catholics: Portrayals in Popular Culture from the Great Depression to the Cold War*. Lawrence, KS: University Press of Kansas, 2010.
Smith, Anthony D. *The Cultural Foundations of Nations: Hierarchy, Covenant, and Republic* Oxford: Blackwell Publishing, 2008.
- *Nationalism: Theory, Ideology, History*. Oxford: Blackwell Publishing, 2001.
Smith, Oswald. *Is the Antichrist at Hand?* Toronto: The Tabernacle Publishers, 1926.
- *The Peoples Church and Its Pastor*. Toronto: The Peoples Press, 1957.
Speirs, Rosemary. *Out of the Blue: The Fall of the Tory Dynasty in Ontario*. Toronto: Macmillan of Canada, 1986.
Stacey, C.P. "Through the Second World War." In *The Canadians: 1867–1967*, edited by J.M.S. Careless and Robert Craig Brown, 275–30. Toronto: Macmillan of Canada, 1967.
Stackhouse, John G., Jr. *Canadian Evangelicalism in the Twentieth Century: An Introduction to Its Character*. Toronto: University of Toronto Press, 1993.
Stepler, Dorothy. *Family Allowances for Canada*. Toronto: Canadian Institute of International Affairs and the Canadian Association for Adult Education, 1944.
Stingel, Janine. *Social Discredit: Anti-Semitism, Social Credit, and the Jewish Response*. Montreal and Kingston: McGill-Queen's University Press, 2000.
Stortz, Gerald, and Murray Eaton. "'Pro Bono Publico': The Eastview Birth Control Trial." *Atlantis* 8 (1983): 51–60.
Swettenham, John. *McNaughton*. Vol. 3: *1944–1946*. Toronto: The Ryerson Press, 1969.
Taine, H.A. *History of English Literature*. Edinburgh: Edmonston and Douglas, 1873.
Tarr, Leslie K. *Shields of Canada: T.T. Shields (1873–1955)*. Grand Rapids, MI: Baker Book House, 1967.
Therrien, Eugene A., ed., *Baptist Work in French Canada*. Montreal: Grand Ligne Mission, 1954.

Thompson, John Herd. "Canada and the 'Third British Empire,' 1901–1939." In *Canada and the British Empire*, edited by Philip Buckner, 87–106. New York: Oxford University Press, 2008.
– *Ethnic Minorities During Two World Wars*. Ottawa: Canadian Historical Association and Multiculturalism Program, Government of Canada, 1991.
Thompson, John Herd, and Allen Seager. *Canada, 1922–1939: Decades of Discord*. Toronto: McClelland and Stewart, 1990.
Thompson, J. Lee, and John H. Thompson. "Ralph Connor and the Canadian Identity." *Queen's Quarterly* 79 (1972): 159–70.
Tumbleson, Raymond D. *Catholicism in the English Protestant Imagination: Nationalism, Religion, and Literature, 1660–1745*. Cambridge: Cambridge University Press, 1998.
Tyner, James A., and Joshua Inwood. "Geography of Race and Racism." In *International Encyclopedia of the Social and Behavioural Sciences*. 2nd edition, vol. 19: 801–6. New York: Elsevier, 2015.
Valverde, Mariana. "'When the Mother of the Race Is Free': Race, Reproduction, and Sexuality in First-Wave Feminism." In *Gender Conflicts: New Essays in Women's History*, edited by Franca Iacovetta and Mariana Valverde, 3–26. Toronto: University of Toronto Press, 1992.
Vance, Jonathan. *Maple Leaf Empire: Canada, Britain, and Two World Wars*. Toronto: Oxford University Press, 2012.
Verhoeven, Timothy. *Transatlantic Anti-Catholicism: France and the United States in the Nineteenth Century*. United States: Palgrave Macmillan, 2010.
Villeneuve, J.-M.-R. "And Our Dispersed Brethren…?" In *French Canadian Nationalism: An Anthology*, edited by Ramsay Cook, 202–14. Toronto: Macmillan of Canada, 1969. (Originally published as "Et nos frères de la dispersion," *Notre Avenir Politique: Enquête de l'Action française*, 1922.)
Wahrman, Dror. "Change and the Corporeal in Seventeenth- and Eighteenth-Century Gender History; or, Can Cultural History Be Rigorous?" *Gender and History* 20 (2008): 584–602.
Walker, Franklin A. *Catholic Education and Politics in Ontario: A Documentary Study*. Toronto: Thomas Nelson and Sons, 1964.
– *Catholic Education and Politics in Ontario*. Vol. 3: *From the Hope Commission to the Promise of Completion (1945–1985)*. Toronto: Catholic Education Foundation of Ontario, 1986.
Ward, Norman, and David Smith. *Jimmy Gardiner: Relentless Liberal*. Toronto: University of Toronto Press, 1990.
Watt, F.W. "Western Myth: The World of Ralph Connor." *Canadian Literature* 1 (1959): 26–36.

Weir, Lorna. "Social Movement Activism in the Formation of Ontario New Democratic Party Policy on Abortion, 1982–1984." *Labour/Le Travail* 35 (1995): 163–93.

Werner, Yvonne Maria, and Jonas Harvard. "European Anti-Catholicism in Comparative and Transnational Perspective: The Role of a Unifying Other: An Introduction." In *European Anti-Catholicism in a Comparative and Transnational Perspective*, edited by Werner and Harvard, 13–22. Amsterdam and New York: Rodopi, 2013.

Whitton, Charlotte. *Baby Bonuses: Dollars or Sense?* Toronto: Ryerson Press, 1945.

– *The Dawn of an Ampler Life*. Toronto: Macmillan Company of Canada Limited, 1943.

Wicks, Donald A. "T.T. Shields and the Canadian Protestant League, 1941–1950." Master's thesis, University of Guelph, 1971.

Wilson, David A. "Introduction: 'Who Are These People?'" In *The Orange Order in Canada*, edited by David A. Wilson, 9–24. Dublin: Four Courts Press, 2007.

– "'Orange Influences of the Right Kind': Thomas D'Arcy McGee, the Orange Order, and the New Nationality." In *The Orange Order in Canada*, edited by David A. Wilson, 89–108. Dublin: Four Courts Press, 2007.

Wolffe, John. "Anti-Catholicism and the Evangelical Identity in Britain and the United States, 1830–1860." In *Evangelicalism: Comparative Studies of Popular Protestantism in North America, the British Isles, and Beyond, 1700–1990*, edited by Mark Noll, David Bebbington, and George Rawlyk, 179–97. Oxford: Oxford University Press, 1994.

– *The Protestant Crusade in Great Britain, 1829–1860*. Oxford: Clarendon Press, 1991.

Woodsworth, J.S. *My Neighbour: A Study of City Conditions, A Plea for Social Service*. Toronto: University of Toronto Press, 1972 [first edition, 1911].

– *Strangers within Our Gates; or, Coming Canadians*. Toronto: The Missionary Society of the Methodist Church, 1909.

Wright, Donald. *The Professionalization of History in English Canada*. Toronto: University of Toronto Press, 2005.

Wurtele, Susan E. "Assimilation through Domestic Transformation: Saskatchewan's Masonic Scholarship Project, 1922–23." *The Canadian Geographer* 38 (1994): 122–33.

Yack, Bernard. "The Myth of the Civic Nation." *Critical Review* 10 (1996): 193–211.

Index

abortion, 11, 25, 94–6, 102; debates over abortion in the 1980s and 1990s, 202, 215, 217–18, 228–32
Anderson, J.T.M., 56–60, 63
Andrew, Jock. *See* BMG Publishing
Anglicanism. *See* Protestantism
Antichrist. *See* papacy
anti-Semitism, 20, 166–7, 180, 218, 234, 241, 246n33; Catholics and, 78, 86
appeasement, 118, 144–5, 269n34

Baptists. *See* fundamentalism; Protestantism; Shields, T.T.
Benedict XVI, Pope, 233–4, 236
bilingualism, opposition to, 41–4, 179, 195, 215, 268n32. *See also* BMG Publishing
birth control. *See* contraception
birth rate: Catholic population, 11, 47, 72, 80–2, 92–3, 98–9, 104–6, 117–20, 146–9, 160, 165, 187–8, 199–200, 205–6, 212–13, 231–2; fear of decline of Protestants, 16, 20, 72, 80–2, 91–106, 110, 127–8, 130–1, 186. *See also* Catholic Church; revenge of the cradle
Blackmore, John Horne, 180–2
BMG Publishing, 203–10
Bonne Entente, 42, 47, 250n55
Borden, Robert, 5–6, 27–8, 44, 47–9, 153
Bouchard, T.-D., 139–41; support for, 141, 143, 148, 208–9
Bracken, John, 142, 148, 152–3, 266n7
Britishness. *See* Protestantism
Bruce, Herbert, 137, 142–5, 154, 274n124–5

Canadian Council of Churches, 191–3, 223–4
Canadian Protestant League (CPL), 18, 181–2, 200, 220–2, 225; and T.T. Shields, 113–14, 118–20, 153
Canuck, Janey. *See* Murphy, Emily
Catholic Church, Roman: as authoritarian and fostering authoritarianism, 7, 13, 17,

22–4, 28, 30, 46, 68–9, 78, 83, 92, 107–8, 113, 123, 125, 130, 136–7, 141, 146, 151, 154–7, 160–7, 170, 178–9, 181, 183, 190, 193, 196–8, 202, 204–6, 209–10, 212–13, 234–5, 240–1; as encouraging high birth rate, 46, 72, 80–2, 91–106, 130–1, 186; as fostering disloyalty or dual loyalty, 7–8, 27, 29, 38, 43, 98, 111–13, 130, 143–5, 151–2; and political power, 3–7, 23, 34–6, 39, 44–8, 54–7, 74–93, 118, 121–4, 129–48, 172–8, 187–8, 193, 204–10, 213–18; in Quebec, 22–4, 27, 34–6, 40–1, 43–4, 46–7, 56, 69–71, 74, 77–87, 92, 99, 102–3, 109–11, 113, 116–27, 129–30, 132–52, 155–6, 164–9, 172–4, 176, 179–84, 186, 188–90, 193–7, 203–10, 232; as regressive and/or medieval, 7, 17–19, 23, 25–6, 28, 35, 39–41, 43, 45–6, 58–60, 70, 73–4, 79–83, 96–8, 99–103, 105–6, 108, 111–12, 121, 126–7, 129, 139, 140–1, 148, 151, 157, 165–6, 175, 200, 206, 210–11, 217–18, 228, 232–8, 242; and sexual abuse, 228, 232–3, 236–7, 294n101; as superstitious and ignorant, 36, 58, 65, 67, 234; as totalitarian and fostering totalitarianism, 24, 70, 79, 82–3, 112–14, 122–3, 150–1, 154–7, 159–64, 167, 209, 233–4, 238. *See also* contraception; fascism; French Canada; immigration; revenge of the cradle

Catholic Civil Rights League, 229–30, 233, 293n94
Cavan, Ontario, 226–8
clerical-fascism. *See* clericalism
clericalism, hostility to, 36, 41, 43–4, 56–7, 74, 80, 136–7, 140–1, 143, 183, 190, 196–7, 258n10; anti-clericalism (from within Catholic countries), 43, 138–41, 188, 196; clerical-fascism, 70, 84–6, 109, 137, 195–6, 217, 234. *See also* fascism; French Canada; Quebec nationalism
Commission on the Church, Nation and World Order, 123–5, 128
communism, 170, 173–4; anti-communism, 70–1, 82–3, 85, 135, 163, 185–8, 192–3; Catholicism as equated to communism, 155–62, 164, 167, 176, 178–9
Connor, Ralph. *See* Gordon, Charles
conscription, 127, 131–3, 137–8, 150, 188, 209; conscription crisis, First World War, 44–52, 113, 251n73, 252n75; conscription crises, Second World War, 115, 119–23, 142–8, 151–4, 268n32, 270n60, 273n108, 277n169; conscription plebiscite, 1942, 119–20, 137–8, 170, 209, 269n39
Conservative Party, 41–3, 88–91, 112–13, 115–16, 121, 142–55, 171–5, 203; and big blue machine, 211–20; in Saskatchewan, 56, 60, 63; as Unionist Party, 27, 44–52

conspiracy theory, anti-Catholic, 3–4, 34–6, 41–2, 46, 48–51, 74–5, 80–7, 96–8, 109, 117, 139–41, 143, 147–9, 175–91, 207–10, 212–15, 221–2. *See also* Order of Jacques Cartier; revenge of the cradle; Shields, T.T.

contraception, 3–5, 11, 23, 34, 71–6, 93–106, 147–8, 165; and A.H. Tyrer, 69–70; and post-legalization (1969), 217, 232. *See also* Great Birth Control Trial; revenge of the cradle

Co-operative Commonwealth Federation, 77–9, 139; New Democratic Party, 219, 237–8

corporatism, 70–1, 77, 83–4, 122, 136–7, 139–41, 208–9

Defence of Canada Regulations, 113, 132, 146

Drew, George, 154, 171–4, 184; and East Hastings by-election, 88–92; and family allowances, 142–7, 150–1

Duplessis, Maurice, 70–1, 77–9, 85–6, 109, 139–41, 167, 171–2, 179, 196

East Hastings by-election, 1936–37. *See* Drew, George; Liberal Party

ecumenism, 76, 120, 124, 128–30, 158–9, 167–9, 191–3, 212–13, 223–5

education, 38–9, 53, 56–60, 62–3, 79–80, 99, 126–7, 136, 193–7, 206–8; separate schools, 87–91, 171, 187, 213–20, 230–2, 237–9. *See also* Inter-Church Committee on Protestant–Roman Catholic Relations; Regulation 17

England, Robert, 57–60

eugenics, 23, 72, 75–6, 94–5, 101; contemporary scrutiny of, 101–3; during Second World War, 142–3; after Second World War, 165. *See also* sterilization

evangelicalism, 31–2, 59–60, 73; conservative evangelicals, 25, 37–8, 178–82, 202, 221–4. *See also* Anglicanism; fundamentalism; Reformation

family allowances. *See* revenge of the cradle

Farthing, Hugh, 9, 147, 173–4, 177

Farthing, John, 9, 174–8

fascism, 68–72, 76–86, 90, 94, 98, 109–11, 113, 116, 123, 126–8, 132–40, 143, 146, 148, 151, 156, 159–61, 179, 193; Fred Ellis and, 195–6, 208, 217, 234

Fellowship for a Christian Social Order, 127, 136

feminism, and/or women's rights, 10–11, 25, 45–6, 75, 95–8, 100–3, 195, 199–200, 224, 230–4

First World War, 38, 43–4, 48–50, 119; and 1917 federal election, 27, 44–8

Forsey, Eugene, 33–4, 84–7, 103, 111, 121, 136–8, 174, 176–8, 194, 234, 265n126

Foster, Kate, 11, 64–6, 106

Francis, Diane, 207–10

Franco, Francisco: and Spain as corporatist Catholic dictatorship, 71, 82–4, 109, 170, 188, 208

French Canada, 12, 22–4, 28–9, 32–3, 41–4, 51–2, 61–3, 82, 89, 91–4, 96–7, 104–5, 108–9, 118, 184, 186, 204–5, 226

French-Canadian nationalism. *See* Quebec nationalism

fundamentalism, 28, 36–8, 88, 113–17, 178–80, 202, 221–3, 225, 248n36, 249n39

Garnsworthy, Lewis, 213–20, 228
Gibbon, John Murray, 64, 106–9
Gordon, Charles, 40–1, 55–6, 66–7
Great Birth Control Trial, 75, 93–101. *See also* Kaufman, A.R.; Silcox, C.E.; sterilization
Groulx, Lionel, 71, 85, 268n68
Guelph Raid, 48–51

Hawkins, Mary: and the Birth Control Society of Hamilton, 95–7
Henry, Fred, 237–9
Hepburn, Mitchell, 74, 87–93, 183–4
Hurd, William Burton, 103–6

immigration, 22, 25, 28–30, 38–9, 52–67, 71–2, 81, 97, 102–9, 126, 130–1, 155–8, 170–3, 181–2, 187–91, 200–1
Inter-Church Committee on Protestant–Roman Catholic Relations (ICC), 182–7, 191–2, 211–13; and Walter Bossy, 188–91
Irish, 28–9, 38, 48, 51, 63, 106, 111, 140, 167, 247n8, 266n2
Islam. *See* Islamophobia
Islamophobia, 17–20, 225, 235, 241

Jehovah's Witnesses, 86, 132, 139, 179–80, 232
John XXIII, Pope, 168–9
John Paul II, Pope, 214, 222–5, 234

Kaufman, A.R., 145; and anti-Catholic illustrations, 3–7; and birth-control trial, 93–9; and Parents' Information Bureau, 94, 101; and support for sterilization, 3–4, 93–5
King, William Lyon Mackenzie, 61, 75, 113–17, 119, 131–4, 136, 138, 141, 143–4, 147–54, 174–7
Kirkconnell, Watson, 27, 46, 108–10, 130–1, 185–8, 271n76
Ku Klux Klan, 5, 56, 60, 63–4, 208, 227, 234, 256n144

Lapointe, Ernest, 114–15, 132–3, 177
Laurier, Wilfrid, 27, 44, 47, 52, 62, 79–80, 140–1
League for Social Reconstruction, 77, 136
Liberal Party, 3–7, 23, 44, 60–2, 85, 109, 114–15, 119, 132–3, 139–54, 172–8, 189, 203, 208–9; David Peterson Ontario government, 218–22; and East Hastings by-election, 87–93; as liberating Quebec from Duplessis, 195–6
Lloyd, George Exton. *See* National Association of Canada
Lower, Arthur, 123–8, 155–6, 162–7, 196–7, 199–200, 201–11

MacDonald, Clarke, 218–19, 224–5
MacLennan, Hugh, 195–7

Manion, Robert James, 113, 147
Maritimes, 12–13, 48, 63–4, 104, 148–9, 186, 244n9, 244n11, 256n46
McAree, J.V., 73–4, 116–17, 134–5, 140
McCarthy, Joseph. *See* McCarthyism
McCarthyism, 193; and connections to Roman Catholicism, 155–6, 167, 179
McNaughton, Andrew, 151–4, 279n187
Meighen, Arthur, 121, 137–8
Methodism. *See* Protestantism
Morgentaler, Henry: clinics, 229–30
multiculturalism, 25, 64, 130–1, 198, 200–3, 207, 220, 271n76, 287n5; as mosaic, 106–9
Murphy, Emily, 30–3, 41, 46, 54–5, 102–3
Mussolini, Benito, 37, 70–1, 76, 90, 94, 100, 109, 155, 161, 197, 208, 257n4. *See also* corporatism; fascism

National Association of Canada, 60–3
nationalism, 8, 13–17, 24–5, 28, 30, 39, 41, 67–8, 109, 156–9, 163, 240–2, 244n12, 245n13, 245n13, 245n15, 245n18
National Resources Mobilization Act, 115, 119, 152
Nazism and Nazi Germany, 82, 84–5, 94, 98, 126, 133–5, 139, 143, 233
New Democratic Party. *See* Co-operative Commonwealth Federation

1917 federal election. *See* conscription; First World War
1929 Saskatchewan election. *See* Anderson, J.T.M.; Conservative Party; Ku Klux Klan
Northern Ireland, 181–2, 222–3
North Grey by-election, 1944–45, 152–4

O'Connor, Frank: as Catholic influence on Mitchell Hepburn, 88–93, 261n66
Orange Order, 12, 18, 20, 42–3, 49, 61, 64, 117, 130, 146, 163, 173–4; and Bill Davis, 215–16; and Morris Zeidman, 74–5
Order of Jacques Cartier, 116, 134, 136, 139–41, 208. *See also* conspiracy theory
Orthodoxy, 158, 201; conflated with Catholicism and Catholics, 29, 57–8, 65–6, 105
Other, the, 18–23, 29, 32, 39, 41, 54–5, 66, 71, 96, 107, 156–7, 159, 161–2, 171, 190, 241–2

Padlock Law. *See* Duplessis, Maurice
Palmer, Dorothea. *See* Great Birth Control Trial
papacy: opposition to papal infallibility, 141, 160, 164, 168, 170; pope as Antichrist, 18, 37, 114, 117, 179
Parents' Information Bureau. *See* Kaufman, A.R.
Parti Québécois, 204–8
Plumptre, Adelaide, 45–6
Prairies. *See* Western Canada
Presbyterians. *See* fundamentalism; Protestantism

Progressive Conservative Party. *See* Conservative Party

pronatalism. *See* birth rate; Catholic Church; eugenics; Great Birth Control Trial; revenge of the cradle

Protestantism, 13–14, 19–22, 49–53, 65–6, 74–5, 97–8, 116–17, 153–4, 184–6, 201, 204–6, 212–13, 215, 219–20, 226–8; Anglicans, 29, 31–5, 60–1, 69–70, 76, 102–3, 174, 183, 189–91, 212–13, 215–17, 223; as basis of individual liberties and progress, 7–8, 17, 28–30, 32, 34–6, 39–41, 45–7, 54–9, 69–70, 76–7, 82–3, 86–7, 90–1, 107–8, 121–2, 125–8, 155–67, 169–71, 178–82, 186–7, 193, 199–200, 210–11, 215, 217–18; Baptists, 86, 130–1, 183, 192, 223–4; and Britishness, 8, 12, 14–17, 28–30, 32, 36, 38–9, 47, 56, 60–4, 66–7, 69–70, 73, 76, 87–8, 104–5, 112, 131, 144–8, 159; Methodists, 33, 46, 57, 67, 164; Presbyterians, 40, 50, 55–7, 67, 74, 87–8, 170, 183, 212; United Church of Canada, 65, 76, 118–19, 123–4, 128–30, 167–71, 218, 223–5. *See also* birth rate; fundamentalism; Inter-Church Committee on Protestant–Roman Catholic Relations; Reformation

public sphere. *See* separation of church and state

Quebec. *See* Catholic Church; French Canada

Quebec nationalism, 23, 44, 56, 71, 78–80, 83, 123, 126–7, 129–30, 138–9, 155, 190, 193–4, 196–7, 206–8

Quebec separatism, 70, 116, 142, 193–4, 196–7, 211–12; and post-1960s, 203–10, 226–7, 268n26

Quiet Revolution, 22–3, 195–7, 200, 266n145. *See also* French Canada; Quebec nationalism; Quebec separatism

race, and/or ethnicity, intersecting with religion, 14–16, 22, 25, 29–30, 39, 45–6, 55, 57–60, 65–7, 72–3, 81–2, 98–9, 102–9, 122, 130–1, 156–9, 164, 170–4, 176–7, 184, 188–91, 194–6, 201–3, 205–6, 226

Ralston, James, 144, 151–2

Rebick, Judy, 230; and rabble.ca, 233–7

Reformation, 37, 88, 128, 223–5; as engine for historical progress, 16–17, 31–2, 59, 107–8, 125–6; as foundational to modern democratic values, 8, 29, 56, 76, 114, 160–5, 170, 175–7

Regulation 17, 41–4, 250n56

revenge of the cradle, 46, 72, 98–9, 110, 118, 120, 173, 185–6; as 1970s conspiracy theory, 204–6; and Dionne Quintuplets, 91–3; and family allowances, 112–13, 142–51; and origins of phrase, 251n69. *See also* birth rate; Drew, George; Silcox, C.E.; Whitton, Charlotte

Robinson, Judith, 120, 174, 177–8, 288n23

Rome. *See* Vatican

St Laurent, Louis, 115, 117–21, 132, 146, 148, 171–4, 177
Salazar, Antonio: and Portugal as corporatist Catholic dictatorship, 71, 140, 170
Saunders, Leslie, 75, 99, 167, 178–9, 283n74
Scott, F.R., 69, 77–85, 98–9, 136–8, 142, 195, 234
secularization/secularity, 16–17, 19, 23–5, 200–3, 209, 214, 217, 228, 234–5, 237–9, 241
Sellar, Robert, 34–8, 42, 46–7, 248n27
separate schools. *See* education; Inter-Church Committee on Protestant–Roman Catholic Relations
separation of church and state, 10, 19, 36, 38, 47, 176, 187–8, 214–15; Catholic violation of "neutral" public sphere, 18, 202–3, 214–15, 229–31
sexual abuse. *See* Catholic Church
Shawinigan Falls: persecution of Christian Brethren, 179–82
Shields, T.T., 77, 88–9, 91, 112–17, 119–20, 134, 153, 181, 267n14
Silcox, C.E., 76–7, 92–3, 95, 98–9, 101–2, 119–23, 147–8, 159–62, 258n14
Sisco, Gordon, 124, 127–8, 183
Sissons, C.B., 42–4
Smith, Oswald, 36–8, 249n38, 257n4. *See also* fundamentalism
Soviet Union, 81, 135, 170, 185. *See also* Catholic Church; communism
Spanish Civil War, 82–6
sterilization, 3–4, 11, 30–1, 102–3, 142–4; and birth-control trial, 93–101; and contemporary scrutiny of, 101–2. *See also* eugenics; Great Birth Control Trial; Kaufman, A.R.; Murphy, Emily
stork derby, 99–102
superstition. *See* Catholic Church

totalitarianism, 131, 149. *See also* Catholic Church
Trudeau, Pierre, 196, 203–9

United Church of Canada. *See* Protestantism
United States of America, 9, 35–6, 81, 83, 96–7, 100–1, 103–4, 108, 112, 119–20, 133–6, 147, 158–9, 172, 174–5, 187–8, 203, 229, 234, 239

Vatican, 9, 33, 37, 71, 117, 134, 221–2, 231, 236–7; as interfering political enemy, 39, 51, 76–7, 81–4, 111, 123, 134, 141, 143, 210; opposition to diplomatic representative to, 172–4, 187–8, 193; as similar to the Soviet Union, 156, 160–1
Vatican II: as obscuring Catholic Church's true nature, 157–8, 167–71
Vichy France, 121–2, 133–7
Villeneuve, Cardinal Jean-Marie-Rodrigue, 78–9, 85–6, 135–7, 141, 151, 260n54
Vlastos, Gregory, 111, 127–8

Wegenast, Francis, 95, 99–100
Western Canada, 12, 38–9, 52–63, 66–7, 131, 189
Whitton, Charlotte, 148–50

Woodsworth, J.S., 6, 27, 38–40, 42, 52–5, 64–7, 106
World Council of Churches, 124, 162, 191–2

Zeidman, Morris, 74–7, 88, 95
Zombies, 119, 137, 151–2, 269n40. *See also* National Resources Mobilization Act